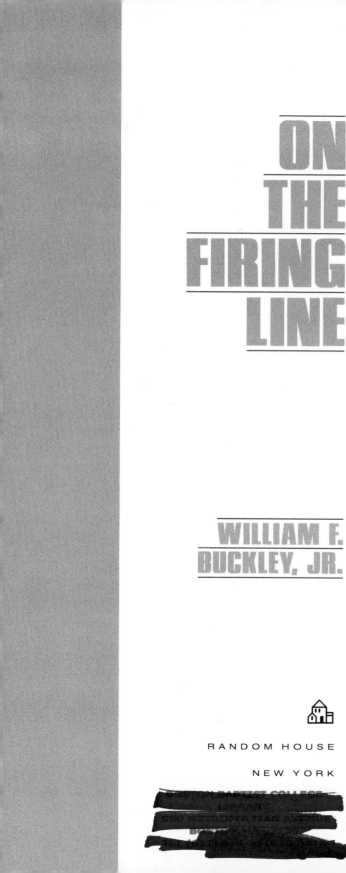

ON THE FIRING LINE

THE

PUBLIC LIFE

OF OUR PUBLIC

FIGURES

WILLIAM F. BUCKLEY, JR.

RANDOM HOUSE

NEW YORK

Library of Congress Cataloging-in-Publication Data
Buckley, William F. (William Frank)
   On the firing line.
   Selected transcripts of, and original commentary on, the television
series Firing Line.
   Includes index.
   1. Firing line (Television program) 2. Buckley,
William F. (William Frank)—Interviews.
3. Journalists—United States—Interviews.
4. Interviewing in television. 5. Celebrities—
United States—Interviews.   I. Firing line
(Television program) II. Title.
PN1992.77.F55 1989 791.45′72   88-43210
ISBN 0-394-57568-7

Book design by Debbie Glasserman

Manufactured in the United States of America
98765432
First Trade Edition

A signed limited first edition of this book has
been privately printed by The Franklin Library.

FOR WARREN STEIBEL
My producer (1966–) and
(*mirabile dictu*)
my friend

ACKNOWLEDGMENTS

When the idea first came to me that there was material in two decades of *Firing Line* that ought not to be neglected, I thought of a dozen categories of what might make especially interesting chapter headings ("Manifest Evasiveness" was one of them; "Brilliant Reasoning" another) and wrote a letter to my friend and associate Elizabeth Altham of New Haven. Stoicism is defined by her conduct on receiving over one thousand one-hour transcripts dating back to April 1966. Nine months later, she had winnowed the material down to about a million words. I am enormously grateful for her diligence and shrewdness.

Before reaching Switzerland for my annual book-writing hiatus it occurred to me that I could not handle what I hoped to do without the aid of a skillful researcher and editorial aide. It happened that the period in question coincided with a vacation overdue from his work as a speechwriter for President Reagan, and through a friend in common I learned that Peter Robinson was willing to take on the work, combined with a little skiing in the off hours. I am grateful to Anthony Dolan, chief speechwriter for the President, for expediting the schedule of one of his assistants, and grateful beyond measure for the extraordinary work of my young colleague, a graduate of Dartmouth College who did graduate work at Oxford, joined the White House as speechwriter for Vice President George Bush (replacing—nice coincidence—my son Christopher, who resigned to work on his novel, *The White House*

Mess). Peter is off to the Business School at Stanford. He is qualified to edit the collected opera of the President he worked for. Some of the editorial insights in this volume which I think highly of were done at his suggestion.

Every photograph in this book is by Jan Lukas. He was a freedom fighter from Czechoslovakia and has recorded the last eighteen years of *Firing Line.* His current book is *The Islanders* (National Review Press).

I have the habitual problem of paying appropriate tribute to the editorial help of my editor, Samuel S. Vaughan. It has got to the point where I am incapable of reading a book—almost any book, no matter how successful—without thinking: Oh my, if only the author had had the services of Sam.

To Joseph Isola, my thanks for his expert proofreading (his twenty-third for me). My special thanks to Ted Johnson, the copy editor, for a fine reading, and for his inventive and pleasing editorial styling of this volume. The research required in this volume put a special strain on Dorothy McCartney, for whom nothing ever appears to be a strain—my thanks, and my compliments. Tony Savage typed the manuscript with skill and enthusiasm. I am blessed to have his friendship and his professional skills. The editorial coordination was, as usual, done by Frances Bronson, without whom I could be reached at the nearest Trappist monastery.

The book was read exactingly by my friends Thomas Wendel, Richard Clurman, and Peter Glenville, for whose comments and encouragement I am grateful. I have dedicated this book to Warren Steibel, with affection and melancholy. The first for making tolerable twenty-two years of an exacting program; the second, because notwithstanding a half lifetime's indoctrination by me, he remains a resolute political liberal. But then somewhere in the text, if memory serves, I ruminate on the subject of invincible ignorance.

And finally, I am indebted to Alistair Cooke for his bouyant and exhilarating introduction. There is no figure in television I admire more; and there are few writers who match the eloquence and shrewdness of his written work.

                                        W.F.B.
                                        Stamford, Connecticut
                                        September 5, 1988

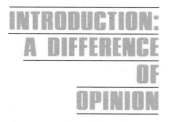

INTRODUCTION: A DIFFERENCE OF OPINION

Civilization began with 'Please?'
and 'Thank you.'
Old Folk Saying

A Constitution is made for
people of fundamentally
differing views.
Justice Oliver Wendell Holmes

My unforgettable headmaster, a dapper, eccentric baldhead with the face of one of the more sagacious Roman emperors, was a man of many cryptic utterances, most of which he delivered impromptu—to uncomprehending small boys—with alarming emphasis on unexpected phrases, as if the listener had just dared him to make a point. Thus, he would seize a boy going along a corridor minding his own business and bellow: "D'you know what a bounder is, boy? You *do not* know what a bounder is?! A bounder is a man who walks along Piccadilly wearing a Guards' tie and *doesn't even know* it's a Guards' tie!!!"

At unpredictable intervals, he would preempt the regular Friday afternoon syllabus of the two upper forms and declare a session of the debating society. Once a year, to the newcomers to the upper school, he would announce: "Never forget that King John debated the barons, and *if he had won,* my school would not even *have* a debating society!" Although this warning was intended to refer small boys to Magna Carta as the source of all their liberties, it almost certainly baffled more of them than it enlightened. However, a hint of what debating was all about would begin to sink in when, at the start of each session, he rehearsed the rules.

The subject for debate was posted on a bulletin board on the morning of the actual events. The protagonists were chosen by lot. The teams—two boys on each side—were "put on your honor" not to accept an

assignment which coincided with their own prejudices. A boy who was
in favor of capital punishment, say, was obliged to declare himself, so
as to be required to speak against it.

In short, the man was—apart from his other, dotty, characteristics—a
man with a settled passion for the idea of contradiction as the lifeblood
of a free society. It strikes me only now that he would have regarded
that latter, resounding, phrase as "high falutin'." Neither masters nor
schoolboys in those days in the England of the middle 1920s bandied
about such words as liberty, freedom, the right of free speech. We took
them for granted, as we took for granted the prohibitions against stab-
bing the teacher. (We also took for granted—without a moment's mis-
giving—the fifty-year embargo on anything the government thought
could be covered by the Official Secrets Act, and the right of the Lord
Chamberlain to censor the scripts of all plays destined for public performance.) As for the word "libertarian," it was not even in our vocabulary, but you could, as Casey Stengel said, "look it up."

From these early, humble encounters, the reader will gather that I
came to accept the airing of differences in a public debate as a routine
procedure of ordinary education. My history master explained the
larger value of all this by pointing to diplomacy—the peaceful resolution
of weighty matters—as the supreme form of debating. (We took him at
his word without pondering the paradox that he, like every other master
in the school except one, was still visibly maimed from a wound suffered
in the trenches of the First World War.) Only many years later, during
a research excursion into diplomatic history, did I discover that the idea
of diplomacy as a means to achieving just, peaceful and moral solutions
is astonishingly recent. Denys Myer remarked, without irony, that so
late as the middle eighteenth century a diplomat was "naturally an
advocate; his object was not justice but the advantage of the country he
represented." And well into our own time (today?) diplomacy, although
conducted according to a precise protocol of politeness, had little to do
with morality. Another historian, whose name I forget, defined the
diplomat as "a protector of real property through a process of exalted
haggling."

Meditating on the long and cynical history of European diplomacy,
from the early Venetians on, Americans will leap with pride to the
reminder that theirs is a nation created in a seventeen-week debate.
Certainly, the records of the Constitutional Convention amount to a
triumph of civilized discourse. And if there is one figure more than
another who comes out of the Philadelphia convention as a shining

exemplar of the magnanimous debater, it is that of Alexander Hamilton, who lost many of the causes dear to his heart and mind, and then sat down to compose a series of brilliantly persuasive essays urging the adoption of articles of government he had hated.

Such a character has not, so far as I know, ever appeared on *Firing Line.* Hamilton, of course, was arguing and pleading before the emergence of the American democracy, but he feared Jefferson's prediction that if that was to be the going system "it will be boisterous." So it has been, and in the era of the sound bite and the TV free-for-all, when nightly brews of subintellectual ferment pass for political debating, we must be all the more grateful for any arena of public discussion that pits the most intelligent and convinced advocates, on different sides of every public issue, and allows them to go on at length, agreeing to disagree short of actual mayhem. Such an arena is *Firing Line.*

It was unique at the start and remains the best of its kind. (We should not forget that *The MacNeil/Lehrer NewsHour* was to come along as a variation of the form: A nightly interview-debate which, conducted with unsleeping intelligence and scrupulous fairness, continues as the incomparable nightly news show, going well beyond the five-second news clip and the quotable one-liner of the three commercial networks.) Without *Firing Line* and *The MacNeil/Lehrer NewsHour* we should be in a bad way.

Mr. Buckley's role in *Firing Line,* and his conception of it, have been vital to the character and life of the program. I myself was worried in the early days, because he seemed to be setting himself up each time as a prosecutor almost more than a moderator. It may be worth considering why this should have been so. Put it another way and say that in the early years, Mr. B. tended to revel in his role as the gadfly of the liberals and often, even in introducing them, put them on the defensive from the start. The frequent result was, as Mr. Buckley concedes, "a bare-knuckled intellectual brawl." But that was in the early sixties, when—in the still powerful wash of Roosevelt and Truman—liberal commentators and columnists were, if not in the ascendant, certainly in the majority and having things their own way; when a conservative columnist of sharp intelligence and possessing a historical perspective was something of an oddity. Of course, there had always been conservative columnists, but from the thirties into the sixties they had been seen, correctly, (with the impenitent exception of Mencken) as flustered defenders of a rearguard action, literally as reactionaries against the Keynesian revolution with nothing very constructive to say on their own. They hectored, they exploded, they moaned. They were old, and they were not very good. We never guessed then that the Goldwater message—so naïve, so barmily Jeffersonian, so floundering in the high tide of the Great Society—would be seized on by younger men and redefined into a formidable philosophy, which eventually, in one of the great and comical ironies of American history, would be greatly simplified and successfully transmitted to a receptive public through the spirit and larynx of a four-time Roosevelt voter and a sixty-nine-year-old newborn conservative.

Throughout the Reagan years, it has been the Democrats, both "moderate" and "liberal," who have been forced to react against the Reagan philosophy by accepting much of it while complaining loudly about the way it was implemented. Failing—as the Republicans failed to resist the sweep of the New Deal and Fair Deal—it was now the Democrats who came, in their turn, to be the "me too" party. Exactly as the Deweys and Willkies grudgingly had to accept the Wagner Act and Social Security and the rest, and promised to "do it better," so now the Democrats have gamely to pretend that they have been for lower tax rates and a tough nuclear defense all along but are pained that these policies are not carried out with "competence." Not the least of Reagan's political triumphs has been to pull the Democrats into *his* mainstream, not the one basked in by Roosevelt and Truman and Johnson, which seemed, when Buckley and Co. surfaced, to be a law of nature rolling along with the inevitability of Old Man River.

Suddenly, eight years ago, Mr. Buckley, the former John the Baptist, found his own savior actually in the White House. The effect on *Firing Line* and Mr. B.'s conduct of the program has been all to the good: endowing him with a newfound benevolence, indulging even the more intemperate arguments of his opponents with almost Churchillian grace: "In victory, magnanimity." (I am bound to say that in this volume, he has relieved the strain of this latter-day tenderness by adding, to the excerpts from the debates, a running commentary, which restores his roles of district attorney, mocker, lover of the last word, and—it must be admitted—confessor of grievous sins.)

This is not to say that the idea of the show, and the way it went along, was even in the early days noticeably one-sided. The original prescription, of opposing the best available protagonists on every social and political issue, was and is more than admirable. It is, as I suggested earlier, a model of civilized discourse. But it seems to me, as one who has watched (or read the transcripts of) 90 percent of the debates since the beginning, that the show has gained greatly in the past decade in seriousness and disinterestedness. Every articulate (and sometimes not so articulate) proponent of one side, or the other side, or a third side, has been heard from.

I don't think I ever appreciated the healthy extent of this catholicity until a party held seven years ago to celebrate the fifteenth anniversary of *Firing Line.* The guests were former participants. I was invited to join the receiving line, along with Vernon Jordan, then president of the Urban League; Louis Auchincloss, the novelist; and Ann Armstrong, former ambassador to the Court of St. James's. I am not myself much of a greeter or, for that matter, a partygoer, having yielded early in life to the pleasures of a skeptical onlooker, always engrossed and rarely inflamed by the wonderful world of politics and suspicious of any politician in a socially embracing posture.

But came the moment for the doors to open, the several hundred invited ones to line up, to patter by, to nod the head, to shake the hands, to mooch on. The shock of the occasion was the totally unexpected social, political, ethnic, professional and temperamental range of the guest list. Compared with it, the Reverend Jesse Jackson's rainbow coalition is a tiny mirage. This was a microcosm of America's dogmatic variety, a gamut of contentious types impossible to imagine in any other room in the country. Shoulder to shoulder stood flocks of amiable men and women who, in another place at another time, would almost certainly have been slugging it out fist to jaw. Conservatives, liberals, socialists, apostles of the Beat, flower people, bankers, Single Taxers, union leaders, right-to-lifers, abortionists, Nixon buddies, Nixon haters, stockbrokers, reporters of every stripe,—*felons!:* the mayor of New York saying how-de-do to a couple of Watergate veterans recently out of jail. An apotheosis of freedom of assembly that would have had the Founding Fathers speechless. All they had in common was that they had been on *Firing Line.*

If this boundless range is not spanned in the book, it is because not all the encounters successfully articulated tenable positions, nor do all of them take easily to explicating Mr. Buckley's manual of debating techniques, from "manifest evasion" to "Go fly a kite!" But there is more than enough to capture and demonstrate the signal value of the program: as an anthology of the arguments, on any serious public issue, that must be met.

So much for the book's extraordinary usefulness as (Mr. B. might say) a chrestomathy for the instruction and enlightenment of the citizen.

What makes it unlike any other book I can think of is Mr. Buckley's remarkable, exhaustive but never exhausted, running commentary, which combines Buckley's *Brief Lives* of many of the debaters, notes the effect of the debates on current politics, sustains a continuous critique of the opposing attitudes, adds sharp and often funny scenes about the social aftermath of the show, and distributes at timely intervals toothsome chunks of the Buckley autobiography. Much of it sounds like *The Life of Socrates, as Told to Evelyn Waugh.* It could well have been entitled: *Buckley's American Nights' Entertainment.*

—Alistair Cooke

CONTENTS

GUESTS: JOHN KENNETH GALBRAITH
         HAROLD MACMILLAN
         PAUL WEISS

A look at the historical background of the program and an examination of the (widely accepted) cliché that yesterday's newspapers are of no interest today. It is arresting how in debate with WFB Professor Galbraith handles, and WFB mishandles, a particular question having to do with U.S. fuel policy. And what about Harold MacMillan's reminiscence about Churchill, one fall day in 1943? Or Professor Weiss's jocular question "Did God found Christianity?" These are only in a purely mechanical sense yesterday's news.

---

*There is participation, throughout the text, by the author, hereafter "WFB" for typographical convenience. There is also commentary, throughout the text, by WFB.

Senator Barry Goldwater doesn't believe (in 1966) that the Vietnam experience will have a decisive effect on behavior in America. Norman Thomas does, thunderingly. Theodore Bikel tries to understand why youth are so uniquely affected, while Enoch Powell lays down the rules without which societies simply do not survive. Al Capp is at his searing, provocative worst/best in discussing student misbehavior, which behavior Timothy Leary undertakes to praise, and imitate.

Here are examples of how very bright people manage ever so skillfully to avoid answering direct questions. Their techniques are varied and, examined in the abstract, amusing and provocative.

Every now and then—maybe once every ten years—you get a guest who proves *truly* impossible. To be impossible you can do one of a number of things. The President of Panama is relentlessly pleasant.

Three or four times a year, *Firing Line* is set up as a formal debate. Here are two, the first on whether we should ratify SALT I (held at Yale), the second on whether "this house" approves the economic policies of Ronald

Reagan (at Harvard). George McGovern is very popular at Yale, J. K.
Galbraith very popular at Harvard. But—well, we didn't ratify SALT I, and
Reagan won forty-nine states a year or so later.

Every now and then you see expert minds go to work on each other with
Socratic skill. Van den Haag does it to Donald Shapiro on capital punishment; Donald MacKay to B. F. Skinner on the presumptions of science.

Muhammad Ali tells how he became a special victim of the sixties when
the draft board denied his "sincerity" in becoming an ordained Islamic
minister in the nick of time to avoid being drafted. William Kunstler has
trouble denying he is in favor of criminal behavior, on being confronted
with an article in *Playboy.* Fox Butterfield, H.D.S. Greenway, and David
Butler share reminiscences of journalists' work in Saigon. Morris Abram,
retreated from the presidency of Brandeis University, confesses his disillusion with some traditional liberal axioms, and Norman Podhoretz tells what
was distinctive about the sixties and why some of those who fell victim to
the Communist-dominated radicalism of the thirties went along with the
sixties fever notwithstanding everything they had learned.

M. Revel probes the structural weaknesses of democracy while Professor
Hollander attempts to explain, with the help of Professor van den Haag, the
special seductiveness of totalitarian societies for the intellectual. Robert
Moss gives concrete examples of intellectual political confusion. Theodore
White applauds U.S. foreign policy up until the ambiguous sixties, and
James Michener, at work on his novel on Poland, speaks of East European
disillusion. Mr. Rurarz, who defected in Tokyo from Poland while serving
there as ambassador, tells what it was that briefly gave hope to Poles waiting
for liberation. Margaret Thatcher says that it is democratic mannerisms,
rather than substantive democracy, that make for national weakness.

Congressman Crane and Mr. Powell believe that the fairness of the marketplace is a communicable truth. Mrs. Pilpel and Jeremy Rifkin disagree, in
part because they see nothing fair about the marketplace to begin with.
George McGovern wrestles with the problem of pragmatic data versus
ideological dogma, as in the Soviet position on privately produced grains.
Jimmy Carter (in 1971) insists that state-federal relations, preeminently the
recently exercised right of impoundment by President Nixon, threaten economic injustice. Michael Dukakis itches strongly for federal aid to states in
temporary distress, and Mayor Koch makes the same point, remarking the
asymmetry of states' debts to one other.

Vice President Gerald Ford is asked: Why doesn't President Nixon suggest that the House unanimously recommend impeachment? That way only one of the two congressional chambers will be tied up. Isn't the impeachment procedure crude? Congressman Pike says that attempts to reform congressional misbehavior have been misbegotten. As it stands—and Dornan agrees—a congressman needs desperately to hang on to his seat; and an overwhelming majority of the incumbents do so. . . . Richard Nixon, in 1967, on the air and off the air, divulges his strategy for becoming President. Clare Boothe Luce doubts, after the defeat of Goldwater, that the GOP will succeed in resuming a distinctive profile. Barry Goldwater predicts that the GOP will get nowhere unless it understands itself to be the conservative party and acts as such. But Congressman Charles Mathias, without saying it in so many words, says: How do you account for such anomalies as myself? A thoroughbred liberal who wins every time? . . . George Wallace pronounces himself aggressively as a populist, and declares that if his host is a conservative, then conservatives are all washed up and damned well ought to be. Brzezinski, on the other hand, warns his fellow Democrats that to ignore national defense and imperial responsibility in the Soviet age will kill the Democratic Party's chances for effective leadership. Mayor Koch agrees, denouncing the hold radicals have on the Democrats, especially during the primaries. . . . Four prominent journalists mix it up: savoring this reform, rejecting that one, laughing at the third, eyeing the fourth suspiciously, but inquisitively.

GUEST: RONALD REAGAN

An ideal situation. It is January 1980. Candidate Reagan is seated down and told: You have been elected President! Now: Tell us how you would react to the following six crises. . . .

Floyd Abrams, as ever, defends the press and its right to refuse to give information at court, with Rusher emphatically disagreeing. Maurice Stans asks how to justify a press that can ruin a reputation and do nothing about its victims' subsequent vindication. Otto Preminger says he thoroughly agrees with the implicit ban on Hollywood sexual exhibitionism. But that was before the days of Harry Reems, the star of *Deep Throat* (the porn film, not the Watergate informer), defended by Professor Dershowitz, who however refuses to see the movie, as a matter of principle. Abner Mikva debates with Robert Kukla of the National Rifle Association the whole question of civil liberties and the right to bear arms. Professor Berger of Harvard says the Constitution simply does not endorse current understandings of the Fourteenth Amendment, never mind the disagreement of the American Civil Liberties Union's Arieh Neyer. And Michael Harrington attempts to bail out the labor union's position—that it has the right to collective bargaining even in dealing with members who are engaged primarily in ventilating their political views.

Always, the haunting question of capital punishment, but talk also of prisons, and prison life. Neyer defends the findings of the Warren Court. Dershowitz admits that the great majority of those who are brought to trial are in fact guilty. Allen argues against capital punishment and Capote suggests that there should be two types of prisons for two types of offenders. Jimmy Hoffa relates his experiences in prison and makes his suggestions for reforms, as does Gordon Liddy, while Charles Colson maintains that half of the people who are sent to prison should be sent instead into community service.

13. ON THE CULTURAL FRONT 252

GUESTS: BENJAMIN STEIN
ROSALYN TURECK
TIM PAGE
SCHUYLER CHAPIN
LOUIS AUCHINCLOSS
HELEN MACINNES
TOM WOLFE
JORGE LUIS BORGES

Screenwriter, novelist, critic Ben Stein says he has never met a conservative in Hollywood, or seen a movie with a decent general or businessman. Rosalyn Tureck, Tim Page, and Schuyler Chapin discuss the merits of recordings vs. public performances, giving illustrations of the best in both areas. Louis Auchincloss and Helen MacInnes jointly deplore novels far gone in inscrutability. Tom Wolfe talks of the tyranny of ideology over architectural art. And Jorge Luis Borges extemporizes a tone poem on language.

14. TECHNIQUE: STYLE AND CIVILITY 278

GUESTS: ABBA EBAN
EDWARD HEATH
NJEROGE MUNGAI

How important is timing in public discussion? How does it bear on civility? How does Abba Eban behave when, seconds before going on the air, he is told that Nasser has died? Or Edward Heath, who announces seconds before going on the air that of course he must not be asked about any British politician? Or Kenya's Foreign Minister, Dr. Mungai, seconds before *not* going on the air—how to respond to his saying that he will not consent to discuss any other African leaders if they are going to be criticized?

15. THE ECONOMIC QUESTION 286

GUESTS: HAROLD WILSON
MICHAEL FOOT
JAMES SCHLESINGER
JOHN KENNETH GALBRAITH
GEORGE GILDER
RONALD REAGAN
JACK KEMP

Harold Wilson is relaxed, looking back on the militant socialism that lingers in the party he once dominated. Michael Foot flatly says it, that no man's economic liberties can get in the way of his duties to his country. James Schlesinger attempts, as Secretary of Energy, to effect a reconciliation between his mandate and the free market. John Kenneth Galbraith confesses—or, better, proclaims—that he loves taxation precisely because he believes in leveling, never mind the economic consequences. George Gilder makes his provocative point, that the risk element of capitalism is precisely what makes it a philanthropic social arrangement. Ronald Reagan makes perhaps his first appearance as an endorser of tax cuts across the board, and intuits the Laffer curve. Jack Kemp, coauthor of the first major tax-cut bill, predicts the consequences of a bill a lesser form of which was enacted in the first year of Reagan's presidency.

Michael Harrington wrestles with his very soul, contending against Charles Murray's position that, in fact, $200 billion of welfare money has worsened rather than improved the plight of America's poor. Jesse Jackson insists that the best way to increase the share of the black minority in the economy is to insist on proportional representation at the levels of ownership and management. James Farmer contends that the plight of the American black is a historical affliction and that it is impossible to estimate the damage done by discrimination. Not so, says Thomas Sowell, who challenges what he considers to be a litany of clichés about the causes of black backwardness.

A view around the world. Yehudi Menuhin has just come back from China, and has found the cultural Esperanto he was looking for. Fox Butterfield speculates on whether China can bury fully the awful memory of its Cultural Revolution. And President Chiang Ching-kuo of Taiwan explains how under no circumstances could Taiwan make a deal with the Soviet Union, never mind the threat from mainland China. . . . Elspeth Huxley speaks of the political problems of the continent she grew up in. Anthony Lewis inveighs against any cooperation with South Africa of any kind, even for the sake of ejecting the Cuban mercenaries from Angola. Why, de Borchgrave asks, should the United States, simply to fight apartheid, surrender its strategic interests in Africa? Alan Paton somewhat reluctantly grants that progress between the races in South Africa will be the result of energetic economic activity, though he distrusts capitalism. And Bishop Huddleston and Paul Johnson fight for fifteen bloody rounds, the bishop urging a total boycott of South Africa, Johnson urging interracial progress through economic activity and the gradual breakdown of apartheid as anachronistic. . . . Carlos Lacerda of Brazil gives it as his opinion that talk about democracy in Latin America tends to be too facile, sometimes neglecting such matters as food, shelter, and work. Lawrence Birns of the State Department quarrels with Nena Ossa of Chile on the effect of Colonel Pinochet, and on the thrust of Allende's government. It is agreed that democracy in Latin America is, well, unstable. . . . And President Ferdinand Marcos explains that the Americans didn't stay around long enough in the Philippines to implant American-style democracy, which is why he had to seize power. Prime Minister Lee Kwan Yew of Singapore explains why the totalitarians are going to beat you if you give them the liberties you would like to give democratically minded opponents.

JOHN MCCAIN
ROGER FONTAINE
GEORGE WILL

A historic encounter in two senses—revealing a division, but among think-alikes. All the participants are equally opposed to softening U.S. hemispheric defenses. Yet here is a roster of well-known conservatives divided on the question: Should we ratify the Panama Canal treaties? Reagan leads the Negative team, WFB the Affirmative. One surmise: If Reagan had taken the opposite position, he would not have been nominated for the presidency (the conservatives would have blocked him). But if the treaties had been defeated, Reagan would not have been elected (developments in Central America would have discredited him).

GUESTS: PAUL JOHNSON
VLADIMIR BUKOVSKY
LEE KUAN YEW
HENRY KISSINGER
JEANE KIRKPATRICK
JAMES MICHENER

Paul Johnson insists that the nature of twentieth-century totalitarianism, particularly at the hands of the Soviet Union, is genuinely unique, and that therefore conventional historical precedents don't tell you very much about how to cope with Soviet aggressiveness. Bukovsky, a famous dissident, describes the means by which a potential opposition is suppressed in the Soviet Union. Prime Minister Lee describes what are the differences between your losing and their losing. Henry Kissinger describes the startling ignorance of the younger generation of geopolitical realities and the dangers implicit in unequal strength between the Soviet Union and the United States. Mrs. Kirkpatrick, freshly returned from Nicaragua, says that she sees for the first time the possibility of the disestablishment of a Soviet satellite state. But such a hope would evaporate if we desert the Contras. And James Michener tells of the dreadful lot of the Poles, who went, without surcease, from domination by Hitler to domination by Stalin.

GUESTS: NADIA ULANOVSKAYA
CLAIRE STERLING
ROY COHN
VERNON WALTERS
ALLEN DULLES
REBECCA WEST
PAUL JOHNSON
CONSTANTINE FITZGIBBON

Nadia Ulanovskaya was a Soviet spy in Washington in the early thirties and worked alongside Whittaker Chambers. Claire Sterling is a close student of terrorism and its interface with intelligence and espionage operations. Roy Cohn angrily defends the FBI against assaults on it and its behavior, stressing the necessary job the Bureau has done to guard the national security. Ambassador Walters regrets the ambivalence so many Americans have about intelligence when it is of supreme importance to know what the enemy's intentions are. Allen Dulles handles with aplomb the matter of President Eisenhower's lying about the activities of our U-2 spy plane. Rebecca West says that the relative indulgence shown Kim Philby, British traitor, by her countrymen is in part the result of his historical association with Arabism. Constantine Fitzgibbon defends strenuous intelligence work on the grounds that we could not survive a nuclear Pearl Harbor.

Two guests who appeared frequently on *Firing Line* (a half-dozen times each), one a liberal, the other a conservative, died, so to speak, with their boots on. Mrs. Luce was not, from her deathbed, voluble during those final weeks. And Al Lowenstein was shot in his office. . . . Two portraits of two great figures and polemicists, together with eulogies delivered at their funerals.

The concluding section, wherein four figures examine the reasons for faith, the causes for faith, the metaphysics of religion, and the serenity of belief.

LIST OF ILLUSTRATIONS

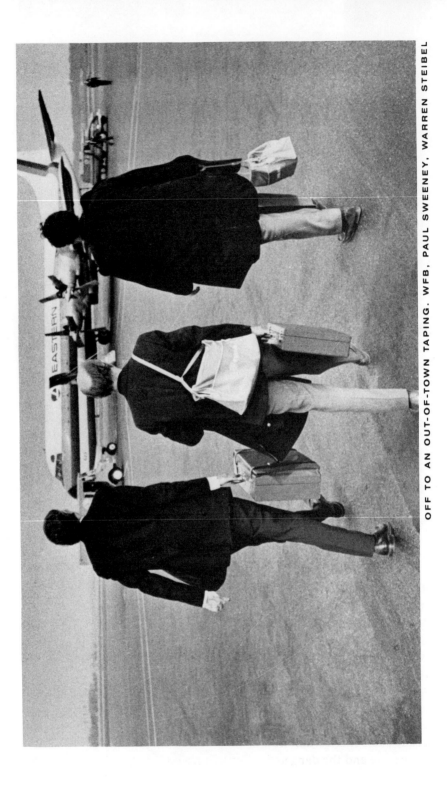

OFF TO AN OUT-OF-TOWN TAPING. WFB, PAUL SWEENEY, WARREN STEIBEL

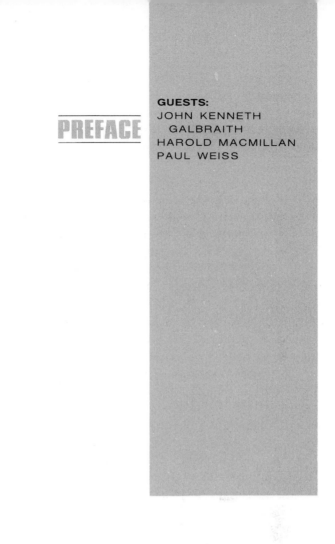

PREFACE

GUESTS:
JOHN KENNETH
  GALBRAITH
HAROLD MACMILLAN
PAUL WEISS

In the spring of 1965, a young entrepreneur approached me to ask whether I would be hospitable to a television program to which I would invite the most conspicuous liberals on the scene, with whom to exchange analyses and impressions of public problems, public policies, and public figures. He had in mind a program that would be booked for thirteen weeks, holding out the breathless possibility that it might be extended for a second thirteen-week period (thirteen was in those days the ruling integer in television). Three networks or syndicates were interested in sponsoring the hour. They were influenced (unquestionably) by the presidential election that had just occurred. Barry Goldwater was the candidate, and his platform reminded many broadcasters that certain traditional presumptions about the limitations of the state and the dangers in overreliance on omnipotent government had not quite died with the New Deal. And then there was the strenuous opposition from the American right to the threat of Communist expansionism. The assumption was that these views might be enough to sustain a dozen hours of television.

But late that spring I decided to "run" (my motives were didactic, not political) for Mayor of New York City, and this put a freeze on the project. No television station would carry a regular program featuring a participant who was an active political candidate. Accordingly, the project was postponed, and was launched in April 1966.

In those days there was no organized public television network. The early sponsor of *Firing Line* was RKO, which owned stations in New York, Boston, Los Angeles, and Memphis. RKO ran *Firing Line* on its own stations and then syndicated it to others. Tapes would be "bicycled" from one city to another. In that way, the cost of "film dupes" (duplicate copies—back before videotape), which was considerable, was kept down.

The series—I remember—began with an hour with Norman Thomas, the grand old man of American socialism. His mood was fustian (his hostility to the Vietnam War incorporated his early distrust of violence in any form—Norman Thomas forsook pacifism only for just long enough to back the war against Hitler), and his eyesight was all but gone (I needed to touch him lightly on the knee to alert him to be quiet for the oncoming commercial, whose imminence was advertised by a director via a hand signal Mr. Thomas could not see). But the hour was bracing, as were subsequent hours with Michael Harrington (successor to Thomas as head of the Socialist Party) and Episcopal Bishop James Pike. The thirteen weeks were renewed; and then again; and then again. Five years later, the general prosperity of commercial television edged *Firing Line* over toward public broadcasting (commercial television could not afford to give up the revenue a program like *Firing Line,* with its exiguous ratings, displaced). As I write, the program has been renewed for its twenty-fourth year (1988–89)—though, at my initiative, it is altering its format to one-half hour. This is an acknowledgment of the hectic metabolic schedule of almost all television geared to public policy. The President of the United States is lucky if a major speech commands four minutes of the evening news. If Lincoln were to recite his Gettysburg Address on any of the morning news shows, he would get the Thank-you-very-much-Abe dismissal before he squeezed in the bit about government of the people, by the people, and for the people.

.   .   .

The cliché about something or other being only as interesting as yesterday's newspapers is for one thing unexamined (yesterday's newspapers, for instance, reveal that the public's reception to Lincoln's Gettysburg Address was—bored). Yesterday's television programs face problems less strenuous than the newspapers', given that kinetic visual material, selected in the first instance for its graphic energies, can continue to divert, move, or solemnize. Television (or movie) shots of the first atomic explosion will continue to engross, as also televised transcripts of Martin Luther King's dream-speech at the Washington Mall. These have the advantage of having been historical events. What is here being undertaken accepts the challenge of highlighting in print excerpts from twenty-odd years of television exchanges that begin in 1966, and continue today, under the logo *Firing Line.*

The project is undertaken out of respect for an enterprise that has been extraordinarily long-lived and in some ways unique. *Firing Line* has devoted an hour to examining the thought (sometimes the attitudes, sometimes the stratagems) of a single guest, sometimes two guests, for a full hour. I have been its host since the outset. And, a distinction extremely important, the hour was never conceived of as an "interview." It was to be an "exchange of opinions."

Polemical styles, and to a certain extent expository styles, have changed since 1966 (I was about to say "evolved," but thought better of it). In that year the Vietnam War became serious in terms of lives lost, Indira Gandhi was inaugurated Prime Minister, Truman Capote's *In Cold Blood* was published, Evelyn Waugh, Billy Rose, and Sophie Tucker died, and Mao Tse-tung ratified the Cultural Revolution with the publication of *Quotations of Chairman Mao.* U.S. population was still under 200 million. The Vietnam War was to be the great geopolitical and spiritual incubus over public affairs for another six years. I say this even though it isn't so that *Firing Line* was so obsessed by the war as to address no other problem. From the beginning, we stressed diversity, for one thing because different people are interesting for different reasons. For another, because tireless repetition of arguments, advocacy, analysis, attitudes, becomes tiresome; and affects, negatively, not only a program's viewers, but also a program's host.

A reason, this last, to confront my own role in this book. There is an unavoidable sense in which the host is omnipresent. It can't be otherwise in a program whose charter specifies an "exchange of opinions." I do not attempt to recapitulate all the arguments used, either my guests' or my own. I do not award equal time, as though the FCC were looking over my shoulder. This is not a *New York Times* archival book of record; it is a needlework of points, made by guests, by friends, by enemies, by me: and a book in which it is here and there recorded what points were *not* made: by others, and by me. It is not a digest of one thousand hours of television exchanges—it is an attempt at distillation of some of the lessons taught by these exchanges, and a reproduction of analytical narrative worth rereading; in some instances, worth committing to memory. Those guests who will complain that some of their best lines were ignored I can only hope to appease by saying that some of my best are also ignored.

I have said that the program was not designed as an interview program, and that proved generally true. There were almost necessary exceptions: I wasn't going to argue with Harold Macmillan about his handling of the Suez Crisis, twenty years earlier.

It should be noted at the outset that in such a program as *Firing Line* the host is at a disadvantage because the subject under discussion is almost always a subject with which the guest is intimately familiar; indeed, a subject with which the guest is publicly identified. I remember when Senator Albert Gore (senior) was my guest to discuss "The Tennessee Valley Authority: Success or Failure?" At the end of the second break for a commercial he leaned over and whispered: "Do you know something, Mr. Buckley? I know more about the TVA than you do. I was one of its original sponsors." There isn't very much you can do by way of professional competition in such corners. One—well, as we shall be seeing here and there, one maneuvers. I remember whispering back to the senator that his only responsibility was to *prove* that he knew more about the TVA than I did.

I have done a great deal of this sort of maneuvering, as in this debate with John Kenneth Galbraith, who is, after all, a professional economist, never mind what some professional economists say on the point.

WFB: I would remind you that most of the mammoth corporations you pointed to in one of your books as dominating us—as though we were mere puppets—are either at this point bankrupt or living off the government.

GALBRAITH: Could I pursue that point and ask which of those companies is bankrupt?

WFB: Well, I exaggerated a little bit. [*Laughter*] [To the audience] The thesis of one of Mr. Galbraith's books was that the huge companies in America have become so important, so vital, and so domineering that in fact they can regulate their own worth by causing people, for instance, to consume their products, by causing the legislature to pass congenial laws, and so on and so forth. Unhappily, his book was published just when the market slid the value of most of these corporations by about eighty-five percent, but this is a datum that Mr. Galbraith, with characteristic savoir faire, has simply transcended. [*Laughter*]

GALBRAITH: I certainly don't want to suggest that Mr. Buckley ever exaggerates. [*Laughter*] What year was it that the market declined by eighty-five percent?

WFB: Well, some of the companies that you mentioned have lost value. As a matter of fact, I think Litton Industries was one of them, wasn't it?

GALBRAITH: Oh, but you said the stock market in general had declined.

WFB: Well, the stock market in general went down forty to fifty percent in the most recent—

GALBRAITH: And you should know that I dined earlier this evening with Mr. Tex Thornton, chairman of Litton Industries, and I didn't ask him, but I could see from the charmed look on his face that Litton Industries has recovered from any temporary misfortune. [*Laughter*]

WFB: Coincidental with your book going out of print. [*Laughter*]

GALBRAITH: One of the marvelous good fortunes of being an author that I share with William Buckley—there are some things that we do have in common—is that authors, unlike automobile companies, are not yet required to recall their defective works. [*Laughter, applause*]

I was relying on memory. It was substantially correct, but in fact I exaggerated. The Dow Jones was at 968.85 at its highest in 1969, and 631.16 at its lowest in 1970. It had, therefore, gone down 35 percent in value.

Sometimes I have just sat back and listened to a few sentences, or to a passage that exercised on me extraordinary power to engross, or to

HAROLD MACMILLAN EXPLAINS

move. Harold Macmillan, Prime Minister of Great Britain from 1957 to 1963, was reminiscing in 1980 about the Second World War. About yesterday, it seemed.

MACMILLAN: In 1943 there was a conference in Cairo, halfway through the war, after Alamein. Everybody was there: President Roosevelt, all the chiefs—the American chiefs, all the British chiefs of staff—Churchill. I was summoned because I was then with General Eisenhower in Algiers.

I remember one night, we had been dining with President Roosevelt in his little villa, and I went back with Churchill—we were staying together in a small house—and he didn't seem in a mood to go to bed. He didn't say very much at first, then suddenly he turned to me and said, "Cromwell was a great man." And I said, "Yes, Prime Minister." "Born and bred in the fear of Spain— Philip II, the great battles of the sixteenth century—yet he failed to see the rise of France. He still thought Spain was the enemy trying to seize Europe, when really it was the France of Mazarin and Richelieu; hence the wars of the eighteenth century; hence the mobile wars." All that was said to me. I knew what he meant. By 1943 he'd lost all interest in the Germans. He knew that we had defeated them and that we had to turn next to the Soviets.

Sometimes it has been a fast sequence of parrying that engrossed me; as, here, with Professor Paul Weiss, as it happens, my sometime philosophy teacher at Yale.

WFB: Tonight, Professor Weiss seeks to inform God that it was a mistake to organize religion. Organized religion, he will argue, has failed.

WEISS: I don't remember when God organized religion. Is there any time when *God* organized religion?

WFB: Well, the situation was like this—there was God and there was Peter, you see—

WEISS: I thought they were distinct.

WFB: They were.

WEISS: Oh, good! Now, then—what?

WFB: Well, then, a church was organized—

WEISS: Fine.

WFB: By God.

WEISS: He did that?

WFB: Uh huh.

WEISS: I don't remember any records to that effect, but let it be. Granted that somebody organized it, now you want to know—has it been a success? Is that it?

WFB: Now you have it.

WEISS: Well, organized religion is rather too easy. It's the only important organization where we say children belong. It's the only important subject where people are able to say they are real adherents, even though they do nothing but perhaps pay some small fee or carry out a ritual without perhaps understanding it. This is not true of art, not true of science, not true of philosophy, not true of any other important subject.

WFB: All right, now, what are you suggesting? That, ideally, organized religion should expel those of its members—

WEISS: No, not necessarily expel, but distinguish between those who are perhaps practicing—

WFB: Well, the Catholic—

WEISS: —who might be equated—

WFB: —the Catholic Church *precisely* does. There are people who *are* in the state of sin, and people who are *not* in the state of sin.

WEISS: *All* are in the state of sin.

WFB: Well, there are people in—

WEISS: —the Catholic Church—

WFB: —different gravities—

WEISS: But they're *all* in the state of sin.

WFB: I agree, and that's why I went on to make a distinction, as I was once taught to do, that—

ANNOUNCER: We'll continue with *Firing Line* in just a moment.

Always there is variety. Some of it, as with Buckley-Weiss above, is of such an order. Some programs are, in a word, better than others; some leave little footprints of an individual's style of thought, and of behavior. Some guests are more interesting than others. And—let's face it—some days the host is in better form than on other days. Sometimes I leave the studio confident that I have planted the cogency of my case. Other times I leave with much on my mind, *en esprit d'escalier* (a wonderful French term describing what you wish you had said by way of devastating retort: typically, a sunburst that hits you as you reach the bottom of the staircase).

·   ·   ·

My church holds that any thought given to the passage of time is a parochialism, that one day "time shall be no more." There is much of that, in a quarter century's *Firing Line*s. You hear some lines uttered in 1988 that are not very different from those uttered in 1966 (neither I nor Senator Joe Biden is disturbed by this). You close your eyes and notice suddenly that much history has slid by without undermining past axioms. Rebecca West, Harold Macmillan, and Clare Boothe Luce are dead, though not by any means all of their thought. Muhammad Ali, so wonderfully, engagingly bright on *Firing Line* (it was the greatest canard in the history of Kentucky that Cassius Clay was "too dumb" to serve in the army), is now, well, weary. Ronald Reagan was elected Governor of California the year *Firing Line* began. He has left the public scene now, having since served twice as governor, four times as presidential candidate, twice as President. Yet all of them are with us still, in the television stacks. They are with us also, I expect to establish, in a running documentary of sorts that gives us a mosaic of life in America (and abroad) over twenty-odd years, giving permanent form to some of the mountainous material uttered in one thousand hours of television. There is a narrative lurking there, in the firing line of public controversy.

The custom on *Firing Line* is to put a topic under discussion in the interrogatory, even provocative, mood, as in: "I should like to begin by asking Mr. Norman Mailer, who has been sentenced to five days in jail for a march on the Pentagon, and is appealing on the grounds that he was sentenced because he is famous, to disclose whether he believes that artists should be immune from the harassments of the law." Or, "I should like to begin by asking Dame Rebecca West whether she has remarked in England or in herself a diminishing resentment of treason." Or, "I should like to begin by asking Governor Reagan, What would you do as President if, say, one afternoon you were advised that a race riot had broken out in Detroit?"

The bored initial response to the Gettysburg Address might, come to think of it, have been accepted by professional students of political rhetoric. Mr. Lincoln had finished by telling his audience that we were engaged in a great national experiment to see whether democracy could actually work. Ambiguities are not conventional political tender; certainly they are not bugle calls to enthusiasm. Conditional rhetoric becomes popular when the optimistic alternative is thought to have prevailed.

ON
THE
FIRING
LINE

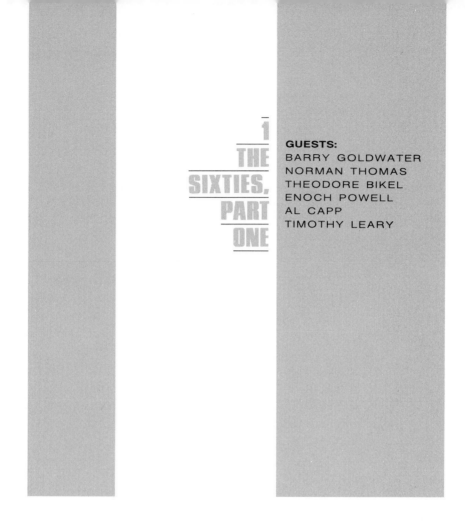

1
THE
SIXTIES,
PART
ONE

GUESTS:
BARRY GOLDWATER
NORMAN THOMAS
THEODORE BIKEL
ENOCH POWELL
AL CAPP
TIMOTHY LEARY

iring Line began (as already noted) in 1966. That was an early high point of the long travail that I (and others) have called the Kid Years, having in mind student riots, college protests against the war, and Woodstock Nation. Vietnam overwhelmed some forums, as it did many campuses; *Firing Line* continued to deal with much else, but, inevitably, spent time in the sixties on The Sixties; on its culture, its morphology, and its implications.

Senator Barry Goldwater, appearing on the program two years after running for President, clearly didn't anticipate the lengths to which The Sixties would go. I asked him whether Vietnam might become "the dominant issue of concern for Americans." He replied, "I would hope this thing could fade away. It won't, but it's not going to have the divisive effect that I think you're getting at." His point (in 1966) was

that there was near unanimity on the matter. "In other words, [Senator]
Jack Javits and I agree pretty much on Vietnam."

But it was also in 1966 that an entirely different reading of what lay
ahead was given. Norman Thomas has already been introduced. Thomas
had become the grand old man of the American left. It was a hot-
tempered exchange. I had several times debated with Mr. Thomas on the
college circuit, and he was progressively displeased with everything I
said, and the positions I took. In retrospect, I regret I dealt with him so
outspokenly. If he had been a younger man, he'd have resented it if I had
been less blunt: Norman Thomas was a veteran of the rhetorical street
brawling in which he delighted. But he was now an old man, and a valiant
figure, even as his causes were surrealistic. I remember the last time I saw
him, a few months later. He and I engaged in a debate at Lehigh College
(he was by then totally blind). The next morning, at the airport to return
to New York, I saw a Piper Cub lifting Mr. Thomas into the air. He was
bound for Ithaca, New York, to preach at Cornell against Vietnam. I can
hear even now the vibrancy of his voice and the stentorian tones of the
preacher denouncing the sinner. . . . His then current ("terminal" is, I
suppose more accurate: Norman Thomas died in 1968) crusade was to
save Vietnam and the United States Marines from each other.

THOMAS: Mr. Buckley, you seem to believe in cruelty as a necessary
             adjunct to this kind of war. Your main point is that some-
             how we're going to contain Communism this way, and we
             aren't. We may *delay* certain events in Communism.
             We're not going to *contain* it. We—

WFB: Excuse me, was the war in Greece cruel? Did we contain
             the Communists in Greece?

THOMAS: You haven't got the same situation by a long ways. For
             one thing you haven't got Yugoslavia—

WFB: Well, for one thing, it's in a different part of the globe; that
             much is certainly different, yes. Proceed.

THOMAS: Let me get a little farther on this. What I am asserting is
             that if we win, Vietnam will be a devastated, broken coun-
             try. Probably this may happen before China or Russia
             comes all the way into the war, which would be a major
             tragedy in the world. We would have to support what was
             left of Vietnam as a colony halfway around the world, on
             the very borders of China, which can no more be done

peacefully than China can do the same thing to a colony in Mexico.

WFB: Why did you support the Korean War, under the circumstances?

THOMAS: —why did I support the Korean War?

WFB: Because in point of fact, if you don't mind, rather than simply—automatically—accept your vaticinations, I'd like to point out that in Korea, we did actually *stop* the aggressor.

THOMAS: All right.

WFB: It cost us many billions of dollars and a hundred thousand casualties.

THOMAS: And several hundred—

WFB: But there were those, including yourself, who thought it was a heroic effort, to try to keep the Communists at bay. Now, is [your change of position] a function of age or is it a function of what?

THOMAS: No.

WFB: You keep talking about the progressions of your intellectual position, from the time you were a pacifist until—it seems to me, [you have become] very nearly a pacifist again. But why did you back the Korean War and refuse to back this one?

THOMAS: Well, give me a chance, and I'll tell you very quickly. There's no question whatever that the Korean War *was* a war of aggression from the North on the South. We acted plainly on a mandate of the UN. There is no such mandate here.

WFB: Now hold it, hold it, Mr. Thomas, please. Do you think there would have been a mandate for the war in Korea if it had happened that the Soviet Union had been present in the Security Council that afternoon in June?* Come on, now.

---

*On June 27, 1950, when the United States proposed before the Security Council that the North Korean invasion be resisted by the United Nations, the Soviet representative was absent. It is generally assumed that he'd have vetoed the motion.

THOMAS: Whatever the reason is—

WFB: Well, I'm *giving* you the reason, so please don't use—

THOMAS: The fact that Russia was away was a very good thing. But it was with the will of the nations outside of Russia that we acted against aggression. You have no similar endorsement now.

WFB: Of course we have a similar endorsement. We have it from England—

THOMAS: And the fact that one—

WFB: —and we have it from the NATO powers, with the exception of France.

THOMAS: You have it—but you know that France, the country that once claimed to own all the countries in Indochina, is very critical of what we've done, and that among outside governments there's a degree of criticism of this war that is very damaging to our leadership of the peace.

WFB: Do you want me to explain the reason for that, Mr. Thomas?

THOMAS: Do you *want* to explain it?

WFB: Yes, would you like to hear?

THOMAS: Yes, I'd like to hear.

WFB: It has to do with a certain infection that comes to societies that tend to shrink from the realities, and it is an infection that causes people to lose all sense, all moral understanding of what is going on.

THOMAS: Did you ever read Edgar Snow? Did you ever read Gunnar Myrdal?* Do you think that the village that he described was ready to overthrow the Communist government, or even—

WFB: No, Mr. Thomas, here is what I think, which is perhaps something that will displease you most. I think that

---

*Edgar Snow (1905–1972) was a resourceful and tireless apologist for the policies of Mao Tse-tung. Gunnar Myrdal, the famous Swedish economist, became famous with his book *An American Dilemma: The Negro Problem and Modern Democracy.*

human beings can be *made* to live like animals. *A Day in the Life of Ivan Denisovich,* which has just been re-outlawed in the Soviet Union, shows how, even in concentration camps under conditions which you and I would rather commit suicide than submit to, people *can* somehow live. Their biological mechanisms continue to work. And I have no doubt this is going on in Red China. I have no doubt that it went on in Nazi Germany. All I am observing is that, by standards that we consider civilized, these are *wretched* people and that we have some sort of sacred mission to hold out hope for them.

THOMAS: I do not think—

WFB: And we can't do that by getting shaky knees every time we throw a napalm bomb on a sniper in North Vietnam.

THOMAS: We don't throw them on snipers, we have to throw them on villages. But what I desire is a situation in which you can substitute negotiation for this kind of terror.

WFB: May I make two observations? One is that I am for negotiation, too. Everyone is for negotiation except the Communists, who usually decline to negotiate. And number two, as a former president of the Americans for Democratic Action, no less, wrote recently in *The New York Times* [I do not remember who I had in mind; probably Professor John P. Roche], the notion is not only romantic but vulgar to suppose that something can be done to build up the economy and the state of civil liberties in South Vietnam during a period when they are engaged in a war for *survival.* He gives you one figure, which I think you ought to concentrate on, or contemplate. And that is that thirty thousand people carefully trained in civics or carefully trained to be mayors and aldermen in their little communities, carefully trained to be agronomists, have been killed—*butchered* by the Vietcong. Now this is an indispensable cadre that takes time to replenish. And for you to suppose that you need only touch South Vietnam with one of Myrdal's books and all of a sudden have freedom sprout up like daisies on the field is simply another and consistent index of your—

THOMAS: I was talking about Myrdal in reference to the state of affairs in China, not at all in South Vietnam.

WFB: But he has *ideas* on South Vietnam, he has ideas on everything.

THOMAS: No connection there. And I don't even think it's very smart debating exactly in that way.

WFB: No, but the utopians who suppose—

THOMAS: I am not that kind of utopian and I am saying—

WFB: It's highly irrelevant for you to talk about the state of freedom or lack of freedom in South Vietnam in the middle of a war as brutal as this one. Do you realize they didn't even have elections in England, the mother of parliaments, during *their* war?

THOMAS: I am saying this, that the only way you will have a chance of freedom is to get peace; it's war that's the great enemy.

WFB: I am for peace too.

THOMAS: I am saying that McGovern—

WFB: But you're not going to have peace—

THOMAS: —says that he went to hospitals in South Vietnam and saw more civilians there who were victims of our proud policy of bombing than he did of the Vietcong terror. I am not for surrendering to the Vietcong. I am for making a kind of effort that hasn't been made for negotiations, which involves recognizing [the Vietcong] as the principal negotiators.

WFB: You're for sending in one of your committees to teach them—

THOMAS: —for reconvening the Geneva nations.

WFB: They wouldn't even *attend,* Mr. Thomas. They certainly wouldn't even *attend.*

It is probably appropriate, after quoting from this exchange from the first *Firing Line* tape, to take up the issue of manners in public debate.

Here is a quotation (from John Judis, *William F. Buckley, Jr.: Patron Saint of the Conservatives,* Simon & Schuster, 1988) that raises the question.

In the sixties, Buckley became best known not as a writer or speaker but as a television performer. Television was the medium through which he projected his own views and personality onto the canvas of the sixties.

The original format of *Firing Line* was that of a debate between the host and his guest. But it was extraordinary in that Neal Freeman's model [Freeman, a young graduate of Yale, who was my assistant at *National Review,* performed also as the program's director] was the prizefights that were shown every Friday night on national television. "I was thinking that *Firing Line* ought to be a challenge to the liberal establishment to see if their champions could go three rounds with the boy wonder. It was the fight of the week." And in its first years, Freeman recalled, *Firing Line* was a "bare-knuckled intellectual brawl."

The debate between Buckley and his guests often became heated and angry, spurred in part by Buckley's ad hominem attacks. The ethic of the boxing ring applied. Buckley was perfectly amiable off camera, but on camera he would do everything he could to discredit his opponent. . . .

In the show's first year, guests were eager to appear, but after prominent liberals saw how their colleagues were treated, Buckley and Freeman, who was helping to line up guests, found it increasingly difficult to find willing recruits. "After about thirty of them had been carried out on a stretcher," Freeman recalled, "the word went out, 'I won't dignify this protofascist by appearing on his program.' It became increasingly difficult to get big-name liberal guests." Asked why Robert Kennedy would not appear, Buckley quipped, "Why does baloney reject the grinder?"

As Freeman recalls, many station executives were "appalled by the level of intensity" of the shows. But what disturbed station executives charmed television audiences. *Firing Line* was an overnight success. . . . The liberal TV critic Terrence O'Flaherty of the *San Francisco Chronicle* said of Buckley, "He's a real honest-to-God personality, one of the few live personalities on a dead medium; he's the best thing on the air."

A few comments:

1. *Firing Line* programs have almost always been governed, temperamentally, by the attitude and behavior of the guest. Norman Thomas

was a highly truculent debater (a running distemper was a part of his public persona). Some of my guests, during those years, were (unlike Norman Thomas) people freshly back from visiting in Hanoi and were siding openly with the Communists. My attitude toward them was as one would expect of a friend of the U.S. Marines, contending with a friend of the Vietcong.

2. Neal Freeman's memory errs. I can remember no point at which we had difficulty in getting guests for *Firing Line.* There were always a few exceptions, some of them conspicuous. No Kennedy has ever accepted an invitation (not Bobby; and not Ted). Neither did Martin Luther King or Nelson Rockefeller. Almost always, by the way, when the producer invites a guest (I have personally invited fewer than six people in twenty-two years, leaving that function to the producer) and the guest intends never to accept, he puts his negative obliquely. No one has ever said: "I will not now nor will I *ever* appear on *Firing Line.*" What the guest says is that, unhappily, the suggested date is not convenient. After thirty telephone calls suggesting alternative dates, the producer gets the message.

3. There were, on active duty during that period, one or two television and radio inquisitors who specialized in plain personal rudeness. One of them (I forget his name—Alan Burke?—and he now has no constituency) said to his guest one night: "Why are you so stupid?" That kind of interviewing-as-scarification was successful during a brief period, the period, as might be expected, of the sixties. Joe Pyne, the Morton Downey, Jr., of an earlier generation, had been much in demand. There are (I am told) regional radio talk-jocks who cultivate hostility toward the people they are interviewing (or talking to over the telephone). Nothing of the sort was ever a modus operandi of *Firing Line.* And in twenty-two years, we have had only a single letter of protest from a guest about the treatment the guest received. That was in 1985, from a cranky academic opposed to easing the marijuana laws, who resented the presence on the program of another scholar opposed to his views.

4. Television exchanges are not properly called "debates." There is, in a public debate, an evolving opportunity for the exercise of rhetoric, which is rare in the rabbit-punching format of the television exchange. In rhetoric, the Schoolmen taught, the disciplines of mathematics and logic (fact and analysis) are sublimely subsumed. They are integrated in an appeal to the moral nature of the audience. But rhetoric of that kind

can only take place serenely where there is ambient quiet: where the
speaker, confident that he has ten or fifteen minutes during which he will
not be interrupted, can build his case, accelerating at his own pace. In
the polemical exchange, facts, analysis, and quick-rhetorical punching
are the rule. When lawyer Joseph Welch said to Senator Joe McCarthy:
"Have you no sense of decency, sir?" it is correct that he wounded
McCarthy, perhaps mortally. But his was, strictly speaking, a verbal
quietus; a parry, not a rhetorical duel. Not a rhetorical exercise. A
format that permits, as television exchanges do, interruptions, or that
in effect limits a participant to a very few minutes' uninterrupted talk,
isn't a debate: it is an exchange. The point is worth noting, given the
frequency of references to *Firing Line* "debates."

To return to *Firing Line* and The Sixties:

In 1966 I questioned Theodore Bikel. Bikel was born in Austria and
was taken to Palestine when Hitler overran his homeland. As a boy, he
worked in a kibbutz. But his parents yielded to the inevitable when one
day they came upon him, pitchfork in hand, standing by a dung pile
reciting Shakespeare.

He was sent to London to drama school, and quickly won fame as an
actor, a folksinger, and a television entertainer. (His most famous role:
Captain von Trapp in the Broadway production of *The Sound of Music.*)
Theodore Bikel was active on college campuses, and much interested in
the causes of student unrest.

"Why are the students unhappy?" I asked him.

BIKEL: We are not dealing honestly with the youth of today,
            because we haven't given them any answers.

WFB: I couldn't agree with you more. But perhaps not for the
            same reasons.

BIKEL: Now I'm frightened. [*Laughter*]

WFB: It seems to me that one of the answers we owe to these
            students is to say from time to time to some of them: You
            are *creeps,* you're doing absolutely nothing in the world
            for yourselves or for your community, you have just
            relapsed into a kind of self-pitying solipsism, you are not
            repaying the community for the great sacrifices made by

your parents and other members of the community to give you a free education, you haven't exhibited any sense of self-discipline, and we feel certain enough of our role as educators to set down a series of rules and tell you that if you break those rules you can just go and break them outside of college. This sounds, I suppose, awfully old-fashioned. But I like to indulge the thought that one of the failures of the adult community—I have, for instance, Berkeley in mind—is the failure actually to lay down limits beyond which you stop talking about activity as defensible protest, and simply call it what it in fact is: totally undisciplined self-indulgence.

BIKEL: Well, in what way? Do you refer to the content of the activity or to its outward manifestations?

WFB: Both. For instance, if I ran a university, I think that I would try very hard to pass and enforce a law saying that my office was *not* available for sit-ins. And that people who chose to sit in my office would not only be forcibly ejected to the ritual little jail where they get photographed and get lots of free lawyers, but get ejected from the campus. And one of the difficulties, as was pointed out for instance by Professor [William] Peterson in his brilliant piece on the Berkeley riots [published in *The Columbia University Forum,* Spring, 1965], was that those students who had a feeling that they had gone too far in some of these protests looked for guidance to faculty, but they found the faculty so very much concerned to be indulgent to the students that they lost any capacity for leadership.

BIKEL: Well, I don't know. Words like "indulgence" are indulgence from one point of view and sympathy or understanding from another. Do you really think that we live in the kind of an age where you can expect children to emulate their parents, where a parent can obstinately cling to the belief that the values of today are not substantially different from the values of yesterday?

WFB: But the parents are *right.*

BIKEL: I knew that you would say that. But the point is that they are *not* right. We cannot possibly assume that there is a continuance of values. People wish to vary, to adapt themselves. Paradoxically, those who wish to have their values endure must do away with obsolete values and retain only the viable. You must adapt yourself, your philosophy and your theory and your practices, to the times. But in Darien, Connecticut, they don't do that.

WFB: Let's say a Tasmanian tribe deserts its particular totem, because over a period of time it has found out empirically that the totem doesn't deliver the goods. Okay. But I don't know of any values that the parents I know of, in our generation, think of as enduring which *have* been anachronized. What is it that has happened in the last ten or fifteen years that has rendered obsolete, say, some of the values that you and I were taught when we grew up? Which values are no longer relevant?

BIKEL: Well, the concept of politeness, for instance, of courtesy.

WFB: This you think is—

BIKEL: Yes. Having lived on a kibbutz, in an agricultural society where we worked darned hard all day long, and you come home dead tired having done your share of the day's work and you have a smile for your neighbor—you don't have to say good evening anymore. That's just a small example.

WFB: That's a terrible example, if I may say so. Do you aspire to rudeness—

BIKEL: No—

WFB: —so that you can be tuned in on the wavelength of student values?

BIKEL: An absence of conventional courtesies is no more synonymous with rudeness than an absence of sickness is with health.

WFB: But there are [different] ways by which courtesy, as I understand it, is expressed. And one of those ways is to *force* yourself to say goodnight to your son or to your wife,

even if you feel just awful. Surely the argument for emphasizing courtesy is more acute than ever today, isn't it?

There were, of course, many campuses around the country where the
problem wasn't a diminution of courtesy, but of order. Enoch Powell,
the provocative scholar-politician from England, best known at the time
for his advocacy of restrictive immigration policies, was well informed
about developments in the United States, and acute in his observations
on them.

POWELL: What has been discovered is the sheer effectiveness of
             violence exerted by those who do not recognize at all the
             framework and terms of reference of a society or an insti-
             tution. Let me take as an example of what I mean the
             university. Now, the life of the university has been based
             until very recently on the assumption that all participants
             desired it to go on. No one, therefore, questioned where
             the force lay—where the legality lay—where the power
             lay. It was an institution by *consent.* But introduce into
             such an institution even the smallest number of people
             who do not recognize those presumptions at all—

WFB: And you have the hijacker's effect.

POWELL: Yes—that's very apt. A very small content of violence
             produces a disproportionate effect. Now all the great dis-
             coveries of humanity have consisted in the discovery of
             how to do a lot for a little. How to make a very small
             amount of force go a long way. *That,* in various forms, is
             the new element which, I believe, is transforming the polit-
             ical arena.

Al Capp, the cartoonist who created "Li'l Abner," appeared on *Firing
Line* in 1969. He had been making his provocative rounds of the campuses, speaking, baiting, ridiculing. He had been, throughout his career,
a political liberal. His reaction to The Sixties was for that reason unexpected, dismaying to the Kids—and bracing to the perplexed bleachers.
His style was the surrealistic put-down ("John Kenneth Galbraith is the
greatest economist since Edna St. Vincent Millay"). He was all too
happy, on *Firing Line,* to diagnose the sources of the trouble and to

answer my question: What kind of reaction was he getting in the colleges?

CAPP: Oh, every now and then some student arises, quivering with rage, and says: "Mr. Capp, you detest us, so why are you speaking here at Chapel Hill?" And I say, "For three thousand bucks and I wouldn't spend an hour with a bunch like you for a nickel less." [*Laughter*] And you know, they're so *relieved*! At Southern Illinois University, just the other day, one of them got up and said, "We detest Mayor Daley, how can we poison Lake Michigan?" And I said, "Why don't you *bathe* in it?" [*Laughter*]

Capp managed a routine compliment for the majority of students who, he said, were uncontaminated by the crazies. I asked him how he accounted for the failure of the majority to discipline the minority.

CAPP: This is a very, very sad state of affairs. One could ask the same question of the city of Chicago, a city of millions which permitted Capone and his gang to terrorize that city. One could ask the same of any group of decent, orderly, busy citizens who permit a tiny, active, delinquent minority to make hell out of their lives. I say that it stems from an event at Harvard about two and a half years ago.

            Now, I live a stone's throw from Harvard. But if you duck, you don't get hurt. [*Laughter*] But Secretary McNamara was invited to speak at Harvard. It's true that McNamara is a member of a despised minority group, the President's Cabinet, but nonetheless he has the rights of any humble man. McNamara attempted to speak. The SDS—Students for a Democratic Society—stormed into that hall and screamed obscenities at McNamara until he was forced to stop speaking. He then got into his car and attempted to leave the grounds. They stopped the car. McNamara then attempted to leave his car. They began pounding him on the head with the poles on which their placards were nailed. It was only because the Cambridge police arrived, surrounded Secretary McNamara, and escorted him through a series of interconnecting cellars of Harvard buildings that he escaped injury.

> Now, the next morning Dean Monroe of Harvard was asked how he would punish those students. And he said, "I see no reason for punishing students for what was purely a political activity." Now, if depriving a man of his freedom of speech, depriving him of his freedom to move, very nearly depriving him of his life—if that's a political activity, then rape is a social event [*Laughter*] and sticking up a gas station is a financial transaction. [*Laughter*]

WFB: Now, what caused Dean Monroe, in your opinion, to make this error in judgment?

CAPP: Because he's a fathead. [*Laughter*]

I have to admit that at that point, Al Capp sounded to me like Aristophanes.

Dr. Timothy Leary was the pope of what he chose to call "a new religion"—a "religion" based on the consumption of drugs, in particular LSD, whose attractions were said to be sweeping the campuses. It was after the drug's initials that Dr. Leary named his new religion, the League for Spiritual Discovery.

Timothy Leary was graduated as a doctor of clinical psychology. He went to school in Alabama and took a Ph.D. at Berkeley. After experiencing nirvana in Spain, he went to Harvard, from which he was in due course fired.

Now, it is not easy to be fired from Harvard, at least not for misbehavior, but it transpired that Dr. Leary had become tour director for a lot of his students whom he was sending on long-distance trips through the mists of psychedelic experience. Dr. Leary traveled widely and had become accustomed to receiving standing ovations as he advanced the position that, as someone observed, "opiates are the religion of the people." Dr. Leary appeared on *Firing Line* in 1967. He had arrived at the studio dressed as a New York businessman might have been dressed. But he emerged from the makeup room dressed as a flower child, a frilly shirt, no jacket or tie, a bleary softness on his features.

WFB: I'd like to ask Dr. Leary why is it that it is the common impression that poorly adjusted people tend in greater numbers to the world of LSD than normally adjusted people?

LEARY: I've never heard that suggested before.

WFB: Then I suggest it.

LEARY: Well, there's no LSD or marijuana problem down in Po-
            dunk Junior College in Arkansas, it's at Harvard, Prince-
            ton, and even at Yale that fifty to seventy percent of the
            undergraduates are seriously experimenting with the most
            important thing that can be experimented with, their own
            consciousness.

WFB: Are you confusing *adjustment* with education?

LEARY: No, I'm not suggesting that.

WFB: Well, why did you mention the difference between Podunk
            U. and Yale University? What makes you think they're
            better adjusted at Yale than at Podunk U.?

LEARY: No, I'm trying to see what your problem is and I think I've
            diagnosed it. [*Laughter*]

WFB: Go ahead, Doc.

LEARY: Your approach to the word "drug," I think, is that of
            many Americans, particularly over the age of fifty, who
            when the word "drug" is mentioned think of some *opiate,*
            something that is an *escape,* something that takes you
            away from reality, something that you take if you're a
            failure. All the statistics that I've seen indicate that the
            people who use psychedelic drugs are people who are
            pretty well adjusted by any standard or criterion you want
            to name: income, education, creativity, productivity.
            What psychedelic drugs produce is not the dull, glazed,
            three-martini haze. Psychedelic drugs *intensify* conscious-
            ness. They're microscopic in their effect and they're used
            by people who are looking for more.

WFB: One thing that fascinates me about you—and there are a
            lot of things that do—is your use of language. There is a
            sort of a nineteenth-century tushery; there's a mysticism
            there that causes you to write sentences like this, when you
            describe dropping out (which you counsel everybody to
            do): "Dropping out," you say, "means to detach yourself
            harmoniously, tenderly and gracefully from worldly com-

mitments until your entire life is dedicated to worship and search."

Now, to the extent that I can understand English—and I have a hard time sometimes—doesn't that really mean that you should abandon a commitment to your family, abandon a commitment to your church, to your country, to superpersonal ideals, and isn't this really a retreat into *yourself* and a failure to come to grips with the fact that the world exists other than merely in yourself?

LEARY: No. Because what you diagnose as the world is actually the fake, prop television studio of New York City and the United States today. The motto of our religion is "Turn on, tune in, and drop out." This happens to be the oldest method, passed on by spiritual teachers and spiritual searchers for thousands of years.

You've got to detach yourself from this situation. Our country was founded on exactly that motto. "Sorry, George the Third, we're dropping out." The Roman Empire fell, as the American Empire will fall in the near future, from exactly the same motives—people turning within and then coming back to found a spiritual and a political and an economic life, not on the IBM-mass-assembly-line society, but on the family and the tribe. I mentioned to you earlier, Bill, in the dressing room, that I consider myself to be much more conservative than you.

At our center in Millbrook, New York, and in hundreds of similar places in the United States today, psychedelic people are leaving the twentieth century. They're leaving this fake prop television studio and going back to exactly the values which have been fragmented and destroyed by American society—we're going back to the family. We teach our kids; we give our kids psychedelic sacraments like marijuana and LSD just the way you would—

WFB: Real old-fashioned, isn't it? [*Laughter*]

LEARY: Well, as a matter of fact, there's nothing that's more old-fashioned than a parent worshiping with his child and sharing in the shrine of the home the deep spiritual mo-

ments of life. Now, your idea—and perhaps the idea of
many of your viewers—is that psychedelic chemicals are
like heroin or perhaps like a super alcohol that you get
drunk on, that makes you *lose* touch with reality.

Of course, this is the myth which we try very hard to
overcome. Like it or not, believe it or not, the LSD experience *is* a philosophic and a religious experience. It does
lead you as any religious experience has in the past to
detach yourself, not from the family or from your ideals,
but from the fake prop society.

WFB: That detachment can be a suicide. Let's go ahead and
agree that LSD seems to be in some particulars different
from other opiates or drugs or chemicals, at the same time
agreeing that LSD is a departure from the normal world—

LEARY: But what do you mean by "normal world"? You mean
Harry Truman? Is *that* normal? You mean "Democratic-
Republican"? Is *that* normal? You mean this sort of tele-
vision studio? This is highly unnormal.

WFB: This *is* the world.

Let's look forward to the possibility that, two years
from now, you will decide you made a mistake by taking,
indiscriminately, a drug as dangerous as LSD—

LEARY: Well, I've never urged anyone to take LSD, and what
we've been doing for several years, Bill, in all our publica-
tions and lectures, is warning people about this power.
See, people seem to think *we* invented LSD. We didn't,
you know. *God* made LSD: the divine process, the evolutionary sequence. Over billions of years these have produced the plants and the vegetables and the molecules
which we now call psychedelic.

But we do tell everyone who wants to listen to us,
"Drop out of American society." We think American
society is an insane anthill, and the human being has been
living for, you know, hundreds of thousands of years
before we had any of the things we consider so necessary
in American life today. You can actually live, you can
make love, you can enjoy food, you can raise children,
without being a computerized mechanized American.

WFB: Well, somebody's got to protect you so that you can be
            free to do this. Without the American marines you
            wouldn't have much chance to make love, you know,
            except maybe in *Siberia*—

    And on & on. But this had been a whiff of the essence of the preadam-
ite tributary that, combined with all the others, poured into the Kid
Years, with special emphasis on Woodstock Nation. Years later, Dr.
Leary made light of his earlier effort at escapism by brain-masturbation.
I had much earlier on concluded that Dr. Leary and his movement had
been dealt one positively mortal blow, from a most unexpected quarter.
A complaint mounted by a flower child in the play *Hair:*
    "Now that we've dropped out, / Why is life so dreary? / Answer my
weary query, / Timothy Leary, dearie." The indictment was, is, unan-
swerable.

NORMAN MAILER, KURT VONNEGUT

2

TECHNIQUE: MANIFEST EVASIVENESS

GUESTS:
NORMAN MAILER
MARK HATFIELD
ROBERTO DE LA
  MADRID
DENIS HEALEY
ROBERT SCHEER
WILLIAM SLOANE
  COFFIN, JR.
CARMINE DE SAPIO
JOHN KENNETH
  GALBRAITH

A subcategory I played with, intending a diplomatic exploration, is what I designated in my shorthand outline as "Manifest Evasiveness." It plays a part in almost every exchange. Techniques of evasion have been studied by rhetoricians, and myriad and strange names are given to such techniques. The most common, I suppose, is classified as *ignoratio elenchi,* which is the technique of acting as though you have answered Proposition A by confuting Proposition B. A common example of this, during the sixties, was the legislator who argued that certain proposed civil rights legislation was unconstitutional, rebutted by the legislator who proclaimed the equality of the races.

In the preface, John Kenneth Galbraith asked me just when major corporations had lost 85 percent of their value: and I evaded an answer

(I did not have the data in the front of my memory; and in any event, I had exaggerated the effect of the Dow Jones dip of 1969–70 by animadverting on one of JKG's books, suggesting that its collapse had coincided with that of the market). Manifestly, I did not get away with this, and ought not to have done.

As I have suggested, there are many examples of manifest evasiveness, and many many more examples of evasiveness not at all manifest: i.e., evasiveness that deceives an audience, carrying it along—successful evasiveness. But in any event, here are a few offbeat examples and varieties.

Norman Mailer. *Evasiveness achieved by a disingenuous and on the whole unsuccessful search for his own shortcomings.* The classic example of this breed, I have always thought, was an interview published sometime in the late forties with Willem Mengelberg, who had been, as conductor of the Concertgebouw Orchestra in Amsterdam, frequently designated as the leading conductor in the world. He continued to perform when the Nazis controlled Holland and after liberation was convicted *in absentia* by a Dutch council of having been a Nazi collaborator. A few years later, a reporter located him, an old man now, living in Switzerland. He asked, "Maestro, it was frequently said of you that you were the greatest conductor in the world. What is your opinion of this judgment?" Mengelberg answered (thoughtfully), "Yes, I have heard that said, but received the accolade very skeptically. But in the years since leaving Amsterdam, I have listened attentively to every other well-known conductor and have concluded, on reflection, that in fact it is so." Norman Mailer's is not quite that direct, but listen in.

In my introductions to my guests on *Firing Line* I endeavor, where it is feasible to do so, to find a little leavening matter when I recite his or her accomplishments. I had had a number of encounters with Mailer over the years, including a great big brawling extravaganza the night before the Patterson-Liston fight in Chicago which the press turned into a kind of polemical prelim before the main athletic event. The theater, seating two thousand, was sold out, and our exchange was published in *Playboy* magazine. For years, Norman had wandered all over the land ventilating his impression that he had won that debate.

WFB: It is safe to say that men of better critical judgment than
         Mr. Mailer now regard him as the best writer in America.
         His technique is one of unalloyed narcissism mitigated by

a recognition of, not to say a devotion to, his own short-comings. One unappreciative reviewer, a couple of books back, summarized that Mr. Mailer "assured us that he, the hero of the work, fought one of his brawls after getting two hammerblows on the head, that he put Kennedy in office, could put Floyd Patterson back on the heavyweight throne, that he outdebated Buckley, that he outwrites everybody since Hemingway, and outloved everybody since Casanova." I should like to begin by asking Mr. Mailer to disclose whether he believes that artists should be immune from the harassments of the law.

MAILER: Whatever gave you that idea?

WFB: What gave me the idea was that you were sentenced to five days in jail, and you're appealing on the grounds that you were sentenced because you are very famous. Now, do I therefore understand that only people who are not very famous should be sentenced when they break the law?

MAILER: I wanted to get out of jail that day for reasons that were quite private and personal. I could have stayed in jail for five days. But I wanted to get out in one day, because I had a feeling there was a book in me, and five days in jail could take the edge off that book. Now, if [my lawyers have said what you said], as far as I'm concerned, it's perfectly pleasant lawyer talk. It has nothing to do with me.

WFB: So you wouldn't—

MAILER: Although there's no doubt that I *was* given the larger sentence *because* I was wellknown. The judge said so. He said he was making a point of me because I was well-known.

WFB: But on the other hand, you went down to Washington *because* you were well known, as your book makes clear, right?

MAILER: Oh, I'm not objecting. If he wanted to give me a larger sentence, because I'm well known, fine. That's the judge's discretion. It's just that the lawyers led me to think that, well, that's unfair.

WFB: Do you as a general proposition believe that when you
                  break the law, you should go to jail?

MAILER: Well, that's an enormously complex matter.

    Too complex, it turned out, to handle even in an hour's exchange.

In 1964, Senator Mark Hatfield, prominent liberal Republican, made it
abundantly clear that he thought it would be a great mistake for the
Republican Party to nominate Barry Goldwater. In 1967, Senator Hatfield appeared on *Firing Line*.

WFB: Senator Hatfield, do you now know, in the light of history,
                  what were, in fact, the principal reasons back in 1964 for
                  your judgment that Senator Goldwater ought not to be
                  nominated?

HATFIELD: I don't think that Senator Goldwater's nomination was a
                  mistake. Decisions that were made in the conventions at
                  the state level and in the primaries of certain states indi-
                  cated very clearly that the Republican Party, as repre-
                  sented by its delegates, wanted Senator Goldwater. Then
                  the Republican Party deliberately nominated Senator
                  Goldwater in open convention.

    If I read that correctly, Senator Hatfield is saying that the Republican
Party cannot make a mistake when it nominates a presidential candidate
if it has followed conventional procedures. He might have said that he
thought it a mistake to nominate Senator Goldwater on the grounds that
he would be slaughtered on election day. He simply did not wish to say
that.

In August 1977, Roberto de la Madrid was elected governor of the
Mexican province of Baja California. Several weeks later, he appeared
on *Firing Line*. There is at least one topic that a Mexican politician
simply cannot touch.

WFB: We know that illegal emigration from Mexico has risen
                  one thousand percent in the last fourteen years. Would
                  your government be sympathetic or not sympathetic to

attempts physically to obstruct that movement by building some sort of a wall along our common frontier?

MADRID: Certainly not.

WFB: Why not? If you accept the responsibility of providing a
home for your own citizens?

MADRID: Any and all Mexicans have the right to return to Mexico
at any time.

WFB: I'm not disputing their right to return to Mexico at any
time. I'm disputing their right to come to the United
States without an American visa.

MADRID: Well, that's the problem of the United States. You're the
one that should try to keep them—

WFB: That's why I say—

MADRID: In other words, if we had it the other way around where
people from the United States were coming into Mexico,
it would be up to us to see that these U.S. citizens did not
come into Mexico without the necessary documents. It
would be our responsibility.

WFB: I'm not talking about Mexicans *financing* this wall. I'm
simply asking, what would Mexican *opinion* be if such a
wall were constructed?

MADRID: We would leave that to the people of the United States.

Denis Healey was Chancellor of the Exchequer in Great Britain's Labour government when he appeared on *Firing Line* (1978). "Heliogra-
phers," I said in introducing him, "record that he has moved from
right-of-center socialist to centrist to left-of-center to center and is today
somewhere between center and left-of-center." This was not surprising,
I now add, because, as you will see, Mr. Healey is always in motion.

WFB: Mr. Healey, you once said that if you were to confiscate
all the money made by Englishmen in excess of twelve
thousand pounds per year, you would raise only enough
money to run the government four and a half days.

HEALEY: What?

WFB: Am I quoting you accurately, or did the British press blunder?

HEALEY: No, I suspect that's probably true.

WFB: In that event, the American, both the pragmatist and the theoretician, wonders why it's necessary to have a ninety-eight percent tax rate unless your purposes are punitive rather than pragmatic.

HEALEY: Yes, a lot of people wonder that. I'd like, myself, to be able to bring the rate down. But dealing with the real world and having had as we have had to do over the last four years to persuade people with very low living standards to accept limitations on their constitutional freedom to get excessive wage awards, it has been—

Here I thought I had him.

WFB: Did you say *excessive*?

HEALEY: Pardon? Yes.

WFB: How is it excessive?

HEALEY: They have had freedom to get excessive wage awards. They can negotiate for them.

WFB: Oh, I see: free in the *extractive* sense?

HEALEY: Of course.

WFB: Non-market-regulated.

HEALEY: Well, I don't know if you've ever heard of negotiations for wages, but negotiations take place between what is called trade unions—labor unions you Americans call them—and employers, organizations. The bargaining power of the individual can be used to achieve levels of settlement which are damaging not only to the local firm but to the economy. Now, if you're to get the consent of people with very low living standards *not* to use the constitutional right they have to bargain for *excessive* wages and to settle instead for *moderate* increases, then you have to prove to them that other people are subject to similar limitations.

WFB: Well, wouldn't this be an argument against permitting
          graduate studies?

HEALEY: No.

WFB: Why not?

HEALEY: Because I think—

WFB: Well, *why* permit graduate studies when there are people
          who can't even *hope* for a bachelor's degree?

HEALEY: No, with great respect, the question is not applying *logical*
          conclusions. The question is, What is required to achieve
          our desired result?

Manifest evasiveness? Or bad logic? B cannot be permitted to earn
a million pounds in the free market noncoercively because to do so
would be to encourage A to earn a thousand pounds coercively. Why
not then argue that B cannot be permitted to linger at college long
enough to earn a doctorate because to do so would encourage A to
demand an unearned bachelor's degree? Are we not applying parallel
logical thought? And if you deny the analogy's validity, aren't you
engaging in simple evasion?

Worth thinking about. I attempted to characterize accurately the
motives of the government that imposed confiscatory taxation on the
economically successful in order to assuage the appetites of the economically less successful.

WFB: What is required, I take it, is to pander to people's *resent-
          ment* of other people's comparative commercial success.

HEALEY: Well, *pander* is a rather pe—

WFB: Political word?

HEALEY: No, "pejorative" is what I was going to say.

WFB: I meant it to be.

Denis Healey is an urbane and civil man, and it was on his own
initiative that the conversation settled back into the grooves of amiabil-
ity. Without, however, any admission from him that some labor union
envy played a decisive role in his government's policy.

HEALEY: Yes, I know you did, but then we do disagree about one
            or two things and I fear that the amenity of our conversa-
            tion probably hasn't succeeded in disguising this from all
            your listeners.

WFB: No, no, when I say "pander" I'm not attempting to say
            that you are in any sense unique. I am saying that the
            movement of which you are a leader very definitely pan-
            ders to certain human instincts, for instance envy. What
            Dr. Johnson called the greatest human pitfall.

HEALEY: I think any democratic politician, however unfortunately,
            has to take account of how people really feel. But also
            every political leader has to try to change the way in which
            people feel and act. I think the government I serve in has
            succeeded in doing that in some important areas.

WFB: Well, I wish you the best of luck.

HEALEY: Thank you very much.

You will notice an abrupt difference in polemical practice between a
Denis Healey and a Robert Scheer, if it is possible to say "a Robert
Scheer," given the happy uniqueness of Robert Scheer. At the time I
thought him manifestly evasive in failing to concede that he was, *tout
court,* anti-American. In 1967, he was the editor of *Ramparts* magazine,
primarily identified for its attacks on the CIA, one division of its general
opposition to American policies, national and international. But "anti-
American" was a designation Mr. Scheer flatly refused to accept.

SCHEER: As to your question about anti-Americanism, I don't find
            the category of anti-American terribly useful.

WFB: Well, would you say that someone was anti-American
            who was pledged, let's say, to remove the United States
            Constitution by force and violence if necessary? Would
            that make him anti-American?

SCHEER: Well, that depends on how you define the term. I assume
            you think there's something wrong about being *anti-
            American*—

WFB: I do.

SCHEER: So why don't we just put the question in terms of, do I condemn someone? Or, do I disagree with the position taken by—

WFB: No, that makes a different point.

SCHEER: If you're trying to ask, should such-and-such a point of view be tolerated, then why don't you put the question to me in that way?

WFB: Well, you see—

SCHEER: —instead of hiding behind "anti-Americanism." You're confusing the discussion—

WFB: I have found the whole concept of "anti-Americanism" increasingly elusive, and I ask myself, Why should that be so? It's possible to use such terms as "anti-Semitic," for instance. Or "anti-Christian," "anti-Negro," or "anti-colonial." But all of a sudden it doesn't seem to be possible to use "anti-American." I tend to believe that the reason for this is that people don't want to face up to the logical implications of the positions they take. Now, for instance—

SCHEER: If you say someone's anti-Negro or anti-Jewish, I assume that you're making a relatively simple comment.

WFB: Not necessarily.

SCHEER: —Jewishness can be rather precisely defined in terms either of religious belief or parentage; and therefore an anti-Semite would be against a person that had that religious belief or parentage. My problem with anti-Americanism is that I don't expect that *your* concept of what the core of being an American is and *mine* would be the same.

WFB: I note and remark your digression, and return to the subject under discussion.

SCHEER: Well, why is that a digression? I don't see—

WFB: Because—

SCHEER: Unless you're willing to define the term "anti-American," we're going to sit here for an hour piddling around. But if you're not willing to define what you mean by "anti-American"—

WFB: I *am* willing to define it—

SCHEER: I've waited for twenty minutes now for you to define it—

WFB: I'm willing to define it, but meanwhile I'm rather enjoying your embarrassment.

SCHEER: I don't feel in the least bit embarrassed.

WFB: You sound it.

SCHEER: If you want to get into that kind of thing, I don't feel that merely by having a certain grin on your face or look in your eyes is the opposite of being embarrassed. If you want to get into this kind of thing, let's *hear* your description of what the core of Americanism is, and then we can discuss the issues involved.

WFB: Let me, if I may, get into the question in my own way. A while ago you wrote an essay on Bertrand Russell. In that essay you quoted a critic of Lord Russell—"an English intellectual," as you described him in *The New York Times Magazine.* It was the critic Mr. Bernard Levin, and he had written that Lord Russell "has turned into a full-time purveyor of political garbage indistinguishable from the routine products of the Soviet machine as a result of his 'rancorous hatred of the U.S.' " Now, this would presumably make Russell, at the very least, "anti-American," would it not? But nowhere in your review did you object to the terminology. All of a *sudden,* you're objecting to it here tonight.

I asked Mr. Scheer why he wouldn't simply settle for the plain fact that Russell *was* anti-American, and proceed to defend Russell.

WFB: . . . [Just say,] "Sure, Bertrand Russell's anti-American, but he has a damn good right to be anti-American because during the 1960s we became a highly unlovely country and anybody who was *pro-* American at that point has an addled wit, to say nothing of an unserviceable moral sense." Now, why don't you say, "Yes, I *too* am anti-American"?

SCHEER: Because you *still* haven't defined the term. And the reason *I* used the term is not because it is a term of *my* choosing, but rather because Russell's critics accused *him* of being systematically anti-American—

WFB: But you didn't jump *them* for using that term. You say you heard Lord Russell express no dislike for the American people, but certainly he must feel a considerable condescension for them. He says, for instance, "I think Lyndon Johnson is just an ordinary murderer." When you consider that the overwhelming majority of the American people support President Johnson—

SCHEER: It's not so overwhelming. According to the latest polls—

WFB: Well, sixty, seventy, or seventy-five percent—

And on & on. One almost always runs into a thicket all but impenetrable when accosting the challenge of defining "American," or "anti-American." For years and years, back in what seems like the Middle Ages, American liberals argued for the discontinuation of the House Committee on Un-American Activities among other things on the grounds that no one was competent to decide what *was* an un-American activity. Prominent among those intellectuals who made that point was Professor Henry Steele Commager, and I remember asking how it was that, having declaimed Americanism to be undefinable, he had written a (very famous) book called *The American Mind.* The trouble with insisting that there is nothing definable about Americanism, it always has struck me, is that it suggests that American history, culture, and idealism are unrelated to anything in any way definable. To say that is to qualify, the cynic would say, to be a member of the Supreme Court.

When William Sloane Coffin, Jr., was my guest he was still chaplain at Yale (we had been old friends-adversaries, having overlapped as undergraduates). He held me, in effect, to be evasive: for refusing to concede that the reason for the creeping de-Christianization of the country was the belated recognition of the Christian church of its obligation to bring about racial equality, at that time one of the two causes militant of the Reverend Mr. Coffin. I tried to suggest that if the Christian church could be accused of irrelevance, surely it had to do more with its failure to accost the transracial tyranny underwritten by the Communist world. Perhaps we were *both* a little evasive.

COFFIN: I'll tell you, Bill, why James Baldwin is down on the church. And Louis Lomax and also many of the rest of [black leaders.] Because they have told me, "Every time we see that cross we think, There's a place where they call us niggers." The primary problem of the church in our time is *not* that people don't believe in God, it's that the prosperous church in our time has failed to make common cause with the sufferers of this world. If the church is not willing to put itself in jeopardy, twenty years from now the average student won't even consider the word of the church *credible,* much less believe it.

Here, I admit, I digressed. I tend to reject the position that the truth of a proposition is an exact corollary of its credibility.

WFB: I don't think it's our role to decide on the credibility of religion. Religion *is.* It's *the* great truth, isn't it? It's presumably not within our power to render the truth more, or less, credible, any more than it is within our power to decree that E doesn't equal MC squared. [I was clearly wrong here. The whole science of apologetics is designed to render religious truths more, rather than less, credible. I should have satisfied myself to say that success in rendering religion credible is unrelated to whether religion is "true."]

COFFIN: Camus talked about people who climb on the cross to be seen from afar, trampling on Him who has hung there so long. It's the self-righteousness of the church [that's the trouble], its incapacity to really feel [along] with the *sufferers* of the world.

WFB: If you're talking about the church's concern for the people of the world, let me ask you this. Why doesn't the church show more concern—here is an area in which I think it has been extremely deficient—for the liberation of those peoples who are permanently subjugated and who are, moreover, conscripted systematically to extinguish other peoples' freedom? It may be that the churches don't have the resources to go out and purify the governments of

Santo Domingo and Peru and South Africa and Saudi Arabia, much though we loathe them. But surely the church ought to be more insistent than it has been on the necessity to do for the Communist world what we did for the Nazi world twenty or thirty years ago, wouldn't you say?

COFFIN: Well, I'll grant you one would be really naive not to be distressed by the addiction to terror that characterizes almost every Communist country—

Note now what one might call (see Chapter 7) the Revel Syndrome at work.

COFFIN: —though in Eastern Europe now it's much less than it was—the incredible drabness of the whole system. [And] at the same time one should recognize there is much less unemployment [in the Communist world]; that medical care, let us say, is much better in the Soviet Union than it is in the United States. And weren't you impressed when the Pope came to the UN? He didn't preach your crusade against Communism. He said, *"Jamais la guerre, jamais plus la guerre."* He was worried much more about a nuclear holocaust. And in a war in which Communism is involved in Vietnam, a Pope has dared to look neutral.

WFB: Come on.

COFFIN: He has.

WFB: Please!

COFFIN: You don't think so?

WFB: I can quite assure you that the Pope is *not* neutral as regards the difference between South Vietnam and North Vietnam.

COFFIN: I didn't say that.

But in fact Bill Coffin had just finished doing so, hadn't he? More like self-contradiction than Manifest Evasiveness.

Once again. Point out that in arguing against A, in fact your opponent was arguing against B. He will argue that in making that point, you were engaged in making point C. You return that nothing said about point C is going to straighten out differences we have respecting point A. Ah, typical of you to come in with point D. . . .

Coffin is a superb debater, but he relies, in my judgment, on points that just aren't quite so. I doubt if one could find a doctor in the Soviet Union who would nowadays come in with the statement that medical attention over there was better than over here. But Coffin has what good debaters greatly need: spirit, a good voice, and an ear for eloquence (a stunningly effective Camus quote, which for obvious reasons I studiedly ignored).

I treat, without quoting him directly, Cardinal Arns. Because to quote him is unproductive. Below, in discussing the onetime President of Panama, I will quote an unproductive speaker in order to make a special point.

Meanwhile, if anyone thinks it is difficult to penetrate the thought of men of the cloth in general, I invite them to submit to the acid test. "If you think it is easy to probe the thought of Catholic socialists," I wrote after a *Firing Line* session in Brazil (1980), "try spending one hour with the senior figure in the Brazilian hierarchy, the archbishop of São Paulo, Paulo Evaristo Cardinal Arns."

He walks into the studio radiating benevolence. Here is a man who studied literature at the Sorbonne, where he achieved his doctorate; who taught petrology and didactics at highly respected universities; who has written twenty-five books, including abstruse treatises on medieval literature. At the end of an hour, one seriously doubts that he knows what a supply-demand curve is, or cares. But, when you come down to it, if you had an hour to spend with St. Francis of Assisi (who founded the order of which Cardinal Arns is a member) you probably wouldn't talk to him about supply and demand; I'd have felt better just sitting and cooing with Cardinal Arns. Come to think of it, he did treat me about as St. Francis did the wild animals.

When the Pope was in town, in 1979, everyone's eyes were trained on him to see how he would handle the problem of Cardinal Arns. The problem of Cardinal Arns is roughly defined by his gentle and plain-spoken contumacy. Two years before, he had egged on the metalworkers in São Paulo, even though they had been striking illegally. Brazil was a dictatorship of sorts in 1979 (Goulart, who was Brazil's Allende, had been overthrown in 1964); and only in the past year or two had there been genuine liberalization. Torture had become, by everyone's admission, a perversion of a dishonorable past; and the 1982 elections were expected, though there were cynics who doubted they would ever eventuate. There were signs of deterioration when I met with Cardinal Arns, including a deterioration in the morale of a breed of people indomitably happy. And there was turmoil in the most stable of Brazil's institutions—the church.

So that when Pope John Paul stood up in the huge soccer stadium, it was everywhere noticed that he hugged with special tenacity Cardinal Arns. To be sure the cardinal was the senior hierarchical figure in São Paulo, but the Pope, it is generally conceded, intended more. What did he intend?

Try to get it from Cardinal Arns. He will smile. His English, though thoroughly functional, is imperfect. (He would rather, he smiled—a smile so warm and ingenuous there is no doubting the sincerity that animates it—he would rather, he says, speak to you in Portuguese, Italian, French, German, or Latin.) But the exchange was being televised, and although the swanks at PBS are pretty proud of the cosmopolitan quality of their audiences, an exchange in Latin would probably have been thought *de trop.*

What concretely, you ask the cardinal, is his economic program for the poor in Brazil? He will answer that neither capitalism nor Communism has helped the poor. You reply that in America capitalism has greatly helped the poor. He will answer that the people must know each other, in small communities, must love each other, and work together, and pool their talents. You agree, and you say that the income per capita in Brazil is on the order of $600, and taking the money from the rich and giving it to the poor wouldn't help the poor to the point where they would even notice it. The cardinal smiles, and says gently that he was invited to talk about religion, and suddenly he is asked questions about economics, which is not his field.

Manifestly so. A number of years ago Robert de Oliveira Campos, Minister of Planning in the government of Castelo Branco (who overthrew Goulart), wrote about the *"profundo desinformação clerical"* in respect of economics. The Austrian analyst Erik von Kuehnelt-Leddihn writes of the present Pope, "He is Papa to the indigent masses, but, alas, he is not an economist. Poets, historians, diplomats, theologians, philosophers, philologists and librarians have occupied the papal throne; but so far—understandable but unfortunate—no financial expert."

Archbishop Pires of Paraíba, before the cameras began to shoot, distributes visual-aid cards to the studio audience. On one of which is a huge bloviated steer. The caption: "The name of the steer is capitalism, and capitalism is the gimmick of the wealthy minority to mislead society into thinking that the most important thing is money and profits. There are actually very few who profit, and they do so by making the poor much poorer. Capitalism puts money in the hands of the few, money that was obtained through the sweat of many poor workers." I read that passage to Cardinal Arns and asked if he agreed with it.

He smiled. Archbishop Pires, he said, is a wonderful man, a holy man. You give up.

Yet somehow you don't wish to call someone like Cardinal Arns a practitioner of Manifest Evasiveness. He's just out of this world.

When the political boss Carmine De Sapio appeared on *Firing Line* (1967) he was down and out. He had been defeated in an important election by the young lawyer Edward Koch in 1963, and Tammany Hall was pronounced dead. The columnist Murray Kempton, ever on the side of the underdog, derisively summed up the defeat of De Sapio by observing that now with "bossism" dead, the lilies would sprout up through the concrete of New York.

The overwhelmed dissenters were trying to make a formal point, namely that a municipal political party could not survive without discipline of some sort. The question is by no means entirely settled whether when Carmine De Sapio was being wooed by John F. Kennedy in 1960, Kennedy was wooing a municipal autocrat or a genuine party leader. It was the distinction between the two that I attempted to isolate. Moreover, it happened that I had become a personal friend of De Sapio (he had even given me tacit encouragement when I ran for mayor in 1965).

I was on his side when we met on *Firing Line.* But Carmine was not going to take any chances. Perhaps I should have stopped the cameras, leaned across, put my arm around his shoulders, and whispered in his ear. Without such reassurance, Carmine, alas, engaged in Manifest Evasiveness.

WFB: Mr. De Sapio, what of a practical nature were you able to do to help guarantee to John F. Kennedy the Democratic nomination?

DE SAPIO: Mr. Buckley, the power that you refer to, in terms of my position as the then Democratic National Committeeman of the State of New York, then Democratic leader of New

York County, came about as a result of, I would say, two decades of internship in politics.

WFB: Mr. De Sapio, I didn't intend to suggest that you rose to your particular eminence by accident. But I think what interests a great many people is the question: Having risen to that position of eminence, what power did you actually wield? Can you sort of level with us and tell us what powers were at your disposal to help Mr. Kennedy?

DE SAPIO: I would say, Mr. Buckley, that all comes within the purview of organization, which in my opinion is the most important word in the lexicon of politics and government today. Organization just simply means what it connotes, and that is organizing people and organizing groups.

WFB: Suppose I had been a district leader and said, "Mr. De Sapio, I love you like a brother but, in fact, I want Adlai Stevenson nominated." What happens to me? Do I get thrown in the East River—

DE SAPIO: You are applauded for your candor.

I could scarcely believe it.

WFB: You are *not* suggesting that you wouldn't put . . . pressure . . . on me? Unless you were in a position to put pressure on me, Mr. Kennedy wouldn't be so concerned to get your support—isn't that the way it works?

DE SAPIO: Not necessarily.

WFB: I am not necessarily *against* pressure, I just want to know more about the mechanics—

DE SAPIO: I don't think that's the proper word; I think that a better word would be an *understanding*. [At this point the laughter from the studio audience became very nearly raucous.] Seriously, the objective and the duty and the responsibility of a leader is to ascertain at the grass-roots level what is the best type of candidate for the particular objective, whatever it may be on the county, city, state, or national level.

WFB: You did have a lot of *power*—did you not?

DE SAPIO: I would concede that in the minds of many people I was identified as having a great deal of power in politics.

WFB: No, I said you *had* a great deal of power, not that you were *thought* to have power, but that you *had* power.

DE SAPIO: Well, it's a question of whether you use power or you abuse it.

WFB: When—for instance—Governor Dewey led the Republican delegation to Chicago in 1952, he got all the delegates together and said to them, in just so many words, in front of a lot of reporters, "Look, you go out there and vote for Eisenhower, or I will have your—neck." Now, he was not considered a political "boss," even though he was using all his prestige as governor, promising to punish any dissenter. But that was considered an okay thing. Could you have done that?

What followed is hard to believe, and belongs in civics textbooks.

DE SAPIO: I would say there is a distinction particularly today in the minds of a lot of people by virtue of some of the recent happenings politically in the past several years that there has been focused in the minds of many people via the media of communication that political leaders who held party position were in many instances more powerful than elected officials. That doesn't necessarily follow.

A day or two later, Carmine De Sapio asked me if I would kindly (he is the politest of men) stop by his office on an important matter. I did. He wanted to know how much it would cost to kill the show, and do another hour. I told him it was out of the question. The program had, in any event, already been distributed. I did not joke about his performance. But there never was a better example of Manifest Evasiveness.

And, finally, an exchange with Professor John Kenneth Galbraith. For several years he declined to appear on *Firing Line,* giving as a reason that the program pays only a pittance as a fee to its guests. He broke down after I had reviewed favorably, and sincerely, his Indian diaries in *Life* magazine. And he has appeared several times, volunteering (nice to hear) that he has more response from an appearance on *Firing Line* than from an appearance on any other regularly scheduled television program.

In this exchange, the question genuinely arises which of us was being more evasive. We were discussing the progressive income tax.

WFB: Let's be *completely* concrete—

GALBRAITH: Would you—

WFB: —for just one second, if it doesn't offend you. There are six hundred and twenty-five—

GALBRAITH: No. Let me ask *you* a specific question. Would you get rid of the progressive income tax *completely*?

WFB: Absolutely.

GALBRAITH: I thought so. Well—would you then distribute the reduced income equally over the civilian and military budget?

WFB: It depends on the extent of the foreign threat. If we'd had a Democratic administration I would say we'd have to go heavy on the military spending.

GALBRAITH: As things now stand, would you take it all out of the civilian budget?

WFB: It depends completely on the nature of the threat.

GALBRAITH: Well, let me rephrase it. Would you reduce the military budget?

WFB: I wouldn't want to have one less airplane than we *needed,* if that's the answer to your question. But let's get back to—

GALBRAITH: No. I understand why you want to get back because I detect a terrible tendency to evade here. You would get rid of the corporation income tax and the personal income tax?

WFB: Oh, absolutely. The corporation income tax is one of those superstitions—

GALBRAITH: No evasion, Bill. Just—

WFB: Now, wait a minute. [*Laughter*] If you reduce the corporate business tax you would have a great incentive to greater employment and therefore greater tax revenues.

GALBRAITH: Not immediately. Not immediately.

WFB: And among other things the need for fewer bureaucrats.

GALBRAITH: I'm talking about next year. Next year we get rid of the corporate income tax, we get rid of the personal income tax. Now—

WFB: No, no, no. I didn't say get rid of the personal income tax. I said get rid of the progressive feature of the income tax.

GALBRAITH: Get rid of the progressive—oh, I see.

WFB: The progressive feature of the income tax. As Professor Milton Friedman—whom perhaps you will not condescend to with quite such flair—has said, you can eliminate the progressive feature of the income tax, have a uniform rate of nineteen percent, eliminate all of the deductions which I'm in favor of eliminating, and raise exactly as much money as we now raise for federal tax purposes. So what's outrageous about that? However, on this business about the economic imbalance that would result—

GALBRAITH: I *still* detect some evasion. I still detect some instinct to protect military expenditures here from—

WFB: If you have an extremely successful foreign policy, you don't *have* to have high military expenses. But you can't have a series of diplomatic defeats as we did after the war and not face up to the military consequences. That is, if you are resolved to maintain your liberty—which some of us feel more strongly about than others.

Now, on the matter of economic dislocation. There are six hundred and twenty-five people in America who made a million dollars last year [1980]. If you were to take the whole of the million dollars—if you were to have one hundred percent taxation [of the very wealthy]—that would pay the federal cost of government for eighteen hours.

GALBRAITH: Oh, yes. I'm quite clear that the purpose of taxation is—

WFB: Is to hurt *them,* not to help *others.*

GALBRAITH: Yes, to provide a general sense of equity, a general sense of fairness in the economy—

WFB: But the progressive feature is not equitable; it calls for treating people differently.

GALBRAITH: —and this is extremely important; the sense of fairness is a very important factor. I would agree with you, Bill, that

"Sh-h-h! It's that William F. Buckley, Jr., show."

it isn't the raising of revenue that is important. As a highly—

WFB: As your friend Professor [Robert] Nozick at Harvard points out, if in fact this were the corporate resolution of a society [to maximize equality], you would begin by genetic interference. You would not allow a bright man to marry a bright woman. If you're really in search of the kind of equality that you want to superimpose, let's do it right. As a matter of fact, that will probably be in the Democratic platform twelve years from now.

GALBRAITH: There is a form of argument that is [known as] *reductio ad absurdum* that I can follow. But there is a *reductio ad absurdum* that I can't even connect with reality. I'm sorry to say your last case is of that sort.

WFB: Well, you are concerned to "connect with reality" but you defend the present tax distribution—

GALBRAITH: How you got over from DNA to—I know why you wanted to evade the issue—but how you got to DNA so rapidly is something that I find absolutely dazzling.

Ah well. "Reality," after all, is what is socially accepted. When the Sixteenth Amendment was passed, a proposed amendment was rejected that a 10 percent ceiling should be imposed. Rejected on the grounds that merely to mention the figure "10 percent" might encourage Congress to levy a usuriously high tax. A 10 percent tax was then a *reductio ad absurdum.* Professor Galbraith's special skill as a debater is to avoid having to evade—by counterpunching. He wants to talk, as the old story goes, about the Negro situation in the South.*

---

*"Evasiveness" is a comprehensive term sheltering what are formal fallacies. These are numerous but are economically described in *Modern English: A Glossary of Literature and Language,* by Arnold Lazarus, Andrew MacLeish, and H. Wendell Smith (New York: Grosset and Dunlap, 1971). Under "fallacies of reasoning" the authors list *ad captandum, ad hominem, ad ignorantiam, ad misericordiam, ad populum, ad verecundiam,* argument against the man, argument from authority, assertion, assumptions (mistaken), begging the question, card stacking, causal reasoning, disjunctive dilemma, equivocation, "every" and "all" fallacy, fallacy of composition, fallacy of division, false analogy, false dilemma, false premise, friend of the enemy, genetic fallacy, glittering generality, half-truth, hasty generalization, inductive reasoning, *ipse dixit, non sequitur, post hoc,* red herring, sweeping generalization, syllogism, *tu quoque,* and undistributed middle.

3
THE
IMPOSSIBLE
GUEST

GUEST:
DEMETRIO LAKAS

People are curious about the Impossible Guest. There was the impossible young man who ended up running Bertrand Russell's political life in milord's dotage. I could name but won't the guest whose entire knowledge of life filled eight minutes, so that when the ninth came along, he simply recycled his *Weltanschauung* for the next eight minutes.

But there is the different Impossible Guest, namely the person who refuses to say anything, anything at all; and seeks to be ingratiating. What follows comes very close to being a Las Vegas comedy skit.

It was September 1976, and I was in Panama to examine the heated question of a prospective Panama Canal Treaty. I arrived there believing wholeheartedly that no such treaty as was contemplated should be undertaken. After five days, I changed my mind.

It is not difficult, in Panama, to Talk to Everyone, since Everyone, meaning the people who run the country, comes down to about twelve people. Yes, I exaggerate, but I talked to Omar Torrijos, the strongman who did run the country, talked to him in his little house surrounded by bodyguards. I talked to the archbishop of Panama, an American. I talked with the ambassador, and with his staff. I talked with all the generals and the admirals. I talked with Panamanian Americans who worked on the Canal. With journalists, native and American. And with Panamanian intellectuals. And no can can dispute that I talked with the President of Panama.

We did two *Firing Line*s in Panama City on the fifth day of my stay and learned to our distress late on day four that the second scheduled guest for the following day—the ambassador—had been recalled suddenly to Washington. Who to substitute? A deputy at the embassy said, Why not President Lakas? He had gone to school in Texas and spoke perfect English. Granted, anyone serving as President, with Torrijos around, was merely a figurehead. But an hour with the President of Panama, we all agreed, would be a useful hour. Could we get him? This proved gratifyingly easy. At first the hour we gave him for the studio was no good because of a Cabinet meeting. He called back to say that he had altered the hour of the Cabinet meeting in order to oblige us.

It was the longest hour of my life. You will see. No, not entirely, because no one could endure in print a transcript of the entire hour, and it is hard to imagine that any viewer stayed tuned in for the entire hour. But I was forced to. Herewith a specimen of what can happen on television when the time that needs filling is inflexible.

WFB: [*Standing alongside a lock of the Canal*] This is William F. Buckley, Jr. We are at the Panama Canal, at the Pacific entrance to it. You can see behind me a Greek bulk carrier. It is part of the traffic that runs through the Canal, and has since it was completed in 1914. As we know now, there is considerable controversy having to do with the future of the Canal and the question of who will administer its future. The guest today will be the President of the Republic, Mr. Lakas.

[*Back in the studio*] In 1968, General Omar Torrijos took power here in Panama, but he was satisfied to name himself Chief of Government, which he remains today. In

1969 he appointed, as Chief of State, Demetrio Basilio Lakas. President Lakas, under the new constitution, was elected in 1972 to a six-year term, and he remains therefore President of the Republic of Panama until 1978.

President Lakas is a Panamanian of Greek descent, who went to Texas to college. There, at several universities, among them Texas Technological Institute, he became an engineer and an architect, returning in due course to Panama to practice his profession. He vows that one day he will return to engineering and architecture; meanwhile, he is Chief of State of Panama during the most exciting period of its recent history, when the renegotiation of the famous Treaty of 1903, signed with the United States, is in prospect. His special skills and his knowledge of America are a considerable national resource.

I should like to begin by asking President Lakas whether he would anticipate, in the event of American disengagement, some kind of a defense treaty with the United States.

President Lakas began immediately to postpone accosting any question that would require him to make any statement that might be interpreted as provocative.

LAKAS: First of all, thank you for all of those nice things you said, and I first of all want to thank the American people for being nice and letting me go into their living rooms through this television set and be able to expose part of my ideas, the way I see things, whether they are right or wrong. They'll be the judges, but at least the way I see them. I would appreciate it very much, Mr. Buckley, if you would repeat the question.

It was too early to panic, but I sensed that we were off to a pretty sluggish start.

WFB: Yes, sir. I was wondering whether you anticipate, in the event that an abrogation of the 1903 treaty is completed, that there would be a defense treaty of some sort between your country and mine.

LAKAS: Things are so hard today, and the way things are shaping,
             we look like we ought to have a treaty in a very brief time.
             The United States has named a good team of men, and we
             have done the best we can in choosing the people we have
             for participating on behalf of a million and a half citizens
             in order to get there and work out a treaty that would be
             equitable to both countries. And it wouldn't work if it's
             balanced one way or the other. I am sure that, as well as
             myself, everybody else would this moment avoid trying to
             predict what will happen after the treaty. But it stands to
             common sense that in the treaty there would be a subject
             talked about and conversed, before any kind of treaty is
             signed.

    The President having said exactly nothing, I tried again.

WFB: Well, let me ask you this, Mr. President. [Sometimes I
             deliberately stretch out a question when I think my guest
             needs a little time to put himself together. As follows:] It
             is, as you know, increasingly an American suspicion that
             explicit acts of friendship between Latin American coun-
             tries and the United States are somehow unfashionable,
             that the public rhetoric in Latin America requires a cer-
             tain anti-Yankee flavor. Now, would it be considered by
             other Latin American countries as somehow undignified
             for Panama to restore a defense treaty, having got rid of
             it during the revisions of the 1930s?

LAKAS: That is a really long question, Mr. Buckley, but I'll try to
             see if I can remember everything and try to cover it all for
             you. Let's start first about Latin Americans disliking the
             United States. Couldn't this just be an attitude brought up
             by people who are not friends—

    I couldn't believe it. Was he actually going to *deny* the existence of
anti-Yanquism? I mumbled—

WFB: I think that's true, yes.

LAKAS: —of the Latin Americans and of the United States, that
             have created this attitude which really does not exist? And

> I can prove it to you. I can prove to you that the United
> States of America and Panama have been true friends for
> seventy-odd years, regardless that Panama's always tried
> to get a fairer deal with the United States. And the United
> States has had people who have worked on it and have
> made it a little better and advanced from different treaties
> that we've had so far. I have all the faith in the world in
> the American people. I believe in the American people.
> The General [Torrijos], every time he talks about the peo-
> ple of the United States, he talks positively and nice about
> them.

Having spent an hour and a half with the General only the day before,
I knew that talking positively and nice about people simply was not his
specialty. Besides, Torrijos had manhandled a number of U.S. politicians and spokesmen. I tried to elucidate.

WFB: You mean the people as distinguished from their leaders?

LAKAS: Not necessarily, because I really don't believe that the
            government of the moment determines the people. I don't.
            I really don't believe much of this here "leaders," because
            to be frank with you, no one man can run any country in
            the world.

Since this was unintelligible, I thought I might just as well go along.

WFB: I agree, yes.

LAKAS: So I think we all form part of a government, and we are
            all liable for that government. It just so happens that it is
            so easy to say when things go wrong, "I had nothing to
            do with it. This leader is to blame for it." When everybody
            else is there pushing, shoulder by shoulder, no one man
            can run a country, so how could one man be responsible
            for it?

I was approaching desperation. I backed up, and tried again.

WFB: Well, that's true. No one man should be expected to be
            responsible for all the policies of a government. But it is

true, I think, that especially in the academic classes of
Latin America, being anti-gringo is a sort of an international sport, isn't it?

LAKAS: I wouldn't say that. A person has to attend— First let me
start this way to say, even though countries are countries,
I work with, and move around with, people, human beings. Have you ever been to a party, a Latin American
party, since you were in Mexico?

WFB: Sure.

LAKAS: Have you ever seen the word *piñata*? You know what it
means?

WFB: Yes, sure. You hit them and everything falls apart.

LAKAS: Then what happens?

WFB: Well, the candies and the stuff—I don't remember.

LAKAS: What happens? Everybody grabs a little bit, right?

WFB: Yes.

LAKAS: All of a sudden somebody grabbed a bunch, a whole
bunch of it, and there's a bunch of them just staring at
him, watching him. All of a sudden what happens? They
jump up. They jump on him, and they try to take it away
from him.

WFB: Yes.

I can only suppose that this "Yes" sounded positively feeble.

LAKAS: That's human nature. But our folks teach us education,
send us to school, and we learn we have to respect things
that belong to others, and we should try to get there and
fight for them to get some for ourselves. I would say it is
just human nature. Then I guess that's what the great
President of the United States tried to say when he said
that we have to help the most, so the few of us who have
a lot doesn't lose it all.

Might I provoke him by reciting from the litany of U.S. aggressions,
as repeatedly adduced by the Panamanian treaty negotiators?

WFB: Well, but the position of your government and of your negotiators if you meditate on it is really grounds for a considerable historical resentment of America. If you believe everything that your negotiators say, then the United States is guilty of having forced you into a treaty without your consent, taken historical advantage of you, exploited your principal natural resource, being indifferent to expostulations by you to revise the treaty, dragging our feet unconscionably over a period of seven decades. If all of this is exactly correct, why *shouldn't* there be a considerable Panamanian resentment of the United States?

LAKAS: Even if all that *was* correct, which I doubt it is, I will tell you something. Our people have shown those who are Americans and lived among us that our people didn't hurt one single American in Panama. Will not then you think that there are true friends among our people, and that we really do *love* each other, and that maybe politics, sometimes for internal combustion, is something else? What do you say? Couldn't it ever occur?

WFB: In other words you think that the anti-Americanism that comes in over the media is fabricated for the purpose of political effect?

LAKAS: I don't know whether there is any of that going on. Because if it's all—

WFB: Well, what do you call it when they burn in effigy the principal press officer of the Canal Zone?

LAKAS: Now, I didn't quite get what this—if you'd just allow me a minute to explain to you what I was trying to tell you. I was trying to tell you that there is no other country in the world where the United States will find friendlier people toward them. Seventy years of not even an intent of sabotage to the Canal. Declaration of war on Japan before the United States did in the world war—all these gestures. Why do they want to charge me if once I went to a saloon and had a drink? What about all the milkshakes I drank? Why just this once I had a drink in a saloon? This is what occurs.

WFB: Well, I think that your analogy, which is very charming,
is a little bit like the man who was up for murder in Ireland
and offered to produce thirty people who hadn't seen him
murder the girl. Inevitably what attracts attention is that
which is unusual, not that which is usual, right? Now,
there certainly aren't riots in Panama every day, God
knows, but you wouldn't expect that a riot in Panama
would not be noticed, would you?

LAKAS: You know what I enjoyed about your word?

WFB: What?

LAKAS: About this "usual." It means that good relations *are* the
usual thing among Panamanians and the United States.

WFB: Right.

LAKAS: *Right?*

WFB: Right.

LAKAS: Thank you, that's what I'm saying.

WFB: Yes.

LAKAS: We agree on that.

WFB: Well, for one thing it would be physically exhausting to
riot every day. There hasn't been, let's say, a Polish riot
against the Soviet Union since 1966. The one before that
was ten years earlier. But we can assume that between '56
and '66 there was considerable resentment on the part of
Poles to Soviet occupation.
    Now, question: There must be very considerable resent-
ment by most Panamanians over the 1903 treaty. What
does that generate? Does that generate animosity toward
the United States, or does it not?

LAKAS: But I don't think the word to use, sir, is resentment. I
mean the word to use is, people are hurt. But they're not
angry at the United States or at the American people.
    You've been with us how many days down here in
Panama? Have you noticed somebody treating you out of
the ordinary, I mean being ugly toward you? Looking at

their face and they're turning around to look at you as a doggone gringo? No.

WFB: Maybe they don't know who I am.

LAKAS: Those blue eyes. You sure don't look very Panamanian.

I had fifty-seven minutes and twenty seconds of this with President Syrup. But what truly astonished was the very last lines of the program. He sat there, pudgy and smiling throughout the hour. And then the *very last* lines—I indicate where the camera and sound went off:

WFB: But it's true that General Torrijos went to Castro's Cuba and signed a friendship pact with him, isn't it?

LAKAS: Yes, it's true we feel we have to get along with everyone. [*Camera, sound off*] And as far as I'm concerned, Mr. Buckley, I just as soon fuck Castro as sign a treaty with him!

He had risen the moment the camera went off, but continued talking in what, I learned, was his normal off-camera idiom.

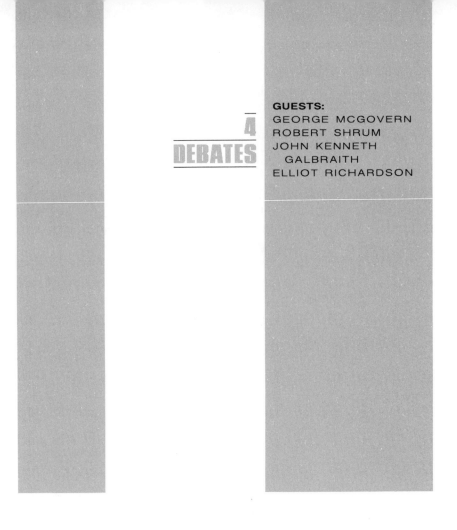

4

DEBATES

GUESTS:
GEORGE MCGOVERN
ROBERT SHRUM
JOHN KENNETH
  GALBRAITH
ELLIOT RICHARDSON

Every now and again, *Firing Line* has presented a formal debate (there have been about ten). Some of these have been jointly sponsored with the Cambridge Union. My first debate in the Cambridge Union was with James Baldwin in 1965, the year before *Firing Line* began.

Much that is interesting happened that day in February 1965. Baldwin had recently published his apocalyptic *The Fire Next Time.* It was quickly accepted as the vehicle of what one might call the totalist black position. The 1964 Civil Rights Act had passed. Barry Goldwater (reluctantly) voted against it on constitutional grounds; and at *National Review* we opposed it for the same reason. Goldwater's negative vote contributed to his overwhelming defeat by Lyndon Johnson in November 1964. By 1965 there was sentiment for an additional civil rights bill.

Baldwin was considered, among intellectuals, to be the prophet, standing even before Martin Luther King, Jr. His position was far more radical than King's. To begin with he was a professed atheist, unlike the Baptist minister who led the political fight in America. And then there was a brooding moroseness in Baldwin's position that was darkly attractive to young Englishmen with large appetites to deplore the United States.

When one is being invited to the Cambridge Union debate, great stress is placed in preliminary correspondence on traditional Union etiquette. Participants are even sent a volume of the history of the Cambridge Union. (I remember primarily from that book a wonderful excerpt from a debate in Cambridge over the question of whether Great Britain should ratify the League of Nations. One student debater had pronounced grandly that, in the end, he was convinced that the case against the League was best summarized by the adage "Familiarity breeds contempt." To which the affirmative student speaker had responded: "But a lack of familiarity breeds nothing at all.")

The invitation stressed that debaters should meet at a stipulated hour for a pre-debate dinner with the officers of the Union and all the debate participants (the two principals, and three student speakers on each side). Absolutely required, the letter stressed, was that speakers should arrive in black tie. James Baldwin appeared dressed in a blue suit. Either at his request or because the hosts intuited an ungovernable personal hostility (by Baldwin, to me), we were placed at opposite ends of a long table.

When the debate began, Baldwin was introduced. Before he had spoken a single word, he received a standing ovation from most of the house. I calculated that this would not be my day, arguing the negative on "Resolved, That the progress of America has been at the expense of the American Negro"—as blacks were always referred to, until a few years later. Baldwin incarnated everything then popular with an iconoclastic student audience. He was a black; he hated America; he was a religious skeptic and a homosexual. Baldwin's speech was followed by thunderous applause. He did not speak again; he did not rebut, nor was any question asked of him. One of the students assigned to endorse my position shook the very foundations of orthodoxy by announcing, as he got up to speak, that he had changed his mind; that he was moved on reconsideration to agree with Baldwin. The house voted affirmatively on the resolution (i.e., that America's progress had indeed been at the expense of the American Negro) by an overwhelming margin.

I was much surprised, on reaching New York a few weeks later, to find Baldwin's prepared talk, and my extemporized talk, both reprinted in full in *The New York Times Magazine.* Baldwin's lawyer telephoned me to say that Baldwin was suing *The New York Times* for breach of copyright—would I join the suit? I went instead to the offices of *The New York Times,* where I spoke to assistant editor Harvey Shapiro. I told him I did not wish to participate in the lawsuit but that I deeply objected to an extemporaneous address being published without my permission (which I'd have granted provided I was given the opportunity to review the transcript of what I had said extemporaneously). Mr. Shapiro, having consulted with Management, told me that the *Times* would not abandon its formal, legal, position that anything spoken over television was public property; but that I had a personal guarantee from Management that they would not do it to me again. The gravamen of Baldwin's complaint was that the *Times'* publication had aborted the publication by *Playboy* magazine of Baldwin's speech, imposing a financial sacrifice on him of the $10,000 he had been told *Playboy* would pay him. I do not know what settlement was finally reached in *Baldwin* v. *New York Times.*

A few months later, Baldwin and I appeared on David Susskind's *Open End,* and later he gave an interview in which he spoke bitterly of my treatment of his position on that show. I answered him in a syndicated column, most sternly:

> Mr. James Baldwin, the author and playwright whose reputation is in part owing to his fine writing, in part to the implacability of his theme (Hate the System), has said a couple of discouraging things on a television program (in which I participated). To wit, that as regards the Negro, "things couldn't be worse." And Negroes who throw their garbage out on the streets are doing so—legitimately, he suggests—as a form of protest against their plight.
>
> When Mr. Baldwin says that the lot of the Negroes could not be worse, one necessarily reacts in either of two ways. He is correct—things couldn't be worse. Or he is engaging in hyperbole; in which case one must ask whether it is useful to the cause of a proper equality to engage in such hyperbole. I conclude, as regards the former, that things could very easily be worse for the Negroes than they are now. Worse, for instance, if the overwhelming majority of the opinion leaders of this country cared not at all about the plight of the Negroes, which manifestly is not the case. And that therefore any suggestion to the contrary goes against realism, and breeds not the galvanic kind of superaction in behalf of equality that Mr. Baldwin presumably seeks to bring about, but rather a feeling of resignation; of despair. If the Negro's lot is not improved by the kind of sympathy he receives,

has received: sympathy registered in legislation, editorials, columns, books, sermons, catechisms, welfare payments, then what *are* we to do? An interesting question, which is hardly answered in apocalyptic statements by such as Mr. Baldwin, threatening us with The Fire Next Time—the "next time" meaning the next time we disagree with whatever poetical locution he comes up with to describe the delinquencies of the white people of this country.

On the program in question, Mr. Baldwin said that he was neither a socialist nor a Marxist. Let us take him at his word—but wonder how, intellectually, he can reconcile his statements with his behavior. In his writing, he deplores the capitalist system, which he holds institutionally responsible for enslaving the Negro. In his political associations, he makes common cause with, for instance, the editors of the magazine *Dissent,* which explicitly identifies itself as an organ of "socialist dissent." The crisis involving the American Negro has much to do with the fear that Negro leaders themselves have of their own most rabid representatives. There is a great deal to disagree with—for those concerned with the integrity of the Constitution—when dealing with the demands of such as Mr. Roy Wilkins of the NAACP, of Mr. Thurgood Marshall, of others who tend to seek out a fresh law to suture every offense against the Negro. But however much one disagrees with them, they are, in context, the voices of moderation: and we must ask them why they do not dissociate themselves from the swollen irrationalities of such as Mr. Baldwin.

The trouble is—and this is brilliantly recorded in the forthcoming book by Mr. Theodore White on *The Making of the President, 1964*—that they dare not do so. For fear that they would thus suggest a lack of militancy in their own approach to the problem. It was exactly so in the twenties, when many of the socialist-humanitarians who backed the Bolshevik Revolution found themselves endorsing the enormities of Lenin, and Trotsky, and subsequently of Stalin—because they feared to alienate themselves from the leadership of revolutionary protest.

But might not the same thing happen in a good cause (equality for the Negroes)—as distinguished from an ungodly cause (the Marxist revolution)? So long as the Wilkinses of this world refuse to turn their back on the Baldwins of this world? The objective of those who seek equality for the Negro is equality for the Negro within the American system. If Mr. James Baldwin and his coterie of America-haters continue to give the impression that such as Roy Wilkins go along with their indictments, then they may very well wind up satisfying the American people that identification with the civil rights movement is an *alternative* to maintaining the American system. How long, one wonders, before the Baldwins will be ghettoized in the corners of fanaticism where they belong? The moment is overdue for someone who speaks authentically for the Negroes to tell Mr. Baldwin that his morose nihilism is a greater threat by far to prospects for the Negroes in America than anything that George Wallace ever said or did.

The second debate was held in October 1970, and my antagonist was John Kenneth Galbraith. Entering the dining hall, JKG leaned over to me and said, "Do you know, I made an awful fool of myself when I last debated in the Cambridge Union." "I am not surprised," I replied, but went on to ask, "How so?" "Well," he said, "I went to the effort of preparing for two entire days to meet my opponent, Enoch Powell. It proved quite unnecessary: I demolished him easily." I was given to understand that Professor Galbraith had not taken any such quite unnecessary pains to cope with me, to debate "Resolved, That the market is a snare and a delusion."

To everyone's surprise, my own especially, I won the debate, by a narrow margin. I am convinced that my victory was primarily the result of an extraordinarily eloquent performance by the senior student debater on my side, delivering one of the rebuttals. Months later I had a letter from him. You will have forgotten, he said, that I am the same student who, five years ago, inexcusably changed my position in the Baldwin debate in the middle of the proceedings. "I tried to make up to you for that ethical delinquency."

My third debate was with Germaine Greer, a few years later, at the height of the feminist fever in the mid-seventies. There was a period of progressive suspense as Ms. Greer refused one after another resolution as suggested by the Cambridge Union. In desperation, the president of the Union called me in New York and asked me to suggest a formulation. I said, Why not "Resolved, The women's rights movement is at the expense of women." I received a telegram from Ms. Greer: she found my resolution "preposterous." This was followed by a second telephone call from the desperate president, asking me please to try again, as the Union was close by an urgent journalistic deadline: the BBC, which had undertaken to co-host the debate with *Firing Line,* absolutely needed the actual resolution for the newspapers.

I remember tapping out on my typewriter a telegram to the president: "How about 'Resolved, Give them an inch and they'll take a mile'?" But good sense intervened: I could not, in any debate involving a *double entendre*, prevail against the formidable Ms. Greer, who during the period was giving interview after interview to various journals, describing her (myriad) sexual experiences. In desperation, I suggested—knowing that the formulation was suicidal—"Resolved, This house supports the Women's Liberation Movement." That proved eminently satisfactory to Miss Greer. Nothing I said, and memory reproaches me for having performed miserably, made any impression or any dent in the argument. She carried the house overwhelmingly. She could have won on "Resolved, Man should be abolished."

GEORGE MCGOVERN

George McGovern does better in debates with me than with the American people. This time around, shortly before the election that brought in Ronald Reagan, we were debating SALT II (he favored it) before the Yale Political Union. The popular vote went overwhelmingly to him, notwithstanding the eloquent analytical arguments of my partner, the man who a few months later was named as chief arms control adviser, Paul Nitze. That wasn't surprising—the pacifist side almost always prevails before a student audience. The last five-minute rebuttal was McGovern's, and he used it brilliantly. He has the voice of a preacher: reasonable, folksy, moralistic, idealistic, pleading.

His last few minutes were devoted to the re-creation of a scene from a household in Hiroshima. We saw the breakfast table, the ash-covered food still on the table. The verbal camera begins to sweep the room. The grandmother is dead, a lick of flame having destroyed her. The mother and father are decomposing on the floor, by the chairs at which they had been seated. You hear the cry of the baby, who lives—for a few hours. "That's the kind of thing I want to labor to prevent for us, and that's why I favor the SALT Treaty." (Explosive, standing roar of approval.)

After it was over I shook McGovern's hand and whispered to him, "George, that peroration is as good as when I first heard you use it at Dartmouth in 1957." "Yes," he agreed. "Very effective, isn't it?"

It occurs to me that the evening was a boon to the taxpayer. George McGovern was running again for President, more or less for the hell of it, and that resulted in the Secret Service's frisking all five hundred occupants of the auditorium and in delaying the program by fifty-five minutes. McGovern was so irritated he dismissed his bodyguards the following day.

A common (though not inevitable) feature of a debate is the interrogation and cross-interrogation of the principals. The idea is that for, oh, six minutes, A gets to ask B questions. The next six minutes belong to B, for the purpose of asking questions of A. There are ways in effect to cheat on this. A can ask a question and B can give a response so windy that precious time is consumed. Or B can answer by presenting a question of his own. For instance: A: Are you in favor of tanks? B: What I want to know, and what I think the audience would like to know, Mr. A., is, Just how many tanks do you think we need?

When that kind of thing happens, one relies very heavily on the moderator (or president, or chairman, or speaker) to intervene, in order to maintain the discipline of the format. The moderator has his own problems: if the audience is clearly enjoying the result of usurpations or evasions, he is reluctant to barge in. We see examples of all of the above, below.

WFB: Senator, you spent the early part of the evening telling us
            we had redundant power, and now in the beginning of the
            second hour, you're telling us that the Soviet Union in-
            tends to deploy seven hundred more missiles. Why do they
            want seven hundred more missiles when you just told us
            how frequently they could kill us with the missiles they
            now have? Either they *are* or they *aren't* sufficient. De-
            pending on whether it is useful to your argument to say

that we shouldn't have any more missiles, you use one argument; depending on whether it's useful to you to say that there are going to be more missiles, you use a contrary argument.

MCGOVERN: Mr. Buckley, what I am saying is that in the absence of an agreement, both sides will continue the pattern they've followed for years—

WFB: Why? *Why?*

MCGOVERN: —of increasing arms. Because of the madness that exists—

WFB: Who's mad? I'm not mad. [*Laughter, applause*]

MCGOVERN: I would suggest that if not mad, you're at least lacking in vision and common sense. [*Laughter, applause*]

WFB: Senator, I accept that as an open question. [*Laughter, applause*] It required *your* peculiar vision and common sense in November 1971 to recommend a thirty-one-billion-dollar military aid cut.

MCGOVERN: Well, let me just say that this is off the point tonight, since we're not talking about the '72 presidential campaign.

WFB: We are here tonight because we *didn't* follow your recommendations. [*Laughter, boos*]

MCGOVERN: What *I* supported—I don't know where you stood at the time President Nixon was signing SALT I, which you now seem to deplore, but *I* supported it. I think that it has saved this country a great deal of funds and we still remain in a position where our nuclear retaliatory capability—which is what deterrence is all about—is untouched. And it's not *my* estimate that the Soviet Union is going to have a thousand additional nuclear weapons systems at the end of this treaty term if we don't ratify SALT II. That's the estimate of the American security establishment, of our top security advisers, of our Defense Department, that if we don't ratify SALT II by 1985 we'll have another thousand missiles aimed at us.

WFB: Why do we care?

MCGOVERN: Now, don't ask me to—

WFB: *Why* do we care?

MCGOVERN: —explain Soviet motives, but this is the best estimate of
                our defense and security experts. Why does anyone sup-
                pose *that's* in our interests?

WFB: Well, I'm asking you, *why* do we care? I know why *I* care,
                but I can't find anything you have said tonight that makes
                it plain why *you* care, except that they cost money. If
                you're saying, Do I care if the Soviet Union spends money,
                the answer is, No, I don't. I don't care if they spend
                money. If you're asking me whether I care if *we* spend
                money, my answer is, Yes, provided it is usefully spent.
                Now, if there is reason to suppose that the Soviet Union
                wants more missiles in order to accentuate its threat
                against the United States, then I want an appropriate
                defense. *What is the appropriate defense?* is the question
                that you haven't asked me.

MCGOVERN: Yes, well, the appropriate defense is to halt an arms race
                that is not enhancing the superiority of either country,
                that leaves us right where we are today, in a state of
                nuclear balance, but at a much higher and more dangerous
                level with more weapons, the enhanced danger of acci-
                dent, of miscalculation, the loss of whatever political and
                moral influence we have in persuading other countries—

WFB: Is *that* my answer?

MCGOVERN: I ask if that is not a reason for another SALT agreement.

WFB: No, no. It's *not* the reason. In the first place—

THE SPEAKER: Mr. Buckley? Mr. Buckley?

WFB: Yes?

THE SPEAKER: While the distinction between questioner and responder
                may have been blurred [*Laughter, applause*], it is actually
                your turn now, Mr. Buckley, to question Senator McGov-
                ern.

WFB: Senator McGovern reminds me of Max Beerbohm's apo-
                thegm that the Socratic manner is not a game at which two
                people can play. [*Laughter*]

Four years later, the subject was Star Wars—SDI—the space shield. The principal debater opposing the development of SDI at the speed recommended by President Reagan was Robert Shrum. Mr. Shrum had appeared as assistant to Senator McGovern in the SALT II debate. He is a gentleman of formidable forensic talents who has served as speech-writer for Teddy Kennedy, George McGovern, and Jimmy Carter, and, in the spring of 1988, speechwriter and adviser to presidential candidate Richard Gephardt.

WFB: Mr. Shrum, you spent a lot of time on a couple of points in the opening program to discuss this question. I would like to take you seriously, but to do so would be to affront your intelligence. [*Laughter*]

SHRUM: Try.

WFB: For instance, you began by saying you don't understand how "Mr. Buckley resists certain forms of domestic ex-penditure" but doesn't resist *this* form of military expendi-ture. So let me ask you to begin with: If you were in a house whose roof was burning down, would you care more about the fire department or about the car that you have in the garage?

SHRUM: If the fire department had no water in its pumps, I proba-bly wouldn't care very much about it, and I'd pull the car out of the garage. [*Laughter*]

WFB: Yes, well, I didn't ask you to give me a discussion about fire departments that have eccentric problems. Most fire departments have water. [*Laughter*]

SHRUM: No, but we're discussing a weapons system that has eccen-tric problems.

WFB: No, no, no, Mr. Shrum. I'm discussing a question of pri-orities. You suggested that it is somehow abnormal for Americans to care more about their security than about the latest project the Democratic Party comes up with, free false teeth or whatever. I have nothing against free false teeth, but as a matter of priorities, I am asking you why did you ask a question that strikes so many people as so, well, untutored? [*Laughter*]

SHRUM: Probably because I haven't been sufficiently tutored by you.

WFB: Well—

SHRUM: No, no, no. I'm going to answer the question. I mean, *you're* going to stop now, and *I'm* going to answer it. [*Laughter*] I think what I'm saying is that neither in domestic policy nor in defense is the solution to throw money at problems. And that if Star Wars has significant problems and if we're spending at a rate which is too fast and if that introduces destabilizing elements into the nuclear equation, then it's—

WFB: Okay—

SHRUM: —not sensible to spend a great deal.

WFB: Okay, okay, thank you.

SHRUM: More?

WFB: Let me ask you this. You confused me, and perhaps you confused the audience—

SHRUM: Oh, good.

WFB: [I do not know whether I paused here. If I did not, I should have.] Was that your intention? You were very good at it. [*Laughter*]

SHRUM: Yes—

WFB: Because you began by saying that the Reagan administration is spending a mere two percent of the [SDI] money appropriated, and then your [debating] partner over here, Mr. Carter, accused us of driving one hundred and twenty miles an hour toward the goal of SDI. Now, do you want to disavow him or does he want to disavow you, or which position do you want to maintain?

SHRUM: I think Dr. Keyworth [my debating partner: George Keyworth, director of the White House Office of Science and Technology] will tell you that by the end of the fiscal year, especially in the last couple of months, they will spend that money very quickly. I think Governor Riley [South

Carolina's governor, Richard Riley] will tell you that that's one of the problems you have with state governments, too.

WFB: At the end of the year we will be going one hundred and twenty miles an hour but right now we're only going two miles an hour, is that right?

SHRUM: No, maybe two hundred and forty. Maybe two hundred and forty. [Shrum here anticipates the counter I am about to make, and attempts to defuse it by, so to speak, seeing me, and raising me 120 miles per hour.] I don't know.

WFB: You don't know.

SHRUM: I don't know whether we will be going two-forty or one-twenty, whatever metaphor you prefer.

WFB: Now, you all seem infatuated with the subject of percentages, and I've dwelled on this question to try to understand what you are saying. I'm having a terribly difficult time. If you want to build a house, you begin by hiring an architect, right? So your bills at the end of that month may be, say, one percent of the cost of the house. And then the architect starts hiring engineers and surveyors, so that at the end of the next month that might rise to five percent. By the time that house is completed, let's say a year from now, you may be spending fifteen hundred percent as much per month as you were spending the first month. This is not an abnormal, eccentric graph, is it? We are all used to it. Question: What *specific* request for an expenditure toward the development of an SDI technology do you think is indefensible?

SHRUM: I think what is defensible is something in the neighborhood—

WFB: No, no, no, I didn't ask you what was *de*fensible. I asked you what was *in*defensible. There is a difference between *in*defensible and defensible. [*Laughter*]

SHRUM: What will be indefensible will be a figure above the defensible figure, which I will provide if you wish. [*Laughter*]

WFB: Would you detail an expenditure which you think is pre-
            posterous?

SHRUM: I think a perfectly reasonable and sensible—

WFB: No, no, a *preposterous* one.

SHRUM: A perfectly reasonable—let me put it this way—

WFB: No, no, a *preposterous* one.

SHRUM: When you deal—

WFB: In other words, you can't. You can't. Can you make him,
            Mr. President?

SHRUM: When you deal with—yes, I can, Mr. Buckley. [*To the
            chairman*] Can you make *him* be quiet for a minute and
            I will *attempt* to answer his question? [*Laughter*]

WFB: No, you *won't* answer the question.

SHRUM: I *will* attempt to answer your question—

WFB: Oh, I know you *can't,* but—

SHRUM: —if *you* will attempt to be *quiet* for about fifteen seconds.
            [*Laughter*]

WFB: Fifteen seconds. Okay.

SHRUM: The same difficulty occurs with domestic spending. You
            would regard spending one dime more than nothing on
            most social programs in many cases as preposterous. I'm
            telling you we shouldn't waste money on Star Wars. I can
            define a reasonable level of expenditure—

WFB: How?

SHRUM: —and to spend beyond that—

WFB: How? *How?*

SHRUM: Because I think we can reasonably—

WFB: Now, Mr. Shrum. Don't try to fool anybody. You don't
            know the slightest thing about—

SHRUM: How did you define *your* reasonable level?

WFB: —what expenses are required to research this program. [*Pointing to my debate partner, General Daniel Graham*] *He* does.

SHRUM: Do *you*? Do *you*?

WFB: No.

SHRUM: I know you don't, but [*pointing to his debate partners*] they do. [*Laughter, applause*]

WFB: But—

SHRUM: Which leads, Mr. Buckley, to the question, what are you and I doing up here talking about this?

A good question. But, in fact, no matter how technical a subject is inherently, it needs to be discussed, and debated, by nontechnicians. It is an application of this principle that makes a President, as of the moment he is sworn in, commander in chief of our armed services.

Years ago, I used to insist that the principals in a *Firing Line* debate be given fifteen minutes each for their opening statements. This for obvious reasons, so that the terrain could be properly explored, and the basic questions planted. Warren Steibel, as several times mentioned the producer of *Firing Line,* kept telling me that this was simply *impossible* on television: that no audience would hang around for fifteen minutes of opening statements. If the time is heavily reduced, to seven or eight minutes, or even twelve, as below, the speaker tends to concentrate on a few points, and to appeal to the audience to groove with him. We are at Pepperdine College in California, and the debate topic is "Resolved, That the price of oil and natural gas should be regulated by the federal government."

I reproduce here the whole of the twelve-minute opening statements, first Professor Galbraith's, then my own. In my judgment, JKG got about as much as one can possibly hope to get from twelve minutes: rapport with the audience; a broad statement of his position, tendentiously given; a sense of wisdom and of realism; and a bite or two to show the audience that the speaker has plenty of ginger, and knows just where, as required, to stick it.

GALBRAITH: Thank you very much, Mr. President. [*Applause*] I am
              sure that it won't take me a full twelve minutes to establish
              my position here this evening because I'm very deeply
              content with the stand that I'm able to take before this
              distinguished gathering here in this hall and beyond be-
              cause, for once in my life, I don't have to bring the voice
              of liberalism over that of conservatism. If I had to do that,
              I might conceivably lose, but it's my good fortune, Mr.
              President, that this evening I bring the voice of reality over
              romance [*Laughter*] and of reason over nostalgia. [*Laugh-
              ter*] And I've only to look at this vast audience here in Los
              Angeles—I have only to look closely at this audience—to
              see that I have reason and also, considering the general
              affluence [the debate's sponsors had raised almost $1 mil-
              lion dollars for Pepperdine College] among this gathering,
              reality on my side.

    Much of the above is simply required in a debate. A genial sense of
leisure, informality, a recognition of the audience and the sponsors . . .

GALBRAITH: I speak at a time when the production of oil and gas, the
              two energy items with which we're concerned mostly this
              evening, both of these the market has been extensively
              superseded by planning. This planning—this superses-
              sion—has been planning not by the federal government,
              not by other units of government, but essentially by the
              large and powerful enterprises which bring these products
              to us. Here in California everyone is closely aware of the
              enormous enterprise which brought petroleum products
              from the Alaska North Slope and which presently, if plans
              proceed, will bring gas similarly from that field, in the one
              case down through the Pacific waters, and in the other
              case down across the wastelands of Canada to the consum-
              ers in this country. It would be insane—and I say this with
              special feeling for the oilmen here in my audience—had
              you done this with reliance on the market. Nearly a
              decade of lead time was required in this enterprise, enor-
              mous investment running into the still uncalculated bil-
              lions of dollars, and had there not been ultimate control
              of price by firms responsible, this would have been an act
              of insanity.

As it was, there is a concentration of power in the oil industry which allows you, among other things, to control price. And I may say that if anything were to go wrong with this process, with this control—were competition to break out and were the investment in the Alaska Pipeline to be threatened—nothing would so manifest itself as that concentration of power.

The counterpart of this power is the need for some assurance that it is not misused. This control, operating either through public opinion or directly, is the inevitable other side of the planning which I think quite confidently you do need in getting these products over these great distances at such great costs. Or we may take, Mr. Chairman, another case—that of the oil imports, the OPEC imports. We have to take that market as it is given to us, and I don't think even Mr. Buckley in his most charmingly romantic moments will suggest that the market operates with the classical freedom, as manifested in the OPEC price making—prices from twenty to one hundred times the cost of production. This very large price increase, combined with the extreme inelasticity of the demand for these important products, has now produced a massive deficit in our balance of payments, and an enormous pileup of dollars abroad which then seek refuge in currencies which seem on occasion to be more secure than the dollar and—a very serious point—threaten the not terribly fragile but still not completely secure structure of international payments.

Mr. Buckley and I are neighbors part of the year in Switzerland. We both have a very personal interest in what has happened to the dollar in relation to the Swiss franc—Bill more seriously than I because he lives at a higher level of living standards. [Laughter] But beyond the immediate concern of the fortunate people who can still afford to go abroad, there is a very great danger in this process. This is the simple result of the fact that the market in relation to oil no longer works, as it no longer works in its consumption.

There is another dynamic which controls the production of automobiles. The people want to buy this particular combination of novelty and banality [the American automobile]. After several hundred millions of General Motors cars, we find an absence, a great disparity, as between what the planning of the OPEC countries takes from us, and the planning the automobile companies require in the form of fuel consumption. And how do we bridge this? Again we're bridging it by an extensive system of public regulation. If there are any strange, neglected Republicans in my audience, I would note that the system of bridging the gap between imports of oil that are too large and consumption that is too large was initiated by Mr. Nixon [even though it] could be associated with any liberal Democrat. And this regulation is what happens when both consumption and production pass into the hands of large planning units, the large planning units which are *essential* if these large tasks are to be performed. We haven't yet come around to calling the very large planning organization that we have in Washington for dealing with this regulatory apparatus a planning department. The man who did that planning, initiated it, was called a czar, the impression being, of course, that that phrase is more democratic than "planning," and I sometimes suspect, Bill, that no one ever told you Republicans what happens after the czars. [*Laughter*]

We should not be fooled. This is what happens as part of the broad thrust of economic development, the broad thrust of mass consumption, and there is no escape from it. I'm enchanted, as you will be, by the vision that is occasionally presented that we are going to be able to turn back the clock and release ourselves from the very real headaches that this sort of thing involves, the lengthy processes of thought which are required by this development. But I warn you that tomorrow will come and when tomorrow comes, you will have to put up with Galbraith rather than follow the much more charming vision that Buckley will now present for you. [*Laughter, applause*]

WFB: Good evening, Professor Galbraith, friends of Pepperdine. I have to confess that the temptation to regulate is not exclusively the impulse of the socialists of this world. I sometimes wonder whether the case couldn't after all be made for regulating the literary production of John

Kenneth Galbraith. [*Laughter*] He says that I live at a higher level than he in Switzerland, which may be a free market's relative assessment of the value of our work. [*Laughter, applause*] Professor Galbraith grew up with earthy biases, both political and extrapolitical. It is recorded that when he was only six years old, his father took him along to a bucolic political rally in Ontario in Canada where he lived. The elder Galbraith began his speech by mounting a manure pile, and promptly apologized for speaking from the Tory platform. [*Laughter*] And then a few years later, well into his teens, John Kenneth accompanied a lovely young girl of literal turn of mind out into the Canadian pastures, where he paused to observe a bull servicing a young cow. "I think it would be fun to do that," said John Kenneth. His girl friend replied matter-of-factly, "Well, go ahead. It's your cow." [*Laughter*] For years we've been trying to remind Professor Galbraith that America is *our* cow. To no avail, he persists in servicing us. [*Laughter*]

It is, of course, his thesis now, as always, that the market has been superseded—superseded by natural events rather than by synthetic events. He refers to his kinship with reality and reason by contrast with my own with romance and nostalgia. I do remember nostalgically that an agent of the federal government reported in 1885 that under no circumstances would any oil ever be discovered in California. Not to be outdone, another agency of government reported in 1920, right after the First World War, that we had already consumed seventy-five percent of all of the petroleum resources of the United States; and, of course, in 1939, Harold Ickes, you may remember—some of you—taught us that we had thirteen years of oil left in our destiny. In 1949 we were told that we had already seen the horizon of our resources. The fact of the matter is that we have a forty-year supply of tested reserves at this moment, but it is also correct that a feeling of finiteness impinges upon us, and, as always, the interventionists reach for that contingency in order—to quote James Madison—"to enhance power in the government."

Now, says Professor Galbraith, it is historically our disposition to turn to the government when and if we get

into any kind of economic trouble. It is certainly historically the disposition of all human beings to turn to *anybody* when they get into trouble. We are here today not
to predict the behavior of American capitalists but to
advise them. It is certainly true, I assume, that the directors of Lockheed and Penn Central welcomed the [recent]
subventions of the federal government. It also happens to
be historically true that if it had not been for the Democratic vote in the Congress of the United States, they
would not have received those subventions. It was the
Republicans who voted in great masses against those subventions. In respect of the Alaskan pipeline, it is certainly
true that in order to secure the credit for it, certain representations had to be made, and on those representations
much good faith rests.

But what actually is the nature of the *crisis,* and to what
extent are the people who actually produce the oil of the
world responsible for it? The nature of that crisis is the
cartelization of oil by American businessmen? No. By
Iranian businessmen? No. By a clutch of governments.
Thirteen governments that oligopolistically took hold of a
great reservoir of the supply of oil and quadrupled its
prices overnight. This was not an economic act, though it
had economic consequences. This was not the doing of the
free marketplace when suddenly the price of oil went from
four dollars to twelve and a half dollars.

This was an *interruption* of the free marketplace by
political forces, combining in restraint of trade and intending to extort to the highest extent possible from the people
of the United States and from other oil-consuming nations
all the money that they could. To react to this crisis by
saying that *we* should impose a synthetic value on the
price of American oil and gas is an attempt to maintain
the level of water at disparate heights. It is, among other
paradoxical things, a means—by reducing demand—of
subsidizing the very oligopoly that has combined to extort
from us. Mr. Galbraith is correct when he says that there
is considerable Republican complicity in the matter of
fixing prices. It was under a Republican President in 1954
that we fixed the price of gas, and under a Republican

President in 1971 that we fixed the price of oil. The fact of the matter is that we made incorrect decisions. The fact of the matter is that the marketplace is constantly there to inform us of the nature of those incorrect decisions.

For every four percent rise in the price of oil, there is a one percent reduction in its consumption. For every five percent rise in the price of oil, there is a one percent increase in its supply. When you consider that there is a thirty percent disparity between the price of oil at which it is regulated in the United States today and the price of world oil at the cartel price, one can break down the figures and see that that disparity causes an eight percent increase in consumption—which [in turn] results in three million barrels per day extra being consumed, and a six-million-barrel shortfall in supply. The net result is that every day an extra five million barrels of oil are imported as a result of that disparity.

We need a program that seeks to comprehend both the political and the economic aspects of this. The United States should declare that it is our public policy to break the cartel. A cartel aimed at us and the other industrial powers is an act of economic warfare against us.

Accordingly, we should categorize the nations, roughly speaking, with reference to the extractive costs of their fuel. Category A would be those nations that spend a dollar and a half approximately, or even less, to pull the fuel out of the ground. Category C at the other end would be those, for instance Great Britain in the North Sea, that spend four and a half to five and a half dollars. Category B would be in between; we should levy then a tax of five dollars per barrel on Category A; three dollars on Category B; and a dollar on Category C, punishing, therefore, those who seek primarily to extort from us and to maximize their profit in surrealistic terms. Locally we should have instant deregulation of oil and gas in order simultaneously to decrease our imports and increase our supply and reassert that majestic impartiality of the marketplace with which Mr. Galbraith, as a result of his failure to reason and failure to reckon with reality, is so manifestly unfamiliar. [*Applause*]

The stage was well set for the debate. At the end of it the president of Union Oil, Mr. Fred Hartley, a gentleman of strong opinions strongly put, approached JKG and me and said: "If you boys ever want to know what the oil business is really all about, give me a ring."

The following is a readable sample of a tight exchange with Professor Galbraith in 1982. The background: Harvard University. The students were extremely vocal, divided approximately 2-1 in favor of the left. The formal resolution was "Resolved, That this house approves the economic initiatives of the Reagan administration." Galbraith's partners were Professor Robert Lekachman, a witty self-proclaimed socialist; and John Oakes, former editor of *The New York Times.* Oakes did not greet me enthusiastically, perhaps because I had written about him in a book recently serialized in *The New Yorker.* I had been ruminating about the active sense of humor of everyone I knew who worked on the *Times,* and entered the qualification "Big exception: John Oakes. But then he retired as editorial page director several years ago, and is understandably melancholy about having to live in a world whose shape is substantially of his own making." On my side were Arthur Laffer (of the Laffer curve) and Robert Bleiberg, editor of *Barron's.*

Audience reaction is important both for participants in a televised debate and for viewers. But only up to a point: Demonstrations that are overprotracted sap the analytical energy of the encounter. There was a point or two, at this *Firing Line* debate at Harvard, where this came close. Especially when my partner, Bleiberg, frowned on the acre of eighteen-to-twenty-year-olds surrounding us and asked with huge, weighty condescension how many of *them* had ever prepared a financial statement. The hoots of derision from the undergraduate audience were hardly unexpected.

WFB: Professor Galbraith, I'd be most grateful if you would answer my questions directly and laconically.

GALBRAITH: That's an example I hope you would set. [*Laughter, applause*]

WFB: Is it your impression that the amount of tax that Americans should pay should be set by Congress?

GALBRAITH: Should be set by Congress?

WFB: Yes.

GALBRAITH: Yes. [*Laughter*] With the support of state legislatures and—

WFB: I'm talking about the federal tax.

GALBRAITH: Yes. —and local governments.

WFB: Okay. Now, if it should be set by *Congress,* then it oughtn't to be set by noncongressional forces, should it? That is to say, the two are mutually exclusive. It's either set by Congress or it's set by an inflationary impact on a tax scale, is that correct?

GALBRAITH: *You're* not setting a superlative example of brevity for me. [*Laughter*]

WFB: I will be as diffuse as I choose, Mr. Chairman. [*Laughter*] [Under debate rules, the questioner can set his own rhythm, but the responder must answer directly.] I am asking you to answer briefly, and I will ask my questions as copiously as I like. [*Laughter, applause*]

GALBRAITH: It should be set by Congress.

WFB: All right. If it's set by Congress, Mr. Galbraith—

GALBRAITH: And there's no question that there should be consideration of the effect of inflation—

WFB: All right—

GALBRAITH: —particularly on the lower income brackets. I would not worry so much about the people of great affluence, as you do.

WFB: All right. In other words, are we to be guided by what *you* worry about or are we to be guided under the rule of law? Make that distinction now permanently, if you please.

GALBRAITH: I would consider myself completely identified with the rule of law.

WFB: Oh, you do?

GALBRAITH: Oh, yes. Wise laws are, as you well know, part of the general expression of the democratic spirit. [*Applause*]

WFB: Yes. Well, having heard that violin cadenza, let me ask you this. [*Laughter*] Inasmuch as during the last year of the Carter administration there was an inflation of thirteen point four percent, would you reason that any taxes that were authorized before that rise were authorized without reference to the anticipation of that inflation and that therefore those people who found themselves moved to a higher marginal rate of taxation were being taxed without representation?

GALBRAITH: I have no doubt about the need for keeping taxes accommodated to the continuing rate of inflation, and I would have had no objection to the tax bill passed last year if it hadn't had this ridiculous three-year presumption, which was supposed to change expectations and which we already know has not—

WFB: You know, I didn't ask you what you found was ridiculous.

GALBRAITH: —and if the—

WFB: I really *didn't* ask what you thought was ridiculous.

GALBRAITH: —and if the tax adjustment had been limited, say, to people with incomes of twenty-five thousand dollars—

WFB: Mr. Chairman, Mr. Chairman, I want you watching closely here. [*Laughter*] All right, now—

GALBRAITH: Just because—

WFB: —we had a—

GALBRAITH: Just because *you* disapprove of answers— [*Laughter*]

WFB: All right, so we had an inflation of thirteen point five percent and along comes Mr. Reagan and he passes a five percent tax cut which is just over one third of the amount of inflation. Now, would you have preferred that that inflation take thirteen point five percent of everybody's money without any tax relief whatsoever?

GALBRAITH: I would have made the distinction as between the lower tax brackets and the upper tax brackets. And I must tell you, Bill, just because *you* disapprove of my answers, you must not interrupt them.

WFB: No, it's not your answers I disapprove of, it's your rhetoric which— [*Laughter, applause*]

RICHARDSON: [Former Attorney General Elliot Richardson was acting as chairman of the proceedings] May I appeal to you both to—

WFB: Your rhetoric is using up my—

RICHARDSON: —recall that you have an audience out there? [*Laughter*] May I appeal to you both to recall you have an audience out there seeking to be enlightened as well as amused? [*Laughter, applause*]

WFB: Mr. Chairman, my point is that his rhetoric is using up my time, and we all draw certain limits on supply-side incentives, so he'll have to contain his rhetoric notwithstanding the supply-side effect.

RICHARDSON: You have three minutes left. [*Laughter*]

WFB: All right. So, therefore, we have a situation in which it is manifest that inflation is taking away the savings of a people and actually depreciating their standard of living. I'm asking you whether, under the circumstances, relief ought to be accorded. Now, don't tell me that you don't like rich people, because this is irrelevant. Extremely irrelevant to *me,* but after all, if there weren't rich people, I don't know how *your* book advances would be subsidized by the publishers. But in any event, my question is whether or not you believe that the rule of law imposes on a government a sense of responsibility for those impositions that economic policy via inflation causes on citizens.

GALBRAITH: Is that a question?

WFB: Yes, it's a question. Do you want me to rephrase it?

GALBRAITH: Certainly not. I go back to my earlier—Specifically I do not dislike rich people. Many of my friends are affluent and I [*Laughter*]—I rejoice in their company. Second, I do make a distinction, which you do not, between the effect of taxation on people of low incomes and middle incomes and the effect of taxation on people of great affluence, and this is something that is well established in law—it goes back to the Taft administration, a Republican administration parenthetically—and I see no reason why we should abandon that distinction now. I would be much opposed to it.

WFB: No, Mr. Galbraith, understand that I concede your right to pursue your socialist militancy in any form [*Laughter*], but I'm asking questions that go to the rule of law, and your whimsical prejudices—

RICHARDSON: You have one minute.

WFB: —against people who are wealthy is not really in point here. What is in point here is whether we approve of Mr. Reagan's attempt to diminish the impact of inflation on the taxpayer.

GALBRAITH: That one has to accommodate your tax system to inflation I don't doubt, but I have said that four or five times. And I feel uneasy about your habit, when backed into a corner and in a hopeless situation, to resort to words like "socialist" and "militant." It's not in the—

RICHARDSON: Gentlemen, Mr. Buckley's time is up.

Everyone, including the questioner, would concede that there was time wasted here in terms of analysis. But public debate doesn't measure ergs of analysis on conventional scales. The entire exercise had one point, and one counterpoint. Mine was that taxation by inflation is a denial of the democratic process; JKG's, that one shouldn't, really, worry about the effect of rising rates on the affluent.

I pause to note that although the exchange was robust, it was conducted between two very old friends. Two hours later I was relaxing in his house, with his wife and one or two friends, talking of this and that. Though he can be acidulous in action, the crowd, in my experience, tends to discover the underlying geniality which Galbraith's friends rejoice in, those of them who aren't broke or in concentration camps, depending on whether our leaders have pursued his domestic or his foreign policy.

5 FINE REASONING

GUESTS:
DONALD SHAPIRO
ERNEST VAN DEN
    HAAG
B. F. SKINNER
DONALD MACKAY

am asked (frequently) (obviously), Who have been my "favorite" or "outstanding" guests? I reply (always) (obviously) that it is not possible to answer that question to anyone's satisfaction, in particular my own, on the grounds that individual guests have individual strengths. When pressed, I do say that I am myself most pleased when, after an hour, I have the sense that analytical construction has actually been going on. That, at the end of a quarter-hour, a foundation has been built on which we proceed in the succeeding quarter-hour to build. And when, arriving at the end of the third quarter-hour, it is intuitively acknowledged that the talk goes on with direct reference to argumentation that came before. I have mentioned Max Beerbohm's crack about the Socratic manner not being a game at which two people can play. And, of course, the paragons—Plato's dialogues—could not have been written if there had been dogged analytical and rhetorical contenders on the scene. Accept, therefore, those limitations, but then ask: Did not the guests I here present argue in such a way as to cause a scaffolding to rise in the mind of the viewer?

In any event, it is pleasant, after so deep a dip into the idiom of politics, to turn for a moment to guests whose interests are primarily philosophical.

Ernest van den Haag (already introduced as a professor of law and jurisprudence at Fordham University) and Professor Donald Shapiro, dean of the New York Law School, were invited to consider capital punishment, a subject much in contentious discussion in 1981. The convicted murderer Gary Gilmore had been working vigorously to surmount his only failing as a killer, the inability to have himself executed. Professor Shapiro had written an article opposing capital punishment.

WFB: On the whole business of deterrence, Mr. Shapiro, you mentioned in your article that it was one of the common jibes of the eighteenth century—I think you quoted Samuel Johnson specifically—that although in those days they would hang children for the crime of stealing a loaf of bread, nevertheless these great public executions would turn out to be field days for pickpockets, and that this was the most melodramatic example you could come up with on the nondeterrent aspect of capital punishment. Is that correct?

SHAPIRO: Right. Indeed, Boswell quoting Dr. Johnson points out it was the hanging of pickpockets which encouraged *more* pickpocketing, at the execution of pickpockets.

WFB: How do you account for that?

SHAPIRO: Well, because I don't think that capital punishment is a deterrent. [Professor Shapiro had already made a logical misstep. I didn't catch it.] What I think is the deterrent—

WFB: It would deter *you,* wouldn't it? I mean, if you wanted to pick a pocket, wouldn't you think twice about it if you saw a guy being hanged for doing exactly that?

SHAPIRO: [Even] going to jail would deter me. I think that what deters people is the certainty and swiftness of punishment rather than whether it's capital or not.

WFB: Yes. Well, but certainly you would rather go to jail, say, for thirty days, than be hanged, wouldn't you?

SHAPIRO: The dean of a law school goes to jail for thirty days? There are social disgraces whose severity depends on each person. A deterrent becomes a very personal thing. I think that in Mr. Gilmore's case we see a man who really *is* seeking death. If death was supposed to act as a preventive to Mr. Gilmore, it certainly doesn't appear [to have worked]. [In fact,] some arguments have been made by psychologists to the effect that some people actually seek the death penalty. [Another paralogism.]

WFB: Well, Mr. Gilmore is famous precisely because of his singularity. If *everybody* in the death house was seeking death nobody would even have noticed Mr. Gilmore, right?

SHAPIRO: No. But there have been other cases where murderers who have been sentenced to death have welcomed death. It's not *that* unusual. Mr. Gilmore's—

WFB: Well, I know of only two, and there are between four hundred and six hundred people in the death houses now. So it's at least *that* unusual.

SHAPIRO: Well, yes. It's not common for people to seek death.

Now Ernest van den Haag, who had been looking on with stern bemusement, moves in. . . .

VAN DEN HAAG: May I point out that murderers are the people who have *not* been deterred, so this discussion is a little bit irrelevant. I would never maintain that *everybody* is deterred. The second point I would like to make about Dr. Johnson is that *he* made a mistake, which does not justify Professor Shapiro's making the same mistake. You see, the deterrent effect of the death penalty, including the hanging of a pickpocket, does not mean that the crime will be eliminated. It means merely that the rate at which it is committed will be diminished. Now, if Dr. Johnson had shown that in two equally sized crowds, the one in which the pickpocket was hanged showed no less activity in picking pockets than the other, he might have made a point.

ERNEST VAN DEN HAAG, TRIUMPHANT

But even there I'm not convinced, because, you see, a
professional pickpocket would have known, in those

days, that if apprehended, he would be hanged. So we did not expect him to be deterred. What we *really* mean by deterrence is that we want to deter *new* entrants into the profession. Those who are already entering the profession, knowing that they run the risk of being hanged, are not likely to be surprised seeing someone else being hanged, and are not therefore likely to be deterred by it. What we *do* hope to do by hanging (or whatever the form of execution is) is to deter those not already committed to their criminal profession. That is, we make that profession so costly that we decrease the number of entrants.

When we discuss the death penalty it seems to me that what we are really discussing is whether the *supplementary* deterrent is sufficient to justify the penalty; and that's a different discussion, one which, I think, imposes the burden of proof on Dean Shapiro. He would need to prove why, suddenly—given that normally the more severe the penalty the greater the deterrent weight—a five-dollar fine would not deter people from rape as much as five years in prison; and why ten years in prison might deter more than five—why that deterrent-enhancement should suddenly stop at the death penalty. Why the death penalty should not effectively add to deterrence has always puzzled me. Further, we wish to proclaim the sacredness and the inviolability of human life, and there is no way in which the law can proclaim that sacredness other than by saying, "He who violates what is inviolable will himself suffer the taking of his own life."

WFB: You sound like the Old Testament.

VAN DEN HAAG: I do indeed.

Professor B. F. Skinner was much in the news in 1971. He had published a book, *Beyond Freedom and Dignity.* It proclaimed that, given advances in psychological science, we might just as well do away with formal affirmations of individual freedom and rise above those superstitions that speak of the dignity of man. Professor Skinner has been the most influential postwar psychologist in America, probably in the

world, in which he is accepted, if not as the founder of behaviorism, as
its principal systematizer and prophet.

Professor Donald MacKay is at the University of Keele, in England.
He is a physicist and a Christian, whose books include *Analogue Com-
puting at Ultra High Speed,* and *Christianity in a Mechanistic Universe.*
Their exchange was remarkable. I present it here with interstitial comments because what both men say repays more reflection than the pace
of their spoken exchange permits.

On the other hand it is only fair to give warning. *Firing Line* does not
Procrusteanize a guest's formal vocabulary. If it happens that the guest
is a jurist, he may start talking about precedents by no means universally
recognized. Here, the two guests use a vocabulary not generally familiar.
The question arises: Should exchanges of such acknowledged philosophical technicality be (a) tolerated, (b) encouraged, (c) prohibited? It is an
interesting question, frequently faced when, together with the producer
of *Firing Line,* Warren Steibel, we pause wondering whether to invite
a particular guest, whose knowledge is specialized.

We compromise. *Firing Line* is not designed as an exclusive seminar,
fit only for graduate students on the *qui vive.* On the other hand, every
now and then, even at the risk of the majority of regular listeners tuning
out, you know that special pleasure is being given to those who are
inquisitive about the discussion under way and the techniques by which
the protagonist, or protagonists, handle themselves. The following exchange is indeed technical, and the reader uninterested in the subject or
unschooled in the special vocabulary used should without either hesitation or self-reproach skip over it. For those who remain, there is the
reward of seeing one of the Big Issues of philosophy argued with intensity and rigor. The question: Whether men can truly be said to have free
will, or whether all our actions can instead be said to be mechanistically
predetermined.

Professor Skinner came right to the point. Freedom, he says, is not
a philosophical concept, it is an evolved biological response:

SKINNER: The traditional struggle for freedom has not been due to
               any love of freedom or any basic philosophical principle
               about the goodness in freedom, but simply to a series of
               modifications which express impulses traceable to the ge-
               netic endowment of the human species to free oneself from
               certain kinds of aversive, coercive, punitive conditions.
               This includes freeing oneself from the annoyances of life

which physical technology [imposes on us] or to free oneself from punitive control by other people, for instance, by
tyrants.

I asked whether human survival was merely a biological mandate,
or whether the impulse to survive could be said to reflect a value option: i.e., could we provide for our survival because we *elected* to do
so?

SKINNER: I'm accepting survival as a value, and I believe that more
                effective cultures will arise through selective action. But
                not because someone in advance says this is going to be
                good for the human race. [I understand him to be saying
                that the techniques by which the chances of human sur-
                vival are enhanced promote human survival, but don't
                reflect any intellectualized desire to improve the prospects
                for the human race.]

WFB: "Effective" is defined *how* in your vocabulary?

SKINNER: By survival. If a culture develops practices which enable
                it to meet current contingencies, and, of course, to take
                care of conflict with other cultures, it will necessarily be
                more likely to survive. And that, as far as I can see, is the
                only value according to which we're going to be judged,
                no matter how much we might prize some others. We do
                not choose survival as a value; it chooses us.

WFB: Mr. MacKay, how do you bounce off these rather extraor-
                dinary assertions?

MACKAY: Well, I think we're going to have to work hard to avoid
                scrambling a number of issues here. Can I take just a
                moment to try to sort them out?
                     First of all, there's the question whether scientific the-
                ory, and particularly deterministic psychological theory,
                concerning itself as it does with brain physiology rather
                than with experimental psychology—whether science in
                this sense has exploded the concept of freedom. Whether
                determinism has made freedom *out of date*—that's one
                issue.

WFB: Have you come to a conclusion in regard to that?

MACKAY: My own conviction is that all the arguments people have
            put up alleging that freedom of action is a myth [nowa-
            days] being exploded, all these arguments are fallacious.
            On the contrary, freedom of action, in a certain quite
            precise sense, is a *fact* that you can *demonstrate,* if you
            think it through.

WFB: But not to Mr. Skinner's satisfaction.

MACKAY: Well, that remains to be seen.

WFB: Maybe he'll convert before the show is over. [*Laughter*]

MACKAY: Well, you never know. But *my* point is that there's quite
            a *different* issue [we need to face] which I think is the
            [issue] Skinner's book is mostly about.
               Suppose you set on one side the question whether free-
            dom is real, that it has not been exploded by mechanistic
            determinism, [and then ask,] Can we afford it?
               I think we [need to] keep those two questions quite
            separate. Skinner convinces his readers that unbridled
            freedom of action doesn't *work.* But the question "How
            much freedom of individual action can a society *afford* to
            have?" is totally different from the question "How far has
            science [taken us in defining a] viable concept of free-
            dom?"
               And then—third point—we've got to separate out the
            question that seems to [lie] behind your probings, namely,
            What presuppositions underlie Skinner's *own* recommen-
            dations? How do we judge the question of what is worth-
            while to do? Mr. Skinner says, for example, that he sees
            survival as—I'm not sure if he said the only, but at any
            rate, the most defensible of values. But I simply don't
            believe from my own personal knowledge of him that he
            would regard [survival] as "good" [by some other crite-
            rion] if the society that managed to survive did so by
            becoming bestially cruel and repressive; if in fact it fos-
            tered all the negative values which are the opposite of
            those that Professor Skinner himself [is guided by] in pri-
            vate life.

SKINNER: [But history has] demonstrated that totalitarian or des-
            potic domination through punitive control [cannot be sus-
            tained].

            The human organism *can't* be controlled—there is
            abundant evidence to this effect—through punitive meth-
            ods. Take Hitler's Germany, for example. It looked, for a
            time, as if [Nazism] might indeed survive and be the domi-
            nant pattern for a long time to come—a thousand years,
            Hitler thought.

            But something was wrong with it. Now, is it not true
            that a culture which uses punitive methods is [ultimately]
            unable to marshal allies in its support? Certainly such a
            society [encourages] its enemies to get support from oth-
            ers. I submit that Nazi Germany, which looked for a time
            to be so successful with [its trademark of a] knock on the
            door in the middle of the night, was actually building its
            own destruction because its techniques create the condi-
            tions which, because of our genetic endowment, we op-
            pose; conditions we draw away from, and attack whenever
            we can.

WFB: Would you say as much about the Soviet Union?

SKINNER: I don't know enough about the extent to which they are
            punitive. I have visited the Soviet Union. The only police-
            man I ever saw with a gun at his side was guarding the TV
            station. I don't know how punitive the culture is, and I
            don't know how punitive the Chinese culture is.

   This was in 1971. In retrospect, I can think of no venture in pro-
Communist apologetics more blatant, done in a single paragraph. This
was fifteen years after Khrushchev had denounced the regime of Stalin,
five years after the beginning of Mao's Cultural Revolution.

WFB: You do acknowledge that there is scholarship on the sub-
            ject?

SKINNER: Oh, yes, of course.

WFB: The [principal] reason I mention this is that it appears to
            me that you are dealing in universals. It becomes impor-
            tant to ask ourselves if there was something *uniquely* vul-

nerable—genetically, if you like—in Hitler's system that caused it to come to an end. One hopes otherwise. If its punitive nature brought it down, we have reason to be more hopeful than we have recently been about bringing to an end the repressive regimes in China and Russia.

MACKAY: Well, there's still a question of whether this [business of overturning repressive regimes because biological survival-instincts react against coercion] isn't actually pious hope. I mean, it sounds like a certain kind of religious view, which perhaps is one that I would share, although I don't often think of it in those terms. That view holds that, given that God is good, and has standards of what's fair and right and so on, evil will not in the long run survive. But I think it would be oversimple to take that metaphysical statement and translate it into a prediction about a particular stretch of history.

One way of putting it is that God's long-suffering is much longer than our logic. We think [for example] that He ought long ago to have wiped us all out because there's so much cruelty in the world. [Instead,] He still waits; and He says, "How long will you kick against the goads of conscience?" So that I personally wouldn't like to take the optimistic view that anyone who goes in for cruelty as a way of insuring survival—anyone who goes in for the destruction of some of the higher values as they were traditionally called, higher than mere survival—is bound to—

WFB: Self-destruct?

MACKAY: I think it would be nice if that were true, [but] I doubt it.

WFB: When you use the word "God" you are using a metaphor—or not?

MACKAY: No, I would take this in the specific Christian religious sense—God as one to be reckoned with.

WFB: Does that make you uncomfortable, Mr. Skinner?

SKINNER: No. [But that's] because when I listen to that sort of thing I'm running a [simultaneous translator] inside. [*Laughter*]

I think that the good, personified in a god, does represent those things which we find, to use a technical term, reinforcing. They're the things which induce us to behave in certain ways. And evil? Well, the ordinary Christian picture of hell is a collection of all the aversive stimuli available. Hell did not have the electric shock [in the classical literature, only] because the electric shock wasn't then available.

But I should like to go back to your opening remark. When Milton's Satan falls from heaven, he ends in hell. And what does he say to reassure himself? "Here, at least, we shall be free." And that, I think, is the fate of the old-fashioned liberal. He's going to be free, but he's going to find himself in hell. [*Laughter*]

MACKAY: Well, that may be true of the *old-fashioned* liberal. [*Laughter*] I think, rather, that what Milton was going on about was the kind of freedom that wanted to be free even from God. We would agree on that, wouldn't we? That that was the theological point he was making? That a man who supposes that his real freedom is to be free of God is a man who is in fact creating hell for himself?

But it seems to me we've really got to try and get clear of the logical fallacy underlying what Mr. Skinner said just now. He said he was [required to] translate when I was talking. And I say that this is a recurrent fallacy in a great deal of reductionist philosophizing based on psychology and physiology. The best way to show this is by analogy.

Suppose that an engineer came into an area where there were computers running. This engineer might develop a complete mechanical explanation of all that's going on in purely electronic terms. In other words, the engineer might say, "You don't need anything but electronics in order to account for what's happening in the computer."

On the other hand, when *mathematicians* watching the computer say that they are watching the solution of, say, Poisson's equation, they are *not* making a translation of what the engineer sees. Nor is he making a translation of what they see. It's a logical mistake to regard the mathematics as a translation of the electronics. And if Mr. Skinner won't mind a little tease, if the engineer were to pursue his fallacy and write a book called *Beyond Mathematics* [*Laughter*] on the ground that he had discovered how to make a translation of "all that the mathematicians were saying" without mentioning any mathematical concepts, he'd just be laughed at. They'd just say: "What can you do with such a man? He's making a fool of himself."

As a matter of logical analysis, talking about reinforcements and so on, talking about them at Professor Skinner's mechanistic level, or talking about nerve impulses and so on at mine—and I practice my discipline just as mechanistically as he does his—these are not "translations" of what people say either when they talk about other people, or when they talk about God. We are talking about the significance of what's going on, at the mechanical level, in the same kind of way that the mathematicians are talking when they talk about the mathematical significance of what's going on in the computer. They are not *translations.* They are *correlates.*

So if I may come back to my point: I believe that God is to be reckoned with in something of the same sense that Mr. Skinner and you and all of us who are alive are to be reckoned with. I.e., not merely as *objects,* but as *people.* And God has got to be reckoned with as one who knows *us* as we know one another. If that's true—and remember, I'm not saying that I'm here proving that it's true—if that *is* true, then it will not do logically to regard talk in these terms merely as a translation of talk at another level, any more than it would do to regard talk at the mathematical level as a translation of electronics. Conceptually, they are *not* saying the same thing, even though they are correlates of one another.

WFB: [I assume I must have smiled at this point.] Would you care, Mr. Skinner, to modify the use of the word "translation"?

SKINNER: Yes, I would. How technical are we allowed to get on this program?

WFB: Oh, help yourself.

SKINNER: I criticized a passage of yours, Dr. MacKay, in a recent book of mine. I don't know if you ever saw it, but you had said something of the same sort about an electric advertisement in Times Square, the bulbs and so on. You could take it all apart and analyze it in terms of circuitry and whatnot and you wouldn't find the advertisement. This suggests to me the fallacy of the structuralist who wishes to take behavior without regarding the situation in which the behavior occurs. Because obviously the advertisement is not to be found in that array of bulbs. It is to be found in the effect on the person who is looking at it. And what that effect is depends a great deal on the viewer's history. What he sees there and what he does in consequence of seeing it.

As to the translation matter: I wasn't translating in the way in which Dr. MacKay thought. I was trying to go back to what I took to be the original version of which theories (as I think of them) of God are "translations." Men have evolved one conception of God to represent "the good." I think this conception can be reduced to what we think of as positively reinforcing. And these people have accommodatingly conceptualized the devil—or evil—to take care of aversive stimuli in general. So that when you were talking, I was trying to get back to what *I thought* was something that came prior to what you were talking about; not something I was undertaking to translate as you spoke.

MACKAY: But [what you just said] doesn't get us away from the fallacy I am trying to identify. I give it the general name of "nothing but"-ery. The No Smoking sign is nothing but ink on cardboard, so we'll go on smoking. Talk about B. F. Skinner as a man is nothing but talk about a piece of meat of a certain size wobbling up and down emitting sound waves. [*Laughter*] So I'll ignore his views. Either that, or I'll merely calculate what I can do to [appease] the nervous system by emitting sound waves in return. This "nothing but"-ery is fallacious.

SKINNER: I agree, you see.

MACKAY: Well, fine. Suppose that there really is God, as there really
             is B. F. Skinner, and suppose that He in some sense is
             aware of us as we are aware of one another. Then it doesn't
             do to suppose it's an answer to His claims on us to say,
             "Oh well, we only came to [believe] these claims [about
             God] through our upbringing and through discovering
             that certain [alternative beliefs] were aversive." Just as, if
             I may take another illustration, Pythagoras' theorem is
             something which all of us, I suppose, came to believe to
             be true through a particular teaching process which could
             be regarded [as deceptive in that it is subject to] manipula-
             tive [design]. But no matter what [the indictment] or how
             complete [the method by which you came by the knowl-
             edge], Pythagoras' theorem *is* true, and that is not affected
             by telling that story.

WFB: You mean it's true irrespective of your perception?

MACKAY: It's either true or false. But if it *is* true, then its truth is
             not affected by how you came to see it to be true. And
             similarly with God. I'm not suggesting that coming to
             know God is as simple as coming to know one another.
             There are all sorts of epistemological barriers, not least the
             truth that Milton was pointing to, that at heart we would
             rather *not* know God. But I am saying that if a man does
             begin to come to know God in a way that's been recog-
             nized down through the ages by those [others] who did
             come to know God, then the mechanical story—how he
             came to know God—isn't going to serve as a logical refu-
             tation of the reality of the God whom he has come to
             know.

WFB: Let me ask you this rather directly, Mr. Skinner. Most
             people understand your book to be saying that there are
             no standards, beyond those culturally accepted—so to
             speak, self-imposed—that would inhibit the planners of
             your Utopia from having their way. Whereas, by contrast,
             there is the distinctively religious notion that there are
             certain things you simply *can't* do to a human being.
                 Some of the antiabortion sentiment is based essentially
             on that religious view. Would you say, therefore, that it

is incompatible with belief in your system simultaneously to entertain religious beliefs?

SKINNER: There is an incompatibility to this extent: Religion, particularly the Christian religion, has emphasized the uniqueness of the *individual* and of *his* contribution. He is self-determined. He can make choices. He is to be held responsible and subjected to the most wonderful rewards in heaven or the most vicious punishments as portrayed in hell and so on. This has been an effort to rally the *individual,* to strengthen *him* to the fullest extent. The Christian religion has been joined by the literature of democracy, which has done a somewhat similar thing with respect to the individual's earthly powers.

This is all part of the literature of freedom, and I don't want to give the impression that I'm against that at all. I think it was terribly important at *one* stage in our culture for the individual to be strengthened against forces of one kind or another. But that does not mean that the individual originates control any more than it means that the despotic forces *originated* it. And to call *all* control wrong, simply because we have emphasized the kinds we don't like, is to overlook the great danger that we are *being controlled, and we don't know it.* When we are doing things that we feel we want to do, we *feel* free. But I don't believe that the *feeling* of freedom is a proper criterion here.

MACKAY: Could I come in on that one?

Christianity comes down on both sides of that fence. On the one hand, it does, of course, say that each individual will have to stand before God and answer for the use he's made of his opportunities and so on. On the other hand, it emphasizes that we are members [of a community]. And Christianity is, indeed, diametrically opposed to the sort of liberal tradition that Milton was caricaturing. But the question in my mind is not "Is it a good idea to *recognize* our freedom?" but "Is it a *fact* that we are free?"

I think it *is* a fact. You see, if you take an outsider's view of a system, whether it is mechanically conceived or psychologically conceived, then in principle you could imagine that if *we* were the outsiders, we could see enough of the game to be able to *predict* the outcome of a man's choice. This might lead us—sometimes it's led Skinner—to suggest that therefore while a man *feels* free, he's just under an illusion.

Oddly enough, this isn't the case. If the prediction of a man's action—an action that he has yet to choose to take—if that prediction depends on the state of the man's brain, then even though we had a complete specification of the actual outcome, that specification couldn't be equally accurate whether or not the man believed in it.

So, even though your brain were as mechanical as the solar system, there doesn't exist a specification of the outcome with an unconditional claim to your assent. Because either it's been predicated on your not believing it—in which case if you were to believe it, you'd be mistaken—or else if you're clever enough, you might be able to cook it into a form in which if you believe it, it would knock your brain into a state which would make it then come true. But then, by the same token, you would not be mistaken if you disbelieved it, because if you disbelieved it, your brain would not be in the condition it presupposed. So that in that sense, a man who faces a normal choice is free, i.e., he is correct to believe in the nonexistence of unconditional specification of the outcome. That makes *us* responsible, and has no tendency whatsoever to deny the mechanistic explicability of the causes from the outside.

What Dr. MacKay is arguing, if I understand him correctly, is that human will, being immaterial, is simply not susceptible to explanations that are entirely material or mechanistic. In other words, free will exists.

6
THE
SIXTIES,
PART
TWO

GUESTS:
MUHAMMAD ALI
WILLIAM KUNSTLER
FOX BUTTERFIELD
H.D.S. GREENWAY
DAVID BUTLER
MORRIS ABRAM
NORMAN PODHORETZ

The challenge, during the sixties, was pretty direct to the law itself, the most popular form for a time being draft-card burning. The act of disobedience to the law that attracted the most attention was the refusal in 1967 of Cassius Clay, reborn as Muhammad Ali, to present himself for service in the army. When he was called by the Selective Service Board to serve in the armed forces, Muhammad Ali took the position that he was immune, given that he had been ordained as a minister of the Islamic faith as taught by Elijah Mohammed. The courts were initially unimpressed (the prosecution insisted that Cassius Clay was simply engaged in fancy-dress draft evasion). The World Boxing Association duly stripped him of his heavyweight crown, and Muhammad Ali was sentenced to five years in prison.

Muhammad Ali had, at that point (1967), defended his heavyweight

crown six times in eleven months, and won each time. Early on, his
ambitions as a boxer had been widely ridiculed: until, in Miami Beach,
he dropped Sonny Liston dead in his tracks (February 25, 1969). His
skills as showman were abundant, and his exploitation of them prodigious. "I am the greatest," he neatly summed up his accomplishments.
"They all must fall in the round I call," he versified. He was in his early
days something very special, and he knew it. As he explained, "I was
the onliest boxer in history people asked questions like a senator." But
then he was touched by the afflatus of Elijah Mohammed. . . .

In 1968, just after he had been stripped of his credentials, he held
forth, on *Firing Line,* with the self-assurance of a senator.

ALI: [In answer to the question "How come you call yourself
             Muhammad Ali?"] First of all, I would like to say I did
             not *take* the name Muhammad Ali. I was just Cassius
             Clay. Muhammad Ali was *given* to me by my religious
             leader and teacher, the Honorable Elijah Mohammed, and
             I would like to say that "Muhammad" means in Arabic
             "one who is worthy of praise," and "Ali" means "the most
             High," but the slave name Clay meant dirt with no in-
             gredients.

WFB: You believe that you were drafted only because you
             changed your name to Muhammad Ali and joined the
             Muslim religion, is that correct?

ALI: Yes, sir. They knew that I wouldn't go. And the govern-
             ment, they *know* the Honorable Elijah Mohammad and
             [who] his followers [are]. [Ali's point throughout was that
             Elijah Mohammed's followers were being systematically
             persecuted.] The jails are packed with Muslims, and this
             would justify, uh, my title being taken, and this—

WFB: If you hadn't changed your name and your religion, in
             your judgment you would have continued to have been
             listed as undraftable?

ALI: I believe so, yes. But it's debatable. You know, you have
             a right to say what you believe, and I have a right—

WFB: Sure. Let's not fight over it. [*Laughter*] But did your
             lawyers in fact ask the draft board to explain how come
             all of a sudden they reclassified you?

ALI: They asked the draft board to explain a lot. As a matter of fact, I have about six hundred and seventy-five documents, handwritten letters by Baptist preachers, some white, and Muslim ministers, and the Honorable Elijah Mohammed, and the question was, Is he really *sincere?* And like right now—I consider myself in court now. I done faced *one* white judge and now I'm lookin' at *you,* and I already had *one* white jury and audience such as I have here now, and it really makes—I have to be real cool and not [be] savage and radical, because it makes me *angry* when I think about it—when I see the white boys, who really are the number one citizens, the future rulers, when I see *them,* by the hundreds, leaving the country, and I see the white preachers breaking into draft board houses in Wisconsin and Baltimore, tearing the files outta the walls and makin' a bonfire out of forty-five thousand draft cards, pouring blood on them, and I see *them* go to court and the juries say *two* years, and I get *five* years for what's *legal*—

WFB: Now, wait a minute. The five years that you're talking about is for doing something *illegal* in the eyes of the courts of the United States, right?

ALI: No, sir. It's not illegal in the court system to *not* take the step [to be drafted], if your grounds are justifiable and you can prove it. [Only] then you can lose.

WFB: All right, but you *couldn't* prove it.

ALI: Yes, we had the proof. Here's what I was gittin' ready to say then, that makes a black man hot, if you understand. My first wife I had to divorce, this was before the draft come up, because she wouldn't wear her dresses long. I think you remember this, this was headline news. *It cost me two hundred and fifty thousand dollars.* I'm paying *twelve hundred dollars* a month now in alimony. I paid *ninety-six thousand dollars* in lawyers' fees. Now if this is not *sincerity,* I don't know what is! [*Laughter*] I'm not tryin' to be funny.

Years have gone by, but I can't think of any other attempt, by anyone, anywhere, in any circumstances, more eloquent to demonstrate his sincerity, than Muhammad Ali's, that afternoon.

WFB: No, no, no, I don't doubt your sincerity. But legality and sincerity are two different things.

ALI: I have to admit that my case did look phony to the public. "Well, at *first* he tried to get by because he's a conscientious objector; second [because] he had to support his mother; now he's a *minister!*" If we had went in with the ministry first, I'm sure it would have been much easier. So, this is why the judges say this and say that—because we made the wrong move at first.

WFB: Well, then, it's incorrect to blame them, isn't it?

ALI: The lawyers?

WFB: No, the judges.

ALI: No.

WFB: But the judges consider whatever argument you present—

ALI: Well, I'm not blaming the judges, and I'm not cryin'. I told them, my bags are packed, and clean out my cell, because I'm *ready* to go to jail. I'm not cryin', I'm not hijackin' no planes, I have my draft card, it's not burnt. What I would say is that the lawyers should have went at it another way. But I'm just playin' it by ear, I'm relyin' on Almighty God, Allah, and whatever happens happens.

It seemed to me clear, after this program (from which M. Ali got a huge kick—he spoke publicly of it for years: "Another knockout"), that Ali was indeed, and obviously, a victim. But not quite in the way he framed his complaint.

Clearly the malefactor was the draft board of Louisville, Kentucky. It had earlier classified him as beneath the intelligence level required of draftees. Now anyone in verbal contact with Ali, as I was for fifty-seven minutes, could tell in the first minute that he was very far from moronic. The motives of the draft board, in retrospect, seemed obvious: They wished him to become the heavyweight champion of the world, which could hardly be done if he became a private in the army. Therefore, find some excuse to make him nondraftable. Local pride.

What then happened was Cassius Clay's reclassification by the draft board. That, I deduce, was motivated by Ali's highly publicized conversion to a racist religious sect that preached a hatred of the white man. "If that's the way he feels about *America,*" I can hear the draft board advocate pleading the case for Clay's reclassification, "let's put him in the army."

Having been reclassified, Ali tried to plead exemption via the progressive steps he outlined on the program. Eventually, the Supreme Court ruled that as a conscientious objector he should have been excluded from the draft. Ali eventually won back his title in 1974, and the fight went on. . . . I think it fair to say that Ali was, however briefly, during The Sixties, a victim of the Establishment.

William Kunstler was probably the best-known of the lawyers who identified themselves with dissent, and who sought a kind of antinomian liberty for dissenters. His engagement with me on *Firing Line* had been whispered about in advance to be an engagement of some consequence. We had exchanged views in public and in debate, and I had been told that he was coming in with hand grenades in his teeth. He did arrive with a boisterous claque, perhaps a dozen followers who egged him on vociferously. I had decided that his Achilles' heel lay in an interview he had recently given to *Playboy* magazine.

WFB: It is important for you to understand that when you make some of the statements that have caused you to become a very well known figure, some people understand you to be urging types of activity that are "illegal." Now, you say you don't deny this?

KUNSTLER: No, I don't deny it; I affirm it.

WFB: You want to distinguish between the kinds of activity that are illegal which you [nevertheless] approve of, and the kinds of activity which are illegal which you disapprove of. Correct?

KUNSTLER: I want to tell you one thing. First of all, I do *not* urge people to take actions which are legal or illegal. In fact, I don't urge people really to do things. I urge people to think of their consciences, think of all the possibilities involved, and then I tell every single audience, "You be your own guide. Nobody can lead you. Not a Bill Buckley, or a Bill Kunstler." I do say that I do not countenance violence against a human being or in any way against property that would injure the life of a human being or the person of a human being.

WFB: Um-hmm. Well, now, when you said in Chicago, "You must learn to fight in the streets, learn to revolt, learn to shoot guns," you meant shoot them into the air, is that it?

KUNSTLER: I don't think I said that in Chicago.

WFB: Well, do you remember *where* you said it?

KUNSTLER: I don't remember where I said it or *if* I said it.

WFB: Did you write a protest against the [newspapers that quote you] as having said it?

KUNSTLER: I think it's wrong. I don't remember ever saying a statement like that. That's Tom Hayden's speech at Chicago, as I recall.

WFB: Oh, it is? In other words, you disavow that statement?

KUNSTLER: It's Tom Hayden's speech.

WFB: I said do you disavow—

KUNSTLER: No, I don't disavow *anything* anybody says. Every man is his own conscience.

WFB: Now, in an interview in *Playboy,* you were asked to be more specific about how certain reforms could be ventured, and you said, "Well, take the students. Students can take over their college by occupying its buildings."

And then the questioner said, "Well, if the administration refuses to grant the students' demands, what should they do?"

You said, "They should move one step further." You said, "Of course, another form of resistance would be to burn down the building—to burn down a particular college building."

This startled the questioner at *Playboy,* and he said, "You condone arson?"

To which you replied, "Yes, if a point has been reached

in a given situation where the mechanisms of society are not responding to serious grievances." Now, these are not words considering which you have any reservations at all; or are they, now?

KUNSTLER: No. But I'd like to tell you that he asked me for certain examples of protest, and I gave him one more which you haven't gotten to. I said, "You could revolt, too. You could go into full-scale revolution." And you didn't read the next thing after my arson remark. I said, "Hiroshima was a pretty good example of arson." And, I take it, *you* must have approved of Hiroshima.

WFB: Well, again, that's—

KUNSTLER: The point is, you say, if it's a war, it's approved; but if a *student* does it, it's something else.

WFB: Mr. Kunstler—

KUNSTLER: I don't like either one, Bill.

WFB: —can I proceed on the assumption that you can distinguish between a declaration of war passed by both Houses of Congress pursuant to an attempt to save the world from the Axis powers; to defend the Jewish population of Germany, to the extent that it could be done; to save people from the Axis aggressions against China— can you distinguish between that and somebody burning down a building in protest against social policies that call for building a gymnasium in that university? Is that a distinction?

KUNSTLER: You usually don't help me so much. You've given me my answer. Because what you've really said is that under certain circumstances any form of arson, mayhem, bombing is justifiable, and you've given an example of World War II. I'm telling you, there are many people in the United States who believe that it's just as justifiable to try to stop the war in Vietnam as it is to prosecute World War II to stop the Germans from doing the same thing we're doing.

WFB: "Do you condone arson?" Answer: "Yes."

KUNSTLER: Under certain circumstances.

WFB: Do you know what arson means?

KUNSTLER: Of course I do—

WFB: Arson means burning down a building illegally.

KUNSTLER: All right, illegally.

WFB: *That's* what arson means.

KUNSTLER: That's correct. Arson means—

WFB: You've been quoted as answering, "Yes." You see, the trouble with you is that you get very resentful whenever anybody reminds you of what you say. If *I* said what you said, I'd feel the same way.

KUNSTLER: Well— [*Laughter*]

WFB: In point of fact, you run around with these bravura statements about revolution and then you come [here] and you say, "I've never urged anybody to burn down a building." What the hell—why did you say *"Yes"* when they asked you, "Do you condone arson?"

KUNSTLER: Under certain circumstances—so do you. Hell, so do you. Are you against the war in Vietnam? There's arson every day there. [*Applause*] *You* condone arson when it fits your purpose.

WFB: You know nothing about the law. You're about to prove it again.

KUNSTLER: Bill, that's another unfair statement.

WFB: What we're doing in Vietnam is *not* arson.

KUNSTLER: No, it's legalized—

WFB: All right, then, if it's legalized, this copes with the problem that we're trying to get to—having to do with the sources of authority—whether or not we are prepared to allow a court and a constitutional system to make the laws or whether you, with your rampant conscience, ought to make the laws of the people. This is the subject before—

KUNSTLER: Now—that's not quite to the subject, but go ahead.

WFB: Now, there are, as you know, certain canons to which lawyers are held subject. One of them—Canon Number One—is listed under the heading "A lawyer should assist in maintaining the integrity and competence of the legal profession." Included in that is a phrase, "He should be tempered and dignified, and he should refrain from all illegal and morally reprehensible conduct."

Now, to the extent that you answered yes to the question "Do you believe in arson?" weren't you, in fact, *condoning* illegal activity, and doesn't that *disqualify* you under Canon One to continue to serve as a lawyer?

KUNSTLER: Not at all. Because first of all you're saying I'm condoning arson as a way of life. I was asked the question "Do you believe in arson?" I said, "Yes, under some circumstances." Arson being the general term for burning—

WFB: For burning illegally.

KUNSTLER: For burning illegally, according to a court of law. All right. I said that. Canon One indicates that my conduct should be free from reprehensible ideas and so on. I think I adhere to that. I think, under the First Amendment to the Constitution, I have a right to say what's on my mind, and I have a right to speak, and I can tell you that the Bar Association has not seen fit at this moment to bring me up to answer that question.

WFB: Do you know why? I think I know why. I have a letter from Francis Plimpton, who was a former president of the New York City Bar Association—I published it—and he said, "I firmly believe that the complaints against Mr. Kunstler are justified; however, I think it would be a mistake to disbar him, because it would only make him a martyr."

In other words, he believes that you're guilty of violating the professional canons of your profession, but he doesn't want to disbar you because he figures that would make you a more effective revolutionary than you are.

KUNSTLER: Well, if Mr. Plimpton wrote that, I'm sure he did not know you were going to use it publicly, did he? Did you ask him?

WFB: He wrote it and *demanded* that I publish it.

KUNSTLER: He demanded that you publish it?

WFB: Yes.

The background here is interesting. Mr. Plimpton was the commencement speaker at my son's graduation from Portsmouth Abbey school in 1970. He gave a talk on the general subject of civil disobedience which I thought rather too indulgent, and the following day said so in a column, stressing the great prestige of the distinguished commencement speaker. He wrote to me, I replied, and toward the end of our correspondence he asked me to make publicly plain his own feeling about contumacious lawyers. I published his letter in *National Review.*

The exchange with Mr. Kunstler gives pretty much the whole encyclopedia, endlessly replayed during The Sixties, of positions on the admissibility of following one's conscience over into illegality: Sure, (a) damage and death by burning are bad, but (b) you advocate exactly that in condoning the Vietnam War, and (c) who is to say that your conscience, in backing that war, is more refined that that of the student who, using the same instruments, does so to dramatize his opposition to that war?

We did not deal with the philosophical quarrel having to do with civil disobedience. This subject was treated elsewhere.

The point came, many years later, when, on *Firing Line,* attention was given to the matter of perspective. What did the sixties, and their preoccupations, look like today?

David Butler, a journalist who has worked with *Playboy* and *Newsweek,* lived in Vietnam for the better part of ten years. In 1985, he published a book entitled *The Fall of Saigon,* a graphic account of the final two months before the North Vietnamese took the city. Fox Butterfield, who appeared with him, was the first *New York Times* journalist to enter Peking, in June 1979, since Mao Tse-tung took over China. His book on Mao's China, *China: Alive in the Bitter Sea,* is a literary and historical masterpiece: After its publication, it was no longer possible to defend the Mao of the Cultural Revolution, even at Harvard. Fox Butterfield was in Saigon on the day it fell. David Greenway, the third guest, was with *Time* magazine for ten years in a half-dozen cities, including Saigon and Bangkok. He visited South and North Vietnam in April 1985 and wrote dispatches on what it was like there, ten years after the surrender of Saigon. I asked Mr. Greenway, Mr. Butterfield, and Mr. Butler to reflect on the war in Vietnam, and, in doing so, to bear in mind the Vietnam of today, ten years after the fall.

WFB: In 1967, Arthur Schlesinger, who was then—well, at least *ambiguous* on the question of America's role in Vietnam—he believed, at first, that there *was* a case to be made for American intervention—had some fun at the expense of those Americans who explained what was going on in Vietnam by saying simply that it was a "civil war." Such people, said Schlesinger, are those intellectuals in America who are willing to believe that Communist practices are okay if inflicted on yellow races. This, said he, was a very subtle form of racism.

Now, did you find this [condescension] infecting a lot of the thinking in Vietnam during that period?

BUTLER: No, no, no, no, no. In my experience, Americans—military men and diplomats and journalists—who actually *set foot* in Saigon quickly made associations and friendships. Once in a while you'd hear a contract worker talk about how life is "cheap" in Asia, but you didn't get many of those clichés. No, most of us who were involved were deeply committed to the Vietnamese *as individuals.* I think the only people who could talk about the Vietnamese en masse, and say, in effect, "Who cares if these thirty million people are Communist?" were never in Vietnam.

WFB: But that "who cares?" attitude is completely consistent with the prevailing attitude among American intellectuals about Mao's China, isn't it? They simply weren't upset about what Mao was doing to China in the sense that they were upset, say, about what Hitler was doing to Germany, forty years earlier? Probably because they thought, "Well, these [Asian] people have to go through their [bloody] rites of passage en route to democracy even as in Africa," where one is only episodically shocked by people like Idi Amin. [Colonel Idi Amin, the tyrant of Uganda, population sixteen million, was thought to be responsible, by intelligent estimates (e.g., Freedom House, Amnesty International) for the death of about a quarter-million people. Amin was overthrown in 1979 and resides now, whether happily or not one does not know, but at any rate securely, in Saudi Arabia.] There is a kind of a cultural ethnocentrism that seems to me to underlie that attitude, and I thought I spotted it among some critics of the Vietnam War who are apparently undisturbed by what has happened in Vietnam since we left.

BUTTERFIELD: I agree with you. I think people back here, people at home—and here we're making a distinction which David [Butler] just made, between those Americans who were in Vietnam and those Americans who stayed at home—there has been a tendency on the part of a number of American intellectuals to say that the Vietnamese—or the Chinese—don't really *need* human rights. They don't *need* democracy because it's not part of their . . . *tradition.*

GREENWAY: Yet *Communism* wasn't a part of their tradition. You could argue that Communism is an alien—non-Asian—phenomenon. It always gave me a shock to see pictures of Marx and Engels on the walls of China. I wonder if we aren't really missing the point here, because what Ho Chi Minh did—and Mao as well, but let's keep our eyes on Vietnam—Ho certainly *did* manage to convince a good number of Vietnamese that his cause, the Communist cause, was the true *nationalistic cause.*

WFB: Why were there so many refugees from his regime, then?

GREENWAY: Because not everyone believed it.

WFB: Like a million and a half?

GREENWAY: Like a million and a half. Especially Roman Catholics. However, I don't think that anyone would disagree that a great many Vietnamese felt that the Communist side was the side of nationalism against foreign presence. And the saddest people one sees in Vietnam today—in my view the most pathetic—are the southern revolutionaries, the Vietcong, whom one meets in Saigon today, who complain quite openly that they have seen their hopes betrayed.

BUTLER: This spring, the tenth anniversary of the fall of Saigon, I
               was surprised that we didn't hear from some of our most
               prominent friends from the antiwar movement.

WFB: Either way? In other words, they said nothing?

BUTLER: Well, what *can* they say, after ten years of boat people and
               reeducation camps?

Well, they could say something, I went on to observe. For instance,
Joan Baez did, and invited Jane Fonda to do as much, to say just a word
about the boat people. She declined. Professor Peter Berger, the sociologist, gave birth to a fine aphorism when he said that anyone who doubts
that there is a difference between an authoritarian and a totalitarian
state would not know the difference between life in Saigon and life in
Ho Chi Minh City.

Twenty-five-odd years ago I was engaged by Emory College in Atlanta
to debate with a local liberal about whom, I now confess, I then knew
very little, other than that he was defiantly liberal, ardently antisegrega-
tionist, a masterful polemicist, and a brilliant lawyer. My plane was late,
the auditorium was packed, and I found myself, on an empty stomach,
facing one of the most ferocious advocates in my experience. It transpired that he had spent days in the library researching everything I had
done and, at least as important, not done. It was a high-pitched evening,
two hours of groin-and-eyeball heavyweight stuff, Morris Abram defending every domestic and foreign salient of the Kennedy administration, I questioning, progressively, the sanity of anyone who could take
Abram's positions.
    The next day I visited his offices, where he showed me an architectural
blueprint for a serene, integrated, happy Atlanta.
    Soon after that, feeling that he had, in fact, outgrown Atlanta, Morris
Abram came to New York, where he joined the firm of Paul, Weiss,
Rifkind. In what seemed no time at all, he had been named head of the
Field Foundation, United States representative on the Human Rights
Commission of the United Nations, chairman of the United Negro
College Fund, president of the American Jewish Committee, and—
president of Brandeis University.
    He had come a long way from his rural background in Georgia. His
intellectual growth began when he was young. He attended the Univer-

sity of Georgia and the University of Chicago, where he took his legal degree, going on to Oxford as a Rhodes scholar. In 1973, he contracted leukemia and was told he had only a few weeks to live. He sat down to dictate an appropriate autobiography and decided, while doing so, to sit up and fight his lethal disease *à outrance*. Seven years later, Morris Abram was still alive, and voting, no doubt under the guidance of the guardian angel who cured him of his bodily disease, for Ronald Reagan for President. He had been cured in every sense of the word. And in 1981, the same book it had been expected would be published posthumously was out. It was called *The Day Is Short: An Autobiography,* and it recounted his heavy disillusionment at Brandeis.

WFB: It will be very interesting to people who read your book, and who know about your career, if you will spend a few minutes on your experiences at Brandeis. Here you were, the most prominent liberal Southerner, I guess, in the United States, placed in charge of a university which is probably the most prominent liberal university in the United States. All of a sudden, an explosion.

ABRAM: Sixty-nine. January '69.

WFB: Would you describe what it is that happened?

ABRAM: What happened was, I suppose, that in those times, after the death of Martin Luther King, a considerable amount of energy in the black community was devoted to the idea that there should be black studies, that there should be black control by students—black students and black professors—of the university curriculum. It was part of a whole mélange of demands that the students were making.

WFB: Question: Why, at the end of two decades in which the vector of intellectual and emotional thought was integrationist, should a sudden demand for separatism have cropped up?

ABRAM: I don't know that I have pondered that question before. But I do know this. Before the eruption occurred, I did get word from Bill Sullivan, whom you probably knew—

WFB: FBI?

ABRAM: —of the FBI; deputy director—that there had been a takeover in a Canadian university and that the people who had stimulated that takeover were on their way to Brandeis. They thought Brandeis particularly vulnerable, first of all because of the close connection—historic and prophetic—between Jews and blacks, and the reluctance of Jews to confront blacks in any decisive way because they felt a deep sympathy for their needs and aspirations.

And, second, they realized that Brandeis was a very distinguished liberal institution. Interestingly enough, you never saw disruptions in institutions that were *not* distinguished. All the disruptions were in the great universities, and Brandeis is, and was, a great university. Columbia, Harvard, Wisconsin, Brandeis, Northwestern, Williams—these were all very distinguished institutions. You didn't have any disruptions at Bob Jones College; you didn't have disruptions at any number of colleges of lesser distinction. Well, anyway, back to the story. Bill [Sullivan] called me and said to me, "They're on their way to Brandeis."

I didn't believe him. Among other things, I felt a little reluctance to be in contact with the FBI.

WFB: Were they black or white? The "they"?

ABRAM: It was *a* black person and *a* white person, and they came one night when I was away from the campus. They got the blacks together and said that if any of the men in the group were *men,* they would stand up and *assert* their manhood.

There was a total uproar, and the next day, they seized Ford Hall, which was one of the ancillary administration buildings. Their demands were absurd. They wanted black control of certain curricula.

WFB: Your predecessor had precommitted the college to accept those demands, right?

ABRAM: My predecessor had agreed to certain things, after Martin Luther King's assassination, which I think were a mistake. One of them was for a black studies program. And I'll tell you why I think it was a mistake. It's not that I think the black experience is properly taught in the Amer-

ican universities. I don't think it is, not for a minute. He
had promised set-aside scholarships—full scholarships—
called Martin Luther King scholarships. He had promised
also an increase in the black student body under a kind of
forced draft. He had promised also a transitional one-year
program in which twenty-six students would be brought
up to qualification, and, if presumably qualified, admitted.

Well now, what actually happened was that students
were brought onto the campus even though they were *not*
qualified. The person in charge of their instruction came
to me. I asked him, "How many of the twenty-six are
qualified?"

"Well, five." He asked me, "You're not going to admit
the others?" "Of course not," I said.

That night I got word that they'd admitted all but
three—because faculties are notoriously tender, and faculties, as you so well know, crave student adulation. It's one
of the coinages of the trade.

The blacks were correct about one thing, and that is,
American history, as I understood it to be taught in most
universities, was never taught in the fundamental respect
that much of our history is a confrontation between whites
and blacks on this continent. Politics and political science
are not taught, in my judgment, in the context of the fact
that the seniority system, among other reasons, was designed to make certain that white Southerners controlled
the mechanisms of Congress. It was not taught that because of racial discrimination, blacks weren't voting in
anything like their proportion of the population, and that
this skewed the political system. There's an enormous
amount of American history and American sociology and
American politics and American economics [relating to
the black-white experience] that I never learned in college.
I wanted that introduced into the *standard* curriculum
that blacks and whites would take.

WFB: I understand.

ABRAM: Not put off in some segregated hole, and taught as black
studies—which only blacks would go to, and which would
qualify them for nothing.

WFB: But it was too late for you to make this point?

ABRAM: I made the proposal, I did.

WFB: But you felt obliged to implement the commitment of your predecessor?

ABRAM: Yes, I had to. I suggested the other [alternative], but the blacks glowered at me, and so did the whites.

WFB: Yes, so then what happened?

ABRAM: Well, I implemented [their program]. But in their judgment it wasn't being implemented fast enough, at least in the judgment of those who came and insinuated themselves on our campus and stimulated the trouble. And, also, there was an additional demand, and this was one no great university could ever meet: that students have some say over the picking of faculty and a *final* say over the curriculum.

            And that I would never agree to. I couldn't possibly. I would have been false to every principle I believe in— every academic principle of any university—had I agreed to that. But I decided [after the sit-in] that I wouldn't call in the police. Harvard had called in the police and it left them in rather a difficult situation. Northwestern University called the police. Wisconsin had called in the National Guard. I just said simply, "Go ahead and stay in the building. I'm not going to accede to your demands."

WFB: In your book you confess to certain trepidations as a lawyer about simply closing your eyes to a continued violation of—

ABRAM: I certainly did. I'm afraid that was one of the reasons why I really think I probably would not be a good university president. I have a love of academia. I love the give and take of Socratic discourse. I love to live in the world of ideas. I went over to Oxford this year after a rather painful experience in this country to teach there for a while, and I loved this. But on the other hand, I am a person who looks at things from the viewpoint, I suppose one would say, of rather stern principle, and maybe you might call it dogmatism. But I could not *stand* the defilement of the ideal of academia as a place that should be governed by the faculty and the administration.

WFB: What about civil disobedience?

ABRAM: I respect it, and I always told the students that Martin Luther King had been a friend of mine and the family had been clients of mine. But Martin Luther King, when he practiced civil disobedience, was always willing to go to jail.

WFB: To take the consequences, yes.

ABRAM: He went back to Birmingham, knowing that he would be placed in jail for something that was unjust, but he knew that the civilized society, with its constraints of law, protected him and protected his movement, and it was too valuable to be forsaken by him. But you see, these students didn't feel that way.

WFB: So you would have distinguished Martin Luther King from, say, William Sloane Coffin and Dr. Spock?

ABRAM: Absolutely.

WFB: Because they were people who practiced civil disobedience but did not want to accept the consequences?

ABRAM: They did not want to accept the consequences.

WFB: Yes. Okay. So therefore, for eleven days you simply ignored [the sit-in], right?

ABRAM: I ignored them.

WFB: You saw that they got plenty to eat and so on and so forth.

ABRAM: I didn't see to it. They—

WFB: Somebody did.

ABRAM: —could come and go.

WFB: Yes, right, right.

ABRAM: And I might add, some of the faculty saw to it that they could get enough to eat.

WFB: Okay. Then the issue arose, should they be punished? And again, your legal instincts agitated you.

ABRAM: Absolutely. I felt that it was *right* to punish them. But here I ran into some extraordinarily difficult decisions. If punishment had been fair, almost every black in that university would have had to be expelled or suspended. And not only that, the black *faculty* and *administrators* would have to be expelled or fired or put under suspension. You would have had a real confrontation, which the community, as we called the campus, would not have supported. I recall saying—

WFB: Was that before or after the Chicago crisis?

ABRAM: Ah, now that's the point I was going to get to. I—this was before the Chicago—University of Chicago—crisis. And Ed Levi, who was the president of the University of Chicago and who had been my teacher when I was at the Chicago Law School—

WFB: And became Attorney General.

ABRAM: Right. He didn't call [when there was a sit-in, similarly motivated, at the University of Chicago]—he followed the model that I had used—he didn't call in the police. He waited them out, and when they came out, *he expelled everybody involved,* and created an enormous uproar. But he *did* it. And later I said to Levi, when he was Attorney General of the United States, I said, "Ed, I wish I could have done the same thing, and I feel bad about it." And he said, "Well, Morris," he said, "I'll tell you something. You would have created a confrontation that you could not have sustained—"

WFB: Why?

ABRAM: "—between Jews and blacks." Because the Jewish—

WFB: There's a heavy Jewish population at the University of Chicago too, so why would—

ABRAM: Yes, but it's not a Jewish-sponsored school.

WFB: So?

ABRAM: "Plus the fact," he said, "your faculty would not have
              supported you." And he's right. *His* faculty was much
              more stern. And then he said something to me that's very
              important. He said, "You know, I grew up at the Univer-
              sity of Chicago. I even went to the lab school there and
              all the way through up to the presidency." And he said,
              "Of course it had a tradition, and I was part of that
              tradition."
                  I felt a little better, relieved; but still I feel very keenly
              that it would have been good for the students who had
              earned it to have been punished.

My instincts were to opine that Morris Abram had been wrong to fail
to act under the mandate of instincts that were refined, experienced, and
liberal. But being told that Ed Levi himself, president of the University
of Chicago, who had stood up successfully to student contumacy, had
said Abram could not have acted correctly because to have done so
would have brought failure in his situation leads one to ask: Shouldn't
one question the postulates of such a situation as immobilized Morris
Abram, the ardent liberal reformer-lawyer from Atlanta, come to New
England to preside over a liberal college, only to be outwitted, or, if not
that, overwhelmed, by circumstances he could neither control nor effectively reform, even as chief executive of the delinquent university?

Well, he wrote his book, and—from the sidelines, now—continued to
fight the same fight he understood himself to have fought throughout
his career. Which, no doubt to the delight of his critics—perhaps his
more thoughtful friends understood him—found him arguing, as a
member of the Civil Rights Commission, on the side of Ronald Reagan,
against racial quotas.

Norman Podhoretz, the influential and outspoken editor of *Commentary* magazine, spoke about The Sixties and the intellectuals: the principal theme of his book *Breaking Ranks.*

Norman Podhoretz, as everyone knows who cares about that kind of
thing, was associated with the left in American politics until some time
in the late sixties, when he gradually, but with that trenchant willpower
which even his critics acknowledge, changed his mind. Since then he has
been a penetrating critic of disorderly thought and romantic views of the
Soviet Union. Under his own signature, he published a great deal about

the Kid Years, and their influence and ramifications. And, under his prodding as editor of *Commentary,* he elicited the views of some of the brightest men and women in town, to give their views on matters not unrelated to the uneven thinking that underlay opposition to the Vietnam War. It is commonly acknowledged that essays published in *Commentary* resulted in the nomination as ambassador to the United Nations first of Daniel Patrick Moynihan, then of Jeane Kirkpatrick.

PODHORETZ: There is a similarity between the challenge that the new radicalism of the 1960s posed for the intellectual community and the challenge that the radicalism of the thirties posed for an older generation of intellectuals. In the thirties, of course, the center of the radicalism was an organized, coherent force, namely the Communist Party. There was no such organized and coherent force in the 1960s. The radicalism of the sixties was diffuse, decentralized, quite chaotic. Nevertheless, by some miracle of communication, the radical line of the sixties acquired a persuasive force and a kind of tyrannical power, over the minds of many people, that was comparable to the force of the Communist Party line or doctrines in the thirties. And among the areas in which this was so was the area of intellectual and cultural freedom.

In the 1930s, the people I considered my elders and mentors—among them—preeminently among them—Lionel Trilling—had all been associated with a then-young magazine, still alive, called *Partisan Review.* *Partisan Review* had begun life as an organ of the John Reed Club, which was a Communist Party literary society. Eventually it broke with the Communist Party—not so much over any strictly political issue as over the issue of the autonomy of art. These were young literary intellectuals, and they found it increasingly intolerable to be told that they were not permitted, for example, to admire T. S. Eliot, whom all of them considered a great poet, because Eliot was a reactionary in his political views, and a modernist in his technique, [when] modernism was regarded as a form of bourgeois degeneracy by the party.

So these young people found themselves breaking with their commitment to the Communist Party in a conflict between political loyalties and loyalty to intellectual and cultural values. They chose loyalty to cultural and intellectual values over political dogma. It seemed to me, when I found myself reliving an uncannily similar experience in the sixties—I had begun the sixties as a radical, and as a sympathetic participant in the spread of the new radical ideas, as you well remember, I think. As the sixties wore on, the same conflict between loyalty to radicalism and loyalty to intellectual values began to make itself felt. The first place in which it made itself felt—visibly, saliently—was at Berkeley [*pace* Al Capp], where, of course, the so-called free speech movement began shouting down speakers who were in disagreement with its views and—you know, in general, in the sixties, you could be sure that *anything* that called itself the "free speech" movement was likely to be anti—

WFB: Free speech.

PODHORETZ: —free speech. If something called itself the antiwar movement, it was probably in favor of the victory of one side.

WFB: Or "liberation" movements.

PODHORETZ: Yes, liberation movements for enslavement. Well, the free speech movement and some of its apologists posed a challenge to those of us in the intellectual community who had been sympathetic to the new radicalism. Were we going to go with this movement because it seemed to be conducive to the progress of our political ideas, or were we going to criticize it, and possibly even, in the end, oppose it? Because it was—I don't know what word to use—subversive; hostile, to *intellectual* values; to such values as free speech and freedom of inquiry, as also to intellectual standards themselves.

WFB: Why is it that some of the same people who had fought free, during the preceding twenty-five years, of the tyranny of the Communist Party ended up being—so many of them—such easy victims? Why were they so easily manipulated? And who bears the intellectual and moral responsibility for that evolution? [In your book] you introduce the leavening factor of fatigue, and it may be that some people simply felt that they had fought just one battle too many and were willing to submit. Is that right?

PODHORETZ: Right. Well, in the case—as I say in *Breaking Ranks,* there were different explanations for what happened to various people. It is true that many of the veterans of those battles in the thirties against the excesses and distortions of radicalism fell victim the second time around the track. I think some of them, I'm sorry to say, were opportunistic; that is to say, they wanted to get onto what they thought of as the wave of the future. Others, as I try to put it, found themselves becoming born-again radicals: I mean, making up for what they now thought had been the mistake of their youth in deserting radicalism. Still others—and here I think Lionel Trilling would be the preeminent example—I think were *tired.* As you say, they were not able to summon the kind of energy, and go through [once again] the kind of agonies, of a battle like this.

What was going on in the sixties and early seventies was the promulgation of a dogmatic creed, dissent from which led to excommunication and worse, as some of us who dissented bear the scars in witness of it. You know, relativism is very often used as a tactic by people who are on the outside seeking power. That is, they begin with a plea of toleration on the basis of a relativistic philosophy. Once they get into power, they find themselves somewhat mysteriously forgetting the relativistic doctrines that suited their earlier stage of powerlessness, and begin being intolerant, and enforcing their truths as absolutes. You see this in the universities, even today.

The experience of the sixties has not been assimilated. Given the inclination in America for self-examination, this is strange, and one must suppose, at the remove of nearly two decades, that there has got to be a reason for it. I suspect that that reason is that no one knows quite what to make of it. Professor Vann Woodward of Yale wrote a few years ago almost in passing that the failure of the intellectual class to deal satisfactorily with The Sixties is the most arresting and disturbing feature of twentieth-century academic life. Just as the intellectuals had failed in Germany when Hitler came to power, so they failed in America when, however briefly, anarchy came to power.

Or is it as Morris Abram so plaintively supposed, looking back on his own situation in Brandeis, that there *was* no solution for such problems as he faced? . . . And yet, in pointing to Brandeis he keeps saying— doesn't he?—that Brandeis is really unique. Well then, why did matters run as they did elsewhere? At Columbia. At Berkeley. At Harvard and Ohio State and Williams. Norman Podhoretz was correct about the failure of the intellectual class. We do not yet know why it failed; nor do we have any sense of contrition, or even any profound experience of self-examination. Which is probably why there is a continuing sense of insecurity in so many colleges and universities.

7

DEMOCRACY

AND

THE

INTELLECTUALS

GUESTS:
JEAN-FRANÇOIS REVEL
PAUL HOLLANDER
ERNEST VAN DEN
  HAAG
ROBERT MOSS
THEODORE WHITE
JAMES MICHENER
ZDISLAW RURARZ
MARGARET THATCHER

eflections on democracy. Can it contend with organized antidemocracy? What are some of its distinctive
frailties in practice? How do its advocates defend democracy against its
performance?

On the first question, there is no one around, this side of the antidemocratic theorists, whose melancholy is more systematic than Jean-François Revel's.

He is one of Europe's profound thinkers. Although it is true that
profound thought is usually traceable to profound thinkers, it isn't
always true that that which is taken as profound comes from profound
thinkers—junk thought can get heavy treatment. Revel, however, is an
original. In 1984 his best-seller *How Democracies Perish* maintained that
democracies don't have the psychological machinery or the mobiliza-

tional resources to stick it out in the long haul against aggressive totalitarian powers that dispose of definitive weapons. And that, therefore, we
are on our way down, and the Communists will inherit the world.

Revel is hardly the first analyst (or poet) to make that prediction.
Whittaker Chambers' formulation is the one found in anthologies: that
on the day he chose to come to the West, he knew intuitively that he
was leaving the winning side in order to join the losing side. It was over
twenty years later that James Burnham wrote his *Suicide of the West,*
whose thesis was that the apparently unshakable biases and inhibitions
in liberalism make it doubtful that the West should prevail. A gloss on
the Revel-Burnham thesis, as one reflects on it, is that if the West does
prevail, it will be not on account of the strength of the West, but the
weakness of the East. What Mr. Revel especially contributed was an
examination of the special attitudes bred by democracy—self-criticism
so pronounced as to induce a relative indulgence of tyranny, a lethal
combination that can lead to self-emasculation.

Jean-François Revel was born in Marseilles, schooled at the Ecole
Normale Supérieure, and for many years taught political science. He
was the dominant editor of *L'Express* for many years. His best-known
books in America, preceding *How Democracies Perish,* were *Without
Marx or Jesus* and *The Totalitarian Temptation.* In appearance, Revel
is the quintessential Gallic intellectual, interested and even passionate
in what he says, but not so much in the consequences, however melancholy, of what he projects. He argues his thesis with total conviction,
but one never has the sense that he is personally depressed by its ulti-
mate meaning for Western democracy.

WFB: You write, Mr. Revel, rather apocalyptically, looking
            down the long historical line. In fact you say, "Perhaps in
            history democracy will have been an accident, a brief
            parenthesis, which comes to a close before our very eyes."

REVEL: Yes. Just after World War I, Central Europe was demo-
            cratic or becoming democratic. Countries like Czechoslo-
            vakia and Poland and Hungary were more or less in
            between; Rumania too. Yugoslavia was half democratic.
            We should have been able confidently to assume that they
            would be democracies today. But now there is just a very
            slim slice of Europe—Western Europe—which is demo-
            cratic. In fact, analysis shows that the totalitarian systems
            have increased their share of the world since World War

II. And why? Because we never learn. We are faithful to an assumed—an alleged—international law whose definition goes back to Yalta or Helsinki which the Soviets simply do not respect; do not implement.

I asked Revel whether there was any reason to exclude democratic coordination in the levying of sanctions, for instance economic sanctions.

REVEL: Democracies cannot implement such sanctions because they are democracies. The United States have their own farmers who want to sell grain. Moreover, America is the most powerful country in the alliance, but cannot impose something on France or Australia as the Soviet Union can impose policies on Czechoslovakia.

But what especially interests me in this economic sanctions problem is that the whole philosophy of economic détente has been turned upside down. At the beginning of the seventies we initiated economic, financial, and technological trade—help in various forms to the Soviet Union and to other Communist European countries because, we reasoned, "They will become dependent on us and this means that they will become more peace-minded and nicer and less aggressive."

But in fact, ten years later, what do we see? That *we* are dependent upon *them,* upon Eastern markets even as we subsidize them, you see? So that you have the Germans, the French, the British, telling the Americans, "We cannot stop the gas pipeline because it means so many jobs for us." So the whole philosophy of détente, accelerated by economic pressures, is completely turned around.

WFB: It's like the old saw about if you owe a bank one thousand dollars, you're in trouble; if you owe the bank one hundred million dollars, the bank is in trouble.

REVEL: Yes, exactly. We have given the Soviet Union a tool to use against us.

Revel had put his finger on something very important in asserting that democracies regularly cripple themselves by coming up with the modern equivalent of "Yes, but what about the Negroes in the South?"

You will perhaps have forgotten that old favorite, which went the rounds thirty years ago.

Scene: the Moscow subway. Soviet Foreign Minister Molotov is showing Secretary of State Dean Acheson the beautiful mosaicized, crystal-clean subways, which Acheson effusively admires. But after waiting for a quarter of an hour Acheson finally asks Molotov, "Where are the trains?" To which Molotov huffily retorts, "What about the Negroes in the South?"

Revel gave many lugubrious examples of the working of the Western mind. He quoted Louis Mermaz, president of the National Assembly in France and a doctrinaire socialist, who replied to a reporter's question about the Soviet gulags: "I am as horrified as you are by the gulags, which are a perversion of Communism. But I ask that you also condemn that monstrosity of the capitalist system: hunger throughout the world that kills fifty million people every year, thirty million of them children."

Revel notes that gulags are, in the mind of a European socialist, merely a "perversion" of Communism: while hunger is postulated as an attribute of capitalism. (The reverse is true. Where there is Communism, there are gulags. Where there is capitalism, hunger diminishes, year by year.) He notes matter-of-factly that given the birth rate, it can hardly be true, as is so widely alleged, that under capitalism the population is increasing year by year, if it is also true that thirty million people per year are dying of starvation. But above all he stresses that the net psychological impact of ceaseless self-critical reaction (our own asking, "What about the Negroes in the South?") has the effect of diluting, if not absolutely castrating, genuine indignation at expansive Soviet barbarism.

Revel insists that there is not one historical occasion in which East-West negotiations have actually improved the Western situation (I would except those negotiations that led to a treaty for Austria in 1956). Revel writes and speaks with analytical passion in forwarding his assumption that democratic countries, bound as they are by rationalist thought, cannot contend with single-minded demonic powers.

One returns to Revel's thesis, namely that whatever democracy's internal weaknesses, its corporate vulnerability is fatal. And this vulnerability grows not alone from democracy's relative rigidity. It is a function also of an addictive self-criticism which is distinguished from dissent in that it can be immobilizing. One supposes that, along the line, the qualifier the "loyal" opposition was coined to distinguish between those who were, when all is said and done, patriots, and those others whose criticisms lead them to defection or, if not to formal defection, to do the work of the enemy often with far greater effect than if they had formally defected. "Clearly," Revel writes, "a civilization that feels guilty for everything it is and does will lack the energy and conviction to defend itself."

It is a matter of record that in our time a significant number of Western intellectuals have been seduced by monstrous regimes, notably those of Stalin, Castro, Mao Tse-tung, and Ho Chi Minh. How come? When Ernest van den Haag, professor of law and jurisprudence at Fordham University, and Paul Hollander of the Russian Research Center at Harvard appeared on *Firing Line* in 1981 to discuss Dr. Hollander's book *Political Pilgrims,* they assayed answers.

I began by asking whether, in their judgment, the number of American intellectuals taken in by Stalin was significant, or whether we were talking merely about "a noisy minority."

HOLLANDER: There is no question that the appeal of the Soviet Union in the thirties was very widespread. Now, when you ask this question, "What proportion of American intellectuals fell for the Soviet line?"—well, we don't know because nobody did a survey of all American academics. But certainly one has the feeling and the impression that of those who were visible—of those who published their views—there was a very large number who at least temporarily went for Stalin and admired him. Now, many of these dropped him later, but they went through this phase.

WFB: Yes, and whatever their number, I think most people would concede that they had considerable leverage—

HOLLANDER: Yes—

WFB: —in a number of very important forums. They had it in the book review media. They had it in Hollywood. So that it isn't as though they were condescended to as merely aberrational.

HOLLANDER: Right. They were influential beyond their numbers—

VAN DEN HAAG: It's not just an American phenomenon. It's an *international* phenomenon. Whether they're intellectuals in France or in Germany, England or the United States, they all seem to be— Let me put it this way. The intellectual as a professional arose in Western history basically as an articulator of religious ideas. Having lost his faith in actual religion, he now is an articulator of pseudoreligious ideas—of a secular religion such as Marxism, which differs from religion in the original sense in that paradise is located not in utopia, but in a particular place: the Soviet Union, China, Cuba. Now whenever the secular utopia gets discredited—

HOLLANDER: They move on to a new one—

VAN DEN HAAG: —a new utopia is found—unless they can go on denying the atrocities in the old one. Would that be your position?

HOLLANDER: Yes, that theirs is a search for some new form of meaning in life. Formal religions are no longer sustaining enough for many intellectuals. Accordingly, they look for secular religious ideologies that serve as substitutes.

But there is a second point. A large number of Western intellectuals who are predisposed to be critical and questioning of their own society gravitate toward critics of their own society. "Something must be right about *that* system," they will conclude, "because its partisans criticize *my* society, which I also criticize." This gives them a certain sense of affinity, a sense of fellowship, with the other country and the other society. Tom Hayden and Staughton Lynd go to Vietnam and China and say, "Well, *they* were revolutionaries. *We* were revolutionaries. *They* reject these things about our society. So do *we*. They *must* be doing something right."

WFB: There is, of course, the subpoint that you make, I think very tellingly. Namely that because people tend not to want to dislike *everything*—in this case, to dislike America—they tend to attach themselves to another society that they can feel good about. This is what you call "a contextual redefinition," which you would define how?

HOLLANDER: It's when you reevaluate a given phenomenon because of its context. For instance, child labor is bad in America for obvious reasons. But you go to Cuba or Nicaragua or wherever, you see the same thing happening, and you say, "Well, this is good because these children are working for a new society."

VAN DEN HAAG: It becomes *revolutionary* child labor, and the intellectuals ask, "What's bad about that?"

HOLLANDER: Or the matter of putting people in prison. That's bad, especially in your own society. But maybe in this other society it's not so bad, because that other society is basically just and idealistic, so they don't put people into prison for the wrong reason. Or take bureaucracy. Bureaucracy is bad, but maybe in a revolutionary society it's not so bad because it's supposed to serve some good purpose in the long run. This contextual redefinition is also often tied in with a kind of future orientation—the future will vindicate what is in the short run unappealing.

   Now none of these intellectuals would go to an American child care center where they may see well-fed children playing happily and on the basis of such evidence go on to say, "Well, that must be a good society because all these happy children are here." But they will do just that in Cuba and the incident is used to vindicate the system as a whole.

VAN DEN HAAG: May I interrupt you for a second?

HOLLANDER: Sure.

VAN DEN HAAG: The rejection of one's own society has all kinds of emotional motives, some of which you explore. But I do wish to point out that there's also an element which is not wholly *ir*rational. The intellectuals feel that in their own society they don't have the position—the standing—that they feel they deserve. Now I'm not saying that they *do* deserve it—but that they feel that they deserve positions of prestige and of power and of income, and they don't have them. Now interestingly enough, in all the societies about which the intellectuals got so enthusiastic and about

which they denied the atrocious actual conditions—in all
these societies there *is* a division between the planners and
the planned, and the intellectuals in some sense are not
wholly wrong if they feel that in such a society *they* would
be among the planners and lesser folks among the
planned.

Generally it is supposed, when one talks of "intellectuals," that one
has in mind only the academics. This is obviously not so. And certainly
it is not so of the critical class. Among the most ideologized critics of
our own society are journalists, polemicists, churchmen. Robert Moss,
the Australian-born British journalist and novelist, made relevant observations on the point when he appeared in 1980.

WFB: Why do the media have so persistent a bias against the free
              societies?

MOSS: Well, let *me* in turn ask *you* a question. Where do journal-
              ists find the easiest stories to write?

WFB: I suppose local scandal?

MOSS: Right, local scandals. Under the Freedom of Information
              Act, secrets come tumbling out. We know how this works
              in America. It's easier to assail your own institutions,
              much harder to get information, let us say, on the KGB,
              or the Soviet defense buildup. You can't file a Freedom of
              Information lawsuit in Moscow.
                 And the second reason is lack of imagination. Now
              most people—not just journalists, but politicians, the man
              in the street—when they try to think their way into the
              minds of the totalitarian dictatorship in Moscow, they
              have great problems. They simply don't know Russian
              culture or Russian history. And consequently, there's a
              tendency to attribute our own hopes and fears to the Sovi-
              ets. I came across an interesting example of this recently
              involving a prominent senator. He said to me that it was
              important that Europe should back the SALT II treaty
              because if we didn't then the hawks in Moscow would be
              stronger and the doves in Moscow would be weaker.
                 I said, "Well, Senator, I understand the demands of
              diplomacy and discretion, but could you perhaps give me

some cases of recent Soviet moderation that might tell us
how our support for the doves is paying off?" He said,
"All I can say is that things would be a lot worse if those
hawks in Moscow took over." I've read many editorials
and columns in the U.S. media which literally transpose
our thinking into the minds of a totally alien group. Since
we have hawks and doves, *they* must have hawks and
doves.

I liked best, of all the generalities spoken on the subject, those by the
late Theodore White, an influential and eloquent journalist and historian, and a political liberal.

WHITE: We are living in a culture of caustic, persistent cynicism
                and criticism, where substance is less important than style,
                and where somehow people have come to believe that the
                United States is the root and the source of all evil in the
                world, at home and abroad. I do not believe that *any*
                government could have moved faster to enlarge civil
                equality, could have moved faster, without bloodshed, to
                enlarge the opportunities of the blacks, than did America.
                I find no reflection in this kind of criticism of the enor-
                mous agony this country is going through, and of the
                enormous goodwill of people both black and white in
                order to make it work. I find a whole record of the U.S.A.
                in the past twenty-five years since the war despised and
                condemned as imperialism. I think our policy in Europe
                between 1948 and 1953 was brilliant and creative. So was
                our policy in Indonesia, so has our policy been elsewhere.
                In the long period of twenty-five years since the war, I find
                the United States has done far more good in this world,
                more people are *alive* today and thriving than there would
                have been had the United States not exerted its influence.

Pitted directly against this soothing buoyancy is the indisputable fact
that a pathological self-criticism makes life at least unpleasant, at most
dangerous for those who wish their democracies to survive. The fact of
it is, Revel observed, "analysis shows that the totalitarian systems have
increased their share of the world since World War II. And why?
Because we never learn."
We never learn. What does that mean? My own inclination is to stress

that we never learn the *advantages* of our system, its weaknesses notwithstanding.

But there are other reasons, other assaults. James Michener, the shrewd and consistent author of best-sellers, made an additional point when commenting in 1983 on his recent book about Poland.

MICHENER: Bill, a very harrowing question arises here which perplexed me and was voiced by quite a few Poles. That is, the present deterioration of affairs in Poland, which is horrible—has that been *fostered* by the Russian masters? There's a real supposition that it may have been—that the Pole was getting too far ahead in the standard of living from what was possible in Russia—and laws were put into motion to bring about a deterioration in the Polish economy.

WFB: That is the thesis put forward by Abe Rosenthal of *The New York Times,* that the best way to exhaust the spirit of people who might otherwise mobilize that spirit in order to acquire freedom is to keep them working as much of the time as possible simply to stay biologically alive.

MICHENER: Yes.

WFB: By that token, if George Washington had had to worry twenty-three hours a day about eating—

MICHENER: Yes.

WFB: —he might not have gotten around to associating himself with the Declaration of Independence.

MICHENER: I have a very gripping passage in the book about that. Give people less and less food till they reach the breaking point, then feed them more so they can work, but be sure then to diminish the food so they go back to the breaking point.

WFB: The gulag formula?

MICHENER: Yes. The gulag formula is operating in parts of Europe today, I'm sorry to say.

[Mr. Michener illustrated Revel's point about the manipulability of the Soviet Union's "allies," by comparison with what can be done by democracies to affect the behavior of *our* allies.]

. . .

There were—there always are—the bright spots. The resonant defection, for instance. Consider Zdislaw Rurarz in 1982. In late December of the year before, he had entered the United States embassy in Tokyo accompanied by his wife and daughter. There and then he renounced his office as ambassador from Poland to Japan. He went further and released a statement: "The present situation runs counter to the interests of the Polish people and serves only Soviet imperialism. I can no longer represent the present regime, which denies the fundamental rights of the Polish people."

He told me, in English as yet imperfect, that a factor that influenced him toward defection was his impression that the United States was, in fact, learning. *Pace* Jean-François Revel. I asked him whether he saw in America a creeping, or indeed a galloping, sense of realism on the nature of totalitarian technique and how to cope with it.

RURARZ: America is in flux, I think. It is quite difficult for me to speak about something I have no authority on. But I used to be convinced that the U.S. is capitulating before the U.S.S.R. somehow, that you are not standing up to their pressure, to their imperialism and so on. Only after I learned that you would be installing Pershing II cruise missiles in Western Europe—this NATO decision of November 1979—*then* I believed that something *is* changing. And after the invasion by the Soviets of Afghanistan and the reaction by the West, especially by the United States, which was missing at the time of Hungary and Czechoslovakia, gradually then I started to believe that something *is* changing. It remains to be seen whether you will really keep up to certain promises or this will end up with rhetoric.

Ten years later, under a conservative President acclaimed as the most pronounced anti-Communist who had ever sat in the White House, the Pershing missiles were on their way out.

The most common cliché in defense of democracy is that except for any alternative system, it is the worst. But we've seen, on *Firing Line,* several

MRS. THATCHER, PATIENTLY EXPLAINING

flashes of courage and felicity in formulation that, for a while, dissipated the antidemocratic clouds. I remember Margaret Thatcher in 1977.

THATCHER: For years now in British politics you have needed to use the word "consensus." "You must have a consensus." It's a word you didn't use when I first came into politics. We had *convictions,* and we tried to persuade people that our convictions were the right ones, and it's no earthly good having convictions unless you have the will to translate those *convictions* into *action.*

Provided you had convictions, politics was more than merely a matter of multiple maneuverings to get through the problems of the day. I often think when you're going for *consensus,* so often it means that those who believe as I believe tend to give in to the left wing.

Now, the previous election [1974] was fought in Britain on what I think is one of the most damning sentiments ever uttered, and it was by the predecessor to Mr. Callaghan—Harold Wilson. What the British people wanted, he said, was *a bit of peace and quiet.* Anything for a *quiet* life. You know and I know that this is the great drag on democracy [this conviction that a quiet life is all that the people wish]. They wish to know, in fact . . . "Does my voice *count*? Can I *do* anything?" Otherwise they leave [politics] to a tiny, well-organized minority. If you do leave it all to that tiny, well-organized minority—

WFB: Unpleasant things happen.

THATCHER: —unpleasant things happen. I understand that one time you interviewed Mr. [Vladimir] Bukovsky. I was very impressed with one of his speeches. He put it marvelously. Back when he lived in Russia, where they had no freedom at all and one or two like him were determined to fight for it whatever it cost, the view he took was not "Does my voice count?" The view *he* took was *"If not me, who? If not now, when?"*

Now that's the view that I want each democrat—and I use it in the ordinary sense, a believer in democracy—to take in Britain.

Mrs. Thatcher was of course right in insisting that democracy, to be successful, depends on energetic political participation by those who resist direct tyranny or creeping tyranny. She does not successfully make the case (no one has; no one can) for democracy as itself the guarantor of freedom. It is after all self-evident that the majority, exercising democratic procedures, can diminish freedom. Even as the minority can err, so the majority can err. There is no constitutional fixity anywhere on which the libertarian can depend with total assurance. Even the Bill of Rights (or its equivalent in other democracies) is subject to amendment. Although it helps to put obstacles in the way of popular distempers, and we have done this in America with the Constitution, we cannot rule ourselves truly safe from domineering government. And as a general rule the more powerful the state, the less free its citizens.

It is under socialism—understood as the government taking primary responsibility for allocations of property otherwise done by the marketplace—that the hazards increase. It is the distinctive characteristic of socialism (or "economic democracy," as he put it), wrote Lord Percy of Newcastle in *The Heresy of Democracy,* that "property should be perpetually insecure." How can a citizen depend on his right to his property if the state has the power to inflate the currency and to tax disproportionately? Those who plead that the Kantian formula of the transcendental imperative is the insight into successful self-government miss the point. Kant told us that no one should do anything which he would be unwilling to elevate into a universal injunction. But how does that injunction affect a state that deals differently with different people, depending on the rate at which they earn income—as an example? A triumphant majority can satisfy the majority and leave the minority bitterly dissatisfied and without effective protections.

Mrs. Thatcher can only appeal to rational conduct. Others, more ambitious (F. A. Hayek, most notably), plead for the abolition of the progressive feature of the income tax, the great instrument of unequal treatment under the law. So Revel was telling us that the democracies cannot effectively resist monolithic and unscrupulous enemies of democracy; while Mrs. Thatcher failed to tell us, no doubt because she could not, that one hundred years after Gettysburg, we had established that government of the people by the people and for the people could be made to endure forever.

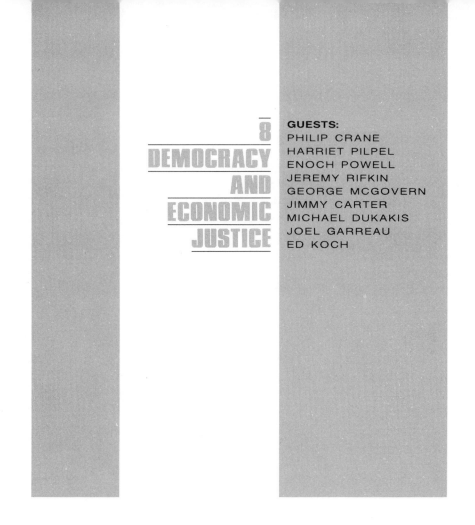

8
DEMOCRACY
AND
ECONOMIC
JUSTICE

GUESTS:
PHILIP CRANE
HARRIET PILPEL
ENOCH POWELL
JEREMY RIFKIN
GEORGE MCGOVERN
JIMMY CARTER
MICHAEL DUKAKIS
JOEL GARREAU
ED KOCH

would label the pessimism of Jean-François Revel as by
no means empirically discredited. But we move to
more particular criticisms of democracy. These are sometimes opportunistic. At the hands of practicing politicians, they have a way of taking
the democratic lady and giving her a little affectionate, flirtatious pinch
on the behind. Consider Congressman Philip Crane, elected to the
House of Representatives in 1969. In 1980, he ran for President. I
remark as an aside that Crane's race for the presidency is one of those
anomalies democracy sometimes hits you with. He went to New Hampshire with sufficient financing to make a good race. Every position taken
by Candidate Reagan was also Phil Crane's, with this difference, that
Reagan was twenty years older. Crane, like Reagan, is matinee-idol
good-looking. He is a Ph.D. He is a splendid orator. He is married to

a beautiful woman and between them they begot eight beautiful children. Crane got about as many votes in the primary as Lyndon LaRouche.

Anyone running for President of the United States is ever so careful in handling the problem of organized, monopolistic labor's union practices. When I was a student at college, Senator Robert Taft ran (1950) for reelection to the Senate. In fact, Senator Taft was running for President of the United States, and much depended on how he would fare, as author of the Taft-Hartley Act, which sought to curb some union abuses. That act had been labeled, by the most prominent Democrats in town, including President Harry Truman, the "Slave Labor Act." Senator Taft brought off a great coup in Ohio. He conducted two simultaneous polls among labor union members. The first asked directly the question "Do you approve of the Taft-Hartley Act?" The answer was something on the order of 90 percent against, 10 percent for. The second poll asked how the individual filling out the questionnaire felt about (a) secret balloting, (b) regular accounting for union expenses, and so on, down the list of the dozen major constituent features of the Taft-Hartley Act. The answers to the second poll were, approximately, 90 percent approval of the act's constituent parts, 10 percent disapproval. With those answers in hand, Taft won the election (against "Jumping Joe" Ferguson: I memorized that memorable name confident that in doing so, I am unique).

WFB: I should like to begin by asking Mr. Crane why, in his judgment, organized labor tends to vote so regularly for the Democratic candidate.

CRANE: I'm not persuaded that they do, Bill. This goes back to a conference that I organized out in Youngstown, Ohio, in February of 1978, to discuss with the union leaders why they felt Youngstown Sheet and Tube had gone under. It was a fascinating exchange. They knew they were meeting with conservative Republicans, and they had almost to be dragged kicking and screaming to come into the room and sit down with us. I don't know whether they expected us all to have horns or what, but we asked them why they felt Youngstown Sheet and Tube had collapsed. And they pointed an accusing finger at me and said, "You people are destroying a climate for investment in this country."

By "you people," Crane's guests clearly meant the Congress of the United States.

CRANE: They said, "You have no idea how much it costs to realign blast furnaces." They said further, "Stop attacking profits. Management may be SOBs, but they're *our* SOBs, and we'll go after 'em for our share of the profits, but don't you people kill profits."

WFB: Well, I don't doubt, as you know, that the objective interests of the American workingman are in living in a society in which the private sector is especially pronounced. Is it a matter of correct labeling?

CRANE: I think it is largely a matter of labeling, Bill. I think that if you present the case for what we conservatives have consistently stood for I would argue that that's the case for economic growth. If properly conveyed to rank-and-file union members, I feel increasingly that we have a unique opportunity.

Crane turned out to be right: that organized labor could be got to vote heavily for a Republican candidate. Ronald Reagan got 43 percent of the vote of organized labor later that year, and 45 percent in 1984.

And, of course, no question having to do with the viability of democracy is more important than the question of whether the truth will emerge in democratic exchange. There is heavy literature on the subject, and the question arises, as in this fragment with Harriet Pilpel, the distinguished (and ubiquitous) feminist–lawyer–civil libertarian. The subject immediately before the house was censorship.

PILPEL: As you know, I have quotations—but I won't bore you with them—from John Milton, whom you cite a lot, and Oliver Wendell Holmes and many others who say, "No matter how pernicious or stupid or evil a book is, if you allow it to get into a combat with other books in a society of freethinking people in the marketplace, the truth will emerge."

WFB: Of course that's rank superstition.

PILPEL: I think it's the actual fact.

WFB: It didn't happen in Germany. It didn't happen in Argentina.

PILPEL: I'm talking about a *democratic* society. If you have—

WFB: But Germany's *was* a democratic society in 1932.

PILPEL: Well, I don't—

WFB: It was *very* democratic, and between them, the Communists and the Nazis won an absolute majority. The plurality was won by Hitler.

PILPEL: I do not think that any theory of the emergence of truth as supreme in the marketplace can work in a dictatorship.

A refinement on the claim that democracy will always usher in the truth is the criticism that the burdens democracy needs to bear are frequently insupportable. The distinction is variously described by different writers. Professor Edward Banfield speaks of those who, impatient, vote for gratification on Monday in place of on Tuesday, intending the distinction that immediate gratification is often at the expense of strategic gratification.

Enoch Powell has appeared several times on *Firing Line.* By nature a maverick, he is a prodigious scholar, unhappily overidentified with a single position, namely the need to strengthen Great Britain's immigration laws. He speaks here about democracy and the free market.

I began by asking Mr. Powell whether he thought that the appeal to confidence in the free market asked the voter for more difficult analytical calculations than are required by asking him simply to repose faith in a political candidate who promises to bring instant gratification.

POWELL: That freedom works can only be proved by *seeing it* working. It's like attempting to prove to a man who thinks he is paralyzed that he can get up and walk on two feet. Where we have freedom—economic freedom I'm talking about—we use it; and the consequences follow unnoticed, like breathing the air by which we are surrounded.

WFB: Can you give me an example?

POWELL: An example, which is a great favorite of mine—it's a small one but perhaps none the worse for that—is that we have

in England a thing called the National Trust, which was
started right at the beginning of this century by the private
sector to preserve historic houses, stretches of country,
parks, and so on. Now, this has become one of the biggest
undertakings in the United Kingdom, privately managed.
It administers a huge acreage and thousands of properties.

Now, let us suppose that the National Trust did not
happen to be founded at the beginning of this century, and
that the government instead had said, "You know, really,
the state must do something about it—we must have a
national commission for maintaining great houses, parks,
and so forth." And let us suppose that that had been done
during the last sixty years—during the whole period that
the National Trust had existed—and then I come along in
the year 1970—Enoch Powell—and I say, "The state
doesn't need to do this! The problem would have been
solved if the state hadn't taken the responsibility on its
shoulders." Everyone would shudder: "But how can you
say such a thing! There's no profit in it, it wouldn't pay.
Of course, people would have to be compelled. Of course,
this has to be done by the taxpayer." It is only because we
have the National Trust that anyone would believe it possible.

So, it is always difficult, particularly when the state has
intervened over a long period of time, to convince people
that the alternative of economic freedom—indeed the alternative of freedom of choice—exists and is viable. That's
the *built-in* difficulty. We must do the best we can.

But the resistance to private-sector enterprise as inimical to abstract
democracy is throughly ingrained in many who think themselves especially sensitive in their understanding.

Jeremy Rifkin was (in 1976) the head of an organization that called
itself the People's Bicentennial Commission. It held the view that we
should seize the occasion of the nation's bicentennial to forward the
American Revolution by accelerating the socialization of the United
States. This, Mr. Rifkin argued, was the true trajectory of the thought
of the Founding Fathers—the founding revolutionaries. Probably the
most publicized maneuver of Mr. Rifkin's People's Bicentennial Commission was the offering of huge cash awards—$25,000 was the posted
figure—to any wife of any major corporation executive who produced

evidence sufficient to put corporate executives in jail. That was certainly a novel idea. Meanwhile, his arguments were of the genus the-rich-get-richer, and the-Founding-Fathers-would-not-have-tolerated-this. In dealing with such as Mr. Rifkin, it probably pays to be provocative. Accordingly . . .

WFB: I should like to begin by asking Mr. Rifkin: Where did you get the idea that the Founding Fathers were premature Communists?

RIFKIN: Well, not having had the advantage myself of a boarding school education and having instead to go through the regular public school system in Chicago, I happened to be taught by my social studies teachers that America was born in revolution. But back when I was in school, our teachers would talk to us about Sam Adams and Patrick Henry and all the firebrand radicals that made the American Revolution.

WFB: I'm not sure that answers my question. I said: What makes you think that revolutionists are necessarily Communists? Probably there have been more right-wing revolutions than left-wing revolutions in the last couple of hundred years.

RIFKIN: I'm well aware that during the Revolution there were many wealthy people that sided with the revolutionists, included among which would be George Washington and John Hancock. But at the same time, the people that made up the corps of the sons and daughters of liberty—the artisans in the city, the small farmers in the countryside— were very much opposed to the concentration of power that Lord North and King George represented.

WFB: The government today can, I think, with a plausibility equal to that with which we used to complain against George III, be documented as being far more tyrannical than George III ever was. So if you wanted to say, on the two hundredth anniversary of the founding of this republic, that we have slipped back into a situation in which there is supergovernment, I think you would have a very substantial following. But the notion that we should fortify that government in order to protect ourselves against Du Pont or—

RIFKIN: No, I don't believe we should. As a matter of fact, I agree with you up to a point—and I hope I don't have to agree with you beyond that. I do believe that the government bureaucracies in Washington certainly reflect a kind of attitude which is destructive to people having access to the political decision-making in this country.

At this point, I was beginning to groove with Mr. Rifkin. But his next sentence brought me up short.

RIFKIN: But I would go one step further: I think that the reason that there's so much concentration of power and so much decision-making in so few hands in Washington is because of the undue influence that the giant corporations seem to wield over our political affairs. Let me throw out a few statistics, and you tell me if I'm wrong. Today two hundred corporations in the United States—according to Senator Hart's committee on antitrust—own two-thirds of all the manufacturing assets of the United States of America. And as a matter of fact, Judd Polk—who you probably know—the former senior economist for the Chamber of Commerce—predicts that twenty-five years from now two hundred corporations will literally own fifty-four percent of everything worth owning on the planet Earth.

Now, I suspect that here in the audience there isn't one person that could tell me five people that head up these companies. *I* don't even know who they are. What I'm suggesting is that we have these nameless, faceless men bestriding these giant corporate institutions that have virtually gotten out of control and dominate American life from the supermarket to the halls of Congress.

WFB: Well, if they're nameless and faceless, why don't you add that they're masochistic? Because as recently as a year or two ago, they lost about thirty-five percent of their capital value on the stock market. It seems to me that if they were controlling the economy of the United States, they would see that that kind of thing didn't happen to them.

RIFKIN: Well, it's amazing. I haven't heard anybody defend the corporations as being in poor financial straits right now. The fact is that of the hundred largest—

WFB: But they *are*. They're in terrible shape. We need thirty-seven or thirty-eight thousand dollars of savings in order to produce a single job. In our highly capitalized international situation it is extremely difficult to raise that kind of money when you're averaging a profit of four point eight percent and when approximately seventy-five percent of all savings of the people are absorbed to finance government expenditures and to service the national debt.

RIFKIN: The reason there's so little capital formation going on in the United States today is because over the past ten, fifteen years, multinational corporations in this country have been systematically dismantling their plants, their equipment, their industrial facilities here and shipping jobs and capital and production overseas to Western Europe, Hong Kong, Taiwan, and across the globe. So we have a situation—

WFB: Are you opposed to free trade?

RIFKIN: Well, I'll tell you what I'm opposed to. I'm opposed to *my* government using *my* tax money to subsidize these giant multinational corporations so they can ship our American jobs *overseas* and our production facilities overseas.

WFB: Excuse me, but how does *your* money get into the act?

RIFKIN: Well, I'm a taxpayer.

WFB: All right. Let's say the Ford Motor Company wants to set up an assembly plant in Mexico. Now, how does your money or mine get into the act?

RIFKIN: Well, there are billions that we would have had in taxes had companies like Ford located new plants here.

That depended, of course, on whether Ford Motor Company operations within the United States were successful and yielded revenue. But I was anxious to pin down the point about Mr. Rifkin's money.

WFB: What is it that makes you talk about *your* money? The investors in Ford hired management who in turn hired skilled labor who put out automobiles, merchandised and sold them. And all of a sudden you're saying that your money is somehow involved in their decisions on where to do business.

RIFKIN: Well, I think what we're really talking about with multinationals locating plant, equipment, production, and markets abroad is just an advanced use of the old colonial techniques that the ancient monarchs used two hundred years ago.

The transcript does not reveal whether, at that moment, I simply slit my throat. The temptation was surely there. That happens, from time to time, on *Firing Line* programs: the difficulty in finding honest engagement. There are even better examples of this kind of thing ahead.

For example, the inevitable question of the many uses of the word "democracy." As in "democratic" justice, or "democratic" distribution. The subject is touched on here in an exchange with George McGovern. We have tackled each other frequently. He is, as noted, a formidable opponent, a crowd-pleaser with a populist-analytical penchant that has carried him a long way, though when he ran for President, he was rejected by forty-nine states. He has the skill (and grace) to yield an occasional point or two, when it satisfies his theatrical and intellectual instincts to do so. The subject immediately at hand was world hunger: Is there a "democratic" way of handling the problem?

WFB: I should like to begin by asking Senator McGovern why the Soviet Union has such a chronic scarcity of food?

MCGOVERN: Well, Mr. Buckley, I've never been very impressed with their system of production in the Soviet Union. As you know, it's basically a system of collective agriculture, over against the so-called family-type farm operation that we have in the United States. I think there is a loss of efficiency, a loss of incentive there.

WFB: Well, under the circumstances, Senator, wouldn't you consider it a part of your responsibility to the anti-hunger cause to make more prominently known what you just said here, your disapproval of collectivized agriculture?

Isn't it plain that there is a correlation between the abundance of food and a free economic system?

MCGOVERN: Yes, I think that's true. I think there's a direct correlation between our capacity to grow food and the other side of the paradox, which is hunger. If we lacked the productive capacity or the purchasing power in this country to feed all of our citizens, hunger would be bad enough, but it's entirely unacceptable at a time when we can produce *more* than enough to take care of all of our people.

WFB: Aren't you just a little bit instrumental in that paradox? Year after year you vote in the Senate to send great gobs of money to rich farmers—like Senator Eastland, for instance—when in fact you are paying them not to grow the food you say is needed for the hungry. Why do you simultaneously complain that some people don't have enough to eat, and yet pay people *not* to grow food?

MCGOVERN: I think that's a good point. I have tried, along with other members of the Senate, to put a limit on the amount of federal payments that go to any one farmer.

WFB: For not growing?

MCGOVERN: That's right.

Time for a little frolic.

WFB: How much would you pay me to stop writing?

MCGOVERN: I don't always approve of your point of view, Mr. Buckley, but I'm one of those that buys your books. But the point is that if we would put a reasonable limit on the amount that we pay to any one producer, two things would happen: We would reduce the cost of the program, and secondly we'd have some funds that we could divert to feeding the hungry.

WFB: Well, now, why do you find it so difficult to press this position inside the Senate?

MCGOVERN: I think it's because many of the senators represent large growers. You referred to my colleague in Mississippi, who himself is a large grower. Many of the senators don't have

that kind of direct tie-up in the farm operation, but they
reflect the point of view, I suspect, of some of the more
articulate and larger and forceful producers in their states,
so when it comes to a vote in the Senate, we ordinarily lose
on that.

A patient, and fatalistic, concession about one of the defects of democracy. You simply accept certain inequities, however gross, as the price
of accomplishing something on which you put a high priority.

In the federalist American situation, I have constantly asked the same
question asked in a different and dramatic form by William Graham
Sumner in his essay "What Social Classes Owe to Each Other." The
question has always seemed to me to be different: namely, What does
one economic entity owe to another economic entity if that entity has
the same or even superior resources? The question goes to the heart of
the redistributionist question, and, of course, to the heart of the meaning
of federalism. It came up directly in a program with Governor Jimmy
Carter of Georgia, in 1973.

There is an amusing sequel to this interview. Seven or eight years later
I was lecturing in Athens, at the University of Georgia. My host was
an associate professor in the history department, as I recall, and he told
me that at the time President Carter had appeared on *Firing Line* there
had been some excitement among his staff. It was Mr. Carter's first
nationally televised program. Accordingly, my host at Athens, who
served Mr. Carter as a press aide, invited the younger members of the
staff to his house for beer, pretzels, and a chance to watch the boss on
Firing Line. "When he came on, I went over and kicked the set and
screwed around with the knobs. He didn't sound like *our* Jimmy
Carter." It developed that for some months, Mr. Carter had been practicing a deregionalization of his accent, in anticipation of his race for
president. "How did he used to sound?" I asked. "Like Billy," was the
short, and sufficient, answer. As a guest, Mr. Carter was fluent, resourceful, and engaging.

I asked Governor Carter to comment on President Nixon's recent
impounding of funds voted by Congress, and how this touched on the
federalist ideal.

CARTER: In the past I and the other forty-nine governors have been
              able to guess, at least, what would be the attitude of the

federal government by seeing what bills passed, what bills were vetoed by the President, what funds were appropriated, what funds were signed into law in the appropriations bill by the President. Then we could make our budget determinations accordingly, submit them to our state legislatures—many of which don't meet but once every two years—and proceed accordingly.

Now, with impoundment and with this extreme secrecy that isolates President Nixon and his decision-making leaders from the public and from Congress, there is no way for us to predict what's going to happen in the future.

WFB: But isn't that the penalty for overreliance on the federal government?

CARTER: But states don't have unlimited funds, and the problem is that with a certain increase in the gross national product, say one hundred percent, local governments are—

WFB: With the gross what?

CARTER: I say with a hundred percent increase in the gross national product, local governments' incomes, based primarily on property tax, only go up seventy percent. The state governments' incomes, based on a combination of sales tax, income tax, and so forth, on the average go up ninety-five percent. The federal government's, based entirely on the very progressive income tax, goes up one hundred and thirty percent.

It's not a matter of the states and local governments not being willing to do our share, it's just an inevitable part of the nation's tax structure.

WFB: It's not inevitable. It's a psychological relationship which—

CARTER: Psychological?

WFB: —you invited. There's nothing in the tax code or in the Constitution of the United States that allows the federal government to preempt the taxing power. You can do anything you want to with your state income tax, and, in fact, the federal government rather obligingly allows your taxpayers to discount all state taxes from taxes paid to the federal government.

CARTER: Well, the federal government doesn't have the right to take any initiative in the tax structure of the state. But the point I'm making, obviously inadequately, is that over a period of years, the interrelationships between the federal and state and local governments have been promulgated first and then accepted as a part of our economic life. And then to have decisions made in secret at the last minute, after many state legislatures have already adjourned, and say, "We're canceling this program which was approved by Congress, vetoed by the President, and then overridden"—you know, this is the kind of thing that concerns me.

In 1976, I asked Governor Michael Dukakis of Massachusetts how he could justify asking other states for money for Massachusetts "given that your resources exceed the resources of the overwhelming majority of those states."

DUKAKIS: I don't think we have to go down to Washington on our hands and knees like a supplicant asking for special aid. We're not in that kind of shape. But I do think generally, where there are states or regions of the country that are having chronic economic difficulties—whether it's the Northeast, or Michigan, or Appalachia in the sixties, or the South for that matter in the thirties—that there is something to be said for federal investments into those areas. It's a shifting kind of thing. I don't think that it's always going to be the Northeast, any more than it was always the South. But it seems to me that's sensible national economic policy.

The governor's answer is plausible, but it fails to take into account the question of whether an economic malady within a particular state or even region oughtn't to be permitted to wrestle with the economic circumstances that brought it down. It was only after a successful encounter of that nature that Massachusetts gradually transformed its economy from that of a manufacturing state to a service and technological-industrial state. There is, moreover, the inevitable tendency in a democracy to consider, as lastingly important, resources (e.g., Appalachian coal) which are of diminishing economic value. Some time after the end of the Civil War it became clear that there wasn't much point in rescuing, on behalf of Massachusetts, the hemp industry there. But under the aegis of macrocosmic redistribution, the decision becomes political, not economic. The point was explored with Mr. Joel Garreau.

Consider, he said, New York, and New York's self-esteem.

GARREAU: New York views itself as the center of the known world. Asia and things like that are barely explored unpleasantnesses.

Now I am certain that Mayor Ed Koch of New York would not publicly permit his views on Asia to be so characterized, but he would never hide his conviction that the city of New York is the center of the civilized world, a perfectly tenable position. But given New York City's resources, does it plausibly ask, say, Indianapolis for financial help? We discussed the question in the context of President Reagan's "New Federalism," a series of executive initiatives designed to return power and money to the states.

Now Mayor Koch's love of New York simply cannot be persuasively challenged. But suddenly we found him expressing a devotion to the state of Texas which I could only accept as revelation.

WFB: Anything that's collected by Washington is collected in the first instance from everybody in this studio. So that it is purely a part of the hallucinations in which liberals deal to suppose that in routing money via Washington, you are in fact getting free money. Yet most of your analyses and rhetoric presupposes that that's the case.

KOCH: No, it does not. Let me [give you an example that] supports my case. [In recent years,] we had a Cuban migration. I was in the Congress at the time. We allocated special dollars to Florida to help with that Cuban migration—just as we [allocated special dollars, in special circumstances] to other states. Perfectly reasonable. Florida was being overburdened by a Cuban refugee problem. Let Texas help also.

WFB: And I'm saying, if I were a Texan, I would say, "Look, it's quite true that we Texans have a lot of oil, but if you New Yorkers want to buy interest in our oil, you can buy it at about four times earnings right now."

KOCH: Now, what—*All* I'm *simply* saying is that people come from *all over the country* to the urban areas. We are the *older* cities, and the federal government has helped the *newer* cities. The federal government, by putting billions into highways, made it possible for industries to leave cities, with the result that jobs were lost. The federal government, by subsidizing one- and two-family homes out in the suburbs, made it possible for middle-class people to *leave the city* with their jobs and with their taxes. And so, we say to the federal government, "You left us with a lot of good people, and a lot of good people means poor people, middle-class people, and some rich people, but a lot more poor people proportionately than we had before. Are *you* now going to say to *us*"—we say to the federal government—"that when *you* put these billions into highways that *you* will not now help us with mass transit in our older cities? When you build dams to create water in the West, is it wrong to create a water tunnel in New York City when we need water?" What we're simply saying is that the formula for the distribution of federal dollars has been notoriously against the Northeast—not New York alone—against the Northeast and against the older cities.

WFB: The figures dispute this.

KOCH: Let me—

WFB: For every seventy-six cents that's taxed by the federal government from New York, New York gets a dollar back, notwithstanding that New York is the sixteenth-wealthiest state in the Union. By contrast, for instance, Colorado pays in a dollar and twenty cents and gets a dollar back, although they are cheek by jowl with New York—sixteenth-wealthiest state per capita—on that particular roster. It seems to me, Mr. Koch, that what you're suffering from is the collapse of the popular notion that other people can pay for other people's expenses. What we've got is simply an implosion of which New York is a characteristic victim. If you want better rapid transit, you should pay for better rapid transit. You shouldn't really expect people in Utah and Mississippi and Texas to pay for your transit.

KOCH: Let me respond to that. [Mayor Koch said that as he recalled the figures, Congress voted $60 for federal highway projects for every $1 it voted for rapid transit during the period he was in Congress and that this was clearly unfair.]

WFB: How do you define fairness?

KOCH: To use dollars where the *need* is. I think that's fairness, don't you?

WFB: [He was missing the point, I said.] People in New York City were paying five cents and ten cents for subway rides at a time when it was costing the city twenty cents to twenty-five cents for a subway ride. So the subway riders were receiving subsidies during that whole period. And on the matter of the highways, isn't it true that people who buy gasoline pay very considerable taxes on it? Now, I'm not saying that people who buy a car oughtn't to recognize that there is a social cost in buying a car. The question is: How to pay that cost? The gasoline tax and the toll charges strike me as the simplest way to do it.

KOCH: It's very complicated, but let me say this: The car—

WFB: It's not too complicated to understand.

KOCH: No, I understand it completely. The car owner, for example, does not pay for the repairs that we do to the highway and the streets of New York.

WFB: Why not?

KOCH: Because he doesn't. There is no special tax that goes into the fixing of potholes.

WFB: I'm not suggesting you ought to stop in the middle of the street and put in a nickel to get through a pothole.

KOCH: But I—

WFB: I'm saying that when the motorist comes into New York City or drives out of New York City, he's going to have to buy gasoline—

KOCH: Yes.

WFB: —he's going to pay toll charges, and that's going to go into a fund; and you, with your sovereignty over these matters, are going to allocate a certain amount to fix potholes, right?

KOCH: I agree, I agree, and I'm simply saying the following: I don't know why it's in anyone's interest, yours or mine, to pit the North against the South, the East against the West, the urban dweller against those who live in the rural and suburban areas.

WFB: But it's been done. You just did it.

KOCH: No, I did not. I—

WFB: You started talking about Texas oil.

KOCH: I say we're one country, and therefore we have a responsibility one to the other.

WFB: We are a federation of states, and the whole notion of Reagan's New Federalism is to invigorate a situation in which communities [exercise relevant authority]. If your predecessor makes life in New York too risky or too expensive, he will encourage people to leave New York—

KOCH: Yes, I *have* changed that.

WFB: Remember, it was Hugh Carey, the Democratic Governor of New York, who said two years ago, and said to [the legislators in Albany], "Don't you realize that people who are leaving New York State aren't leaving to go to Tennessee? They're leaving to go to Pennsylvania and New Jersey and Connecticut—because the taxes there are less." Now, this is a good [example of federalism at work], isn't it? It's the means by which adjacent states can in effect exercise some control over excesses in adjacent states. But what you're doing is encouraging the superstition that if you just get the money from Washington, it isn't costing the people in New York anything.

KOCH: You are perpetuating myths, and you shouldn't do that. You would give the impression, for example, that New York is, you know, like number one in welfare. It is not true. For example—

WFB: I didn't say that.

KOCH: I know, but that's the implication of all of these things, that somehow or other we're profligate and we're taking other people's monies. Nothing could be further from the truth. Now, what we have done in New York City—we're very proud of it—firstly, we thank the country for helping us. We think we've made a contribution to the country. The fact is, most of the country, or large parts of it, were populated by people who came through New York City. I think the rest of the country has a greater affection today for New York City than it had years ago.

WFB: Well, I do too. And there's been a lot of people not only leaving New York, but coming into New York. And a lot of people came here using Texan oil to get here.

KOCH: I love Texas. There's nothing wrong with Texas. I wish *we* had the Texas oil. But if Texas were ever in trouble, New York will help you.

Firing Line is naturally attracted to hard political questions, and these tend to rise when the national curiosity is especially aroused. "Will Richard Nixon be impeached?" was as hot a question as the program—as any political program, editorial, column, whatever—has asked itself in a quarter century. It was on June 28, 1974, that one aspect of the question seemed especially relevant to put to the man who, in the event Nixon were impeached and convicted, would become President of the United States.

Gerald Ford—it is quickly grasped, both by interviewer and viewer—is one of those unusual creatures about whom it can be said with conviction that they appear to have nothing to hide. Granted that any man serving as Vice President would rather be President. Prince Charles would surely like to be King Charles, but to acknowledge human ambitions in heirs presumptive is not to suggest that they would consent to reach for power in the manner of Lady Macbeth.

Vice President Ford, in the summer of 1974, was acting as dutifully as the Prince of Wales when he sings "Long Live the Queen." The question I thought to press on Vice President Ford was the equivalent, I suppose, of asking Prince Charles, were his mother to succumb to senility, whether loyalty to the sovereign might not be overdone.

Specifically, was Gerald Ford's loyalty to Richard Nixon overdone— to the detriment of the republic? Was the pull of Ford's attachment to the President blinding him to some of the political problems caused by so inextricable an attachment?

Suppose (I said to Gerald Ford) that it became clear that the House of Representatives was going to return a bill of impeachment against President Nixon. Might it not then make sense for President Nixon to urge House Republicans to accept the findings of the Judiciary Committee, rather than submit the country to a huge procedural fight in the House which Nixon was bound eventually to lose, all of it before the final question went over to the Senate?

I made the point that President Nixon was hardly *obliged* to burden Republican congressional loyalists seeking reelection that November by putting them on the spot. President Nixon could take the position that the question of executive authority was under the circumstances one for the Senate to handle, and that the House could, whatever the predispositions of its dissidents, with a clear conscience turn the matter over, by unanimous vote, to the Senate. I hardly succeeded. . . .

FORD: I don't think there is sufficient evidence to contend as an impeachable offense that the President was involved in the alleged cover-up, or in the cover-up. Now, this is what four hundred and thirty-five members of the House have to decide. I don't think there are enough that will vote for it.

I attempted for a full hour to get the Vice President to talk simply about the questions I had in mind. He had clearly resolved that to do so would suggest to the public that even to entertain the hypothetical possibility that Nixon would be impeached would suggest that he favored his impeachment. He would not budge from his position. Six weeks later, Gerald Ford took the oath of office as President of the United States.

. . .

Some hard questions, asked of two bright congressmen, one of them a liberal Democrat, the other a conservative Republican. On the institution of the Congress, Otis Pike and Robert Dornan were in uncharacteristic agreement. They had asserted that Congress was deteriorating as an institution, and I asked why.

PIKE: Well, I have my own pet theory. It was the alleged reforms of 1975. They required everybody in Congress to cut off all their outside earnings, all of their outside interests. In many cases congressmen *have* to get reelected in order to feed their families. They don't have a law practice to go back to because they had to saw off the law practice. They don't have another way of earning a living except to get reelected. I predicted at the time that this was going to wind up with a whole bunch of people who were afraid to make tough decisions for fear of losing the election.

WFB: How did it used to be?

PIKE: From the days of the founding of our republic a lawyer could go to Congress and still keep his law practice going back home; a farmer could do the same thing; a doctor could do the same thing—

WFB: You can't now?

PIKE: No, you are cut off—

WFB: You can't own a farm and be in Congress?

PIKE: Well, you can own it, but you can't earn money farming and be in Congress.

DORNAN: You have to play games. It's a disgrace.

PIKE: It is a fraud. There are all kinds of ways of getting around it. For example, if I wrote a book and collected royalties on the book, that would be proper, because they made an exception for book writers. If I wrote the identical words in twenty articles and sold them as articles—which is what I [would be inclined to] do—that is illegal, because that is earned income.

DORNAN: Or if a congressman goes on a show and strays beyond a
             certain point in talking about his book, then he is engaging
             in oral history, and isn't allowed to keep income from that,
             either. They protected those dead-asset congressmen who
             get books ghostwritten by exempting book royalties—and
             that's all.* The other exemption was for dividends for the
             millionaires in Congress.

PIKE: Oh, yes. *Un*earned income. Unearned income is legiti-
             mate. *Earned* income is *ill*egitimate.

WFB: Okay, let me see if I understand you. What you are saying
             is that given the attenuation of means by which congress-
             men can eke out a living by doing other things, they end
             up by putting such an emphasis on their jobs—

PIKE: —they *must* get reelected—

WFB: —and that there is a tendency to prostitute themselves in
             order to appease their constituents.

PIKE: Absolutely.

That problem—the dependence of the congressman on political office—is well focused. One does wonder why such obvious legislative
fiascos don't get corrected. It has to be that the same legislators needed
to correct them are afraid. I remark, in passing, that in my adult lifetime
I have seen only two political firestorms that resulted in sharp and
immediate political response. Odd, odd ones. The first was the sentenc-
ing of William Calley, the antihero of My Lai who undertoook to wipe
out the civilian population with his machine guns. The crowd simply
insisted that the penalty was inordinate, insisted on this for a congeries
of reasons, primarily (I think) a frustration with the length and conduct
of the Vietnam War. And so President Nixon ordered that Calley be
released from the stockade and returned to his base apartment, pending
reevaluation. (In due course, the army lessened the sentence.) And the
other? The protest after the 1982 tax law demanded that interest be
taxed while en route to the bank's depositors. A strange cause militant,
but that is exactly what it became, mobilizing primarily the retirement
community. The protest overwhelmed Congress even though Ronald

---

*This program, aired in 1985, anticipated by three years the mess in which Speaker Jim Wright
found himself, involving his "book" and the royalties paid to him.

Reagan was in favor of the 1982 law. I don't expect, in my lifetime, to see a true revolt of that potency against the legislative accretions that have glued congressmen into their safe seats, calcifying so much that is tacitly accepted as unsound public policy.

Occasionally we have guests who look at American politics as though they were guest lecturers at the Constitutional Convention in Philadelphia . . . *we should limit senators to two terms, congressmen to four terms, Presidents should serve one six-year term.*

But such normative looks at American political architecture happen less frequently than workaday discussions about: the situation right now . . . *at this moment. . . .*

Within the Republican Party.

The Democratic Party.

And what will it mean to the future of American politics? Or, for that matter, to the future of individual parties?

In the first section we listen to Richard Nixon, Clare Boothe Luce, and Barry Goldwater. The subject, almost necessarily: the GOP.

What *about* the Republican Party?

In September 1967, Richard Nixon was reemerging as the dominant presence within the Republican Party. He was touching necessary bases. In several books about Mr. Nixon, published, so to speak, posthumously, it has been noted that he made it a point to meet with me privately and to participate in a *Firing Line* program in order to firm up his position with the conservatives. He had always been popular among us, but Goldwater had captured the heart ("In your *h.,* you know he's right") of the right.

It is amusing to recall the evening of September 14, 1967. Mr. Nixon not only agreed to appear on *Firing Line,* he agreed to have a private dinner with me, and with columnist James Jackson Kilpatrick, who was preparing a portrait of Nixon for publication in *National Review.* That was a heavy contribution, by Mr. Nixon, to the Life & Work of WFB, but little did he know, when he came to my apartment at six o'clock, just how heavy a contribution it would turn out to be.

We chatted for a few moments with Kilpatrick and with my old friend and personal lawyer C. Dickerman Williams, who for a year or two served as moderator of *Firing Line.* Mr. Williams and I had a glass of wine; Kilpo (as he is known by the profession in which he is eminent) a bourbon on the rocks; Nixon iced tea. At six-thirty we drove down to the studio. We had calculated that we would be back at seven forty-five, to proceed with our scheduled dinner. We got two minutes into the program when—technical breakdown. These happen every now and then (perhaps a half-dozen times in twenty-two years) and usually require five or ten minutes to fix. But ten fidgety minutes later we were told by the producer that, alas, the problem was grave: it would require two to three hours (!) to remedy.

I turned ashen-faced to my guests, apologized and suggested we go back and have dinner, postponing the television show for another day. Ah, but I knew not the iron-butted Nixon, who did not get where he has got by lack of fortitude.

No, he said, we will go back to your place, and do the show later.

At least, I thought, we could give him a good meal to make the time pass. But no. "I don't like to eat before I work." So we sat in my comfortable living room until we got the call from the studio—two and a half hours later, during which Mr. Nixon had consumed a whole lot of iced tea, and Kilpo a whole lot of bourbon. We went back to the studio, did the hour, and traveled back to 73rd Street to begin dinner just before midnight. At that point Mr. Nixon permitted himself a half-glass of sherry, I think it was, and a cigar, which he never lit. Kilpo, feeling absolutely no pain, was asking him such questions as "Dick, do you *really* want to be President? I mean, there are a lot of other people out there—why should it be *you*?" I will never forget the utter serenity with which Mr. Nixon handled that and fifty other questions, some of them deeply personal (nor will I forget the startlingly eloquent and penetrating portrait Kilpatrick wrote for us the following week). Well after midnight I asked if I could hail him a taxi. No, thanks very much, he would walk home; get a little exercise. We shook hands goodnight at the door.

At the studio I had introduced him—

WFB: In 1946 at the age of thirty-three, Lieutenant Commander Richard Nixon was doing a little legal work for the navy in Baltimore. Six years later he was Vice President of the United States. Eight years later he lost the presidency in the closest election in American history. Two years after that he lost an election in California. And as if to prove the depths of his despondency he went to live in New York City.

Four years later, Mr. Nixon suddenly emerges as the

RICHARD NIXON, DELIBERATING

leading Republican in all of the speculation having to do with the forthcoming presidential election. I should like to begin by asking: Mr. Nixon, last year for the first time, registration of Republicans went up a little, and Democrats down a little. Is it the Democratic Party that's running out of steam, or is it liberalism?

I thought this a very nice opening for Mr. Nixon. He was treading a delicate line. He very much needed the enthusiasm of Goldwater's legion. But he could not be Goldwater's successor in any palpable political way. An aspiring politician does not want to be the successor of a candidate who captured six states. He turned the question into one of political mechanics.

NIXON: Well, I would say first that there are some technical reasons. Last year the Republicans had better candidates across the country generally than the Democrats had. They were better organized, more—

WFB: Wouldn't you say that of *every* year?

NIXON: Of course I would tend to say that every year, but looking at it in retrospect, last year we just happened to come up with a very good crop, and they came up with a group of candidates who—well, just a bunch of turkeys, really.

Now, under the circumstances—not all of them, of course, because some of them did win—I would say too that last year, in terms of the way the two parties presented their cases across the country to the people, the Democratic Party seemed to be the party of the past. They were applying the various programs of the thirties to the problems of the sixties. Whereas the Republican Party seemed to be more in tune with what people believed in now.

WFB: What's an example of this—of the intuitions of the Republican Party that were communicated last year?

NIXON: There was a tremendous disillusionment, for example, with the poverty program. The poverty program, of course, was a throwback to the programs of the thirties. And across the country Republicans who stood up and pointed out that these programs were costing a great deal of money but were not dealing with the problem of poverty. The Republicans were taking what I think you might call a conservative line.

They won, and they won even though many political pundits thought they would lose, when they were in effect attacking Santa Claus.

WFB: Well, but aren't you then caught up in this difficulty? Aren't you saying that people are tiring of the old remedies of the thirties, and therefore going back to the remedies of the twenties?

NIXON: I think that the Republican Party today does not present that posture. Naturally I'm a prejudiced witness, and I would be expected to say that. But I believe that as this campaign in 1968 unfolds, that the nation will see that the new Republican Party is one which advocates change, but advocates change in a different way from the irresponsibles. And I mean by that, that in changing those things that are wrong in America, we must not destroy the things that are right. That to me is the essence of true conservatism.

Nixon had confided to Williams, Kilpo, and me that if he won the New Hampshire primary he would almost certainly win the primary in Wisconsin. "After that, it will be a quick succession. By the time I win Indiana, I will have clinched the nomination. And if I do, I will beat Lyndon Johnson." By the time the program was over, I felt relatively certain that it would go exactly as Nixon had predicted. Except that he ended up beating not Lyndon Johnson, but Hubert Humphrey.

When Clare Boothe Luce first appeared on the program in 1977, the pollsters gave the figure 20 percent for Republican registration compared to 49 percent Democrats. Those figures reflected the composition of elected officials—though, to be sure, most elected Southerners were "Democrats" of the pattern of Harry Byrd. There were one-half again as many Democratic as Republican senators, twice as many congressmen, three times as many governors. I asked Mrs. Luce, what to do? (Mrs. Luce always had an answer to any question at the tip of her tongue. Though this, I came to know, was polemical training: she was often dissatisfied, after consulting her private intellectual conscience, with the answer she gave.

LUCE: The Republicans come into power ultimately [she was speaking of the presidency] only because the Democrats make *terrible* mistakes, and the people *demand* someone there at the national level to redeem Democratic errors. But each time the Republicans come in simply as critics and tinkerers and repairmen and plumbers—I'm not invoking the spirit of Watergate there, by the way—each time they come in, they go out a little weaker. Because what is needed is not only carpenters to repair the holes in the Democratic roof. What is needed is a new architect that gives the people a vision of a better future.

But by the time Mrs. Luce made that *Firing Line* appearance, the struggle within the Republican Party for precisely that—a new architecture—had been going on for almost two decades. The nomination of Barry Goldwater in 1964 was the decisive event. The Eastern Seaboard Liberal Establishment never again controlled the Republican Party. Richard Nixon told me, driving to the studio in 1967 to appear on that program, that he had discovered in his gubernatorial campaign in California in 1962 "two things." Of course, I asked, "What?" And he answered: "A Republican can't win without attracting the conservative votes. But the second lesson I learned is that a Republican can't win by attracting *only* the conservative votes."

In 1977, Gerald Ford had been defeated by Jimmy Carter, and conservative intellectuals disagreed on exactly why. Granted, Ford was never a Napoleonic political figure. But he was competent, good-natured, and conservative in inclination. Even so, he had been actively opposed in the primaries by Ronald Reagan—who very nearly took the nomination away from him, and who almost certainly would have won against Carter. But Mrs. Luce had her eye on the new architecture. And she acknowledged that Barry Goldwater, her old friend and, up until she moved to Hawaii, her neighbor in Phoenix, had been if not an architect, an architect *manqué*.

During the campaign in 1964, Barry Goldwater had been heavily treated. George Meany, head of the AFL-CIO, charged that Goldwater was "liable to drag us into a nuclear war." Senator William Fulbright said that "Goldwater Republicanism is the closest thing in American politics to an equivalent of Russian Stalinism." Martin Luther King saw "dangerous signs of Hitlerism" in the campaign.

The celebrations when he lost so overwhelmingly (he carried only Arizona and five Southern states) for a while suggested that the Republican Party had lost its head, as one critical book published in 1966 (*The Party That Lost Its Head,* by George Gilder and Bruce K. Chapman) concluded. Goldwater was entirely impenitent a few months later:

GOLDWATER: I think the time is approaching when we have to stop fooling ourselves in the Republican Party. Historically, it's been the *conservative* who's perfectly willing to go along with a liberal. He'll work for him, raise money for him. We just have to honestly ask ourselves, wouldn't some of these [liberal Republicans] be better off if they

were with the Democrats? Today the Republican Party is
a *conservative* party.

That may have been true, but it was not true that the liberal element
within the Republican Party was willing to hand the party over to the
right. There was no gainsaying the political influence of such prominent
Republican liberals as Senator Charles Mathias of Maryland. Senator
Mathias, on *Firing Line* in 1981, was at the height of a considerable
career as an undiluted, unapologetic, liberal Republican. In 1980, the
ADA had given him a 72 percent rating, along with his brother Republicans Senators Chafee and Weicker; the AFL-CIO gave him 100 percent,
a vote of comprehensive confidence he shared only with Senator Javits
(defeated in a Republican primary in 1980). In 1980, Senator Mathias
had voted 16 percent of the time with his own party, 55 percent of the
time with the Democrats.

MATHIAS: It seems to me that a member of Congress of either party
             is ultimately responsible to the voters. We come under the
             aegis of a party. But we only owe that party our first vote.

WFB: You mean to organize the Senate?

MATHIAS: Yes, to organize. In the House of Representatives that first
             vote is the vote for speaker, and in the Senate that first vote
             is the vote on the president pro tempore of the Senate. But
             beyond that we are answerable to our constituents and to
             our conscience.

WFB: In 1963, in my presence at a dinner party, Senator Javits
             addressed twenty-five people and said, "If the Republicans
             nominate Barry Goldwater, the probability is that the
             Republican Party itself will cease to exist." Now, Javits is
             a very smart man, but he was simply wrong on that, right?
             He was not only wrong, he was perversely wrong, because
             although Goldwater was defeated, Goldwaterism, so to
             speak, was picked up by Goldwater's most conspicuous
             champion, Ronald Reagan, who now sits in the White
             House.

MATHIAS: Jack Javits was wrong in predicting that the Republican
             Party would fall apart totally. He was not totally wrong
             in predicting that the Republican Party would fall apart

to some degree. There were a number of very able young
Republicans who left the Republican Party in 1964.

WFB: Yet Goldwater in effect was elected. As George Will has
            pointed out, the 1964 election was finally adjudicated in
            1980.

MATHIAS: I don't know that we can transpose time in quite that way,
            but the fact is that I could name you a long list of people
            that we lost in '64 who might have made a difference to
            the Republican Party. We might even have avoided the
            Carter experience. So I think Jack Javits was more right
            than you give him credit for being.

WFB: Yes, but how many people came *into* the party or were
            attracted by it as a result of Goldwater's experience with
            it? Compared to how many people left it?

MATHIAS: I invite you to look at the returns that year. I think that
            we carried—what?—five states in '64?

WFB: Yes, but it's also true that a higher percentage of the public
            made cash contributions to Goldwater than had been true
            of any other candidate in American history, showing that
            he had a lot of grass-roots support. And indeed we saw
            this develop—did we not?—during the succeeding fifteen
            years. But something happened to the Charles Mathias/
            Rockefeller/Percy/Javits/Case view of where the Repub-
            lican Party ought to go, and I think as a survivor—the
            only survivor—it's extremely interesting for us to hear
            your—

MATHIAS: No, I don't claim to be the only survivor. In fact, I'm—

WFB: Well, Chafee. John Chafee, I guess. You're both in the
            Senate. Everybody else [of your persuasion] has been
            beaten or has retired or died. Now, do you feel nervous,
            or do you feel that one of those historical reversals is about
            to happen?

MATHIAS: I feel fine.

    His good health and high spirits notwithstanding, Senator Mathias
elected to step down from the Senate in 1984 to return to private life.

His seat in Maryland was then contested by a liberal Democrat and a conservative Republican. The Democrat won. Is there something a little . . . odd about Maryland? Always a possibility. Senator Mathias may have had a practical point. If you are a Republican surrounded by Marylanders, win the approval of the AFL-CIO and the ADA if you want to stick around.

The Democratic Party was having its own difficulties. There was, of course, the erosion of voters to the Republicans when time came for fresh Presidents and the voting public went Republican. But another problem had to do with the evanescence, from within the Democratic Party, of pervasive, credible foreign policy planks aimed at the strategic problem posed by the Communist world. The death of Senator Henry Jackson left the party not only without a leader representing that traditional Democratic position but, oddly, without anyone else who apparently hoped to assume that position.

And on the Democratic Party's right, George Wallace presented a special problem. As he eased away from his obsession with racial segregation, he began to emerge as, well, a New Deal populist. But there was much that he said, and could continue to say, that reminded the critical Old South of days gone by, with the result that he continued to hold out an appeal to conservatives.

We were in a studio in St. Louis. It was January 24, 1968. About a month later, George Wallace confirmed that he would run for President on a third-party ticket. Over a period of several years I had written sharp commentary on Wallace and his movement, stressing its ties, which I judged ineradicable (I was subsequently proved wrong), to the Jim Crow movement. When he entered the studio he was calculatedly brusque in his dealings with me, to whom his greeting was perfunctory (followed quickly by warm handshakes with everyone in the studio), before sitting down to get on with the program.

A week or so earlier, the right-wing weekly journal *Human Events* had published the results of a poll of "two hundred prominent conservatives." The poll unearthed a "surprising hostility toward George Wallace." Why? I asked him.

WALLACE: Well, Mr. Buckley, you said that two hundred "prominent conservatives"—that's typical of those who write to magazines. Who *are* these prominent conservatives?

WFB: Suppose, Governor Wallace, that you name one promi-
            nent conservative outside the South who's in favor of you.

WALLACE: Mr. Buckley, I run my politics like I do in Alabama. I
            never went to the county courthouses to see the county
            governing bodies. I just went to the *people*. I go out to the
            masses of the people with the message that I have, and I
            don't [even] *know* any prominent conservatives.

I tried to suggest that the reason prominent conservatives weren't
endorsing Wallace was that they didn't believe that his activities had
been in the conservative tradition. Sophisticated conservatives believed
that Wallace's passion for states' rights derived from his conviction that
this was the only way in which to administer a racially segregated state.
Wallace replied that an enormous number of Negroes had voted for his
wife, Governor Lurleen Wallace, at the last election; that he was no
longer a member of the official Democratic establishment; that he had
broken with John F. Kennedy after Kennedy's election as President and
hadn't voted for Johnson in 1964. (He was, I took his point to be, free
of any organizational ties.) And anyway, what could a conservative find
to criticize in his program for Alabama?

WALLACE: Name *one thing* in Alabama that I have supported on the
            governmental level that you are against.

WFB: You want the state to take care of hospitalization, you
            want the state to take care of old people, you want the
            state to take care of the poor . . .

WALLACE: Are you *against* caring for the poor and the old?

Wallace knew that my quarrel was with statist remedies to social
problems. It crossed my mind that he would abandon his disingenuous
approach if I ridiculed it. So I answered him mock-solemnly: "I hate the
poor."
    It didn't work.

WALLACE: I am *for* looking after destitute elderly people. I'm *not*
            against that *at all*. So if conservatism is against looking
            after the elderly who are destitute, I might say that no
            conservative in this country who comes out against look-

ing after destitute elderly people ought to be elected to *anything.*

WFB: You call yourself a populist, right?

WALLACE: If you mean by a populist a man of the people, yes, I'm a populist. Let's get back to the old-age pensions. Let's see, you're against Alabama's looking after the elderly, destitute citizens of the state?

I had written that, on the record, George Wallace favored federal welfare programs but then went on to resent Washington's interference. To this charge, Wallace replied that Alabama was only getting back in welfare what Alabama had put out in federal taxes. Partly true, I agreed, but in fact Alabama got more back from the federal government than Alabama gave to the government, by a long sight. He was extremely defensive on this point.

WALLACE: Where are your figures? You've made a charge against Alabama, give us the *figures.* . . .

WFB: My guess is that you take in at least five times as much from the federal government as you send out in taxes.

WALLACE: . . . that's *totally* untrue.

The then-current figure for Alabama was 51 cents taxed by the federal government per $1 received from the government. I.e., two times as much, not five times as much. I was wrong on the figure, not wrong on the general point.

So it went. Wallace seemed to be arguing that state welfarism is altogether desirable provided the relevant administrative unit is the state, not the federal government. He seemed to be saying that something suddenly happened halfway through John Kennedy's reign that justified Wallace's sudden disillusion with the national Democratic Party. And that whatever that disillusioning thing was, it had nothing to do with the race question; and that the vote of so many Negroes for Lurleen Wallace in 1966 absolved him of any reasonable suspicion that his program was based on race.

What proved especially interesting about George Wallace was less his views than his techniques. Here are a few that I discovered during our *Firing Line* session.

1. *Exaggerating the South's Plight*

WALLACE: . . . We had five generations of people who didn't go to school because there were no schools for blacks or whites. All they could do is eke something out of the ground to eat. . . .

There *were* public schools in Alabama, and for that matter private schools, during the five generations in question.

2. *So's Your Old Man*

WFB: Certain politicians grew up in the South and lusted for participation in a type of government which is distinctively anticonservative, the type of government of which Mr. Roosevelt and Mr. Kennedy and Mr. Johnson are representative. Then all of a sudden, something happened. The consequences of that federalization also meant that they couldn't continue in their segregated ways, and that's when Governor Wallace was born—

WALLACE: Of course, I was not even voting in the days that you're talking about. I didn't even vote in those elections, but when you say that, because the people of the South voted for Mr. Roosevelt, that made them anticonservative, well, New York voted for Mr. Roosevelt all four times. . . . [And back to the theme of his extra-Democratic Party popularity:] It doesn't make any difference to me whether some prominent conservative is not for me; seventy percent of the people last night on a poll on the television station in St. Louis said they would support me. The fact is that I won the television poll on WIIC in Pittsburgh the other day and defeated Johnson, Kennedy, and Reagan by almost three to one.

WFB: They might have given even more votes to Perón than they did to you, right?

WALLACE: That's a real smart answer.

3. Nobody Ever Lets Me Talk

WALLACE: Why don't you let me *talk* on this program? After all
             . . . I thought you invited me to get my opinion. But when
             you get on this show, the man that puts on the show wants
             to do all the talking.

At that point in the program, I had spoken 269 words, Wallace 845.

4. There Ain't Nobody Loves the Nigra Like Me an' Lurleen

WALLACE: In fact, we *don't have* segregation in Alabama. . . . I've
             always made speeches in my state in which I said any-
             body's entitled to vote regardless of their race or color.
             And we had Negro citizens by the *thousands* who voted
             in 1958, when I first ran for governor. And, I might say,
             in the run-off for governor, they voted for *me.*

WFB: Is that because they didn't have the education you're talk-
             ing about?

WALLACE: You reflect on the Negro voters of Alabama if *you* want
             to, but *I* won't.

On reflection, twenty years later, my judgment is that Wallace out-
pointed me in our exchange. In part because he handled with facility the
populist argument, in part because my antagonism to him was rooted
in the great event of 1963 when he emerged as the most adamant
American political figure standing in the way of desegregation. That was
when he sent state troopers to the University of Alabama to block the
entry of two Negro (as they were then called) students.

What then happened was that, slowly perhaps, but very surely,
George Wallace began to abandon segregation as his primary political
objective (he had once declared, "Segregation *forever*"). He ultimately
was so successful in superintending the transformation of his own position from segregationism to populism that in 1982 he capped his
career by winning the overwhelming majority of the black voters in
Alabama.

In 1968 I, along with, I suppose, most "prominent conservatives,"
never mind George Wallace's resistance to the term, judged him at heart
a segregationist and a populist and, for both reasons, undeserving of

conservative support. The general feeling among political conservatives, in 1968, was that George Wallace was a social pariah. I shared that feeling, and clearly acted as if I did.

It was in 1972 that the image of George Wallace began to change. The triggering political event was the visit by Senator Edward Kennedy to the hospital in which the wounded George Wallace was recuperating. He having passed through that tripwire, it became safe for others to do so. And so, before that summer was over, Hubert Humphrey, Vice President and candidate for President, was photographed with his arm around Wallace.

From his wheelchair, Wallace addressed the Democratic Convention in 1972 when George McGovern, unanimously viewed as the fundamentalist-liberal alternative to relatively moderate Hubert Humphrey, was nominated the Democratic candidate for President. At that moment (I wrote), George Wallace could have walked away from the convention formally abandoning his ties to the Democratic Party. If he had done so, Republican politics in the South would have changed, and many Democrats with formal ties to the party would have crossed the line, registering as Republicans. Instead, they stayed on as Democrats, and tended to vote for the Republican presidential candidate.

. . . I wish that, on *Firing Line,* I had charted more clearly the trajectory of the Wallace movement.

The evening after taping the Wallace show, back in New York from St. Louis, I met with Nelson Rockefeller at his apartment. It was the first time we spoke, and the meeting had been arranged by Henry Kissinger, a friend of both of us. Its purpose was quickly evident: to give Rockefeller an opportunity to tell me how inventively anti-Communist he had been at the Chapultepec Conference preceding the planning of the United Nations. The whole design was to dilute my traditional anti-Rockefeller position (I had opposed him for advocating domestic policies I thought more properly Democratic than Republican) in the event (however unlikely) that he, rather than Richard Nixon, succeeded in winning the nomination for the presidency in Miami the following summer. Rockefeller was fascinated by my account of the afternoon with Wallace, and opined that the Wallace vote could end up deciding the election in November. It very nearly did, reducing Nixon's lead to hairline size.

ZBIGNIEW BRZEZINSKI, LISTENING

Zbigniew Brzezinski had been a frequent guest of *Firing Line* up until he became the National Security Adviser for President Jimmy Carter, when for obvious reasons he had to clam up. I note in passing that guests are much more interesting before they are in office or after they are in office than while they are in office—during which time they need to be so . . . *measured.* In 1983, Brzezinski was back.

WFB: You are, after all, a Democrat, and you are identified therefore with a party, one projection of whose center of gravity is that it is moving in the direction of unilateralism. Now, do you think that the Democratic Party can survive these suicidal impulses?

BRZEZINSKI: The Democratic Party really *does* embrace that kind of an orientation. Endorsement of the nuclear freeze is an example of what should be avoided. Otherwise, in my personal judgment, the Democratic Party is going to make itself less attractive electorally and less able to assume the responsibility for protecting the national interest.

WFB: It will go the way of the Labour Party in Great Britain?

BRZEZINSKI: Well, let me give you one very, to me, telling example. Since World War II, eight Democrats have run for the presidency. Four lost, four won. Stevenson lost twice, Humphrey lost, and McGovern lost. Truman won, Kennedy won, Johnson won, and Carter won. What differentiates them is the attitude on foreign policy issues. The four who won by and large were seen as centrist or tough-minded. The ones who did not were viewed as somewhat different. I don't want to put labels on them.

WFB: Yes. [I said; while wishing he *would* go ahead and put labels on them. But I knew better than to try to get him to do so.]

BRZEZINSKI: And I think Democrats should not forget that. Only *centrist* Democrats can forge the needed bipartisan collaboration.

An odd use of the word "centrism," by the way. A "centrist" foreign policy, by Brzezinski's reckoning, is one which appeals to more Democrats than could be rounded up to defend a nuclear freeze. It is a clumsy designation, but the political vocabulary is not rich in these matters. Thus the "conservatives" in the Kremlin are those who desire a return of Stalinism. Sometimes these anomalies bite back. A dozen years ago, *The New York Times* ran a sober account from Moscow about a crackdown by "Kremlin conservatives" against the importation of foreign books. One of the proscribed titles was *The Conscience of a Conservative* by Barry Goldwater.

In pursuit of my mission to save the Democratic Party from itself, I took up the subject of its leanings to the left with Edward Koch, Mayor of New York, already visited above. In between the two programs, Koch had made the signal error of his political life, namely to run for the Democratic gubernatorial nomination against Mario Cuomo. (His subsequent account of what had happened: "I was wrong, and God punished me.") Koch was concerned, in 1983, when all the presidential political talk within the Democratic Party was of Walter Mondale or Gary Hart or Teddy Kennedy, about the drift of his own party.

Koch has always been careful with me, though absolutely ready to argue: he is uncomfortable with demagogy perhaps because he knows that just as he can spot it in others, so can I in him. Our personal relationship goes back many years to when, as a congressman, he wrote and asked me to testify on behalf of a bill he was backing to set up a federal commission to investigate the marijuana problem. The bill had practically no sponsors when first Koch introduced it. "Then,"

Koch had told me happily, as we walked toward the committee room, "half of my colleagues realized that any federal measure imposing prison for first-time marijuana users would put all of their own children in jail!"

By 1983, Koch was less the center of enthusiasm of the Democratic reform movement than he had been when he ousted Carmine De Sapio twenty years earlier. But his feelings were quite obvious, namely that the Democratic Party was *his* party, not that of the ideologues who had taken charge of it.

I began by asking him to comment on one or two positions recently taken by Democratic presidential candidates.

HIS HONOR, MAYOR KOCH

KOCH: We're all capable of foolish statements. For example, there are people who take the position that groups ought not to hold conventions in states that haven't adopted ERA [the Equal Rights Amendment]. If that were so, those groups couldn't come to New York State.

I then asked him how come the intellectual community didn't take a corporate position against this kind of intellectual intimidation.

KOCH: Fear.

WFB: Fear?

KOCH: Yes.

WFB: Who is Arthur Schlesinger afraid of?

KOCH: I think he would be fearful—I don't want to talk about
           him in particular, but people like him—

WFB: I'm using him as a synecdoche.

KOCH: Okay. —would be fearful of losing his credentials in the
           academic community or the community that sees him as
           a guru. And so, while such an individual might *recognize*
           the foolishness of a statement of that nature, he might not
           want to take on that battle. I'll give you another illustra-
           tion, if I might.

WFB: The ACLU?

KOCH: Yes.

WFB: But you were talking about *fear.* You think fear intimi-
           dates intellectuals from taking *obviously* indicated stands?

KOCH: Sure. I'll give you another illustration of it. You know the
           vast majority of people in this country, black and white,
           are *against* racial quotas.

WFB: Yes.

KOCH: But there are leaders, black and white, who are *for* racial
           quotas, and most people will simply not speak out against
           racial quotas. Out of *fear* of being perceived as an-
           timinority.

WFB: If it's correct that there is that kind of intimidation of the
           academic community, aren't you terribly concerned? It's
           the academic community that is supposed to have the
           special intelligence and specially refined conscience to
           warn us about dangerous trends.

KOCH: There are individuals who feel that you have to support
           things which have been perceived as liberal. And they
           become sort of sacred cows which cannot in any way be
           assailed or criticized. I happen to believe that's foolish. I've
           never been bound by those strictures and I will never be.

True. On the other hand it is also true that the Ed Koches no longer
dominate the Democratic Party. Yet I suppose it has been more or less

true that the majority of the people continue to reject the Democratic Party, though only at the national—presidential—level.

Interesting journalists are always, in my experience, worth listening to. They combine the passions of late-night sessions at college with experience gained as professional observers of the political scene.

Jeff Greenfield—of ABC, I suppose I am obliged to say—is a major figure in the history of *Firing Line.* He attracted my attention when, while a student at the Yale Law School, he wrote a withering essay, gleefully published by the *Yale Alumni Magazine,* about an appearance I made at Yale which had begun with a press conference and went on to a formal speech. His piece was a stretch of arrant scorn for my thought, logic, diction, and cosmology.

Jeff had been a crusading liberal editor, in charge of the campus daily of the University of Wisconsin. Although he finished his courses at the Yale Law School, his interests were always in journalism and politics. I was not surprised that when I next heard of him, in 1968, it was as a journalist, commissioned to do an interview of me for a new, and short-lived, Hearst magazine, *Eye.*

I wasn't surprised to find that he should be what he was: a bright young Jewish intellectual, then feverishly ideological (Jeff soon found himself on the staff first of Senator Robert Kennedy, then of Mayor John Lindsay).

For fifteen years, *Firing Line* had a regular battery of three students who asked questions of me and of my guests during the last fifteen minutes of the broadcast hour. I asked Jeff, after the *Eye* interview—I admired his tough interrogatory style and his keen intelligence—if he would serve as one of those panelists. Enjoying his witty and trenchant questions, I kept him on as a regular in the student panel for over four years.

Perhaps because it is here and there said of me that I have "mellowed," I feel free to say of Jeff, without fear of being thought condescending, that he too has mellowed, no longer adoring the state as the only vessel of civil grace. He has become, of course, a leading commentator on ABC, and has a syndicated column besides. Every couple of years I treat myself to his presence on *Firing Line* as an interviewer: Two or three times a year, *Firing Line* turns the tables and I am, so to speak, the visiting guest. My job is to defend what I have written and said, against grilling by liberal experts. Jeff serves in that capacity.

As also, frequently, does another young man. I gave up the student

panel in favor of an "examiner," because the quality of the student panel
had declined. Mark Green became a regular examiner. He is, well,
unreconstructed: a lawyer who served for ten years at the right hand of
Ralph Nader. He ran for Congress in Manhattan and lost; ran for
senator in New York, succeeded in winning the Democratic nomination, but lost to Al D'Amato in 1986. He runs something called the
Democracy Project, writes a book every six months or so, and is wittily
and informatively engaged in furthering the cause of the Devil.

Together we discussed the state of the parties as the 1984 campaign
approached.

WFB: Have the media begun to miss the story [I was looking
                back] of the 1980 campaign?

GREENFIELD: There are some encouraging signs. The media have awak-
                ened to the fact that ideas count in politics. What are the
                Democrats saying about the nation, the world, the econ-
                omy, that validates their claim to return to power? To the
                extent that Democratic candidates can or cannot answer
                that question, I think, we will know what happens in 1984.

WFB: Does this signify an evolution in the maturity of the Amer-
                ican voter or does it signify an intuitive burst of recogni-
                tion by politicians that in fact ideas do count?

GREENFIELD: The example of Ronald Reagan awakened both the press
                and other politicians. The notion that Ronald Reagan won
                because he was an actor, as I have mentioned before, is
                about as relevant as that Harry Truman had been a haber-
                dasher. Ronald Reagan was and is a superb political ani-
                mal, and the most ideologically committed candidate of
                the last half-century to seek that office, much less win it.
                Also, he is a fellow who managed to translate many of his
                ideas into legislative action. That, I think, alerted the press
                to the fact that something other than the last straw poll
                in Wisconsin may have an impact on how people think
                and how they vote. And I think you're going to see people
                starting to ask the Democratic candidates and the Demo-
                cratic Party: What is it you mean to do?

WFB: Is there that side of you that is saying that the strategic
                prospects of the Democrats might benefit from their losing
                the election, this time around?

GREEN: You can only say that retroactively.

WFB: To say it at all, you have got to assume that the Democrats will survive.

GREEN: I don't think terribly much of Mr. Reagan. It's not worth the risk of four more years of Reagan just to give us a twenty percent better candidate in '88 than '84. I'm a public Democrat, unlike Jeff Greenfield, who's renounced his party card—

GREENFIELD: No more party status.

GREEN: —because he's now an objective television commentator.

GREENFIELD: That's me.

WFB: Might it be better, are you saying, for the Democrats not to win back America until 1988?

GREENFIELD: It is true that there are certain campaigns they might better not have won. I think that the Democrats in 1976 [Ford vs. Carter] is an untypical case. They elected a guy who was a mile wide and an inch deep and the party crumbled beneath him. And then, by 1980, they not only lost an election—a presidential election—but the Senate, and an ideological majority in the House. The Democrats have had a problem for decades, a hidden one. And if you think back and look at the numbers, in the post-Roosevelt era, the Democrats have won *one* decisive election: 1964. The other two presidential races were squeakers. The Republicans have won four landslides, or near landslides—and only one squeaker.

WFB: But without getting the House or Senate.

GREENFIELD: Yes, I'm talking just the presidential thing. At the presidential level since the death of Roosevelt, this tends to be a Republican country. What Horace Busby has called an "electoral lock" may be developing. The Democrats have some very hard political work to do if they're going to reverse that.

WFB: A Gallup poll points out that college graduates tend to vote Republican.

GREENFIELD: I mean, you lay the last eight or nine elections out on an electoral map and what you find is that the Republicans go into any presidential election more likely to win than the Democrats.

WFB: Because of the increase in education? [*Laughter*]

GREENFIELD: No, because of an increase in age—

GREEN: The correct correlation is that the more wealthy, the more Republican.

GREENFIELD: Given your attacks on higher education, Bill, I'm not sure what you're saying. Ill-taught college students may vote Republican while populist salt-of-the-earth working people vote Democratic. You don't want to extend that too far.

GREEN: By the way, there are *two* nightmares. The Democrats' nightmare is that there's a Republican lock because population is going west and south and they have a majority of the electoral college. The *Republican* nightmare is that they start ten million votes in the hole—

WFB: Blacks?

GREEN: Right. When you look at the gender gap, females, and add to it ninety-five percent of blacks voting for the Democratic candidate—

GREENFIELD: That's right.

GREEN: So that the problem for Democrats is that a large part of their constituency *doesn't vote.* They're not even *registered* to vote. This isn't only minorities: poor people, disproportionately, don't vote. So no matter what the lineup is in '84, one suspects ninety percent of minority voters will vote for the Democrat, but ninety percent of how large a universe?

If the universe expands, Southern states could go Democratic because blacks are registering and voting in greater numbers in the so-called hard-core South. The division is pretty automatic when you are discussing minority groups and Ronald Reagan. They see the administration as hos-

tile to their economic interests and their civil rights interests, and one suspects that Mr. Reagan or Bush won't be
able to overcome that by '84.

Greenfield warned of a potential danger here. If, he said, the Democrats, capitalizing on monolithic black support in the main cities, attempted to extend to the country at large this appeal to the black voter,
the Democratic leadership would need to go one of two ways. If its
appeal to the blacks was restricted to assimilating them into Mainstream
America, that would be one thing. But if the party's appeal was based
on an invitation to the black community to accept special status—to
exempt itself from responsibilities but to lay claim to perpetual indem-
nifications for past injuries—that would be something else. "I think,"
Greenfield said, "that would produce a backlash among people who
didn't used to be backlashable before. That's the great hidden question
for '84."

1984 did not produce an antiblack backlash. But it did suggest a cement-
ing of the electoral lock Mark Green was referring to.
    I remember hearing the results come in in a hotel room at Hilton
Head, South Carolina, where I was because of a lecture date the following day. The morning brought the final count: Ronald Reagan had won
every state in the Union except for Minnesota.
    I began my lecture by recalling an episode dating back to 1956. That
year, the dry populist Estes Kefauver astounded the political world by
beating the silver-tongued, witty Adlai Stevenson in the Minnesota
primary. Asked to comment on this surprise, the professor-politician
Raymond Moley answered with a simple comment: "Did you ever try
to tell a joke in Minneapolis?"

Charles Peters is the founder and editor of the *Washington Monthly.*
Michael Kinsley, his sometime editorial assistant, is now editor of the
New Republic, and a syndicated columnist and essayist. In 1986, they
made provocative political suggestions.

KINSLEY: I have a reform for you, and it sounds so perverse I think
             you'll like it. [*Laughter*] Free up rich people to give as
             much money as they want to political campaigns, and I'll

tell you why this would actually serve to *reduce* selfishness. The ironic effect of the contribution ceilings in the post-Watergate reform laws has been to eliminate all disinterested contributors of large sums of money.

The only people who have large sums of money to give to political campaigns now are the PAC [Political Action Committee] managers. The PAC managers could almost be fired, or possibly even sued, for dereliction of duty if they did anything *but* use that money for the narrowly focused self-interests of the groups that are contributing.

So, you lose the potential for the occasional gifts by rich people—they gave huge sums of money in the old days. I think in part they were, yes, they were serving their class interests. But in part they were on ego trips—and in part they were idealistic. Whereas with the PAC people, there is *absolutely* no hope.

WFB: And by the way, the rich donors were heavily Democratic, interestingly enough. The overwhelming number of big-money gifts during the last twenty years were from Democrats.

KINSLEY: Yes, but that has almost completely reversed itself now.

WFB: As recently as in 1976, Democratic PACs outnumbered Republican PACs. It turned only in 1980.

KINSLEY: It was the unions who really invented the PACs, and then the corporations ran away with the idea.

PETERS: And of course it's the incumbents in political office who primarily benefit. The PACs serve the interests of the incumbent.

The theoretical view is, of course, that as the boundaries enlarge within which the politician is making his appeal, so special interests diminish. Vote-gathering in central Massachusetts might cause the candidate to come out for protection against foreign shoe manufacturers. Extend the radius a few hundred miles and the concern of the shoe manufacturers attenuates, as does the attention paid to their special concerns by the politician. Ergo, it is supposed, the larger the forum, the less the appeal to the special interest.

WFB: But do you believe that a regionalization of primaries
            would have the effect of diminishing the appeal to special
            interests?

KINSLEY: I don't think so necessarily at all. I mean, if you define
            Mrs. Loeb [the editor of the *Manchester Union Leader*] as
            a special interest, that is an extremely narrow special inter-
            est. In fact, the really paralyzing special interests in our
            political system are *precisely* regional. Are you going to be
            able to deregulate natural gas if the New England primary
            comes first? No. Are you going to be able to get rid of farm
            price supports—which are bankrupting the country—if
            the Middle Western primary comes first? No.

            After every election since at least 1976, which is when
            I started paying attention, the Democratic Party forms a
            commission which thinks through all of this stuff and they
            [always] come up with some new set of rules. Then, after
            the next election, they conclude: "The reforms didn't
            work. We ought to try something else." I think this obses-
            sion with procedure is one of the problems the Democratic
            Party is facing. It is *paralyzed* with procedure. There is an
            entire generation of Democratic Party apparatchiks who
            only know about *procedure* and only think about *proce-
            dure* and only stand for *procedure,* and I think they ought
            to stop fiddling and start thinking about substantive is-
            sues.

As of the moment, nothing "substantive" has been done in the direction of civilizing the primary process, or revising in an intelligent way
the means by which many Americans achieve political office.

10
RONALD REAGAN ANTICIPATES HIS PRESIDENCY

GUEST:
RONALD REAGAN

In January 1980, Ronald Reagan did an hour of *Firing Line.* He had appeared on the program before he became governor, while he was governor, and after he was governor *(pre partum, in partu, post partum),* and there had been the two-hour debate on the Panama Canal Treaty (see Chapter 18). This time around there were a few formal differences in our encounter. He arrived in a limousine (large, but in the circumstances normal) and with a rather energetic and concerned entourage (small, but conspicuous). It was obvious that he was running for President of the United States, that he took himself seriously as a candidate, and that enough others did so to guard him as one would guard a dauphin.

Our close personal friendship had not been affected by his accelerating political career, but in planning the program I thought it would be

BARRY GOLDWATER, RONALD REAGAN AT *FIRING LINE* AFFAIR

fittingly exploitive to ask him very direct questions on the assumption
not that he was a *candidate* for President, but that he *was* President.
"What would you do if . . ." was the generic nature of the questions
asked. We got, in response, a series of "This is how I would handle the
problem if I were President" from someone who, one year and one week
later, was inaugurated President.

I introduced Reagan with a view to provoking his critics.

WFB: Those who oppose Ronald Reagan cite, exhibiting tradi-
            tional American ingenuity, almost everything they can
            think to say against him. Careful attention is given to
            avoid citing his record as governor of the largest state of
            the Union, to which office he was reelected—in a heavily
            Democratic state. Careful tabulation reveals that, in order
            of their frequency, Mr. Reagan is criticized (a) for having
            been born too long ago, (b) for being inexperienced in
            foreign affairs, (c) for standing by a series of propositions

no different from those he articulated in 1964, and (d) for being lazier than other candidates, who travel more frequently to New Hampshire and Iowa.

And I toyed, with the advocate's delight, with the quotidian criticisms of Reagan.

WFB: These criticisms are difficult to confute objectively. If Ronald Reagan were to enter the 1980 Olympics and win the hundred-yard dash, there are those who would say that that was the last effusion of a discharging battery. If tomorrow he were to write a sequel to Machiavelli's *The Prince,* there are those who would say that here finally is proof that Ronald Reagan's mind is rooted in the Renaissance. If tomorrow he announced that in the next six weeks he would visit every town and hamlet in New Hampshire, there are those who would find here concrete evidence that Governor Reagan has finally recognized that he is not the front-runner.

And I announced the format (I had not told Reagan what I proposed to do).

WFB: Accordingly, I propose to spend the hour discussing not so much the forthcoming campaign, but rather: How would a President Reagan, were he now safely inaugurated, handle himself? What are the priorities that guide him? What techniques of government appeal to him? What is his view of the responsibilities of the chief executive? I shall offer him hypothetical problems.

I should like to begin by asking "President" Reagan: What would you do if, say, one afternoon you were advised that a race riot had broken out in Detroit?

REAGAN: Well, I would be inclined to say that that was a problem for the local authorities in Detroit, unless those local authorities were unable to control the situation and had called on the federal government for martial help. And maybe one of the things that's been happening too much is the federal government has been interfering where they *haven't* been invited in.

WFB: Do I understand you to say that the actual role attempted by, say, President Johnson during the riots of his administration might have exacerbated the situation rather than helped to mollify it?

REAGAN: Well, when I was Governor of California, it was in the roaring sixties, when the campuses were in ferment, and we were talking about long, hot summers, and there would be more cities burned and more rioting. Those were handled, in the first place, by local authorities, even in war-torn Berkeley. The state was not involved until the local authorities—as they did one day, calling from the university president's office—told me, as governor, that they could no longer assure the safety of the people of Berkeley, and they asked for the National Guard, and I immediately sent the National Guard in.

A fair question, a good answer, but not one that proved of historical interest during 1981–1988. There were no race riots during Reagan's presidency to test the Reagan position on how to handle them. I went on.

WFB: President Reagan, Tito is dead. The pro-Soviet faction in Yugoslavia has urged the Soviet Union, citing the Brezhnev Doctrine, to send its armies to restore order, and you are advised that in fact Soviet columns are on their way south.

REAGAN: Well, I would hope by that time, the United States would have given enough signals to the Soviet Union, beginning with, say, Afghanistan—such as an American presence now in the Middle East; an American presence in the Indian Ocean and the Persian Gulf area; the restoration of arms sales to Pakistan and an American presence even there (because we have a treaty with Pakistan)—that the Soviet Union would have received enough signals that a move of the kind you've just described would run the very serious risk of a direct confrontation with the United

States. And I don't think the Soviet Union *wants* a direct confrontation with the United States.

WFB: Is it your opinion that those historians are correct who say that when the Soviet Union marched into Czechoslovakia it was President Johnson who kept them from going on into Rumania by saying that they should look out lest they "loose the hounds of war"?

REAGAN: This is the first time I've heard that. I did not know that he'd said that. The goal is world peace, and therefore the United States cannot recklessly put itself in a position where the confrontation does take place. But I think the United States must make it plain to the Soviet Union— which it has not done for the three years of this [the Carter] administration—should make it plain that they run that risk of having such a confrontation if they continue with their imperialism and with this kind of expansion.

To me—the reason I use the Afghanistan example, right now—the danger and the thing that we should be very conscious of is that outside of their own circle of satellites, this is the first time the Soviet Union has used its own forces, its own troops. And it seems to me it's kind of showing off that they think they are [reaching], or have reached, a level of strength vis-à-vis the United States in which they can become a little more reckless than they've been.

I know that President [Carter] has said he's just discovered that the Soviet Union can't be trusted. That's something that a great many people would have been happy to tell him anytime over the last several years.

WFB: So therefore, if I understand, your position is that you would so order the foreign policy as to make it an impermissible risk for the Soviet Union to enter Yugoslavia.

REAGAN: You put it better than I could. Thank you.

Historical afterthought. When Nicaragua became the freshest Soviet salient, early in Reagan's administration, Reagan did as much as he could do, short of recommending the use of U.S. troops, to stop the

Soviet juggernaut. But it is also true that when, in 1988, he went to the great summit in Moscow, he addressed the leaders of the Soviet Union as if they were in critical respects different from those predecessors he had accused Jimmy Carter of failing to understand. Whether Reagan #2 was wiser than Reagan #1 remains, as of this writing, to be seen.

WFB: Representative Kemp of New York State proposes that all future United States bonds be issued on a guaranteed-purchasing-power basis. What is your reaction, Mr. President?

REAGAN: That sure would make the government honest for a change. Today we even use patriotism to induce people to buy bonds, and yet the federal government knows that as long as we maintain this inflation rate, they are going to pay the people back with dollars that, even plus the interest, will not buy as much as the dollars that the people who are investing in those bonds put up—

WFB: And then tax the interest.

REAGAN: —and then *tax* the interest. And of course the answer is to . . . stop inflation; and government should be doing that, and it hasn't. But yes, that sure would give the government something to think about. In other words, if it had to index and give back to the people dollars that had the same purchasing power as the dollars that they had invested.

WFB: Well, that is a very specific proposal that has been made by Milton Friedman. The notion is not to sell this as an anti-inflationary weapon, because it won't necessarily control inflation—

REAGAN: No.

WFB: —but at least it will keep the government from defrauding the people.

REAGAN: That's right.

WFB: It would also hugely lower the interest rate, obviously, because if you were going to get your inflation back, you'd be disposed to buy bonds at a lesser carrying cost.

REAGAN: Yes.

WFB: The carrying cost would be implicit in the sense that the government would have to bear the burden of its own inflation. Are you favorably disposed to such a reordering?

REAGAN: Well yes, because I've often thought, Bill, that— Well, last year the American people reported capital gains for tax purposes of four and a half billion. An economic study has revealed that those capital gains, if they were computed in constant dollars, actually represented not four and a half billion profit, but a one billion loss. Now, by what right does the government make you pay a tax on a *loss*? If we're to have a capital gains tax, I think that tax should be computed in constant dollars. You shouldn't have to pay a tax on inflation.

WFB: So in brief, you would not veto any act by Congress that authorized the issuance of guaranteed-purchasing-power bonds?

REAGAN: No. I'd laugh all the time I was signing it. [*Laughter*]

And we know that, in respect of indexation, the Reagan administration implemented it for taxpayers, ending the bracket creep; a tax reform judged by Milton Friedman (and others) as the most important of the Reagan administration. But there was never any serious effort made to issue constant-purchasing-power bonds. On the other hand, inflation was, of course, greatly reduced under Reagan.

WFB: Mr. President, the OPEC powers announced yesterday afternoon that the basic price of a barrel of crude oil will be fifty dollars. What is your reaction to that announcement, and what do you propose to recommend?

REAGAN: Well, I've been recommending for a long time that the only way we're going to make ourselves independent of OPEC oil is not by telling people to drive less, or by keeping the farmers from getting enough diesel fuel to run their tractors and plant their fields. It is to restore *incentives* for the energy industry to find the sources of energy we need here in *this* country so that we're not dependent on OPEC.

On the other hand, I have to say this with reference to the OPEC nations. Some years ago it was decided that the OPEC nations would price their oil based on American dollars. And at that time, thirty-five dollars would buy ten barrels of oil and thirty-five dollars would buy one ounce of gold. Is OPEC raising the price, or is OPEC still saying, "We are figuring that ten barrels of our oil is worth an ounce of gold, and we're not going to follow the American paper dollar downhill"?

WFB: It's one thing if OPEC were to say, "We are going to index the price of a barrel according to the depreciation of the American dollar." But however badly the dollar has fared, it has not in fact reduced in value by ninety percent, but the price of a barrel of oil has increased in the last seven years by a factor of two thousand percent. Now, how would you, as President, cope with the apparently unfettered power of the OPEC nations to set any price they want to for oil?

REAGAN: Well, as I've said, right now, here in the state of California, there are sixty-five thousand oil wells; twenty-three thousand of them are closed down because they cannot afford to pump the oil for the price the government says they can charge for it. And instead of giving us lectures on conservation—even though conservation and saving may be good in and of itself—isn't it time for the government to recognize that it has created this crisis, and the government can uncreate it if it will make it once again profitable for American independents to go out there exploring, finding more oil wells, producing more oil in this country?

Historical observation: President Reagan did indeed end price controls on native oil and gas, and the effects were to the consumer's benefit. But soon after his term of office began, the organizational discipline of the OPEC cartel broke down, and the price of oil tumbled. The question then became: Should imported oil be taxed, to encourage the pursuit of fresh oil deposits within the United States and to dis-

courage the reformation of OPEC's cartel power? Reagan never advocated this measure.

WFB: Mr. President, the Department of Commerce announced
                yesterday that during the preceding quarter unemploy-
                ment had gone to a level of ten percent. What do you
                propose, by way of remedial action, to Congress?

REAGAN: Wait a minute. That unemployment had gone—

WFB: From six percent to ten percent in the last quarter.

REAGAN: Well, that's probably due to some of the massive layoffs
                in the automobile industry, and again aren't we getting
                to a—

I was fascinated by what had just happened. Clearly, Mr. Reagan had
suddenly shifted out of the hypothetical mode that had protected the
entire program up to this minute. This was owing, so far as I could see,
to two (and only two) possible explanations. The first, uh, was the
histrionic authenticity of my question, as posed. The second, Mr. Reagan's autohypnotic walk back into the theater scene in which he had
served as a professional. Clearly, he had suddenly become Julius Caesar,
advised of a catastrophe in the provinces.

WFB: This is hypothetical, you understand.

REAGAN: What?

WFB: This is hypothetical.

REAGAN: Oh, this is *hypothetical.* Well, I don't think that *would*
                happen—

WFB: You can't challenge a hypothesis.

REAGAN: —in this administration that we're talking about—be-
                cause by that time we would have gone to work—

WFB: But suppose it happened the day after you were inaugu-
                rated, so you could still blame the preceding administra-
                tion?

REAGAN: And I would. [*Laughter*] Without question, I would.

WFB: What would you propose, to turn the economy back to-
            ward fuller employment?

REAGAN: Well, we would start an immediate program of cutting
            income tax rates across the board for everyone, to provide
            incentive for individuals. We would go after some of the
            punitive taxes and the tens of thousands of regulations
            which are keeping American industry from being as com-
            petitive as it could be in the world market. Our rate of
            increase in per-man-hour productivity is only a third what
            it is in Japan, half what it is in West Germany—not be-
            cause our working people aren't as good as their working
            people, but because we have the highest percentage of
            outmoded industrial plant equipment of any of the indus-
            trialized nations. This is so because federal government
            practices have kept us from having the capital we need to
            modernize, but what capital investment we do make is in
            answer to government mandates to meet environmental or
            safety standards, ideas that the bureaucracy has.
                I have in speeches around the country been pointing out
            there are seventeen United States Steel company plants
            closing in this country. We once produced forty-seven
            percent of the steel in the world. We now produce nineteen
            percent. But there are twenty-seven government agencies
            imposing fifty-six hundred regulations on the steel indus-
            try.
                I would also like to eliminate the tax on interest on
            savings accounts to encourage thrift, because the Ameri-
            can people are saving at the lowest percentage of their
            earnings that they ever have saved and lower than the
            workers in other countries. Thus we're reducing the capi-
            tal we have for research and development, to develop new
            products that will employ those people that are no longer
            needed in the steel mills and so forth.
                If we'd do all of those things, I think we'd begin to see,
            because three times in this century—four times in this
            century—three times under Republicans, once under a
            Democratic administration—we followed that policy of
            an across-the-board tax reduction, and the burst of pros-
            perity was so great that even in the first year even the

government got more money at the lower rates than it had been getting at the higher rates. And I just have faith in the *marketplace,* and I believe that this is the way we must go to curb inflation. This is the way we must go to put us back where we were as an industrial giant.

WFB: While you are encouraging these tax reductions, there is inevitably a deficit in the cost of government operations. This you would cope with how?

REAGAN: Well, since the General Accounting Office says that there's probably fifty billion dollars lost at the federal level alone through fraud and waste, we might start with that. That would certainly eliminate a deficit right now, if you could eliminate that. And from my experience in California as governor, I found out that you can eliminate things like that. Balancing the budget is a little bit like protecting your virtue: You just have to learn to say no. [*Laughter*]

WFB: You would propose to say no to future programs or would you say no retroactively, by asking Congress to repeal some existing programs? If so, which?

REAGAN: Well now, pardon me, but you've just reminded me of another facet of my program that I hadn't given as yet and I should have. Part of that program calls for a reimplementation of the Tenth Article of the Bill of Rights— the one that says the federal government shall do only those things that the Constitution calls for, and all others shall remain with the states or the people. I propose and would have already started, if your hypothesis is correct, a planned and orderly transfer back to the states and local communities of functions the federal government has usurped, and which it has proven it is incapable of operating. And one of the first of those would be welfare.

One of the second would be in the field of education. I would like to dissolve the ten-billion-dollar national Department of Education created by President Carter and turn schools back to the local school districts, where we

built the greatest public school system the world has ever
seen. I think I can make a case that the decline in the
quality of public education began when federal aid became
federal interference.

Waal, now. The world knows that the Reagan administration did
indeed reduce taxes—and that these tax reductions did indeed increase federal revenues. But we learned also that these increases were
vastly insufficient to balance the budget; that President Reagan's
dreams of reinstituting federalism failed almost without notice; that
no serious effort was made to eliminate the Department of Education,
although when, in the second term, it was headed by Mr. Reagan's
appointee, William Bennett, serious efforts were made to say the right
things respecting a restoration of literacy and learning—from a bully
pulpit.

WFB: Mr. President, yesterday the union of postal employees
            went on a nationwide strike. Now I know you well enough
            to know that your instinctive answer would be "How can
            you tell?" [Laughter] Having got past that, what would be
            your official policy toward a strike by federal and munici-
            pal employees?

REAGAN: I have thought for a long time that by law they should
            not be allowed to strike. Government is not the same as
            private business. Government cannot close down the as-
            sembly line, and isn't it significant that when govern-
            ment employees first began to unionize, and they had
            the support of organized labor but then organized la-
            bor supported them only on the condition that their
            unions would contain a no-strike clause—their constitu-
            tion, I mean—a no-strike clause. The public employees
            should *not* be allowed to strike. Government *can't* close
            down.

Here Candidate Reagan foretold exactly the action of President Reagan, who, eight months into his administration, fired the air traffic
controllers who were striking illegally. His act, against contumacious
organized labor, deeply affected, in the desired direction, organized
labor union's routine disdain for the public.

WFB: Mr. President, the Supreme Court ruled yesterday that
            opening congressional sessions with prayer is a violation
            of the First Amendment to the Constitution, and that the
            practice must be discontinued instantly.

REAGAN: Do you mean, bad as Congress has been all this time *with*
            praying, they want us to take it now *without* praying?
            [*Laughter*]

WFB: I think that what you just said is so homiletic it might *itself*
            be unconstitutional. But what would your reaction as
            Chief Executive be, in a situation of that sort; or do you
            see any role for the Chief Executive where the Supreme
            Court of the United States issues its own exegesis of the
            Constitution?

REAGAN: Well, Bill, I think it is high time the presidency—I
            don't know all the legal powers that the President might
            have in regard to a Supreme Court decision—I'm not a
            lawyer. But I do know that the President has a great
            power of moral persuasion, and I think it is time for a
            President and for a great many people in this country to
            start pointing out that the First Amendment was never
            intended to *outlaw* religion, that the separation of
            church and state does not mean that the state should be
            separated from religion. We are a nation under God,
            and to suggest—I suppose the next step—well, we know
            that there's already been a movement on the part of
            some atheists that there shouldn't be chaplains in the
            armed forces. I think this is being carried to a ridicu-
            lous extent.

WFB: Well, would you endorse a constitutional amendment, the
            effect of which would be to reverse the Supreme Court's
            policies on prayers just described and some of its preced-
            ing decisions that call it a violation of the First Amend-
            ment to provide state aid to religious schools?

REAGAN: State aid to religious schools—I have always supported
            the idea that—and this, I think, would be the kind of aid
            that would not run the risk of interfering, because govern-
            ment aid is usually followed by some measure of govern-

ment control, and therefore I would not like to see our parochial and religious schools, independent colleges, and so forth losing their freedom because of government constraints. But I have always favored the idea of parents who are paying their taxes to support all of the public ventures, but then who take it upon themselves to send their children to a school of a [religious] kind, I think should be allowed to get either a credit or take a deduction for the tuition that they pay—

WFB: A voucher system of sorts?

REAGAN: —for that education. But I would support, yes, I *would* support a change in the Constitution, I would support a constitutional amendment to restore prayer—voluntary prayer—to the public schools. I don't think anyone should be forced to pray, but I think that we have—we are actually, in a way, violating the spirit of the First Amendment in that the government is now *interfering* with the practice of religion. If the members of Congress feel that they can do a better job and that their day will start better if they open with prayer, what in the First Amendment bars them from doing that because they're in a government building?

President Reagan never changed his views on the question, and related questions. He backed a constitutional amendment that would permit prayer in the schools. But it got pretty well swamped by the secularists and separatists.

WFB: Mr. President, the National Security Council, having conducted extensive studies, has reached the conclusion that that which the free world has that the Soviet Union most urgently needs is agricultural products. Are you prepared to use the agricultural surplus of the United States, and attempt to use the surplus of other free countries, to the extent that they will cooperate with us, in order to exert strategic pressure on the Soviet Union?

REAGAN: Yes, provided that this would be a united effort, and provided that it would involve other things, and provided that

we would then, if we are going to use that as a strategic
weapon, [pay] some compensation to the people who raise
that food. You can't make them bear the burden of national defense.

Now, I have been critical [of President Carter] for the
seventeen million tons of feed grain that he is withholding
right now from the Soviet Union. The Soviet Union's
going to be able to get what they need in the rest of the
world, and so we've just aimed our blow at the American
farmer instead of at the Soviet Union. And there are other
countries in the world that are *not* interrupting their sales
to them. This is again a little bit like us shutting off the
Iranian oil and only having to reduce our oil supply by a
small percentage.

I regret to conclude that this (and more, not here given) was largely
spinach, and the hell with it. To be sure, in his fourth month as President, Mr. Reagan canceled the agricultural embargo imposed by Carter
in response to the Afghanistan War. It may be that agricultural boycotts
simply do not work. On the other hand, neither do agricultural subsidies, and Mr. Reagan, by his own reckoning, became the greatest philan-
thropist to the farmers in U.S. history.

WFB: Finally, Mr. President, the CIA has complained to you
            that it cannot discharge some of the recent directives that
            the National Security Council has given it as a result of
            its having been hamstrung by a number of provisions
            initiated by Senator Church three or four years ago. How
            would you handle that dilemma?

REAGAN: Why, I'm surprised that they're complaining, because one
            of the first things I did when I took office was ask Congress
            to repeal those restrictions that were put on by Senator
            Church.

WFB: And what threats did you use if Congress didn't comply?

REAGAN: That I would take my case to the people and tell the people
            that we were flying blind with no counterintelligence
            whatsoever and that the Congress was to blame.

WFB: Thank you, Mr. President. [*Laughter*]

THE PROGRAM IS INTERRUPTED. THE PRESIDENT HAS BEEN
SHOT. TO WFB'S RIGHT, DOROTHY MCCARTNEY, CHIEF
RESEARCHER. BEHIND, WARREN STEIBEL, PRODUCER; TO THE
LEFT, ANTHONY LEWIS, GUEST

Of very considerable historical interest. President Reagan did not ask
for a repeal of the War Powers Act, restricting the freedom of the first
executive. And he never directly challenged the act in the courts—he
simply ignored it, having pronounced it unconstitutional. And he mined
the harbors in Nicaragua, an act subsequently ruled by the World Court
as in violation of international agreements. It is safe to say here that
President Reagan proceeded as Chief Executive as though the laws had
not been written; but he did not challenge them in court.

And then the Examiner was heard from, Thomas Plate, editor of the
Los Angeles Examiner. He asked a question which, using a different
subject, would be asked time and time again—was Ronald Reagan his
own boss?

PLATE: Governor, I would imagine you'd be distressed by the
opinion of some people that John Sears, as your campaign
manager, has Rasputin-like qualities in terms of relating
to you, and that this would raise questions in the minds

of some as to if, when you do become President, as Mr.
Buckley suggests, the style of your presidency—will it be
an adviser-oriented presidency, if you follow that logic?

REAGAN: No. I've read those, too, and the idea that someone is
moderating me or changing my positions— First of all, no
one's trying to, and second of all, no one could. That's one
of the advantages of age. There wouldn't be any point in
running for that job if I were willing to change the things
I believe in in order to get the job. I'm only seeking it
because of what I believe and what I would like to attempt
to do.

A final note. Six weeks later, Reagan discharged John Sears. In respect of the failure by Ronald Reagan to consummate so much of what
he declared himself determined to do, one quotes from Mr. Reagan
earlier on *Firing Line* in 1972, six years after his election as Governor
of California.

WFB: I should like to begin by asking Governor Reagan: What
does he consider the most clearly impractical demand
regularly made by conservative theorists on men of affairs?

REAGAN: I think, Bill, the thing that happens is this. The belief
develops that simply by electing a President or electing a
governor, suddenly all the things that group supported—
[all the things that the individual voter] wants changed in
government—*will* be changed. It overlooks the fact that
this government of ours has grown in these last forty
years, and you just don't elect someone to office who [can]
take over this gigantic machinery of government. The
great bulk of that government is unchanged. The permanent structure, the permanent employees of government—
they're there in their various departments, and they tend
to think of an elected official as a temporary aberration.
They're going to go on doing things the way they had
always intended to do them—and the result is that you
can only try to whittle back. You have to point out that
no one man, no one administration, can make all the
changes that these people want.

11
CIVIL
LIBERTIES

GUESTS:
FLOYD ABRAMS
WILLIAM RUSHER
MAURICE STANS
OTTO PREMINGER
HARRY REEMS
ALAN DERSHOWITZ
ABNER MIKVA
ROBERT KUKLA
RAOUL BERGER
ARIEH NEYER
MICHAEL HARRINGTON

t is not disputed that in the sixties and seventies there was more discussion than in any two other decades over the nature and the reach of civil rights. The triggering question was the long suppression of the rights of those who were then called Negroes. The conclusive battles over their civil rights were fought in Congress during the sixties. But some people elaborated some these rights, reaching a point, e.g., in the quota-system extension of affirmative action, that in the opinion of many aggressed against the rights of nonblacks, and could set back blacks in the long term.

During the same period, there was also what, as we look back on it, one might call very simply the End of Censorship. It seems otherworldly to imagine back to the day when one could not buy a book by de Sade (if one wanted to), or *Lady Chatterley's Lover* (many wanted to), at a bookstore. But the arguments for the *status quo ante* were never entirely discredited.

What did the Constitution say, or fail to say, about the traditional right of the American citizens to bear arms, even Saturday-night specials? Labor unions having attained formidable institutional powers under the New Deal, including—even before the New Deal—an immunity to laws against the restraint of trade, were they going too far, for instance, by insisting that I join the American Federation of Radio and Television Artists (AFTRA), their union, before being permitted to appear on the air to expound a political point of view?

How to define civil rights, indeed how to enumerate them—these questions have been a staple of *Firing Line* discussions.

In 1979, William Rusher, my colleague (he was publisher of *National Review*), a prominent conservative journalist and a lawyer, joined me in discussing freedom of the press with Floyd Abrams, a New York attorney much associated with press liberties, and something of an absolutist on the subject.

WFB: Mr. Abrams, would you be good enough to describe the Branzburg decision of the Supreme Court?

ABRAMS: That's a six-year-old ruling of the Court [1972] in which by a very slight majority the Supreme Court ruled that journalists did *not* have the right to refuse to appear before a grand jury to bear witness to evidence they might have, bearing on a crime. The case involved a reporter—Paul Branzburg—who had seen hashish being made, and reported a story to expose the conditions, in Kentucky, in which it was being made. He was called to testify in front of a grand jury, and he took the position that he should not have to testify about material he had learned in confidence. The Supreme Court held five to four that he *did* have to testify. Mr. Branzburg subsequently left the state, and so far as I know has not returned to Kentucky.

WFB: Is that condign punishment? [*Laughter*]

ABRAMS: It is a very, very serious thing—

WFB: No, I mean against Kentucky.

ABRAMS: Well, it was like Humphrey Bogart in *Casablanca*. He cannot return to his country.

WFB: I have seen *Branzburg* referred to as the "anchor" decision.

ABRAMS: It is an "anchor" decision in the sense that it is the only ruling of the Supreme Court about the confidentiality of journalists' sources, confidentiality, that is, of information learned by journalists [on duty]. And because it was a close decision, it remains a somewhat open question as to precisely what the law is today about what protection journalists have, if any, for the confidentiality of their sources.

WFB: May I ask you to comment on one or two clauses from Justice White's opinion? He said that from the beginning of our century, the press has operated *without* constitutional protection for press informants, and even so the press has flourished. Is that a true statement?

ABRAMS: That is true. Something can be added to it, however, which is that from the beginning of the century, journalists were *not* routinely called as witnesses. It was at least an accepted practice that journalists were not considered by judges—by lawyers—a part of the legal system. They were reporters. They reported. They were *not* called as witnesses. But I see in my own practice how routine it has now become for journalists to be called as witnesses. That does make a difference, it would seem to me, in terms of the need for legal protection.

WFB: Do I understand you to be taking the position that somebody who is a journalist inherits the right to immunize someone who gives him information?

ABRAMS: Yes, in much the same way that someone like myself, who is a lawyer, inherits the same right to immunize a client, where the client gives information.

WFB: So therefore you would say that the rights of lawyers and priests should extend to journalists.

ABRAMS: As a general matter, yes. There are some differences, but as a general matter, yes, I—

WFB: That's sort of a revolutionary accretion and yet, in assert-
            ing that point, you tend to do so as an exegete of the
            Constitution rather than as somebody who wants to
            amend it.

ABRAMS: Well, I do, and for this reason. It seems to me that most
            of the privileges we have—attorney/client at least, doc-
            tor/patient for sure—do not have constitutional roots
            at all. One can look in vain through the Constitution
            for any way to extend privilege to a person who is a
            doctor. It seems to me that because of the role played
            by the press in our society, and the need of journalists
            in order to make it possible to play that role, that the
            First Amendment itself, as four Supreme Court justices
            said—

WFB: So yours is a utilitarian argument—

ABRAMS: Well, it's utilitarian in the sense that if the press didn't
            need it in order to function, [the journalist's immunity]
            should not be sought, and should not be granted.

WFB: Your arguments are empirical then—

ABRAMS: I can't go back to the framers of the Constitution and
            say—

WFB: Or rooted in the common law.

ABRAMS: To the common law, certainly not. The common law is
            almost the antithesis of the First Amendment in so many
            areas that I wouldn't want to go to the common law. The
            common law, as [Justice Hugo] Black said, is what we had
            a revolution to get away from.

WFB: Did Warren repeal the common law too?

ABRAMS: No, Warren didn't repeal it. But now and then there were
            majorities, in past days at least, for the proposition that
            the First Amendment was drafted so as to get away from
            the English common law with respect to press rights—or
            lack of them.

WFB: Mr. Rusher, do you see what is happening here as a natu-
            ral evolution that corresponds with the demonstrated use-

fulness of the press as a guardian of domestic liberty, or
do you see it simply as pressing a vested interest?

RUSHER: I think it's not evolution but an *attempt* at evolution.
Historically, journalists did not claim [such] rights as
those they have been seeking to establish in the last few
years. It was only ten or fifteen years ago that the press,
and particularly the Washington press corps, moved into
a position of serious adversary posture with regard to the
administration—first, the late Johnson administration
over Vietnam, and then, of course, the Nixon administration.

Since they do the reporting in this country, I can forgive
anybody who [mistakenly] thinks that they had had these
rights for two hundred years, and that the Supreme Court
and other courts fell upon them with berserk fury in the
early 1970s and began taking them away. This is not true.
On the part of the press, this is a power-grab.

When Maurice Stans, Richard Nixon's Secretary of Commerce, appeared on *Firing Line* (1979), he had been through hell.

The question was whether he had been to hell and back. That was the
point he was really pressing in his book, *The Terrors of Justice.* It's one
thing to be exonerated by the courts, another to work your way back
into the esteem of the community. It is news if someone is found guilty
of obstructing justice, much less so when he is found not guilty of having
obstructed justice. Moreover, in the case under consideration, there is
the comfortable inclination to assume that anyone as closely connected
as Maurice Stans was to the Nixon enterprise must have been somehow
guilty of something. And, finally, why go to all that trouble to find out?

Maurice Stans was always regarded as something of the Resident
Puritan in Nixon's reelection operation. His background was exem-
plary. He was a self-made man, a former president of the Professional
Society of Public Accountants, a citizen of demonstrated public spirit
with two decades of service in and out of government, a director of
numerous public companies, recipient of ten honorary degrees, trustee
of several colleges, and honored by numerous awards in recognition of
philanthropic and civic work. He resigned as Secretary of Commerce in
order to take on the chore of finance chairman for the Committee to

Reelect the President, and in May 1973, along with former Attorney General John Mitchell, he was indicted for obstruction of justice, charged with having attempted to straighten the way at the Securities and Exchange Commission for Robert Vesco,* in exchange for $250,000 in contributions to the Nixon campaign.

The court found him not guilty. He *was* found guilty of several irregularities in reporting, and fined $5,000. By virtually unanimous agreement, these infractions were trivial. A reviewing panel of the professional CPA society, surveying the record, decreed that he was morally blameless.

Stans' experience had not made him a fan of the press. He makes the case that unbridled press freedom can levy heavy costs on innocent people. He set out to make the case for restricting press freedom.

STANS: Hundreds of other innocent people were swept up into this Watergate hysteria—and that's what it was—in which the press went to great extremes, created news—there was a great deal of fabricated news at the time, because of the competition between investigative reporters to get ahead of each other. And many times stories were printed as fact which had *no* factual basis whatever.

WFB: But isn't it a fact, Mr. Stans, that you're the *only* person who was prosecuted and found innocent?

STANS: Actually, as I point out in the book, there were fifteen people charged with major crimes who were [subsequently] acquitted.

WFB: A moment ago you said hundreds of innocent people. You were making a nonjudicial point, right? You were not intending to imply that hundreds of people were actually prosecuted?

STANS: Right. Hundreds of people were *smeared,* their reputations injured, they were put to great expense in time and anguish in order to defend themselves in a way and at a time when defense was impossible. It's almost impossible in the kind of hurricane that existed there to prove the negative.

_____

*Robert Vesco, a large-scale crook, on the international lam since trying to steal a few hundred million from Investors Overseas Services.

WFB: But the seeds of the hurricane were dropped by Nixon, weren't they?

STANS: Believe me, I am not an apologist for Richard Nixon. I don't defend what he did. I don't second-guess any of the conclusions of the court as to the people found guilty. What I am saying is that in the search for the guilty, there were hundreds of *innocent* people who were swept into that dragnet and left out there to *prove* their innocence; that it was a witch-hunt–type operation that should never again happen in this country.

WFB: Let me ask you, Mr. Stans, is it possible to conduct such an investigation without finding suspicious the behavior and conduct of people who are in fact innocent?

STANS: I think you are absolutely right. But the question is, What do you do with that information? Do you print a leak as a fact? Do you print a rumor as a fact? Do you surreptitiously get the records of the grand jurors, so you can go to their homes and solicit information from them as to what's going on in the supposedly sacred grand jury room? And when it gets to the side of the prosecution, do you threaten witnesses? Do you intimidate witnesses because they happen to be witnesses for the defense and associated with Richard Nixon?

         That kind of thing went on, and that was inexcusable. It seems to me that if anyone here—anyone in our audience—were to get up and say, "I think Jimmy Carter's a crook," then Carter ought to have the right to take action against that person. There is absolutely no reason for an open, unlimited hunting season against a public person just because he is a public person.

Freedom of the press, freedom of speech—these cognate liberties are, of course, routinely construed to extend not only to journalism but also to expression of a more subtle kind, namely, artistic expression. That is the subject examined in these next two excerpts. They are separated by only nine years, the first in 1967, the second in 1976, but the contrast between them in attitudes is striking.

Otto Preminger had vast theatrical experience. Born in Vienna, he

was the son of the attorney general of the Austrian Empire. At twenty-
nine he left for the United States, where he lived the rest of his life,
producing many successful movies, including *Laura, The Moon Is Blue,
Angel Face, Carmen Jones, The Man with the Golden Arm, Anatomy of
a Murder,* and *Advise and Consent.*

Preminger liked to tease the censors. He was reportedly delighted that
the Motion Picture Production Code was denied to *The Moon Is Blue.*
It is difficult, in today's perspective, to understand a public fuss over
such a movie, but instructive to remind ourselves that it was exactly that
controversial, in 1962, as was *The Man with the Golden Arm* in 1956.

WFB: Mr. Preminger, you are quoted as saying, "Many people
                think that because I have had censorship trouble, I am in
                business to make dirty pictures. This is not true. Nobody
                can make a success with immoral films. The public will
                not accept them. No one ever got rich selling French
                postcards. I want to make adult films, not immoral films."

                Now, you seem to be saying there, as I understand it,
                not that you're against immoral films because they are
                unsuccessful, but that you would be against them even if
                they *were* successful.

PREMINGER: I would be against them under all circumstances.

WFB: You would? All right—

PREMINGER: Only in the context of this quote, I have said that an
                immoral film also could not *be* successful. I think there is
                morality built into any dramatic medium, whether it's a
                play or a television show. You cannot mention one suc-
                cessful play or film where the bad principle won. This is
                morality, the bad principle must always lose in the end.

WFB: I think that's extremely interesting, but I want to find out
                what it means when you say, "I, Otto Preminger, am
                against immoral films." Does that mean that, assuming
                the existing obscenity laws were to come up for review
                tomorrow, you would vote yes or no that you wished those
                laws to continue in being?

PREMINGER: I would want them to continue in being.

WFB: Well, then you are in favor of certain kinds of censorship—

PREMINGER: No. No. Censorship is different. Censorship is if the government wants to see the film *before* it is shown to the people. That is censorship. If, on the other hand, somebody publishes a film and permits in the film or through the film a violation of the law—let's say, the obscenity laws—then he has committed something which is *against the law* and then—you know. It's like stealing, or like any other violation of the law; and the normal agencies start to do their job, arrest him and confiscate the film. That is not censorship. It is the responsibility of the picture maker to decide whether he offends the law or not. Certainly I wouldn't do anything *deliberately* to offend the law. If then a judge in a court decides that I have offended the law, I must take the punishment. It's very simple; it's just like any other crime.

WFB: Right. But you do reject then the position of so many people, for instance, the American Civil Liberties Union, who believe that those obscenity laws shouldn't *be* on the books, that they—

PREMINGER: I don't think that anybody should want the laws on obscenity changed.

WFB: I assure you, quite a few people do.

PREMINGER: Really?

WFB: Yes, sir.

PREMINGER: Well, *I* don't. I can only speak for myself.

That is an altogether coherent position: that the state must not, on the one hand, intrude in the creative process, but that the state is competent to enforce the will of the people with respect to obscenity. In fact, although the legal prohibitions survive—obscenity statutes continue on the books, and you can get copies of them in the same bookstores where you can buy obscenity—given current readings of the First Amendment, they are for all intents and purposes a dead letter, which, for all the good it does, can become at times a Hydra-headed monster. It creates "right" after right after right, against which organized contention is progressively impotent. In any event, it was quaint to hear from Mr. Preminger that people could not get rich making obscene films. It was obviously otherwise well before Otto Preminger's death in 1986.

One day, in 1972, Harry Reems gave over his private parts to a movie studio, for the sum of $100, for one day's use. The resulting movie went out as *Deep Throat* and became the *Gone with the Wind* of the smut circuit. The film grossed, it has been estimated, over $20 million. The government decided *this* was the one to go after.

It did so by filing charges against a dozen of the persons involved in the venture and charging them individually with conspiracy to violate the law that prohibits interstate commerce in obscene materials. The feds shrewdly decided to try Harry Reems (the principal defendant) in Memphis, Tennessee, a venue not given to latitudinarianism in matters of obscenity. The defense (Professor Alan Dershowitz of Harvard) made much of the dark mischief in choosing Memphis (why not Miami, where the movie was made? or New York, where it ran day and night? or San Francisco, where variant sex is available at all but McDonald's hamburger stands?).

The implication was that only in Rubesville would a jury find *Deep Throat* obscene. Alan Dershowitz was being a good lawyer, which is to be distinguished from a plausible lawyer (*Deep Throat* would have been found obscene if shown in Sodom and Gomorrah). Reems was tried and convicted.

The so-called Memphis argument went on, in the appeals phase, to contend that if the conviction of Reems was upheld, the federal government would have at its disposal a means of setting obscenity standards for the whole nation by the simple act of finding the chastest corner of the republic and prosecuting all off-color films or books in that city (or hamlet), getting quick and secure convictions, and going on to drive products uncongenial to the parochial minds of the Justice Department out of the country, out even of the most cosmopolitan sections of the country.

Then—the defense went on—there was the *ex post facto* problem. In 1972, when Harry Reems made the movie, the courts were being guided by the *Roth* standard. That decision, handed down by Justice Brennan in 1957, held that something was obscene if it appealed exclusively to the prurient interest and had no "redeeming social importance." It wasn't until 1973 that the Supreme Court revised that definition, doing away with the social-importance clause. As of *Miller* v. *California,* that which was legally obscene was any book or movie which, read or seen by the "average person, applying contemporary community standards," would be judged as, on the whole, appealing "to the prurient interest." That meant that, in 1976, Reems had been indicted by the stricter 1973 standards for doing something he did in 1972, under more permissive standards. Where were we left?

It was proposed (I forget by whom) that *Firing Line* invite Harry Reems as a guest, along with Alan Dershowitz.

No, I said. Maybe Harry Reems will survive as a great constitutional figure, like Guy Fawkes, but as far as I am concerned, he is primarily (exclusively?) a sex exhibitionist and he can ply his wares and make the case for doing so elsewhere, say on the Donahue program. But I would be happy to have Alan Dershowitz. . . .

Came back the answer from Dershowitz: You get us both, or none at all.

I had had several experiences with Dershowitz. There had been a *Firing Line* program, disputing something or other, and also a lively public debate at Harvard before a packed audience at the Law School, on the general question of law and obscenity. I knew his range and theatrical resources, and I had the feeling he was deploying one of them at this moment. Either that, or else Reems was insisting on his right to appear on television in his own defense. That is an initiative, I pause to note, that, in court, Dershowitz would have been quick to deny his client if he thought it prudent to keep him off the stand. But whatever the strategy, Dershowitz was (a) anxious to be on the show, but (b) un-budgeable in his insistence that Reems also be on it.

I conferred with producer Warren Steibel and said: Okay. Invite Reems. I'll simply ignore him.

Which I did, addressing not one word to him throughout the hour. Occasionally he bleated in with a self-serving irrelevancy, which I made it a fastidious point to ignore. My feeling, as suggested above, was that although Reems might emerge as the vehicle on which an important constitutional point would emerge, a public judgment of his chosen occupation need not be suspended. He deserved (was my point) the ostracism anyone deserves who makes his living by exhibitionistic ob-scenity. I was amused, though not surprised, that Alan Dershowitz revealed on the program that he himself had never seen the movie *Deep Throat*. That was a piquant touch: it enabled him to say, in effect, "I am defending a man for taking part in a movie. What is in that movie is so irrelevant to the defense that I shall not even bother to view it."

We began with the basic question: Were films entitled to the identical protections promised by the Constitution to the press?

DERSHOWITZ: If we simply passed a law saying, "From now on, films are not covered by the First Amendment," that wouldn't convert us into a totalitarian society automatically. But it's a better society which [gives] vigorous support of *any* media, any film, no matter what its content.

WFB: Well, *I* don't think it's necessarily a better society. Surely a society that condones—it having the presumed power not to condone—the reduction of sex to its exclusive biological dimensions is no more commendable than a society that reduces liquor to its pure alcoholic effect?

DERSHOWITZ: See, here's the essential fallacy of your view. Your view suggests that by *allowing* something under the First Amendment, the society condones it. My view is that society does not condone something just because it *permits* it. Now, if you take the view that it condones it by permitting it, then you're going down a slippery slope. Then the society always has to ask the question: Is this something we want to condone and encourage? You and I would probably agree that we don't want to condone a great many of these things.

WFB: I shouldn't have said "condone." That's a legitimate point. I should have said "licenses," and I think that's an important distinction. The whole approach of the Genocide Convention, for instance, whose impulse came after a bloody experience thirty years ago in Germany, assumes that words have consequences.

DERSHOWITZ: I believe they do.

The distinctions here being approached are socially critical, legally elusive. Under the Genocide Convention, it is legally prohibited to advocate genocidal attitudes. Under *Beauharnais* v. *Illinois* (1952), the Court confirmed the constitutionality of a statute that made it a criminal offense to advocate genocide. Dershowitz was examining, quite properly, the question of whether the law could deny anyone's right to advocate anything. The two-decades-long fight over the Smith Act,

which forbade the advocacy of the overthrow of the government by
force or violence, suggests the general confusion on the subject. In any
event, Dershowitz was here correct on the narrow point that in refrain-
ing from illegalizing obscenity, the Court was not implying that the
law—or the society that makes those laws—advocates obscenity.

WFB: And certainly anyone, a substantial part of whose vicari-
                 ous experience in sex is encouraged in the kind of reduc-
                 tionism that the porno market caters to, is a target of
                 coarsened human sensibilities. And if indeed *no* freedom
                 can survive—as was predicted by *The Federalist Papers*—
                 except in a *virtuous* citizenry, it becomes a legitimate polit-
                 ical concern of society to discourage such sentiments,
                 whether they are genocidal or whether they are reduction-
                 ist in respect of the human body.

DERSHOWITZ: I don't disagree with you on that. You may be surprised
                 to hear that. I really do believe that words have impact on
                 conduct and that pornography, in fact, may coarsen sen-
                 sibilities. I think that there are a great many things in our
                 world that coarsen sensibilities, and that I would prefer to
                 do without. On the other hand, the real issue between us
                 is whether it is an appropriate tool of society to ban the
                 kind of speech which may, in fact, coarsen conduct. And
                 I would draw a sharp distinction, as I think the Constitu-
                 tion does, between courses of conduct which encourage
                 genocide, which encourage racial hatred, and those that
                 have much more subtle, much less discernible, much more
                 questionable impact. Because to move toward a regime of
                 censorship on the ground of heightening sensitivities—I
                 think the cost simply isn't worth the very, very prob-
                 lematic benefits that one might expect in return.

Two further questions stood out. First, is the government legitimately
concerned with obscenity? If so, then clearly it had to be concerned with
Deep Throat. The objection that a government permitted to move
against *Deep Throat* will tomorrow move against the Song of Solomon
is the generically antigovernment argument that, ultimately, only the
anarchist is comfortable with. On most questions of government authority I am much nearer to the anarchists' position than Dershowitz tends

to be. But the intellectual argument—*Thou shalt not stand in the way
of a reader and the reading matter that reader elects to read*—tends to
estop other, graduated considerations. The slippery-slope argument is
widely ignored by those who nevertheless adduce it when convenient.
A government given the uninhibited right to tax can end up taxing 100
percent (Communism, in the raw, does this in effect). But it is also true
that, in some areas, government has retreated from the temptation to
enhance its power, as, for instance, government in the United States
retreated from the exercise of capital punishment as a sanction against
unlawful behavior.

The second question had to do with the prospective universalization
of the standards of the discrete community. Does the definition of a
federal obscenity crime, pronounced as such by a jury in Memphis,
defensibly set standards for San Francisco and New York? The 1973
ruling (*Miller* v. *California*) of the Court spoke of "community standards," and it can hardly be denied that these are different in Memphis
and in Venice, California. What emerges is the technical difficulty of
regulating the distribution of material deemed acceptable in Sodom, but
not in Middletown. And then one runs into the question: Whom do you
consult, in San Francisco, in deciding whether a movie appeals only to
the prurient interest? A jury of whose peers? Harry Reems'?

The Supreme Court, in short, enunciated an unworkable criterion for
judging obscenity. Perhaps because there is no workable criterion. We
have here one of those bridges, impassable, between intellectual refine-
ments and dolichocephalic law. No sober American could judge *Deep
Throat* to be other than obscenity, pure and simple. But that judgment
doesn't animate a stillborn law, as Dershowitz demonstrated when, in
due course, he got Reems out of trouble: a federal district judge over-
turned his conviction.

On a later program, Dershowitz and I discussed the question of AIDS
and civil liberties. It was that discussion that gave rise to the whole
business of Buckley-wants-to-tattoo-all-homosexuals. It is instructive
for personal and professional reasons to study what was said and, subsequently, written, in a column in *The New York Times.*

At the time of the Dershowitz discussion (December 1985) we knew
less about AIDS than we now do. Mr. Dershowitz believed that only
10 to 20 percent of those who carried the virus would die of it, and I
had no grounds to challenge that estimate (we now know it is much
much higher: perhaps, if Dr. Norman Ross Tamarkin is correct, even

as high as 100 percent). And it was not known with certainty whether contamination could be effected by casual encounters (we now know that it cannot be). It had recently been announced that the army would test all two million of its members for AIDS. Dershowitz agreed that such a test was reasonable even if, in order to confirm a positive test, it was required to test again and even a third time. Did Dershowitz agree that an AIDS-infected soldier should be (honorably) discharged? He had no trouble with that, "so long as we have some assurance that it [the discharge] is not being used as a subterfuge to simply discriminate against gay men."

WFB: What would be your attitude toward some kind of ineffaceable mark on a human body to be implanted in the event that AIDS were recognized?

DERSHOWITZ: We're making the jump now from the virus to the AIDS, right?

WFB: Well, he's got the antibodies and as I understand it, we don't know (a) whether he will die himself, or (b) whether he will communicate it; but he can. . . . In either case, we both agree that if John Jones were in every sense of the word moral, he would inform his sexual partner that he had it, right?

DERSHOWITZ: That's right.

WFB: Okay. Now, hypothetically, what would be your response to a law that required that person to carry on his body—and presumably it could be on a remote part of his body under the circumstances—some sign that would alert—

DERSHOWITZ: A scarlet letter—

WFB: A scarlet letter. Yes.

DERSHOWITZ: But one that was far less visible—

WFB: A scarlet letter was supposed to be very visible.

DERSHOWITZ: This would be a kind of bluish, a little letter, a kind of little arm-thing that you might wear but you put it somewhere else?

WFB: Yes, but something that would be visible to somebody who
                was engaged in a practice in which it was likely that he
                would see it.

DERSHOWITZ: And it would say in the small print, basically, "If you're
                close enough to read this, be careful."

WFB: That's right. . . . I am asking you whether the idea of
                required identification of that kind—some people, for in-
                stance, when they get driver's licenses and need glasses,
                have to have on there that they need glasses or else they
                can't drive. Now this becomes very relevant when you're
                driving. When you are in the business of homosexual sex,
                presumably there is a counterpart to that point.

DERSHOWITZ: Would you let me throw the question back at you? If, as
                has happened, a rector of a church or—as happened in one
                case—a priest or a nun got the AIDS virus through blood
                transfusions, would you require that priest or nun or vicar
                or somebody who you would have no reason to believe
                would be (a) immoral, (b) dishonest—would you require
                them to carry that demarcation too? Or would you only
                limit it to people who had AIDS—

WFB: No, no, no. I would be impartial in the application of this
                law. I'd have a twelve-year-old child do it if he had gotten
                the disease from his diseased mother. It seems to me the
                idea is to protect people we have a public obligation to
                figure out a way of protecting.

DERSHOWITZ: Why shouldn't [everybody] be required to subject himself
                to the tests?

WFB: I share an instinctive dislike for that kind of thing, but at
                the same time I recognize that we have been doing it
                [compulsory social hygiene] for a long time. Every time I
                fly on an airplane, my baggage has to be inspected. Every
                time I marry I have to get a Wasserman test. All children
                have to have polio shots.

DERSHOWITZ: We would require [if we had compulsory testing] two
                million people to know something that they didn't want
                to know.

WFB: . . . If [the identifying mark] was on a concealed part of the body, then most people would not know.

DERSHOWITZ: No no, I'm saying the person himself—if you are going to have it put in a concealed part of the body, it seems to me the next step is mandatory testing, because otherwise what you are going to do is you're going to create a disincentive for testing. If you are going to say that anybody who tests positive on this has to do things and carry certain signs, everybody is going to say, "I am not going to get tested unless they make me get tested."

WFB: Oh, I don't know, because that's the same person who *wants* to avoid contamination by somebody else. And after all, if this is going to become increasingly a heterosexual problem, with infected men passing it along to women and—God help them—to little children, it seems to me that we have something very like a common concern crystallizing.

A few months later, at the urging of *The New York Times,* Dershowitz and I shared an Op-Ed spread on combating the AIDS epidemic. In that column, I spoke of two hypothetical schools of thought. The first (School A) is concerned primarily to protect the homosexual, i.e., to gain for him civil rights and general respectability. The second (School B) argues from the mandate to guard against an epidemic threat. I wrote that School B was influenced by "currently accepted statistics, [e.g.,] *The Economist* [which] recently raised the possibility that 'the AIDS virus will have killed more than 250,000 Americans in eight years' time.' Moreover, if the epidemic extended to that point, it would burst through existing boundaries. There would then be 'no guarantee that the disease will remain largely confined to groups at special risk, such as homosexuals, hemophiliacs, and people who inject drugs intravenously. If AIDS were to spread through the general population, it would become a catastrophe.' "

On that basis, I wrote, in my hypothetical exchange between a spokesman of School A and one from School B,

> *"Is it then proposed by School B that AIDS carriers should be publicly identified as such?*

"The evidence is not completely in as to the communicability of the disease. While much has been said that is reassuring, the moment has not yet come when men and women of science are unanimously agreed that AIDS cannot be casually communicated. Let us be patient on that score, pending any tilt in the evidence: If the news is progressively reassuring [as it has been, 1985–1988], public identification would not be necessary. If it turns in the other direction and AIDS develops among, say, children who have merely roughhoused with other children who suffer from AIDS, then more drastic segregation measures would be called for.

"But if the time has not come, and may never come, for public identification, what then of private identification?

"Everyone [this is the spokesman for School B speaking] with AIDS should be tattooed in the upper forearm, to protect common-needle users, and on the buttocks, to prevent the victimization of other homosexuals.

"You have got to be kidding! That's exactly what we suspected all along! You are calling for the return of the Scarlet Letter, but only for homosexuals! [Italics in the original.]

"Answer: The Scarlet Letter was designed to stimulate public obloquy. The AIDS tattoo is designed for private protection. And the whole point of this is that we are not talking about a kidding matter. [If] our society is generally threatened, then in order to fight AIDS we need the civil equivalent of universal military training."

Well then. The record is pretty clear that the effort was never to "stigmatize homosexuals," though that charge has been made, over and over. In due course, having been told that the mere mention of "tattoo" brings to mind Nazi extermination camps (my response: Because they used barbed wire in Buchenwald to keep men and women from freedom ought not to stigmatize ranchers who use barbed wire to separate, say, bulls from cows), I formally withdrew the suggestion even though it was never more than hypothetical. But I have permitted myself to wonder how many men and women have died, or have been sentenced to death, since 1985, by society's failure to come up with a means of protecting the uncontaminated and unknowing from the contaminated who knew.

The issue of gun control is not unrelated to the larger view of civil liberties. Stated bluntly, those who have guns and wish to continue to have them see in the Second Amendment ("The right of the people to keep and bear arms, shall not be infringed") a "right" to own such guns. The conflicting position bases itself on civil liberties, in that its proponents can point to the number of innocent people killed or maimed by guns used by irresponsible persons.

The simmering issue began seriously to boil after successive political assassinations and attempted assassinations during the stormy decade. John F. Kennedy. Martin Luther King. Robert F. Kennedy. George Wallace. In 1968, reacting directly to three assassinations, Congress passed a law placing severe restrictions on interstate commerce in certain kinds of weapons (Lee Harvey Oswald bought the rifle he killed Kennedy with from a catalogue published in another state). In 1977, Congressman Abner Mikva was widely acknowledged as one of the most eloquent and resourceful advocates of gun control. His proposals fell short of requiring Americans to hand in all their guns (though he favored a bounty on guns handed in), but he backed a prohibition against any further production or sale of most categories of guns.

I remember shortly before this program reading and being greatly influenced by an article published in *The Public Interest* by B. Bruce-Briggs (1976). I found it a devastating challenge of the feasibility of prohibiting guns in the United States. He made one original point of special interest, as we will see.

Robert Kukla was the principal source of polemical energy behind the National Rifle Association, and as such the most conspicuous opponent of further gun control legislation. His book *Gun Control* is a most comprehensive study of the subject, done from the position of an opponent of legislation (he wanted existing laws restricting firearms to be relaxed).

I asked Congressman Mikva whether he thought the 1968 law, given the concessions Congress had made to the gun lobby, all but useless.

MIKVA: It doesn't perform many useful purposes. Part of the problem—whenever I hear Mr. Kukla and the others who advocate the repeal of the existing gun laws—is that I really wonder whether they mean what they say, and how far they would go. I heard Mr. Kukla use the word "inconvenience"—that the '68 law has inconvenienced some sportsmen and others who want to own guns. Ten thousand people were inconvenienced to the maximum last year by handguns. They were killed by them. I hear him say that he really thinks there should be no controls on adults who don't fall under psychotic or criminal [disqualifications]. I challenge that. Does he *really* mean that a three-year-old should be able to go out and buy a gun? I don't believe that. Does he *really* mean you should be able to carry a gun down the streets of New York, just in case somebody wants to rip you off?

WFB: We will have no *reductio ad absurdum* on this program. [*Laughter*]

MIKVA: Well, isn't that what the NRA is basically saying? As I've heard them from time to time? That they are opposed to what's on the books, by and large, and are opposed to anything we propose to put on the books? Now, I have read most of your own books, Mr. Buckley, and I subscribe to the doctrine that government ought not go beyond where it is essential and where it can be proved to be performing an essential common good. I think the common good here is to get rid of handguns, which are not a hunting weapon.

WFB: I happen to have hunted a great deal with handguns.

MIKVA: What kind of hunting?

WFB: Woodchucks, snakes.

MIKVA: What kind of handguns? Those little baby .22s that they sell on Saturday nights?

WFB: No, six-shooters.

MIKVA: Pretty long barrel, right?

WFB: Yes.

MIKVA: I'll let you have *your* gun. That isn't a gun that's scaring people off the streets of Detroit and Chicago and New York.

WFB: You mean you will amend your act right now to permit a six-inch barrel? [*Laughter*]

MIKVA: If you will help me pass it, yes. [*Laughter*]

WFB: But, Congressman, have you ever meditated on the statis-
          tic of how many people's lives are *saved* in virtue of their
          having guns and discouraging people to burglarize or rob
          them?

MIKVA: Yes. There, too, a couple of studies were made recently.
          The odds are six to one, approximately. You might as well
          play Russian roulette with a gun. You are six times more
          apt to kill your wife or your children or yourself than you
          are to shoot a burglar. But besides that, as a gun owner
          and shooter, wouldn't you agree with me that if you really
          want to defend yourself in your house, wouldn't you
          rather have a double-barreled shotgun than a baby .22?

WFB: Well, I have both, as a matter of fact. There's a certain
          mobility that a handgun gives you. But the figure of six to
          one is called "ingeniously specious" by Mr. Bruce-Briggs
          in the current issue of *Public Interest,* and he points out
          that it does not take into account such statistical factors
          as how many people are in fact discouraged from coming
          into a house in which it is known that there are handguns.
          For instance, there's much less burglary in the South and
          the Southwest because it is widely assumed by putative
          burglars that to break into a house is to invite some sort
          of a firestorm. Now, the fact that six times as many shoot-
          ings occur in houses that *have* guns as *don't* have guns
          seems to me—well, the tautology is, you [obviously] can't
          have a shooting where—

MIKVA: No, no, no. This isn't against houses that don't have guns.
          This is for every person who successfully defends himself
          against an intruder with a gun.

WFB: But how do you know if he hasn't been successful preemp-
          tively? If you decide—you, as a burglar—not to *enter* a
          particular house because you know that that person is
          armed, how does *that* datum work into your statistics?

MIKVA: Well, the preempting point is answered, as far as I'm
          concerned, by pointing out that you're more likely to be
          broken into if you own a gun, statistically, than if you
          don't own a gun.

WFB: Why?

MIKVA: Well, that's just the way the statistics break down. I'll tell you why.

WFB: The statistics are idiotic if they say that. How on earth— [*Laughter*]

MIKVA: Well, more houses where guns are owned are broken into than houses where guns aren't owned—

WFB: But that's like saying more people die of tuberculosis in Arizona—

MIKVA: I'm speaking—you won't even let me finish the statistic. Taking into account the fact that a lot of people don't own guns—a lot more people *don't* own guns than *do* own guns. One of the reasons is that a gun is a valuable thing to steal, isn't it?

WFB: No.

MIKVA: No?

WFB: No. Twenty-five dollars? Not that valuable.

MIKVA: It's valuable for lots of other reasons. They are a very, very fungible kind of item.

WFB: I've read your speeches and I've never heard you represent that they are difficult to acquire.

MIKVA: No, they aren't, but they're *nice* to acquire—

WFB: There are forty million handguns around.

MIKVA: They're nice to acquire and whenever you acquire one you usually can get rid of it for scratch. As I said, it's a very fungible item. You can exchange it for all kinds of things on the street, with a fence, you name it. And even—

WFB: The last thing I want is for you to strain your credibility. If you're telling me that somebody is going to try to break into a house because he knows that there is a twenty-five-dollar loaded pistol there waiting to shoot him if he breaks in—

MIKVA: No, I don't want to—I thought the rule of *reductio ad absurdum* applied to the host, too. [*Laughter*] No, the point I'm making very simply is that as a defense weapon, the handgun, the concealable weapon, is a very, very inept and inapt weapon, and the reason is that it is not effective.

WFB: Mr. Kukla, you wanted to comment on that.

KUKLA: Well, yes, as a matter of fact it's exceedingly difficult to know how many individuals have successfully defended themselves with a firearm in their home, not only for the reasons you cited, but because there are no statistical records kept of such incidents, particularly if the firearm is not fired. If a person happened to be living in the city of New York, for example, where people are not allowed to have a gun except by permit, and if they happen to have an [illegal] firearm, and if they were successful in routing someone who attempted to break into their home or apartment, it's unlikely that [the incident] will be reported to the police. Now even in *those* instances, where a firearm had to be discharged to scare off an intruder or in fact to shoot an intruder, police statistics simply are not geared to maintaining that kind of record.

WFB: Fired for self-defense?

KUKLA: For self-defense, for [testing] a collection, for target shooting, for informal recreation, for side arms while on hunting trips, or any number of reasons. And I submit that it's not the business of government to decide for you whether or not you should do that.

It was this point, made by Bruce-Briggs, that I was especially anxious to insert—

WFB: How do you handle that argument, Mr. Mikva? Suppose you've got, say, a seventy-year-old couple in the Bronx—and there have been some rather arresting stories about things that have happened to people in the Bronx recently, causing one couple finally to commit suicide as an act of desperation, having twice been mugged and tortured.

MIKVA: Well, first of all, they were mugged once on the *street,* as
            I recall. Now, I want to know, Mr. Buckley or Mr. Kukla,
            do you think people should be allowed—

WFB: No. Well, maybe they were mugged on the street also, but
            I don't think they were tortured on the street. That would
            be unusual even in New York. [*Laughter*]

MIKVA: No, they were mugged once. Most fear, at this point, is
            fear of *street* crime, much more fear of being mugged on
            the street.

WFB: That's right. They don't walk on the street, most of these
            people. They just stay home.

MIKVA: So when you *do* walk on the street, should you be allowed
            to carry a handgun? That's when you need it the most.

WFB: Well, I think there's an interesting argument. The respon-
            sibility of the state is to protect you.

MIKVA: Right.

WFB: If the state doesn't protect you, what do you then do? This
            is a problem that has been faced by political philosophy
            for two millennia.

MIKVA: For thousands of years, right.

WFB: Now, the chief of police of Los Angeles says that in his
            opinion—and I quote him—"Anybody would be a fool
            not to arm himself in Los Angeles," even while the *sheriff*
            of Los Angeles County wants stricter gun control. The
            head of Scotland Yard says that in his judgment it's a very
            interesting argument [whether to outlaw handguns in
            America] but purely academic—because you just don't
            undertake to disarm a nation with forty million arms. You
            just can't do it. An anthropologist points out that in Japan
            there is very little crime and they have very strict gun
            control laws, but among Japanese-Americans, where there
            is no gun control law, the crime rate is even less.
                If the police will guarantee some sort of a safe passage
            between your apartment building in the Bronx and the
            Grade A Market and back—we're for that, right?—that's

one thing. But since you *can't* have police around the clock, there's a case to be made for looking after oneself.

MIKVA: But not with guns.

A good example of a moot point: Both sides, really, have unanswerable arguments. As it happened, nothing came of the Mikva bill, and he sits now on the U.S. Circuit Court of Appeals, appointed to that position by President Carter, opposed, but not shot down, by the gun lobby.

Then—yet another civil liberties question—there was the question of forced busing and related measures designed to integrate racially the schools. In New York City, the Lindsay administration separated public school teachers by race and then assigned them to schools in rough proportion to the school's racial population.

Protest against such abstract remedies (what if there weren't enough qualified black teachers?) was traditionally associated with segregationists and untamed libertarians. Quietly, however, the critical scholarly juices were running, and with the publication in 1977 of *Government by Judiciary: The Transformation of the Fourteenth Amendment,* by Professor Raoul Berger of Harvard, apologists for judicial authoritarianism in teacher-student-racial composition cases have had the burden of the case. On reading this book, Professor Philip Kurland of the University of Chicago Law School wrote, "Professor Berger has made a historical effort addressed at what is surely—if not yet recognized—to be the most immediate constitutional crisis of our present time—the usurpation by the judiciary of general governmental powers on the pretext that its authority derives from the Fourteenth Amendment."

Professor Berger had made a big name for himself in extrascholarly circles with the publication of his book on presidential impeachment. It was an invitation to Congress to proceed against Nixon after Watergate. To be taking, now, a line associated with antebellum conservatism shocked his professional colleagues into relative silence. But his case was arresting. He said, on *Firing Line,* that when a President of the United States, after conferring with the Black Caucus of the Congress, calls in an Attorney General and dictates to him the line he should take on a pending constitutional question (as President Carter had done in the case of Bakke), we cannot be said to be living under the rule of law; and constitutional language, in such circumstances, has lost its meaning.

Professor Berger, who believes ardently in racial equality, stressed the point that his own, or anyone else's, advocacy of this or any other social or political program does not entitle him to interpret the Fourteenth Amendment as a mandate for a policy that did not issue under that Amendment's auspices. There is a difference between saying "Any right granted to a white man must equally be granted to a black man" and saying "Here is a right previously granted only by this or that state legislature. Henceforward, we shall universalize it."

Berger warned those who thought the shortcut to racial equality was to make their own paper doll out of the Fourteenth Amendment to the Constitution that the strategic security of the people's liberties was at stake. Madison warned, "If the sense in which the Constitution was accepted and ratified by the nation . . . be not the guide expounding it, there can be no security for a consistent and stable government, more than for a faithful exercise of its powers." And Jefferson: "Our peculiar security is in the possession of a written constitution. Let us not make it a blank paper by construction." "When Chief Justice Warren asserted that 'we cannot turn back the clock to 1868,' " Berger warned, "he in fact rejected the framers' intention as irrelevant."

BERGER: It still is incumbent under traditional canons to look at the intention of the legislatures, because from the Middle Ages on, the meaning of the law is always to be ascertained in what the fellows who wrote it meant. If you say that what you meant doesn't matter—and some libertarians have been so intoxicated that they've said it—it's like Humpty Dumpty telling Alice, "When you say something, it means what I say it means."

WFB: That's where you get the idea of the roving constitutional convention that you made so many references to?

BERGER: Yes, that's what the Court's been doing. I am a liberal, but I will say defiantly that my commitment to the Constitution rises paramount to every other consideration. It's not that I love segregation. In fact one of the very painful things that I had to confront was that I find myself in bed with people I detest. They're going to applaud me whereas those whose respect I esteem are going to criticize me.

The argument over original intent ("original understanding," Robert Bork prefers to call it) raged on into the next decade and probably reached its rhetorical peak during the hearings on the nomination of Judge Bork in 1987.

I became a letter-writing friend of Raoul Berger, eighty-seven years old at this writing. I was fascinated among other things by his background. In 1927, he was a violinist of the Cleveland Symphony Orchestra! One day he laid his violin to one side, and went to the academy. I asked him if he had ever heard about the meeting at Versailles of Clemenceau and Paderewski:

> Clemenceau: *You, Mr. Prime Minister, are the same Paderewski who was the greatest pianist in the world?*
>
> Paderewski: *The same.*
>
> Clemenceau: *And now you are Prime Minister of Poland. What a comedown!*

I assured him I thought him as fine a jurisprudential historian as he had been a musician.

I got involved in another civil liberties suit, this time as the plaintiff.

One day, as I was walking out of the television studio after an appearance on the Merv Griffin show, a man in his forties, rather seedy in appearance and just a little menacing in manner (probably he was hired to perform this duty), approached me and told me that unless I joined the American Federation of Television and Radio Artists I would be prohibited from appearing on television. This was in *1972*.

So I filed a lawsuit. I took my complaint to a federal court in New York and invited the American Civil Liberties Union to back *my* civil liberty for a change. I heard back from the executive director of the New York Civil Liberties Union, Mr. Arieh Neyer, that the ACLU had many years earlier adopted the position that a requirement of union membership was not a violation of civil liberties. However, he acknowledged that my own case, insofar as it introduced the question of free speech, might be exceptional; accordingly, he agreed to take the question to the directors.

Arieh Neyer, a graduate of Cornell, had been with the ACLU for years and had played an important role in its affairs, becoming executive director of the New York Civil Liberties Union. Michael Harrington, whom we have met above, dismissed my lawsuit as a threat to union security (which, in a way, it was: If nobody wants to belong to a union, its security is certainly jeopardized). Harrington was simply one of the legion, mostly of the political left, who confer upon labor unions rights (e.g., to close down a newspaper, or a public school, or a fire department) they would refuse to confer upon Congress, the Executive, the Supreme Court, or God. For the socialist (Michael was then the chairman of the Socialist Party of the United States), the labor union is the mythical vehicle for the emancipation of the working classes, never mind the historical nuisance that (effective) labor unions (Solidarity in Poland is now illegal) are not permitted in Communist societies.

NEYER: Since you wrote to me I've been doing some thinking about the old ACLU position—

WFB: Which distinguishes you from Mr. Harrington.

HARRINGTON: I don't think there's a free-speech issue involved in the least, because it's not a question of one's *having* to be a member of the union as a prerequisite to *appear* on television. I am not a member of the union and here I am appearing on television. When you were a candidate for Mayor of the City of New York, Mr. Buckley, you were not a member of the union, yet you were on television all the time. The issue is, what you have to do when you go into *business* to be on television in a jurisdiction where a majority of the employees have freely voted to protect their job security by way of the union. Under those circumstances, not as a *political* speaker exercising First Amendment rights, but as a *businessman* under the interstate commerce clause, you're required to join a union where the employees freely vote so, and I think it's a good idea.

WFB: Well, that's very reassuring; the trouble is that AFTRA doesn't agree with you, because, for instance, when I wrote them on the third of November, 1964, to tell them that the scheduled *Firing Line* [I referred to the postponement of *Firing Line*'s inauguration because of my candidacy for mayor] had been put off and I then asked whether I could proceed as I had been doing—as you do—without joining the union, I got a letter which said, "Dear Mr. Buckley: In answer to your letter, please be advised that you are *still* required to be a member of AFTRA notwithstanding that the television series which you were to have hosted has been canceled."

HARRINGTON: I'll let AFTRA speak for themselves. All I *do* know is that no political candidate exercising his right under the First Amendment is required to belong to the union. Free for you, free for me, free for any serious candidate.

WFB: *Serious* candidate? That excludes us, doesn't it? [*Laughter*]

NEYER: Can I respond to Mr. Harrington?

WFB: Yes.

NEYER: I think the point he raises is a defensible position. But it seems to me that he's suggesting that the free-speech aspects of communication through radio and television are limited to those segments of radio and television which are specifically news-broadcast times, or times that are used to interview candidates for public office.

I'm not entirely persuaded of that. I think there may be some free-speech aspects to regular programming on television. I assume, without knowing a great deal about AFTRA, that the distinction that AFTRA makes between Mr. Harrington and Mr. Buckley is that you, Mr. Harrington, don't have a regular program on television; Mr. Buckley does have a regular program. But clearly, Mr. Buckley uses his regular program as an opportunity to air points of view. Clearly, his point of view would have less access to radio and television if he were limited to an occasional guest appearance and could not have a regular program.

HARRINGTON: What I'm saying is I would be delighted to support a law that would provide free television time for William F. Buckley's points of view and all other points of view on a democratic basis. The issue we are facing *here* is in the area of *employment*—hiring [policies] where workers in

an industry have freely decided to follow this policy. Now,
I think that there is something somewhat disingenuous in
Mr. Buckley's lawsuit in the sense that he invokes it under
the auspices of the First Amendment–newsman–political
free speech. He even says, in a column, that perhaps a
union shop is good for steelworkers. But, interestingly
enough, Mr. Buckley is supported in his lawsuit by the
National Right to Work Legal Defense Fund; that is to
say, by an organization which is not concerned simply
with First Amendment freedoms, but which is out to *destroy* [the unions] altogether. And I think the *real* point
(hiding behind a First Amendment question on television,
which I think is spurious) is an attack on the principle of
union security and trade unionism itself.

   Harrington was saying that there are those who oppose compulsory
unionism, and that I was probably one of them; and that therefore my
pleading the First Amendment was disingenuous—the Bill of Rights
serving merely as a crutch for my anti-union bias. Fair enough. But it
became necessary for me to move in heavily.

WFB: Well, let me talk a little while here. In the first place, you
              managed, with extraordinary serenity, to slide over the
              fact that you had gotten the history [of my dealings with
              AFTRA] exactly wrong on this particular lawsuit. Your
              opening statement was based on a distinction being drawn
              between people who work regularly on television and
              radio and people who don't. I shattered that distinction by
              quoting from a single letter of AFTRA. You regrouped
              rather successfully, but immediately went on to cite a
              whole other series of dissatisfactions which are irrelevant
              to that particular point. The record remains that AFTRA
              said that *anybody,* irrespective of whether he has a regular
              [or irregular] role on television or radio, *must* be a mem-
              ber of that union in order to be permitted to proceed to
              work on radio or television. Now your saying that Na-
              tional Right to Work's [backing] makes the whole thing
              disingenuous is the equivalent of my saying that the
              ACLU is disingenuous to the extent that it is in favor of
              civil liberties because here and there it is concerned with—

with the protection of somebody who doesn't *believe* in civil liberties.

HARRINGTON: No, the—

WFB: Now, there's nothing hidden about National Right to Work's positions. It is a committee that says that people ought to be able to work, irrespective of whether they belong to any private organization. It is a position which was rather ringingly endorsed by the ACLU in 1954 when it argued against the boycott of the Hollywood Ten, you will remember, in which the ACLU said "The right to work is a human right, a personal right, a constitutional right, and the opportunity to earn a living cannot be unjustly withheld from a man without doing violence to the constitutional guarantees protecting his life, liberty, property, and assuring him equal protection of the law."

HARRINGTON: Well, I completely agree with that.

WFB: Now, it makes no difference whether the Right to Work group believes that unions should be abolished, or whether the Right to Work group is a useful vehicle in the instant case. I don't have to believe in anything the ACLU believes in to ask the ACLU to make common cause with me on this particular—

HARRINGTON: Well, let me—could I pursue the question?

WFB: Yes.

HARRINGTON: You mentioned in a column that newsmen and analysts are different from steelworkers.

WFB: Yes.

HARRINGTON: Are you in favor of the union shop for steelworkers? Or put it this way: Are you against the right-to-work law in the case of steelworkers?

Harrington knew that I was in favor of right-to-work laws, and I knew that he knew I was: I had declaimed from the rooftops on the subject. But I thought to deny him an easy departure from the more difficult argument of AFTRA vs. me—

WFB: You know what? I'm going to refuse to answer that—
                 because for me to answer it would distract from the point
                 I'm trying to make. The point is that when the people who
                 wrote the Constitution of the United States sat down to
                 enumerate rights they chose certain rights to emphasize:
                 the right to practice your religion, the right to speak freely,
                 and the right to assemble. Now I don't say, on the princi-
                 ple of *numero unius exclusio alterius* [the lawyers' adage
                 that by enumerating the few, you exclude the many], that
                 they meant to say that *steelworkers* have no rights; but I
                 do mean to say that a body of positive law grew up,
                 post-Constitution, on the basis of which we decided what
                 are the respective legal rights of unions and steelworkers.
                 But the right I'm talking about—free speech—is a *very*
                 distinctive right, which is ringed around with protections
                 which it is your professional and personal obligation to
                 guarantee; and I'm wondering why you're so indifferent to
                 it.

HARRINGTON: I will fight like the dickens for your right to express your-
                 self in any way you want, or anybody else: a Communist,
                 fascist, anything in between. I will fight for your right to
                 get access to television, free. That's not the question you're
                 raising; you're raising the question: Do you have a right
                 in following a *commercial* pursuit—

WFB: Why do you call it a commercial pursuit?

HARRINGTON: —to act in such a way—

WFB: Why do you call it—now *wait* a minute; why do you call
                 it a *commercial* pursuit? Because AFTRA does not distin-
                 guish between the two.

HARRINGTON: Now look—

WFB: On the contrary, they *want* to commercialize [television
                 appearances]. If you tell AFTRA, "Look, I guarantee to
                 appear on these stations, and these offers [to appear] are
                 for *nothing* [i.e., for no compensation]," they will tell you
                 that's *precisely* what they *won't* allow you to do!

HARRINGTON: I have no idea—

WFB: *They're* insisting on commercializing it.

HARRINGTON: I have no idea what AFTRA's position is.

WFB: I'm telling you what it is. Now you do know.

A not uninstructive exchange. On the one hand I kept out of the discussion my hostility to those labor unions that insist on membership by all workers; on the other hand, Michael stressed his belief in the right to speak, alongside the right of the union to organize. Precisely the point of the AFTRA suit was that it involved a case of either/or.

The lawsuit went on for years, from the courts, to the National Labor Relations Board, back to the courts. The final result was an agreement, more or less forced on AFTRA by the Court of Appeals. No one henceforward needed to join AFTRA or to obey its instructions. But anyone regularly appearing on television had to pay AFTRA dues. I had substantially, though not wholly, won my point. AFTRA could not order me to strike, or punish me for crossing a picket line. On the other hand, I am still required to contribute to the union. The precedent became important in the news and entertainment world. AFTRA hasn't, since the concordat, called a national strike, or sought to fine a member for crossing a picket line.

PHOTOGRAPHER JAN LUKAS IN THE CONTROL ROOM

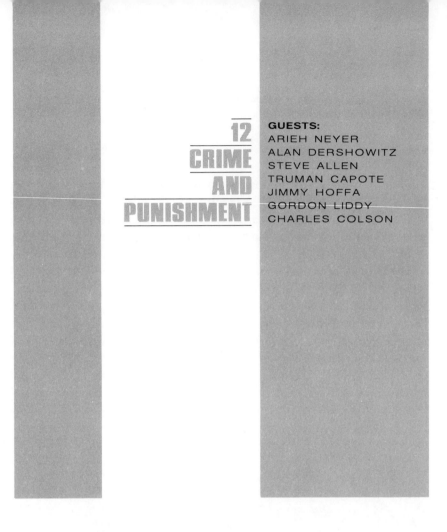

12

CRIME AND PUNISHMENT

GUESTS:
ARIEH NEYER
ALAN DERSHOWITZ
STEVE ALLEN
TRUMAN CAPOTE
JIMMY HOFFA
GORDON LIDDY
CHARLES COLSON

H ave you noticed that most people have emphatic ideas on how to cope with crime and punishment? Probably the reason for this is that crime is everywhere, and everywhere deplorable. From this it follows that criminals are everywhere. But the treatment of them?

The questions one would expect, arise. What about the right of the defendant, the fruits of the adversary process, the question of capital punishment? Many of our guests have addressed themselves to this or that aspect of crime and punishment. Herewith a collection special in that it is, as these things go, almost entirely devoid of clichés, but by no means devoid of drama. Try to get that from your neighbor, on the subject of Crime and Punishment.

. . .

Arieh Neyer (previously mentioned) made several appearances on *Firing Line.* We discussed at one point the rights, progressively expanded by the Warren Court, of the defendant.

WFB: Mr. Neyer, isn't it true that the Supreme Court seems to be saying, "Look, what's important is the *procedures* by which guilt or innocence is established, and the only way to see to it that the procedures that we insist on be constitutional is to release even people who are palpably guilty."

Let me give you an example. There's a fellow called Townsend, as you probably know, who was arrested for murder, and in the course of his stay in jail it was discovered that he was suffering from pleural disorders because he was a narcotics addict. So the police obligingly gave him a drug that helps people in that condition, a drug called biosine. Well, it turned out that biosine had a most remarkable effect on the prisoner! It made him truthful. And in the course of consuming biosine, he confessed to having murdered this particular person.

Now, there it was: proved to the satisfaction of the courts, (a) that he was indeed guilty, and (b) that the police did not with malice aforethought give him biosine, intending in that way to circumnavigate the Fifth Amendment of the Constitution. Nevertheless, he was let go.

Now, as far as I can see, there's no justification for his having been let go, other than that procedure is [deemed] paramount in any confrontation between procedure and truth.

NEYER: Well, my interpretation of the Court's reasoning is that it is concerned *simultaneously* with means and ends. Even so, the Court is not saying, "Release the person." They are saying something else. They are providing *exclusionary* rules, rules which state that the fruits of an illegal search may not be used in order to convict. In a way, this was always true. There was never any authority for police to engage in illegal searches and seizures, and today, the Supreme Court—

WFB: How come customs agents can search your baggage?

NEYER: Well, I think that there are some considerable questions in that whole area involving customs agents [but] I think those are so complex that we would need a number of separate programs to discuss those. But in the general search-and-seizure cases, the exclusionary rules basically deprive the police and prosecuting officials of the *incentive* to engage in illegal search and seizure. They never did have the authority, constitutionally; but now, since they can't use the fruit of an illegal search in a court proceeding, they no longer have the incentive, and thereby they are prevented to some extent.

WFB: But don't you sometimes get the impression, Mr. Neier, that what's really happening is that the Supreme Court and you are engaged in a search for an exquisitely symmetrical means of dotting all of your i's and crossing all of your t's and coming up with some sort of a divinely [fair] judicial system, without really much reference to the problems of crime and punishment?

NEYER: I don't think it's we who are engaged in the search for the symmetrical or the ideal system. I think the search was engaged in when the Bill of Rights was incorporated into the Constitution.

And so on. It has always seemed to me that the correct balance of police power and individual rights should reflect the crime rate. The interdiction by the airlines of terrorist weapons, conducted at the expense (however trivial) of every American who steps foot on an airplane, can be demonstrated statistically to be nugatory in its accomplishments (a search of seventeen- and eighteen-year-olds going into school would probably be more productive of crime aborted). But the arguments tend to flow in on ideological barges. The largest single cause of crime in the eighties is the high price of illegal drugs. To legalize drugs would eliminate this crime, but would leave society with the social consequences of coping with its drug addicts, presumably in greater number. Even as the Civil Liberties Union is not prepared to abandon the exclusionary rule in exchange for an increase in the number of criminals apprehended, society isn't prepared to make the exchange of free drugs for less crime. The reasons are cultural, philosophical, and other: and, where possible, those who make their points attempt to tie their position to their reading of the Constitution.

ALAN DERSHOWITZ

In 1985, long after the Warren Court had given way to the Burger Court, Professor Alan Dershowitz (on to other things, after springing Harry Reems) probed some of these same issues with me. He gave his views in the coin of legal realpolitik.

WFB: I should like to begin by asking Mr. Dershowitz to explain what he means when he says that "everyone" lies in the courtroom, in the sense of telling only partial truths.

DERSHOWITZ: Well, if you start out with the assumption in criminal cases that the vast majority of people charged with crime are guilty, and I certainly start out with that assumption. My God, think of living in a country where the vast majority of people charged with crime were innocent! That may be the Soviet Union, Iran, Saudi Arabia, but it is *not* the United States. If you start out with that assumption, and then you follow that with the assumption that the job of the criminal defense lawyer is to do his or her best to present the case *for* the accused defendant, then obviously the criminal defense lawyer's job is not to help bring out the truth, the whole truth, and nothing but the truth. His job is by all lawful, proper, and ethical means to *limit* the truth from coming out. So the criminal defense lawyer certainly is *not* paid to bring the truth out.

Now. Is the *prosecutor* paid to bring the truth out? Well, surely that's his job. But with the exclusionary rule that we now have—a rule that says that even if the defendant is guilty, if the evidence was obtained unlawfully, it can't be used—there are many cases where the prosecutor [fearing that his evidence will be inadmissible] has an interest in making sure the whole truth about the manner in which the state obtained its evidence *doesn't* come out. And so there is really nobody in the process who is the Chairman in Charge of the Truth. [The truth] tends to get last place in the adversary system.

WFB: Well, then, are you [suggesting] that it is also the responsibility of the judge so to frame his charge as to induce the result that he seeks?

DERSHOWITZ: That happens often. But the judge is *also* constrained, by rules of evidence which prevent the whole truth from coming out. For example, hearsay. We all operate with hearsay in our daily lives. If we hear from a particularly reliable source, secondhand, that a statement was made, particularly a statement that the person wouldn't make unless it were true—a self-demeaning statement, for instance—we believe it. We act on it. And yet courts of law require the judge to instruct the jury not to listen to hearsay as if it were the truth. So there are all kinds of rules that operate to send the message. The adversary system of justice, though it has been proclaimed as the greatest engine of truth since the beginning of history, is *not* single-mindedly designed to pursue the truth.

WFB: Well, is it correct or incorrect to view the adversary process as an epistemological process? I.e., will it lead us to the truth, or is it more likely to be described as something which leads us to the only bearable means by which we will agree to proceed in deciding whether to put this guy in jail or not?

DERSHOWITZ: The second is much closer. It reflects both an epistemology, but also clearly a series of compromises in values. Yes, we want to get to the truth. But we want to get it through certain means. Even the Bible talks in terms of

"Justice, justice, shalt thou pursue"; and the Commentaries ask the question, "Why does the Bible mention justice twice?" Why the redundancy? And the answer given is that the *means* of justice are deemed as important as the *ends* of justice. Therefore, our legal system entails that compromise in many ways.

WFB: I forget who it was who commented on the exclusionary rule. . . . His quote was "Only a system with limitless patience with irrationality could tolerate the fact that where there has been one wrong, the defendant's, he will be punished, but where there have been two wrongs, the defendant's and the police officer's, both will go free." That truth has always struck me as paradoxical. But usually people who defend that exclusionary rule say there is no other [suitable] punishment for the prosecutor. Is that your judgment also?

DERSHOWITZ: Well, my judgment is slightly different than that. It's not a question of punishment. It's a question of incentive. If we were to eliminate the exclusionary rule, the prosecutor—by the prosecutor I mean primarily the police, people who are perhaps less well trained and less sympathetic to the Constitution—would have no incentive to comply with the Constitution. The Constitution is not a self-enforcing or obvious document.

WFB: Couldn't the court discipline him?

DERSHOWITZ: No. The problem with that is that we also have an amendment to the Constitution that says nobody can be punished without a jury, and you just won't get the juries that are prepared today to punish criminal policemen. To give you an example, in Washington, D.C., a few years ago, two FBI—high-ranking agents—broke into the homes of relatives of Weathermen and other radicals. They were clearly in the wrong in doing so. President Reagan pardoned them, to the great relief of most people, because it was felt that they were doing their job.

My feeling about the exclusionary rule is, I'd like to see it gradually wither away as we see fewer and fewer violations. Because the exclusionary rule can only operate when the police in fact violate the Constitution.

But today the exclusionary rule is a necessary evil. Some people emphasize the necessary, others emphasize the evil.

It is not, I think, that clear-cut. As witness that the courts continue to divide on whether a particular act does or does not violate the principle of excluded testimony. A recent example was the Supreme Court's ruling that the discovery of drugs in the garbage of a man's home, put out for collection by a public agency, is not an unconstitutional act of illegal search and seizure. Accept the general terms of Professor Dershowitz's schemata and you will still divide a roomful of bright students of the law on such questions as whether a drug packet discovered while legally searching for a concealed weapon validates prosecution for carrying illegal drugs. Nor would the legal fraternity unite in believing that a jury trial would be needed before administering disciplinary rebukes against police officers who violate citizens' rights.

We have heard Donald Shapiro and Ernest van den Haag discuss capital punishment. There have been others who have addressed the question on *Firing Line*. I recall that a poll published a dozen years ago seeking to accumulate and taxonomize differences of opinion between "conservatives" and "liberals" came up with capital punishment as the count on which the disagreement is most conspicuous. I.e., if there are twenty points of public policy which tend to separate the two camps, capital punishment appears first, polarizing conservatives and liberals in the greatest number under different columns.

Steve Allen, the entertainer, made reference to this hard ideological division. Allen has been a pronounced liberal ever since his anti-epiphany. He wrote, in his autobiographical *Mark It and Strike It* (1960), that at a point in his youth he resolved to jettison his inherited cultural and religious baggage, preferring to spend his life in other, looser pastures. He is a fine entertainer, married to an actress (Jayne Meadows) who for a spell in her late teens taught dancing (she was then "Jane Cotter"). Among her students were me and my siblings, attempting to learn ballroom dancing, in which she is expert.

When we met at the studio, Steve Allen approached me a little warily, because, a few months earlier, in a conversation at my parents' home in Sharon, Connecticut (he and his wife were visiting his in-laws across the street), I had persuaded him in the course of a discursive afternoon that the logic of his adamant stand against nuclear weapons (he was national cochairman, along with Norman Cousins, of the Committee for a Sane Nuclear Policy) committed him to backing a preemptive strike against the nascent nuclear-bomb facilities of Red China (as we used to call it). I promptly wrote a column ("Steve Allen/ Favors Bombing/ Of Chicom Nuke Facilities") which was widely commented on, causing among Steve's Nuclear Committee Colleagues a reaction not far removed from mass suicide. Anyway, the *Firing Line* show went on at a moment when executions had practically stopped, with the hanging of Perry Smith and Dick Hickock—done, as I think I put it at the time (on Johnny Carson's program)—primarily for the convenience of Truman Capote. Steve Allen is a lively sparring partner. . . .

WFB: Mr. Allen has asked that the conversation tonight be confined to the subject of the death penalty, and I must confess that I shall emerge as an inadequate adversary because my own thinking on the subject is confused, which, come to think of it, should make Mr. Steve Allen feel quite at home. [*Laughter*]

ALLEN: I share your confusion. It's good of you to concede it. One of the things that I hope we will get into tonight, Bill, because it interests me and I think it may reveal something about the whole issue, is why this particular issue should be one concerning which in general, granting all due exceptions, the right seems generally [on the side of] capital punishment.

WFB: I think it has to do with a general tendency in the right wing to subscribe to the notion that each person is his own decisive moral agent. I think it is correct that people who are generally associated with the left have more [frequently] adopted the theme that it is society rather than the individual which is ultimately responsible for the commission of the crime.

ALLEN: They attribute more significance to the environmental factors.

WFB: That's correct.

ALLEN: Yet man in general seems to have concluded that the will is not as free as he would have insisted it was, say, a century ago. He might a century hence conclude that it's somewhat less free than he now thinks it is. I also would assume that the will is less or more free from individual to individual, and even within the same individual at certain times, based on my own experience and study and conjecture.

I think there are probably various reasons why conservatives generally favor capital punishment. I think one of them may be so obvious there is the traditional risk of overlooking it, and that is simply that it exists and that it has existed for a long time. And there is—

WFB: A venerable sanction.

ALLEN: Yes. There is the Presumption in Favor on the part of most conservatives, and even most middle-of-the-roaders with some conservative tendencies, to sort of go along with whatever has been around for a long time.

WFB: Of course, if that's the case, then don't we agree that, as in certain other matters, conservatives seem to be losing out? Because the incidence of capital punishment, as you no doubt know, has reduced enormously—

ALLEN: Yes.

WFB: —in this country during the past twenty years. Seven [executions] last year, compared to, what, one hundred and ninety in 1935?

ALLEN: I'll be gracious enough to concede that the very fact that the trend on the chart is down by no means establishes the correctness of the direction—

WFB: Excellent point. You save me from making it.

ALLEN: But to circle back, there are variations within the same individual, concerning the degree to which the will is free. It's entirely possible for a man to be recognized by society, his peers, as sane for say forty years, and nevertheless for one, say, twenty-four-hour period, become so overwrought, so jealous, so furious, so envious—whatever— that the degree to which his will is free might go a few notches down on the chart.

WFB: But then it's a circular argument. If you say, look, every-
        body's normal, up until the moment he commits murder,
        and then he's not normal, how can I go on to say anything
        interesting?

ALLEN: That's your problem, not mine. . . . Perhaps we can just
        let this part of the argument rest and try another avenue
        of attack?

WFB: Okay. What is the *matter* with capital punishment?

ALLEN: Well, I am against capital punishment, period. The classic
        arguments *for* it just seem to me not convincing. The most
        common argument, as I'm sure Mr. Buckley knows, is
        that it serves as a deterrent.

WFB: Let me ask you, if I may, whether you've ever heard of
        what I call the van den Haag dilemma.

ALLEN: I don't believe—

WFB: Professor [Ernest] van den Haag uniquely, so far as I
        know, makes a point of devastating consequence. Now
        listen very carefully.

ALLEN: I'll do my best.

WFB: The way he puts it is this. The figures don't prove con-
        clusively one way or the other whether capital punish-
        ment is a deterrent to certain kinds of crime. About this
        everybody seems to be agreed, so says he. The dilemma
        is as follows. If a convicted murderer is *not* put to death,
        in the absence of statistics which absolutely establish
        that capital punishment is *not* a deterrent, he *may* go on
        to kill again. So that, in practical effect, a judge who, let
        us say, has before him the discretion of ordering the exe-
        cution of a convicted murderer must ask himself, in the
        absence of evidence to the contrary, "Will my failure to
        execute this man, who is guilty, result in the murder of
        an innocent person who might not otherwise have been
        murdered?"

ALLEN: That constellation of ideas is accurately described as a
        dilemma.

WFB: Yes. [*Laughter*] How would you crack it?

ALLEN: I don't think I can. If I do, I'll call you. [*Laughter*]

Truman Capote came to me in 1967 to say he wanted me to put in a good word for him with two governors, John Williams of Arizona and Ronald Reagan of California, both personal friends.

Capote had in mind to do a television documentary on convicted killers, waiting in the death houses for execution pending action by the Supreme Court.

I did as he asked, introducing him first to Governor Ronald Reagan (with whom in subsequent months and years he became friendly, as also with Mrs. Reagan). Only a few weeks before their meeting, the Reagan administration had been rocked by a scandal. Drew Pearson, the columnist, revealed that the administrative assistant of Governor Reagan had been apprehended engaging, in the Lake Tahoe area, in a homosexual orgy with various partners. (I learned—much later, and not from Reagan—that after an hour's interview in his office, Reagan had reacted to Capote's exaggerated effeminacy by opening his door and calling out to his aides along both sides of the corridor, "Somebody call that feller back and troll him up and down a couple of times in case there's anybody else left around here.")

After much work, Truman Capote's one-hour documentary was completed; but to his chagrin he did not succeed in selling it to any of the networks. He brought his problem to me and I agreed to discuss it, and his views on capital punishment, on *Firing Line.* Capote was confident that, after much study, he had come to know something conclusive about the psychology of killers.

CAPOTE: I've never met a *single* murderer who said that the death penalty was a deterrent to him in *any* way. In fact, two of the most interesting murderers that I've ever interviewed both said that though they had spent all of this time on death row, if they were released into the general population, they would kill *again,* because they simply were under a *compulsion* to do it.

              Now concerning Perry and Dick [Perry Smith and Dick Hickock, the killers of the Clutter family, whom Capote had written about in *In Cold Blood*], you ask, "Would the

death penalty have been a deterrent to them?" Well, they
were very aware of the death penalty and after they committed the crime they were increasingly aware of it. They
were *terrified* of being caught in Kansas. But nevertheless,
all the time they were planning other murders and crimes,
so one can't say that it would have been a deterrent.

My point about it is, and I'm not being a proponent of
the death penalty, don't misunderstand what I'm saying.
I'm saying that if the death penalty *were* imposed in a
genuine and authentic way, then I think that it would be
an effective deterrent against violent crime. But since it is
not, and in fact is almost a masquerade in which people
are selected very arbitrarily and occasionally executed,
then I think it should be completely abolished.

WFB: Uh-huh. Well, as between its total abolition or its systematic restoration, which, for instance, would you approve
of?

CAPOTE: At the moment, abolition—because the other is absolutely
impractical—

WFB: Oh. You mean, impractical for political reasons?

CAPOTE: Um-hm.

WFB: But you propose a reform that involves nothing less than
a constitutional amendment, so you're not against politically impractical solutions, are you?

CAPOTE: Ah, yes, but my solution to the whole problem of capital
punishment—

WFB: Which we will go into in a minute, but in fact [abolition]
also requires a political upheaval, doesn't it?

CAPOTE: Not a political upheaval. An amendment to the Constitution.

WFB: Well, Mr. Capote, I wish you would elaborate your notion
of how killers ought to be handled in the new state where
you don't have capital punishment.

CAPOTE: Well, how I arrived at this theory is that a boy that I knew
was in death row, in a Midwestern state, and he'd been

there for quite some time, five years, I guess, and he received a commutation of [the death] sentence, and was returned into the regular prison population. Well, about four or five days after this happened, he stabbed to death another prisoner in the yard, and of course when that happens in prison, and it's very common as you know—I mean, there are numerous murders in every prison, every year—and they can never get a conviction on it, because no one will testify, you know, against another prisoner.

But I'd known this boy was a psychopathic murderer, and I had known that if he went back into the prison population that it was inevitable that he would kill somebody again. So, I mean, there he is *loose* in the prison population still, and, of course, *cannot* be returned to death row and cannot be executed having got a commutation. So what is the answer to this problem, where you have compulsive homicidal minds who are incapable of controlling this violence of theirs?

I envision two federal prisons whose operation would be the handling of homicidal cases. Now, when a person is sentenced in a homicidal case, he would be sentenced to an indefinite term, never to any specific thing, so that—and these two prisons, I sort of envision one being in the East and one in the West—would be really in effect *hospitals* with *bars.* You would have the person who is sentenced to an indefinite term, like, for instance, say, a woman who in some extraordinary rage with a drunken husband killed him—she would go to the hospital really for treatment and she could be released in three weeks or three months. Whereas a person with a genuine homicidal mind, like say Perry Smith from my book, he would *never* be released. But he would never be *told* that, you see? They would always think, and this is the thing I've always noticed in prisons, as long as they can *hope* that they're going to be released, they constantly are changing and evolving, and in many cases they make quite extraordinary rehabilitations. But if you once remove the element of hope of getting out of prison, then you would have destroyed the possibility of rehabilitating the person.

WFB: Well, aren't you contradicting yourself? Because if you say that you're dealing with somebody of such a homicidal mind that in fact he will never be released, how can you then go on to say that there is an evolution there which you want to encourage the acceleration of?

CAPOTE: But no. You see, in my theory of things, from talking and interviewing these people, I think, a homicidal mind is incurable, you know.

WFB: I see.

CAPOTE: What I'm talking about is what the person then *does* with himself. For instance, there's this boy called Michael John Bell, who is in prison in Colorado State Prison, who's had six, seven dates of execution. Well, he's really a most extraordinary young man, and he became quite an accomplished painter, and reads, and grows rather amazing gardens. But Michael John Bell would tell you himself, you know, that he is *very* dangerous.

WFB: You mean, he's told you?

CAPOTE: Well, in effect, yes. The point is that Michael John Bell shouldn't be outside of the prison.

It is my judgment, after talking several times with Capote on the subject, that his thought combined analytical toughness and considerable insights into crime and punishment. And that although he could involve himself as directly and emotionally as he did with the two Clutter killers (he is said to have wept for two days after their hanging), he could also outcon a killer in conversation, and laugh about the experience.

I must imagine that it is apocryphal, but I need to tell the story, untold until now, to my knowledge. It was January 1968, and our twenty dinner guests included Governor Reagan and Truman Capote. It was toward the end of the centuries-old season when men and women were routinely separated after dinner, at cognac-and-cigar time.

Truman accosted Reagan: Had he heard what happened after Truman left California and went down to Arizona?

No, Reagan hadn't.

Well, listen to this, said Truman.

"I got Bill to call Governor John Williams in Tucson, and he said, 'Mr. Capote, you can go up to the Arizona State Penitentiary, but the warden who runs that place won't take any suggestions from me very kindly, so you'll have to persuade him yourself to let you interview and film the death-house people.'

"So, I went over there with my crew. Walked into the warden's office, introduced myself, told him I had had a good visit with you, Ronnie, and you had opened up the death house in Sacramento for me, and I asked him, Could I go upstairs with my crew and do a little interviewing?

"An' he said, 'That's simple. The answer is no.' So I jus' said, 'Do you mind if I use your telephone, Warden?' And I say'd to the operator, 'Please get me Governor Williams on the phone.'

"Well"—Capote rose to complete the story, while a dozen of us fastened on his every word—"I am not kidding you, Ronald Reagan, at jus' that moment we heard a great shout in the jail corridor outside! Then we saw a guard chasing a prisoner! The prisoner ran down the stairs, fas' as he could, and the guard was holding out his pistol, taking aim. Just when the prisoner got close to the warden's office, the guard shot, and the prisoner fell dead, *right over my lap!*"

"What did you do?" Reagan asked, on behalf of all of us.

"Well, I still had the telephone in my hand, so I jus' said, 'Operator? *Cancel* that call to Governor Williams.' "

There were others who shed light on life, and death, in prison.

Jimmy Hoffa maintained, right into 1972, that he had been framed by Bobby Kennedy and would soon be going into court with some kind of affidavit to the effect that the principal witness against him was lying. When, in 1964, he was convicted, it surprised nobody in particular: the Teamsters Union had been notoriously corrupt for a generation and had been kicked out of the AFL-CIO in 1957 by the union's Ethical Practices Committee (calling to mind the telegram sent, sometime in the late fifties, to the same committee by CIO boss John L. Lewis on the third consecutive day of their session: "HAVE YOU DISCOVERED ANY ETHICAL PRACTICES YET?").

On the other hand, it was generally acknowledged that Attorney General Robert Kennedy wanted, above most earthly things, the conviction and imprisonment of Hoffa. This had been accomplished. Now seven years later, President Nixon had ordered Hoffa's release from prison on bail. Shortly after, Hoffa came out for Nixon in the 1972 election. That might have been a political quid pro quo. On the other hand, Hoffa had also come out for Nixon for President in 1960, a misdeed Robert Kennedy had presumably never forgotten.

Hoffa's experiences in prison had made him a zealous advocate of reform. He had been in Lewisburg, Pennsylvania, considered among the two or three most genteel prisons in the federal system. But even there, Hoffa charged, 85 percent of the guards were mere time-servers, most of them incompetent, a significant number of them sadists. He said that the medical treatment given to inmates of Lewisburg was so bad that a principal fear of the prisoners was that they should take sick. Homosexuality—he said—was so rampant that 45 percent of the inmates were either sexual aggressors or their victims. The food, he maintained, was almost artistically inedible. And the dehumanization all but systematic, ranging from silly and arbitrary rules governing the length of the inmate's hair to protocols concerning the inmate's dress (if you were five feet five inches tall, and it happened that the day you came in for trousers the supply room had only a set designed for a man six feet tall, the solution was simple: the guard cut off the bottom seven inches of the pant legs).

It isn't news that no prison system (Sweden's may be an exception) is successful as a school for rehabilitation. "Our prisons should be humane," says New York's sociologist-author Roger Starr, "because they should be humane." Quite right. But it is wrong to assume that because they are humane, they will transmit a concern for humanity to their inhabitants.

Hoffa appeared to believe that the proper organizing principle for reform was segregation. To begin with, he said, prisons oughtn't to hold more than 350 inmates. And these should be carefully segregated according to age, the nature of the offense, and temperament. Above all, homosexuals should be grouped together. One sometimes got the feeling that all these reticulations, finely drawn, would have isolated James Hoffa as the sole occupant of one federal prison; but however exaggerated, he made a compelling case. Why hasn't it been acted on? Presumably, (a) because he made it; (b) small prisons cost money; and (c) with the onslaught of drug-related prisoners, the traffic is simply too great to control.

HOFFA: I served fifty-eight months, behind a forty-foot wall, in a twenty-seven-acre walled-in space, in a prison that was

built for nine hundred and fifty people which now contains
eighteen hundred people. Not one stick, one stone, nor one
addition has been added to that building. In talking to
individuals who were in there in 1932 when the prison was
built, as against 1971, and asking them what has been
changed in the prison, either by the system or by correction of the system, I learned that the only thing that had
been changed from 1932 to 1971 was that they moved the
control tower from the right-hand side to the left-hand
side.

The criticism I have of the prison system in the United
States, particularly the federal system where I served
fifty-eight months, is very simple—that, even though a
man is incarcerated and convicted of a crime, you have no
right to take away the dignity of a man, nor have you any
right to attempt to destroy any initiative that he may have
and regulate him as though he were some oddment.

Our program was on September 22, 1972. On July 30, 1975, Jimmy
Hoffa disappeared. It is commonly conjectured that he lies imprisoned
somewhere in concrete.

The hour with Gordon Liddy was productive. I remember that, via the
producer, he relayed a few conditions before agreeing to appear, primary
among them that I was not to ask him any questions about who was
finally responsible for Watergate, the historic operation he and Howard
Hunt had executed, or rather sought to execute. My reply was that he
could of course decline to answer any question I put to him—in fact I
had no intention of going over the old ground, intending rather to talk
to him about prison life and the courts, and the judge who sentenced
him.

It was an engrossing hour. It was quickly obvious that for Gordon
Liddy, as for other inmates—mostly members of the criminal class—
informing was the supreme sin. On this point Liddy was inflexible.
Consider:

WFB: If, for instance, you were a member of a terrorist gang, the
                 business of which was, let's say, to kidnap and mutilate
                 systematically, and one day you woke up the beneficiary

of a changed view of life, I understand you to be saying
that you would not inform on the continuing activities of
your former confederates—notwithstanding that in your
new perception you understood them to be despicable, and
that, therefore, the kidnapping and the mutilation and the
rape and the murder would continue rather than cause
you to act out the role of an informant.

LIDDY: No. The way you have just stated it would lead someone
to believe that were I the beneficiary of this changed point
of view, the only alternative to the continued killing and
mutilation and so on and so forth would be my turning
informer, and that's not so. I could turn and make war
upon my former associates by honorably attempting to
meet them in battle and kill them.

I say Liddy was *almost* inflexible because he did concede that if he
had been a Jew, mistakenly caught up in Hitler's genocidal enterprise,
upon seeing the light he would have informed against his former associates—but not on moral grounds. "On the grounds that they were, after
all, really trying to kill *me.*" Otherwise Gordon Liddy's views on informants were unequivocal. They were captured, almost as if in a haiku,
in the opening sentences of his article for *Esquire* magazine (December
1977), "Serving Time in America."

> For those whose understanding of prison life is predicated upon early
> Warner Brothers films depicting George Raft banging a tin cup
> against his cell bars or, more recently, the introspective musings of
> John Dean in *Newsweek,* based upon his four months of tender loving
> care as the prize canary of the Watergate Special Prosecution Force,
> I offer first my credentials. . . .

Liddy spent fifty-two months in nine prisons, and was released finally
by President Carter. He told us that in prison there were roughly
speaking five classes of inmates. Beginning at the bottom were the
informants. These needed the protection of solitary confinement or
else sanctuaries in other prisons where they were not known—otherwise, said Liddy, they were quite routinely executed. The free-market
cost of arranging for such execution, he reported, was five cartons of
cigarettes.

Next there were the homosexuals. These were men (however many
the exceptions) who were considered weak, and therefore contemptible,
given over to tawdry and perverse pleasures: a society within a society,
treated as an isolated unit.

Then there were the drug users. These were less contemptible, one
gathered, because in order to indulge their habits it was necessary that
they use their wits.

A class above these was what Liddy called the knock-arounds—men
of a high level of competence; unattached, usually; smart, able, generally
aloof, and fiercely independent. One gathered that Liddy belonged to
that class. Which was not, however, the aristocracy. These were those
"accused"—as Liddy carefully put it—of being members of "organized
crime rings." Once again, these tended to be intelligent men. More
important, they were men whose contacts in the outside world were
sufficient to make them a credible force even within prison.

WFB: For five cartons of cigarettes, you relate, you can arrange
            for the killing of anybody in prison.

LIDDY: Assuming that inflation has not increased. It was what—
            two or three when I first went in, but—

WFB: Well, let's say seven. [*Laughter*] Indexation in killing.

LIDDY: Yes.

WFB: Well, these categories of rather sharp, highly freighted
            words—

LIDDY: It's a highly freighted place.

WFB: Yes, it is a highly freighted place, but it is a highly
            freighted place that seems to have adopted a scale of val-
            ues that is not entirely alien to your own nature, for in-
            stance.

LIDDY: Well, *au contraire,* I would say it doesn't adopt a scale of
            values not entirely alien to my nature. I would say that it
            simply possesses, in microcosm, the scale of values that
            predominate. Now you may feel that that ought not to
            predominate, and that's a valid distinction, but it is a
            distinction nevertheless.

WFB: No, let me— You have a very subtle piece here, and I
            don't want to vulgarize it at all. You tell the American

reader what it is in prison that constitutes the sort of a natural ranking of people, and the lowest are the informers. The highest are the organized members of crime.

LIDDY: *Accused* members of organized crime.

WFB: Excuse me?

LIDDY: *Accused* members of organized crime.

WFB: Accused members of organized crime. And in between are these various other categories. Now, you really talk almost as though this were a state of nature. This is really how you'd end up if you didn't suffer from all of the impositions that we've been taught by Margaret Mead or whoever. According to your scale, the most base are informants. Then after that it's homosexuals. Now, do I understand that you would rank the practice of homosexuality in prison as the second-most-ignominious classification of activity—more so, for instance, than murdering people, which is done rather routinely by people up in category two?

LIDDY: That's not considered ignominious by those people. We're speaking now of that particular society, and there's no ignominy there unless it's done unnecessarily. For example, an unnecessary killing—one which brings heat, which is defined as undue attention—will be regarded as something that's wrong.

WFB: For instrumental reasons? It has nothing to do with sentimental reasons? It has nothing to do with taking somebody's life?

LIDDY: No. There's no sentiment there.

WFB: Yes. Well, is the ordering of a class structure in which sentiment plays no role one with which you can feel even intellectual sympathy?

LIDDY: Well, as I said in the piece, I went into prison, and I found in prison what I find outside of prison, except in microcosm.

WFB: Well, how would you make the comparison in this particular taxonomy with the taxonomy outside of prison?

Would you say that homosexuals outside of prison are the second-most-despised category of men?

LIDDY: What I'm attempting to convey is not that particular category, but I find outside of prison an ordering of categories in which the weak generally *are* on the bottom and the strong are on top. Now, I think—in discussing something like this with you—it's important to say that we must always bear in mind the distinction between the world as it is—or as we perceive it to be—and as we might like it to be or we think it ought to be.

The Christians, after all, are still waiting for the second coming of Christ. The Jews are still waiting for the Messiah. The Communists are waiting for that day when socialism will be converted into pure Communism, and the millennium will be here. But the millennium is *not* here. The Bible speaks of the meek inheriting the earth. It says, "shall." It uses the future tense. They haven't yet, and when one makes decisions on important matters—life-and-death matters, let us say—one must bear in mind how the world *is.*

WFB: I'm not suggesting that it is widely thought as working that way, but neither is it widely thought that only the powerful are in a position to survive in the world, and you seem to edge increasingly to that thesis, don't you?

LIDDY: Well, it's a matter of degree. I certainly wouldn't say that only the powerful are in a position to survive, but only the powerful are in a position to exert power and to change the world as they ought to attempt to change the world with any reasonable expectation of success. The unpowerful can *survive,* of course, by being out of the way, if they can. But very often they get underfoot of the powerful, and they *don't* survive. I would think that the experience of mankind—at least as I perceive it to be—would indicate that the big fish still eat the little fish—that Jaws is still out there in the Atlantic, not Charlie the Tuna.

Charles Colson, who worked Watergate from the White House and was an intimate of President Nixon, went to prison and in the summer of

1973 experienced a call from Christ. Pursuant to it he founded an organization, the Prison Fellowship. It has a staff of one hundred people and is bent on prison reform.

Colson appeared on *Firing Line* in 1981. Asked whether he would be living the life he was living unless animated, as he had been, by Christianity, he said no; he would not otherwise spend his days in prisons, conducting seminars, evangelizing, agitating for reform—he is driven by a concern to please God. But he conceded that the specific reforms he favors could be argued for using exclusively secular reasoning.

Colson was much influenced by Yochelson and Samenow's masterwork *The Criminal Personality,* in which Samenow (a practicing Jew) concluded that criminals were for the most part criminals because that was their nature, and that in order to change, they needed to expose themselves to "deliberate conversion . . . to a more responsible lifestyle." This is, as a matter of fact, best accomplished by a religious conversion; but Colson was prepared to admit that the hypothetical possibility exists that criminals can change their appetite for crime by experiencing a transformation outside of any religious experience.

That much having been disposed of, Colson explained his ministry, one part devoted to persuading criminals to believe in Christ, the other to persuading the American public for God's sake to listen to reason. To wit:

—The prison population has been expanding fifteen times as fast as the national population. And this notwithstanding that only two out of every one hundred agents of crime are apprehended, convicted, and put away.

COLSON: We've had a sixty percent increase in the prison population during the decade of the seventies and about a hundred percent increase in crime. Now, if prisons stop crime, how come we've got so much crime?

—The prisons were bursting at the seams, with over 200,000 more criminals inhabiting quarters than our prisons were designed for, resulting in a gruesome intensification of the awful experience of prison and a resulting increase in recidivist crime.

COLSON: I worry about this summer terribly, because with the heat coming—I don't like to say this because then it becomes self-fulfilling, but I've been in these places where the human excrement is out on the floor and the food and the containers have been there for three weeks because there's a dispute between the guards and the inmates and the men are triple-deckered in cells built for one and men are living in tents and there's—you just can't put human beings that close together.

We have been cramming these pits that we call prisons full of humanity. Put them in where they have to live with a knife; they lie, cheat, steal; they are homosexually assaulted; they see violence and corruption pervasive around them. And then after a period of time, we let them back out on the street, and we say, "*Now* we've taught you how to behave." They taught you how to *behave*? They taught you how to be a dangerous criminal.

You could put a person through Yale—room, board, tuition, and give him five hundred dollars a month to boot—for the same price that you're spending—

WFB: And teach him to be an inflationist, too. [*Laughter*]

COLSON: It's a question of what kind of education you want him to get: in prison or at Yale.

—An interesting statistical coincidence: About 53 percent of men behind bars were there for having committed a crime that did not involve violence or cause physical danger. Meanwhile, 53 percent of Americans report that they are afraid to walk one mile from their residence after dark. To some extent, then, it can be said that half of America is imprisoned by virtue of the impulses of half the criminal population.

But what to do with criminals caught and convicted?

COLSON: Well, there are plenty of jobs to be done where people need help—

WFB: Okay.

COLSON: —in our society that could be performed rather than have that person sit in a cold cell, staring into the emptiness, getting angry and bitter, at a great cost to you and me as taxpayers.

WFB: Okay. Oh, by the way, simply on figures, you use fifty-three percent for nonviolent inmates, right?

COLSON: Yes. It varies from state to state. New York's figures would be closer to twenty, twenty-five percent, which I think you used in a column, but then you go into other states where seventy percent—for example, I think, Georgia, Oklahoma—would be nonviolent; and so the place you start with reform is to get the nonviolent person out of prison and into some sort of a community-based corrections program where he is doing something that is redemptive for himself and for society.

Colson's manner is quickly engaging. He is a graduate of Brown University, a trained lawyer, a survivor (more accurately, a victim) of a vicious school of political practices, and an extrovert convert to Christianity. His faith is repeatedly confirmed by personal experiences (many of them brilliantly recorded in his book *Kingdoms in Conflict,* Zondervan, 1987).

COLSON: I just preached this Sunday morning at the Indiana State Penitentiary, and when I arrived, an inmate came running up to me—a great big, tough convict—and he said, "You were here a year ago. You told me to go back to my cell and think about what you'd told me and to try a commitment to Christ." He said, "I did."
            And he said, "For the last year they've had my body in here, but not *me.*"
            We [the Prison Fellowship] make it plain what we stand for, but we put no pressure on people. I think Kant is right in one sense, and that is that people can be motivated by a variety of things and good ethical standards and do good work. But in my experience in the prisons—in two hundred and fifty prisons that I've been in, seven months as a prisoner myself—I've never seen anything that really *transforms* a person's heart unless it's the power of God.

13
ON
THE
CULTURAL
FRONT

GUESTS:
BENJAMIN STEIN
ROSALYN TURECK
TIM PAGE
SCHUYLER CHAPIN
LOUIS AUCHINCLOSS
HELEN MACINNES
TOM WOLFE
JORGE LUIS BORGES

Mostly, *Firing Line* is about public issues. And, of course, "public issues" generally involve focus on politics or economics, war and peace. There are other issues that separate us: cultural questions, high and low. Herewith an introduction to one of the latter, namely, What is Hollywood up to?

Benjamin Stein (a son, by the way, of Herbert Stein, chief economic adviser to Nixon, and a former guest of *Firing Line*) had written television criticism for *The Wall Street Journal,* speeches for President Nixon, articles for *Esquire, Playboy,* and *The New York Times,* and three books. At that point he had decided to go to Hollywood, responding to the most unexpected invitation conceivable—one from right-wing–dragon killer Norman Lear (the genius who produced television's *All in the Family*). Poor Lear/dear couldn't find *anybody* in Los Angeles who could write required witticisms for a right-wing character in the contemplated series *All's Fair.* Ben Stein's book *The View from Sunset Boulevard* gave a portrait of the ideologically homogenized television-producing industry in Los Angeles.

It was Ben Stein's position, ten years ago, that Hollywood engaged in ideological stereotypes. Businessmen and military men were bad, small towns tended to be provincial, superstitious, and easily corrupted; religious figures tended to be either buffoons or helpless fuddy-duddies. My impression is that the situation has changed, if not dramatically: one does see patriotic military officers on the screen, and here and there a likable businessman.

WFB: How about newspaper publishers? [*Laughter*]

STEIN: Well, they used to be bad, but now they're good.

WFB: Post-Watergate, they're good?

STEIN: That's right. My book had nothing to do with whether the shows are good or bad or fun to watch or boring to watch. The point is just that there is an enormous amount of *background noise* on these TV shows, which is a fully alternative view of American life. People watch TV so much that it's like a second life for them, and in this second life, conditions are very different from what they are in *real* life. That is, in real life, one occasionally finds a businessman who is not plotting to murder his go-go dancer girlfriend. On TV [this is] a standard episode of *Starsky and Hutch—*

WFB: Normal people just don't pass the screen test.

STEIN: Right. On TV, a standard episode of *Barnaby Jones* or *Starsky and Hutch* will be that a go-go dancer has been murdered. There are three suspects. One is her boyfriend, who has just gotten out of jail after serving twenty years for murder. The other one will be the janitor who cleans up the club and is a heroin addict. And the third one will be the head of the local utility company who stops in there for a drink on his way to the train. Invariably, the killer will be the head of the local utility company. [*Laughter*]

            This is a reality on TV which it seems to me tends to

screw up most people's perceptions of real life. I often think that a lot of people's anger at the oil companies is based on the fact that all they've seen on TV are villainous, scheming, heartless businessmen. So they begin to think that all businessmen in real life are like that.

WFB: What about, say, *M*A*S*H,* a show that has received considerable critical acclaim?

STEIN: Well, *M*A*S*H* is a perfect example of what my book is about, because one of the parts of the book is that on television, military men come in two different categories. If they are enlisted men or draftees, they're saintly, virtuous people. If they are professional military officers, they are killers. Their whole aim in life is to kill—

WFB: What about the officer in charge, the colonel? He's a very nice guy, as I recall.

STEIN: But he is a *draftee.* All of the people in the Mobile Surgical Hospital are draftees. The people who come over from headquarters are only concerned to bomb civilians. *M*A*S*H* is the absolutely pluperfect example of how on television a professional army man is one inch away from being an SS man.

But television, usually through the public channels, brings us also fine music, and every year or so I have tried to do a program based (however obliquely) on a point of musical contention. Here is an excerpt from a discussion with Rosalyn Tureck, Schuyler Chapin, and Tim Page, respectively a performer, a musical director, and a critic. Normally, *Firing Line*'s screen credits are accompanied by the same few bars of music (from Bach's Second Brandenburg). For this program, we altered the opening notes to reflect the special theme of the program, which would examine the question of live vs. studio performances. We played Glenn Gould.

The springboard for the discussion was the dicta of the late Mr. Gould (he had died in 1982). He was a great virtuoso, but infamous for his decision, reached at age thirty-one, never again to perform in public. Why go through the hassle of public performance when there is the alternative of a recording? Why settle for the vulnerabilities of a live performance when, with the aid of recording technology, you can get it just right? Authors can edit their work before publishing, Gould wrote; painters can meditate and put final touches on their canvases; why should musicians expose themselves to the vicissitudes of public performance?

ROSALYN TURECK

WFB: We have with us three guests, selected with a jeweler's eye. The first, Rosalyn Tureck, is first and foremost a live performer. She has performed on the piano and the harpsichord in every civilized country in the world and in one or two less than civilized countries. She elected a generation ago to play only the work of Johann Sebastian Bach, her mastery of which is universally acknowledged.

Schuyler Chapin was the dean of the School of Arts at Columbia University. He is a figure associated with live performance, having served as general manager of the Metropolitan Opera Company. There is nothing more like

a live performance than one that features one hundred and
fifty singers, ninety-five orchestra players, eight soloists, at
least one prima donna, and occasionally a few live ele-
phants.

Tim Page, although he studied at Mannes and Juilliard,
elected not to perform but to criticize. He won in 1983 the
Deems Taylor Award for music criticism, which he wrote
as music and cultural affairs editor for *The New York
Times* before going to *Newsday.*

PAGE: Some people take joy in live concerts. [Mr. Page addressed now the question: Are live concerts progressively
obsolete?] I think Miss Tureck most certainly does. I
know Artur Rubinstein loved doing live concerts. At the
same time, I think the most important way to *encounter*
either a composer's work or a performer's re-creation of
that work is via the media, and I would like to give one
example of this. A few years ago, Birgit Nilsson sang
Richard Strauss's opera *Elektra* at the Metropolitan
Opera. On that one evening, broadcast by television,
more people saw *Elektra* than the sum total of every
man, woman, and child who had ever seen or heard
Elektra since 1909.

WFB: I remember Leonard Bernstein saying the same thing
about Bach's B Minor Mass back during the days of *The
Ford Hour* in the late fifties. He said more people would
now hear the Mass than had ever heard it. But nobody
that I know of wants to put an end to studio technology.
What we're disputing is whether Glenn Gould makes a
point of a kind that *ought* to put an end to *public* performances, as he suggested in one or two of his essays.

PAGE: Well, Glenn said really, categorically, that the concert was
dead, period. Now, I'm a music critic and I see as many
as ten or twelve concerts a week, so I know it is most
definitely not dead. But I think that it *has* been *replaced*—
I think that technology has most certainly superseded the
concert.

WFB: Well, Miss Tureck, how do you bounce off that? You flatly
reject the Gould position, don't you?

TURECK: No, I don't flatly reject the Gould position. There are three fundamental ways of performing: in a studio, in live performance, and alone personally with a few close friends. One plays differently in all three situations, and I don't believe that any one can be judged absolutely superior.

WFB: Why is that so?

TURECK: Because of the essence of the artistic process. When one plays in a concert hall with an audience, in my view the audience and I are really one. The audience is not an entity beyond the stage, hostile or friendly or bloodlusting for whatever they may find to disagree with. They are one with this whole experience.

WFB: Well, why wouldn't that be so if you were playing for two or three people?

TURECK: One plays in a different way. That is one of the reasons why artists and musicians and music lovers like to sit and listen to an artist play in a small room in a private home. That has a very special, not only external atmosphere, but an internal kind of spiritual atmosphere.

               I just would like to expand a little on the concert experience, because that to me is the main pillar of the discussion. I feel that at such moments one reaches the highest level of communication with other human beings. One reaches into their innermost thoughts, their innermost spirits, their innermost strivings and aspirations . . .

WFB: Would you feel the same way toward the television viewers? Or is there an interruption in the vibrations that you are talking about?

TURECK: Yes. There we move into another world. That's the third aspect. I think at this point, even though I would not agree with Glenn that the concert is absolutely dead, I think it has become an important sidelight rather than the main event. I don't see, necessarily, anything wrong with a musician taking the time to tinker and perfect a conception of a work to his very best ability. Nobody holds it against, say, a great screen actor who does not want to be on the stage.

Gould is now there for us forever on film, he's there for us on disk, and the fact that he spent the rest of his life working very hard on these creations rather than running to meet the train and running to get on the stage is, I think, good. In the long run he has left us more than a lot of people who did not record, and who trod the boards.

WFB: Well, Mr. Chapin, in your experience, is there a significant difference between the recorded product of a successful opera singer, say, who also performs onstage, and that of the reclusive type like Mr. Gould?

CHAPIN: When you deal with opera performances, perhaps they are really the only musical performances that are *gladiatorial.* There is an antagonism, whether it is expressed or not— not an antagonism as much as a competition—between the singer on the stage and the audience. In many instances, and I remember sitting in the auditorium during performances where you really knew that most of the people there were anxious as to whether the soprano was going to hit the high note or the tenor was going to—

WFB: To say nothing of the general manager. [*Laughter*]

CHAPIN: Yes, exactly. And you had almost a sense of *combat,* a sense of *tension* between the two. Whereas in a recording studio, in an opera production made for a record, the concentration is on the music and the interpretive part of the artist in reaching out to do that music. So I think in the opera world you have this unusual situation of a tension in a live performance which often militates against the artist being at his or her best, as opposed to working in a studio to record an opera where the dramatic musical content of the piece is all that is under consideration.

WFB: Well, that's a fascinating concession. So that the best opera recordings would be of nonlive performances?

CHAPIN: Yes, I think so. Now, there are always exceptions to statements like that. I mean, moments when a performance is captured where in and of itself it will simply never be surpassed.

WFB: It just took off?

CHAPIN: It just took off. There is a pirated recording of the Metro-
            politan Opera's only performance, for example, of *Tristan
            and Isolde* with Birgit Nilsson and Jon Vickers. They only
            sang it seven times during their active lives with that
            opera.

WFB: And the black-market tape cost you sixty-five dollars? [I
            had heard Chapin tell this story.]

CHAPIN: Yes. Yes, it did. [*Laughter*] As a matter of fact, when I
            bought it, I went to a shop that I knew specialized in these
            things—I waited several years after my reign at the Met—
            and I said to them, "By any chance do you have a copy
            of the Nilsson—"

WFB: Did you wear a mustache? [*Laughter*]

CHAPIN: No, I didn't. The man looked at me and said, "Mr. Cha-
            pin, we've been waiting for you." [*Laughter*]

WFB: But these are anomalies, right?

I asked Miss Tureck to give us her word on studio recording. She
came in with a *locus classicus.*

TURECK: Some people redo many, many passages. I know of one
            very famous artist who performs the C-minor Chopin
            étude in about three thousand takes, and what he did
            was—

WFB: Three *thousand?*

TURECK: Yes. What he did was to play four measures at a time
            about twenty or thirty times. And when he finished the
            four measures all that many times, then he went on to the
            next four measures.

WFB: *I* could do the C-minor that way! [*Laughter*]

TURECK: And not only that! When he finished, it was up to the
            engineer to sift out each four-measure portion and corre-
            late them—

WFB: I can't *believe* it sounded like a whole—

TURECK: —and it came out and it received *excellent* critical reviews!

WFB: You're kidding.

TURECK: —and it was praised because it was said that his endurance was *phenomenal*. [*Laughter*]

WFB: He should have left in one mistake to make it *plausible*. [*Laughter*]

TURECK: Yes, like the Siamese, who have one god upside down. But the point is that there is so much to be said for studio performance because it is infinitely more *comfortable*. You are alone, you do not have the hazards of— For instance, in Chicago at Orchestra Hall all the lights went out the first two minutes of my beginning to play.

WFB: You kept on playing, I hope?

TURECK: Yes, absolutely.

WFB: Myra Hess played during the London bombing, didn't she?

TURECK: Yes, she did. And I kept on playing through absolute blackness.

WFB: Good for you!

TURECK: But that's the kind of thing that happens at live performances. And when . . .

WFB: I want you to know I can do that with a typewriter. [*Laughter*]

An interesting point. I had, that day, three guests, two of them intimate friends. However close I might personally be to one of my guests, I tend always to begin by treating him formally. Mine was an early reaction, made back in 1966, to the cloying informality of TV exchanges. I may have carried my rule too far (I had a problem when my brother, Senator James Buckley, was my guest. I could hardly call him "Senator Buckley"). But personal familiarity, as between Tureck-Chapin and me, can pay off. Intercommunication becomes informal not in the Gee-whiz-what-did-you-do-today? sense; but in other ways; as, for instance, in the way easy familiarity, within formal protocol, catalyzed Rosalyn's account of her performance in the dark dark.

We had an interesting go discussing the novel. This was in 1969, and my guests were two formidable literary producers. The critic J. Donald Adams referred to Louis Auchincloss, twenty books ago, as "our Trollope." His regular output is so exhaustingly good, the critics seldom get around to noticing it anymore, rather like one more ode to Niagara Falls. Helen MacInnes's first smash triumph was *Assignment in Brittany*, in some eyes the greatest spy story ever written. Twelve books later came *The Salzburg Connection*, which was leading the best-seller list at the time we convened.

I asked—or, rather, ventured—"Why do people take less satisfaction from novels than they used to do? I assume it has something to do with the availability of alternative ways of spending one's time, and television would be the principal enemy, I suppose. But another might be that the current appetite is for something that gives you quick, continuous sensations; that there isn't, among people seeking distraction, the kind of spirit that obtained in another age disposed, say, to engage a Dickens or a Trollope or Jane Austen. Somebody who would take his or her time in taking you through a considerable experience. Now, there are people who buck that particular trend. You certainly are one of them, but you get a lot of flak for it too, don't you?"

AUCHINCLOSS: Yes. There's a constant demand for forms that are relevant to our age. The screen, painting, and sculpture can change their form. The novel tried to change its form. The French novel carried it to the point where Nathalie Sarraute has eliminated characters. Plot is of course being commonly eliminated today. But it seems to me that the novel is not capable of this adjustment to new forms. There isn't very far a novelist can go. I really don't think Nathalie Sarraute is successful in eliminating characters.

MACINNES: But she isn't writing a *novel*. Why doesn't she call it something else? People never used to get confused about what the novel was for. A novel was a certain form, and if they were good at being essayists, they wrote essays; or if they were very poetic, then they would concentrate on writing poems. Perhaps we have tried to do too much with the novel.

WFB: Doesn't it strike you as possibly the case that the twentieth century, being the century where the intellectual and romantic odysseys usually begin from yourself and end up with yourself, that it becomes therefore the age of solipsism? Only the author is truly interesting?

MACINNES: That's it.

WFB: Whereas before, God was interesting; nature was interesting; humanity was interesting. A novelist who more often than not finds now that on the one hand he is interested exclusively in himself, now wants his readers also to be interested—in himself. Therefore he's asking his readers to violate his own rule. Now, Norman Mailer *is* interesting. But suppose he weren't? It would be fatal, wouldn't it?

MACINNES: Well, now, I really do think, looking back at the history of the novel, there came a point when people suddenly discovered the interest [out there] in writing about yourself, and it was marvelous when it was begun—at *first.* And done very well. There was less of a need for a plot. But in the end, if you don't want to be a storyteller, you want to be something other than a novelist. Go find another form of writing.

WFB: Become a journalist?

We traveled around that question for a bit, and I reminded my guests (or rather myself: Auchincloss knows everything) that G. K. Chesterton was very fussy in designating himself as a journalist by trade. By so doing, he elevated the profession.

As have several of the New Journalists in America, foremost among them Tom Wolfe.

Tom Wolfe had published *The Painted Word,* a defi hurled in the face of the art critics, challenging their taste, questioning their originality, and lamenting their power. We had discussed that book on

Firing Line, and this season (1981) he had turned his withering attention on modern architects, in a book called *From Bauhaus to Our
House.* Bauhaus was the name given to a compound of architects
gathered together after the First World War in Germany to remark
the general desolation, which they sought to shrive by a kind of architectural asceticism celebrating (right word?) a cleanness of line, an
absence of ornamentation, the blandness of color, and the "honesty"
of generic building materials.

Wolfe records the rapacious success of the Bauhaus school, which
within a generation had captured almost the whole of the American
architectural academy, bequeathing us such megatonnage as, say, the
World Trade Center. He saw in a few architects signs of genuine independence, but most of these remain prisoners to the vocabulary of
Bauhaus, as we shall see. ("As we shall see": that phrase—more orna-
mental than instrumental—would not have been used by a Bauhaus
architect.)

WFB: I should like to begin by asking Mr. Wolfe to describe why
            it is that the rubble of postwar Germany brought on a felt
            need for drabness in German architecture.

WOLFE: At that particular moment it was very *exciting* to people
            in a place like the Bauhaus to have rubble all around. They
            were young men and they could point to the ruins of their
            own civilization. After all, at that point the Kaiser had
            fled, inflation was worse than anything anyone had ever
            experienced. Germany was an absolute shambles, and to
            be young and to be brought together under a figure like
            Walter Gropius—who was designated by Paul Klee, the
            painter, as the "Silver Prince"—and to be told to start
            from zero is like saying, "You are the young gods of the
            future." And a part of their program was that the past was
            discredited.

            Now, to me the irony of this—whether or not you like
            it is another question. The great irony is that all of these
            forms were created for the *workers* in the ruins—the rub-
            ble of Germany after the First World War under a social-
            ist government. I'm not talking about a Communist
            government, but a social democratic government. And
            somehow, as if they bounced off Telstar, they land—these

same forms—now land on Sixth Avenue, *Park* Avenue; practically any avenue you want to name, in any large American city—

WFB: Landed in a country that did not lose the war, and whose income was rising, not falling—

WOLFE: Right. Far from being ruined in the First World War, it was the First World War that, you could argue, made America a world power and created a tremendous boom that lasted for about ten years. Far from housing *workers,* these structures which are now pitched up—the same forms are now pitched up fifty, sixty, and, in the case of the World Trade Center that you mentioned, *one hundred* stories high, are housing the corporate giants of America. In other words, you're looking at the very Babylon of capitalism.

WFB: Our Medici.

WOLFE: Our Medici. And they're all in worker-housing forms. And I love, going to the great law firms of New York which are housed in some of these buildings on Park and Fifth and Sixth Avenue, to see offices with ceilings about seven feet high or maybe seven feet six, with corridors thirty-six inches wide, which is also part of the Bauhaus program. Gropius, incidentally, felt that high ceilings and wide hallways were bourgeois grandiosity expressed in the void rather than the silence, so the ceilings were first lowered dramatically for the worker housing in Berlin. In these pygmy spaces you'll see the law firms send out their search-and-acquire girls and their cabinetmakers and their carpenters and they—

WFB: Okay. I'm going to quote a sentence from your book in which you express the reaction of workers and of all those people who were given this kind of house to live in. Apparently what developed was an absolutely irrepressible hunger for something just a little bit more picturesque.
        "I have seen the carpenters and the cabinetmakers and search-and-acquire girls hauling in more cornices, covings, pilasters, carved moldings, and recessed domes, more

linenfold paneling, more (fireless) fireplaces with festoons of fruit carved in mahogany on the mantels, more chandeliers, sconces, girandoles, chestnut leather sofas and chiming clocks than Wren, Inigo Jones, the brothers Adam, Lord Burlington and the Dilettanti, working in concert, could have dreamed of."

Now, this does suggest that there was no hospitable response to these dwellings, and makes all the more interesting why it is that people who were in charge of the marketplace, in every sense of the word, yielded to this tyranny. Why is it that there wasn't a popular *revulsion*?

As a matter of fact, there was a popular revulsion. That is to say, people didn't build their own houses to look like Le Corbusier's Villa Savoye, did they?

WOLFE: In domestic architecture there was constant guerrilla warfare and rebellions and so forth. But not in great public structures. Not at all, no.

WFB: What does that tell us about the response of public men— this sort of mimetic response as against the relative individualism of the consumer?

WOLFE: Here we get to the heart of my particular argument, which is that today in this country, in the midst of what could certainly be called the American Century, we remain the most obedient in matters of the arts. Any questions of the higher aesthetics—architecture, serious music, serious dance, the novel even—we remain the most obedient little colonial subjects of Europe. We are a little Nigeria of the arts. I pick out Nigeria because that was the only British colony that *didn't* revolt. They had to form a committee to create a national anthem, another committee to choose the national colors, and so on.

We have never to this day had our revolution in the arts from Europe. It's supposed that we got over that in the 1920s, and V. F. Calverton coined the term "the colonial complex," which he used as if the complex was over—had been cured. His book, in which that term was used, was published in 1932; and the thing was just getting rolling.

TOM WOLFE

And when a baffling design, whose forms were originally created for workers in Germany and Holland after the First World War, would be presented to Exxon or to whatever other great corporation—that's one of the companies that has one of the glass boxes on Sixth Avenue—all the heads at the walnut conference table gleaming there would turn to the architect, and he would have the perfect vocabulary for why this was a terrific design. He would say, "You have to notice that the *morphemes* of the *infrastructure* of the *semiology* of the language of the vocabulary that the architect was using provide the *perfect* screen through which—" [*Laughter*] And this also happened to be the age of the *expert,* and by the 1950s we believed that architects were experts. They were part scientist, part artist.

WFB: They were experts, but never geniuses, right? Very important, isn't it, to emphasize, as you do here in your book, the collectivization of the architectural firm?

WOLFE: By this time, the genius—the individual genius in the sense of the solitary artist who finds his own exclusive path—was very much denigrated within the architectural profession. The idea was that there was a *spirit of the age.* Mies van der Rohe, one of the Bauhaus architects who had such an influence here, used to say that "there is no such thing as architectural style; there is the spirit of the age." And this creates a uniform style, which he wouldn't even refer to as a "style."

            Now, this was much believed in, and when somebody like Eero Saarinen or Edward Durell Stone, or someone like Morris Lapidus (an interesting figure), would go off in some exuberant, wild, decorative direction, using pure screens and cornices and gold leaf and marble and all sorts of things that were banished as bourgeois from the—

WFB: They just ceased to exist, didn't they?

WOLFE: They would either cease to exist as apostates who are no longer spoken of, or they'd be treated as heretics. Or they just were no longer seriously *talked* about. And that spirit was very much alive. This brings us to a point about the clients, which was that by this time there was a great premium put within the American corporate world on "cultivation." Cultivation had become the antisepsis of success. If you could endow the right buildings, buy enough art, show your appreciation for the world of art, it tended to kill, like penicillin, the spirochetes of the greed of commerce. So this was one of the ways of making yourself look cultivated, a part of a higher spirit.

            You know, Max Weber predicted back in about 1890 that in the twentieth century, aesthetics would replace ethics as the standard by which men live; and we begin to see that when it becomes part of corporate policy to go to the world of the architects and ask, "Who are the important architects? What are the important forms? [Whatever they are], we'll use them."

    I knew he would tell the story well, and in any event it was a story that dramatized his case against instrumental architecture—which turns out not to be instrumental at all, if one grants that that which is uninhabitable is not, after all, instrumental.

WFB: Tell us now about the sad, sad fate of the Pruitt-Igoe
            project, which is on page eighty-one [of your book]. This
            practically made me weep by the time I was through with
            it.

WOLFE: This was a housing project which was designed by Minoru
            Yamasake, the same man who was the major designer of
            the World Trade Center. Even before the buildings had
            gone up, in St. Louis, his designs had won an award from
            the American Institute of Architects, just for the brilliance
            of the concept and the drawings. And the picture that
            we're looking at is the scene as the building is *blown up,*
            in July of 1972. Only about ten or twelve years after the
            project had been built.

            Now, the project had been built along the lines of Cor-
            busier's idea of having "streets in the air." The notion was
            that you should take workers—this was built for workers,
            incidentally; I mean all of this type of building was built
            for workers—you should *stack* workers up—you
            shouldn't have them sprawled all over the landscape. So
            you put them in skyscrapers, and to keep them away from
            the fetid atmosphere of the streets—from Gin Lane (Ho-
            garth's, not Southampton's)—you'd have streets in the air
            which would be kind of boulevards on the tenth floor.
            They were great open porches, is what they really were;
            so that the workers wouldn't get into trouble in the nonan-
            tiseptic life down below.

            As a result, you have thousands of people in a building
            like this—and this was repeated in many, many places—
            with no place to *sin*! No place even to commit *minor* sins!
            So if you wanted to shoot some dice, or if you wanted to
            shoot up, or if you wanted to make love or anything that
            might be on your mind in the way of that sort of recrea-
            tion, they would end up doing it in the *streets in the air*!
            I mean, those were the only streets that they *had*.

            Well, these were the same streets that everyone had to
            use to get from one part of the building to the other, and
            life just became *impossible*. And the workers? Workers
            never lived in "worker housing." They all went to Islip,
            Long Island, or to the San Fernando Valley outside of Los

Angeles, and lived in houses with clapboard siding and sort of fake gaslights on the front and pitched roofs and all the rest of it.

And, finally, a gentle titan.

Jorge Luis Borges (1899–1986) was living in Buenos Aires. I had lunched with him a few years earlier in Boston while he was visiting professor at Harvard. A friend—Herbert Kenny, then the literary editor of *The Boston Globe*—had brought us together. Borges was already blind. He did not mind it, he said, because now he could "live his dreams with less distraction."

He took early to his craft, translating at age six from English into Spanish Oscar Wilde's demanding *The Happy Prince*. That translation was thought to have been the work of his father, and was used as a school text. He began to publish in the twenties—poems, essays, short works of fiction. In the late thirties he got his first job, as a menial assistant in a library. When General Perón, against whom Borges had signed a declaration, was ousted, Borges was made director of the National Library. He traveled and lectured extensively, and was for decades the writer who for some unknown reason had not been awarded the Nobel Prize.

We met in Buenos Aires, in 1977, during the reign of the military junta. He seemed astonishingly frail, but he spoke without hesitation.

I did not interrupt him. The following pages I think of as the fairest ever minted by *Firing Line.*

WFB: You have been compared to both Milton and Homer in terms of a highly illuminated internal vision. Is this a correct judgment, as far as you're concerned?

BORGES: Well, I do my best to think it a correct judgment. At least, I try to put up with blindness. Of course, when you are blind, time flows in a different way. It flows, let's say, on an easy slope. I have sometimes spent sleepless nights— night before last, for example—but I didn't really feel especially unhappy about it, because time was sliding down that—was flowing down that easy slope.

WFB: You mean, you'd have felt more *un*happy if you *had* been able to see?

BORGES: Oh yes, of course I would.

WFB: Why?

BORGES: I can't very well explain it. These are the thoughts of years. When I first went blind—I mean, for reading purposes—I felt very unhappy. But now I feel that being blind is, let's say, part of my world. I suppose that happens. One's heard about it. When one is in jail, one thinks of being in jail as part of one's world; when one is sick, also.

WFB: How do you refresh yourself, as someone who is blind?

BORGES: I'm reading all the time. I'm having books reread to me. I do very little contemporary reading. But I'm only going back to certain writers, and among those writers I would like to mention an American writer. I would like to mention Emerson. I think of Emerson not only as a great prose writer—everybody knows that—but a very fine intellectual poet, as the only intellectual poet who had any *ideas*. Emerson was brimming over with ideas.

WFB: Well, you did a great deal to reintroduce many Americans to many American writers, including Emerson, isn't that correct?

BORGES: Yes, yes. I've done my best. Emerson and also another writer I greatly love.

WFB: Hawthorne?

BORGES: Well, but in Hawthorne—what I dislike about Hawthorne is, he was always writing fables. In the case of Poe, well, you get tales; but there was no moral tagged on to them. But I think of Melville, one of the great writers of the world, no?

WFB: How do you account for the failure of Melville to achieve any recognition during his lifetime, any significant recognition?

BORGES: Because people thought of him as writing travel books. I have the 1911 edition of the *Encyclopaedia Britannica*. There's an article about Melville, and they speak of him much in the same way as they might speak about Captain [Frederick] Marryat, for example, or other writers. Melville wrote many travel books; people thought of him as writing in that way, so they couldn't see all that *Moby-Dick; or, The White Whale,* meant.

WFB: Yes. Well now, you say that you spend most of your time reading the older writers now. Is it because you reject the new writers, or because you choose to continue to be unfamiliar with them?

BORGES: I am afraid that I'd find the new writers more or less like myself.

WFB: You won't.

BORGES: I suppose I will. I suppose all contemporaries are more or less alike, no? Since I dislike what I write, I prefer going back to the nineteenth, to the eighteenth century, and then, of course, also going back to the Romans, since I have no Greek, but I had Latin. Of course, my Latin is very rusty. But still, as I once wrote, to have forgotten Latin is already, in itself, a gift. To have known Latin and to have forgotten it is something that sticks to you somehow. I have done most of my reading in English. I read very little in Spanish. I was educated practically in my father's library, and that comprised English books. So that when I think of the Bible, I think of the King James Bible. When I think of the *Arabian Nights,* I think of Lane's translation, or of Captain Burton's translation. When I think of Persian literature, I think in terms of Browne's *Literary History of Persia,* and of course of Fitzgerald's. And, frankly, I remember the first book I read on the history of South America was Prescott's *The Conquest of Peru.*

WFB: Is that right?

BORGES: Yes, and then I fell back on Spanish writers, but I have done most of my reading in English. I find English a far finer language than Spanish.

WFB: Why?

BORGES: There are many reasons. Firstly, English is both a Germanic and a Latin language, those two registers. For any idea you take, you have two words. Those words do not

mean exactly the same. For example, if I say "regal," it's
not exactly the same thing as saying "kingly." Or if I say
"fraternal," it's not saying the same as "brotherly"; [then
there is] "dark" and "obscure." Those words are different.
It would make all the difference—speaking, for example,
of the Holy Spirit—it would make all the difference in the
world in a poem if I wrote about the Holy Spirit or I wrote
"the Holy Ghost," since "ghost" is a fine, dark Saxon
word, while "spirit" is a light Latin word.

And then there is another reason. The reason is that I
think that of all languages, English is the most *physical* of
all languages. You can, for example, say "He loomed
over." You can't very well say that in Spanish.

WFB: *Asomo?*

BORGES: No; they're not exactly the same. And then, in English you
can do almost anything with verbs and prepositions. For
example, to "laugh off," to "dream away." Those things
can't be said in Spanish. To "live down" something, to
"live up to" something. You can't say those things in
Spanish. I suppose they can be said in German, although
my German really isn't too good. I taught myself German
for the sake of reading Schopenhauer in the text. That was
way back in 1916. I had read Schopenhauer in English; I
was greatly attracted to Schopenhauer, and then I thought
I would try to read him in the text and then I taught
myself German. And at long last I read *Die Welt als Wille
und Vorstellung* in the text, and *Parerga und
Paralipomena* also.

WFB: Do you write your poetry in English or in Spanish?

BORGES: No, I respect English too much. I write it in Spanish.

WFB: Do you pass on the translation? Do you personally pass
on the translations, or do you simply entrust them to
people like Kerrigan or di Giovanni?

BORGES: No, I have people like Alistair Reid, di Giovanni, and
Kerrigan, who are greatly better than I am at my texts.
And then of course in Spanish words are far too cumber-
some. They're far too long. For example, if you take an

English adverb, or two English adverbs—you say for instance "quickly," "slowly," and then the stress falls on the
significant part of the word. *Quick-*ly. *Slow-*ly. But if you
say it in Spanish, you say "lenta*mente,*" "rapida*mente.*"
And then the stress falls on the *non*significant part. And
all that makes a very cumbersome language. But still,
Spanish is my destiny; it's my *fate,* and I have to do what
I can with Spanish.

WFB: Well, does the fact that the Spanish language is less re-
          sourceful than the English language necessarily make it
          less complete as poetry?

BORGES: No. I think that when poetry is achieved, it can be
          achieved in *any* language. It's more than a fine Spanish
          verse that could hardly be translated to another language.
          It would turn to something else. But when *beauty* hap-
          pens, well, there it is. No?

          What Whistler said—people were discussing art in
          Paris. People spoke about, well, the influence of *heredity,*
          tradition, environment, and so on. And then Whistler
          said, in his lazy way, "Art happens." "Art *happens,*" he
          said. And I think that's true. I should say that *beauty*
          happens.

          Sometimes I think that beauty is not something rare. I
          think beauty is happening *all* the time. *Art* is happening
          all the time. At some conversation a man may say a very
          fine thing, not being aware of it. I am hearing fine sen-
          tences all the time from the man in the street, for example.
          From anybody.

WFB: So you consider yourself a transcriber, to a certain extent.

BORGES: Yes, in a sense I do, and I think that I have written some
          fine lines, of course. *Everybody* has written some fine
          lines. That's not *my* privilege. If you're a writer you're
          bound to write something fine, at least now and then, off
          and on.

WFB: Even Longfellow?

BORGES: Longfellow has some very beautiful lines. I'm very old-
          fashioned, but I *like* "This is the forest primeval. The

A WEARY PRODUCER, AND WEARY HOST

murmuring pines and the hemlocks." That's a very fine
line. I don't know why people look down on Longfellow.

WFB: Is it in your experience possible to stimulate a love of
literature, or is it something that also just happens, or
doesn't happen? Is it possible to take twenty people and
make them love literature more?

BORGES: Of course. I was a professor of English and American literature during some twenty years, at the University of Buenos Aires.

WFB: That's why I asked you.

BORGES: And I tried to teach my students not literature—that can't be taught—but the *love* of literature. And I have sometimes succeeded, and failed many times over, of course. If the course has to be done in four months, I can do very little. But still I know there are many young men in Buenos Aires—maybe they're not so young now—young men and young women, who have their memories full of English verse. And I have been studying Old English and Old Norse for the last twenty years. And I have also taught many people the love of Old English.

WFB: And so there is a pedagogical art? It isn't simply a matter of—

BORGES: But I think literature is being taught in the wrong way all the time. It's being taught in terms of history and of sociology. And I wouldn't do that. I have seen many teachers who are always falling back on dates, on place names.

WFB: You don't do that?

BORGES: I do my best to avoid it.

WFB: On the grounds that it is distracting?

BORGES: Yes, of course. Yes, I feel that it's irrelevant. For example, if I give you a beautiful line of verse, that verse should be as beautiful today as it was centuries ago. Or had it been written today, it should be beautiful also.

WFB: Well, doesn't the context in which you read it attach a certain meaning to it?

BORGES: Yes, but I suppose if a line is beautiful, the context can be safely forgotten, no? If I say, for example, that "the moon is the mirror of time," that's a fine metaphor, don't you think?

WFB: Yes.

BORGES: A mirror as being something round; it can be easily bro-
            ken; and yet somehow the moon is as old as time, or half
            as old as time. Now, were I to add that that comes from
            Persian poetry, it wouldn't really add to the beauty. Per-
            haps it might add in a certain way. But still, had that
            metaphor been invented this morning, it would be a fine
            metaphor, no? The moon, the mirror of time? It happens
            to be a Persian metaphor.

WFB: But certain things are accepted as beautiful in part de-
            pending on the prevailing style. The kind of enthusiasm,
            for instance, that was shown for Restoration comedy.
            Some of that stuff isn't very funny now. Some of the
            romantic excesses of the nineteenth century aren't—

BORGES: But I suppose all that's rather artificial, no? That's one of
            the reasons why I'm so fond of Old English poetry. No-
            body knows anything whatever about the poets [other
            than] the century they wrote in, and yet I find something
            very stirring about Old English poetry.

WFB: It has to stand on its own two feet, you mean?

BORGES: It has to. Or maybe because I like the sound of it. "Maeg
            ic be me sylfum sothgied wrecan, / Sithas secgan"—now,
            those sounds have a *ring* to them.

WFB: What does that say? What does that mean in dollars?

BORGES: That would say—in dollars that would be: "I can utter a
            true song about myself. I can tell of my travels." That
            sounds like Walt Whitman, no? That was written in the
            ninth century in Northumberland. "Maeg ic be me sylfum
            sothgied wrecan, / Sithas secgan"—and Ezra Pound
            translated it as this (I think it's a rather uncouth transla-
            tion): "May I for my own sake song's truth reckon, jour-
            ney's jargon." Well, that's too much of a jargon to *me,* no?
            Of course, he's translating the sounds. "Maeg ic be me
            sylfum sothgied wrecan, / Sithas secgan"—"May I for my
            sake song's truth reckon,"—"sothgied wrecan." He's
            translating the sounds more than the sense. And then
            "Sithas secgan"—"tell of my travels"—he translates
            "journey's jargon," which is rather uncouth, at least to me.

WFB: Whose translation did you say?

BORGES: It's Ezra Pound's translation. From the Anglo-Saxon, yes.

WFB: How would you have translated . . .

BORGES: I would translate it literally. "I can utter, I can say a true song about myself. I can tell my travels." I think that should be enough.

English can receive no higher tribute than that it was so loved by such a man, who used it from time to time to tell of his travels, in the world, and in his mind.

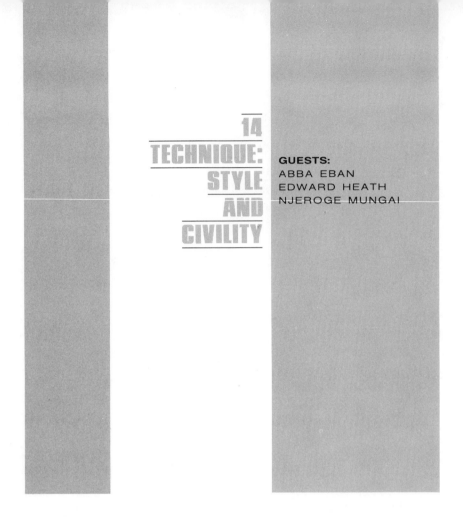

GUESTS:
ABBA EBAN
EDWARD HEATH
NJEROGE MUNGAI

A television exchange is successful, or not, with intense attention to timing. The guest who makes a bewildering point is often best treated by an instant's pained silence, before you remark on what he has said or not said. The guest who never stops talking invites staccato interruptions—and, sometimes, conspicuous inattention. There was the young man, briefly mentioned above, who was a guest of *Firing Line* for the sole reason that he had become, at age twenty-seven or thereabouts, the de facto manager of the mind and body of Bertrand Russell. That this could have happened at all is a melancholy observation on the reaches of senility. But here was this puerile ideologue sending out invitations in Lord Russell's name to statesmen and scholars the world over to attend a War Crimes Trial of Americans for pursuing an objective in Vietnam, quoting Lord Russell to the effect that there were no differences, really, between the United States and the Nazis.

Moreover, it was impossible, on the set, to stop him from talking for the purpose of commenting on what he said, or for asking for elucidations. He simply continued to talk. Finally, I picked up my bundle of notes, extracted from them an issue of *Time* magazine, and proceeded to read from it while he went on. Timing.

Consider the implications of timing in the experience of Morris Abram (Chapter 6). If he had moved *more* decisively? . . . If President Levi of Chicago had moved just a *little* slower? Just a *little* quicker? As it happened, Levi captured the perfect moment, and Chicago University became an oasis of academic stability.

And with that stability comes the quality indispensable, within a university, to the life of the mind: civility. A civility not unrelated to the success, or lack of it, of democratic life. It is, in a sense, an exercise of civility that causes the minority to accept the majority after an upset election. It was noted by a Latin American journalist with awe, on August 9, 1974, that that morning there were only two policemen—the usual number—outside the White House. Inside the White House, a President of the United States was being forced out of office for the first time in American history. An interaction of timing and civility. *At just the right moment,* Richard Nixon concluded that the time had come to go. Although one would hardly classify as civil all the ambient shrieks and yells demanding that he should go, the propulsive move was a calm visit to the White House by three Republican senators. They told him he had lost his political base; and, there and then, he decided he had to resign his office.

It has occurred to me (after modest ratiocination) that style is, really, a matter of timing. Here is a case in point.

It is a story by one of the nineteenth-century Russians, and timing here is one factor for not going to the trouble of finding out which one it was, since it doesn't matter. Chekhov, I think. In any event, the story I read sometime during my teens was about a very rich young prince who one evening engaged in a drinking bout of Brobdingnagian dimensions with his fellow bloods, which eventually peaked, as such affairs frequently did in that curious epoch of genius and debauchery, in a philosophical argument: this time, over the limits of human self-control. The question was specifically posed: Could someone succeed in voluntarily sequestering himself in a small suite of rooms for a period of twenty years, notwithstanding that he would always be free to open the

PRIME MINISTER EDWARD HEATH

door, letting himself out, or others in? In a spirit of high and exhibitionistic dogmatism, the prince pronounced such hypothetical discipline
preposterous, and announced that he would give one million rubles to
anyone who succeeded in proving him wrong.

You will have guessed that a young companion, noble but poor, and
himself far gone in wine's litigious imperatives, accepted the challenge.
And so with much fanfare, a few days later, the rules having been
carefully set (he could ask for, and receive, anything except human
company), "Peter" (we'll call him) was ushered into the little subterranean suite of rooms in the basement of the prince's house.

During the first years, he drank. During the next years, he stared at
the ceiling. During the succeeding period, he read—ordering books,
more books, and more books. Meanwhile the fortunes of the prince had
taken a disastrous turn, and so he schemed actively to seduce Peter to
leave his self-imposed confinement, dispatching letters below, describing
evocatively the sensual delights Peter would experience by merely opening the door. In desperation, as the deadline neared, he even offered
one-half the premium to abort the experiment.

The night before the twentieth year would finish, at midnight, half the
town and thousands from all over Russia were outside to celebrate and
marvel over the endurance of Peter, at the instant of his emergence. But
one hour before midnight, the startled crowd saw the celebrated door

below street level open, prematurely. And saw Peter emerge. He had, you see, truly *become* a philosopher; and in all literature I know of no more eloquent gesture of disdain for money. One hour more, and he'd have earned a million rubles. What style, you say; and I concur.

But what is it about that one hour that speaks so stylishly? Had Peter emerged one year before the deadline, much of the drama of his final act would have been drained. Or, at the other end, suppose that Peter had emerged exactly one minute before midnight, forfeiting his reward? We sense immediately that a mere one minute's edge before the twenty-year term formally matured is overfreighted in melodrama.

It is a question of style, surely.

It is even so in the matter of the speed of human responses which, indicating spontaneity, communicate integrity. "Is it all right if I bring Flo's sister and her husband along for the weekend?" demands *instant* assent; the least pause is, to the quick ear, lethal. When such a proposition is posed, the man of style will make one of two decisions, and he must here think with great speed. He will either veto the extra guests, going on to give whatever reason he finds most ingenious; or he will accept them on the spot. Absolutely nothing in between. In between is many other things, defined as lacking in style.

It is so, I think, with language in a television studio, whether written or spoken; as also with that aspect of language on which its effectiveness so heavily relies, namely rhythm. It matters less what exactly you say at a moment of tension than that you say it at *just* the right moment. Great speed might be necessary, as above; or such delay as suggests painful meditation, as required to ease, console, or inspirit the other person. Style is not a synonym for diplomacy. Style can be infinitely undiplomatic, as in the stylish means selected by John L. Lewis to separate his union from the CIO ("We disaffiliate," he wrote on the back of an envelope, dispatching it to headquarters). It is sometimes stylish to draw attention to oneself, as Lewis was doing. But in other circumstances, the man of style will be all but anonymous. Some men are congenitally incapable of exhibiting a stylish anonymity. Of Theodore Roosevelt it was said that whenever he attended a wedding, he confused himself with the bride. The Queen of England could not feign anonymity; neither could LBJ, or Mr. Micawber. But whichever is sought— being conspicuous or inconspicuous—timing is the principal element of success. Arrive very early at a funeral and you will be noticed, even as you will be noticed arriving at the very last minute. In between, you glide in, on cat feet.

In language, rhythm is an act of timing. "Why did you use the word 'irenic' when you tell me now it merely means 'peaceful'?" a *Firing Line* guest once asked me, indignant. To which the answer was: "I desired the extra syllable." In all circumstances? No, for God's sake. In the peculiar circumstances of the sentence uttered, and these circumstances were set by what had gone just before, and what would probably come just after that. A matter of style. A matter of timing.

Timing, style, civility. . . . Abba Eban, Foreign Minister of the state of Israel, was in the makeup room: the taping would begin in a few minutes. Suddenly a messenger arrives at the studio, demanding to be taken to his superior. He is admitted, and advises Eban that the news has just been received: *Gamal Abdel Nasser is dead!* Abba Eban sits stony-faced, assimilating a piece of news of historic importance for Israel. Israel's principal, full-time, fanatical tormentor is suddenly— dead. His face is immobile for another few moments. Then he rises, proceeds to the designated chair in the studio, and our exchange proceeds. He has by this time integrated the implications of Nasser's death for the state of Israel.

Or: Edward Heath, former Prime Minister of Great Britain, contender for future Prime Minister in an election only a few weeks ahead. He arrives at the studio and talks amiably about the America's Cup race that day, being fought in the waters off Newport. Just before we enter the studio he turns to me and says: "Oh, you do understand, Mr. Buckley. No criticism of any kind can be made of any British politician. I am, after all, in a foreign country." To spend one hour with a principal British political figure without any critical attention being given to the leaders of the Labour Party or to his critics within the Conservative Party would make for an epicene hour. I stammered that *something* would need to be said, for instance about the criticisms of Mr. Heath made during the preceding days by Enoch Powell?

Mr. Heath simply reiterated his position.

The show went on; the timing of Edward Heath was, in a true sense, an exercise in incivility.

Three experiences in Africa. On Monday, I did John Vorster, Prime Minister of South Africa. It was his first appearance on television in his own country. He rushed from the studio chair to a playback machine to evaluate his performance. I watched for a moment or two, and decided not to interrupt him and his attendants. And so left without shaking hands with the Prime Minister, a gentleman of formal habits, but engrossed, now, in seeing himself for the first time on the tube.

The following day I was in Rhodesia. I was told by an aide to the Prime Minister that he had grave misgivings about accepting my invitation to go on *Firing Line,* which, finally, he had agreed to do. "The Prime Minister was on television only once before, with David Frost, and Frost gave him a very hard time," Mr. Smith's aide confided to me. I told him to reassure the Prime Minister. As a former RAF fighter pilot who served gallantly in action during the war, he would certainly survive an hour on *Firing Line.*

Which he did. Following the hour came a memorable few seconds illustrating the electrical question of timing. When the music ended and the program was over, Ian Smith stood up and his face broke into a tight smile. He was clearly delighted by his performance. A man of preternatural social stiffness he nevertheless turned to me and said with forced, labored effusion: "Mr. Buckley, er, you must come back to Rhodesia! Yes, you must come back to Rhodesia and *stay* for a while! And bring Mrs. Buckley with you! And I don't want you, when you come back, to treat me like the Prime Minister. I want you to . . . [his face suddenly, dramatically, sobered] to . . . [more slowly] come and have *tea* with us."

The Prime Minister, obviously, had suddenly espied contingent thunderclouds coming in from America. *"What am I doing! This Yank is undoubtedly going to call in a few weeks and announce that he and his wife and his kids are going to spend the hols with me!"* The timing was delinquent; the effect, hilarious.

The following day I was at a high school in Nairobi, waiting in the cloistered wings, in the headmaster's study, to do a *Firing Line* on the theme "Black Africa Looks at White Africa," featuring Njeroge Mungai, a medical doctor, and Foreign Minister of Kenya.

He told the producer he wished to talk with me briefly before we walked into the studio, already packed with several hundred students waiting to see the taping.

He was a half-hour late (people outside the television world have no idea what agonies, nervous and financial, lateness imposes on a producer). Dr. Mungai sat down casually and good-humoredly in the waiting room, and we exchanged pleasantries.

What, I said finally, looking a little apprehensively at the clock, did he want to discuss in advance of the program?

Well, said Dr. Mungai, as Foreign Minister I would be very embarrassed if you were to get into the subject of Nixon and Watergate.

No problem, I said. Anything else?

PRIME MINISTER HAROLD WILSON (TWO VIEWS)

Well, he said, as Foreign Minister I couldn't be a part of any program in which criticism was expressed of any other African state or its leaders or its policies.

We were there to criticize white Africa, which is to say South Africa, Rhodesia, Mozambique, and Angola (this was a month before the coup in Portugal that decolonized Mozambique and Angola; six years before Rhodesia became Zimbabwe). How could we neglect to discuss other African states?

"Those are not states," Dr. Mungai corrected me. "They are *colonies*—white colonies." All right, I said, but the argument against these—colonies—is that their policies are racist in foundation, but to explore this question requires us to probe definitions, and in order to do that, it becomes necessary to probe the policies of other African states that might also be called racist in character.

Dr. Mungai just sat there and repeated his proscriptions. The producer, desperate at the prospect of losing an entire program after all the trouble that had been taken and money spent, intervened to suggest that perhaps a suitable formula would be for me to criticize, say, Idi Amin, and for Dr. Mungai to reply that he could not participate, as Foreign Minister, in any criticism of chiefs of African states. That way, I could have registered my point, and Mungai could invoke protocol to abort any discussion of it.

No, said Dr. Mungai: the criticism can't be uttered even to be ruled out of order.

I told Dr. Mungai that people watching the program would think I had taken leave of my senses if I spent an entire hour in Africa discussing white racism without mentioning the racism of such as Amin and Bokassa.

Bright idea—Could Dr. Mungai suggest a prominent Kenyan journalist, or academician, who, uninhibited by protocol, would be able to discuss freely the policies of other African countries?

Nobody in Kenya—Dr. Mungai smiled, but the steel was now showing through—would be willing to criticize another African country.

Dr. Mungai smiled. "It is," he said, "my country."

I returned his smile. "And," I said, "it is my show."

To the consternation of everyone, including, I happily report, Dr. Mungai, I extended my hand, shook his, waved at the producer, and left the studio to return to my hotel.

Timing, timing. We would never have traveled all the way to Kenya if we had been given timely notice of the Mungai Reservations.

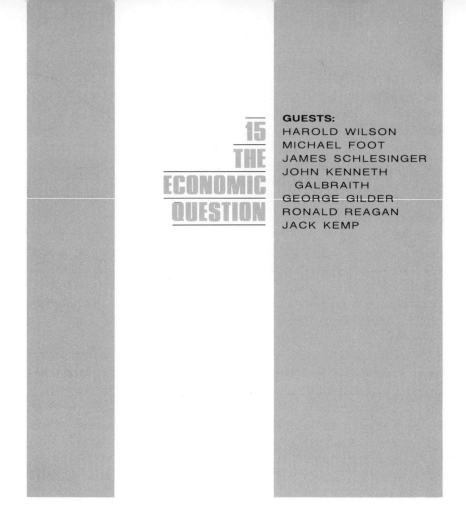

The eternal economic argument. It has raged unceas-
ingly, on *Firing Line* and off *Firing Line.* But although
there have been wide swings, the central question has always been one
or another modality of the question: the private, or the public sector?
The political problem is that of the ugly reaches of the omnipotent state.
There are the supply-siders vs. the redistributionists. It is not wide of
the historical mark to say that during the years *Firing Line* has been
produced, socialism has collapsed. No causative link is suggested,
though I think socialist theology collapsed not only on national stages
in the Third World and in much of Europe but also at *Firing Line*
studios, more or less contemporaneously.

    We begin in England, whose socialist experiment has been, well, more
thorough, and more dogmatic, than our own. In 1976, quite suddenly,
Harold Wilson announced that he would retire as leader of the Labour

Party, and therefore as Prime Minister. He had been elected in 1964, as Britain's youngest postwar Prime Minister. In 1970 he was defeated by Mr. Heath, but in 1974 won again. After his resignation in 1976 he was succeeded by James Callaghan, who in 1979 lost to Mrs. Thatcher. Mr. Wilson appeared on *Firing Line* in 1983 as Sir Harold Wilson. Not much later he was elevated again, and now he was Lord Wilson. I made the (innocent) mistake, at one point in a later program, of referring to him simply as Sir Harold. He paused quietly to correct me: "It's . . . *Lord* Wilson." Lord Wilson was still formally an enemy of the class system, and a "socialist," though his arguments were, really, rather relaxed.

WFB: Do you believe that eighty-three percent taxation, the level at which taxation was imposed under Mr. Callaghan, is an obstacle to productivity?

WILSON: It's very high. It's not necessarily an obstacle, because people may work harder in order to transform that seventeen percent into more cash in the pocket. But, yes, it was too high. We had very little alternative, and we were still running pretty heavy military expenditures, not least under the pressure of certain distinguished countries the other side of the Atlantic from us.

All very pleasant, and it was nice that Lord Wilson thought an 83 percent taxation rate on the high side. What was most revealing was two premises, one explicit, the other implicit. High tax rates, he said, would make people work harder. And a heavy military burden justified a tax rate of 83 percent. I.e., high taxation does not discourage industry or individuals; high marginal tax rates are the necessary means of financing such burdens as the military. But these are basic socialist premises.

Michael Foot, who succeeded James Callaghan as leader of the Labour Party only to lose in the general election to Mrs. Thatcher in 1983, had peaked, as adamant socialist, on *Firing Line,* in 1968. His reputation, as protégé and biographer of Aneurin Bevan, was as a doctrinaire leader of the British left.

WFB: Isn't it a part of the general objection to socialism that unless you have total control of your own affairs in the international money market you *can't* carry out your own experiments internally?

FOOT: Of course, you would have more control over economic policy if you had a socialist plan. You would stop the freedom of [money] movement in some respects: the freedom, just to give an example, of capitalists to take their capital out of the country and invest it wherever they want to—in South Africa, or wherever they please. You would, of course, control that *much* more strictly. There are controls now. I would like to see those controls much stronger. It seems to me an *absurdity* and indeed an offense against humanity that we should insist on "freedom" for our capitalists to be able to take capital out of the country at the price of putting a lot of people on the dole queues. It's much better to have everybody working and to control the capital which is produced—not very much by the capitalists, if at all, but by the whole community. The capital of the nation belongs to the *whole country* and shouldn't be regarded as purely a "private" property which can be used to the injury of the nation.

WFB: But surely *any* freedom can be used for the injury of the nation? An eloquent case could be made for the government to regulate publishing—on the grounds that people can use their right of freedom of speech to injure the nation. I don't deny that an individual could use his "capital," which is another word—an ugly word—for savings, and use it in such a way as to offend *you*—

FOOT: But I don't—

WFB: —by taking it to an economy where people can live with more privacy than they can in a socialist economy.

FOOT: I—

WFB: I think one of the criticisms of socialism in *general,* at that level—the philosophical level—is precisely that you find nice, civilized people like you suggesting that there ought to be laws which have the effect of regulating human movement.

FOOT: No, well, as far as—let's clear this out of the way first—as
             far as freedom of speech or freedom to print goes, of
             course, I am *absolutely* in favor of both. And indeed most
             of the fights for the maintenance of freedom of speech and
             freedom to print fought for in this country were fought
             for by people on the left, not by the right.

WFB: That's because you were the dissident class.

FOOT: Hmm?

WFB: The question is whether you would protect the dissident
             class if *you* became a majority. Wherever one has, in fact,
             entrenched socialism—for instance, in the Soviet Union—
             the dissident class all of a sudden loses its rights. And the
             kind of thing I'm worried about is the kind of thing that
             Orwell worried about. He wasn't talking about Russia—
             he was talking about *English* socialism when he wondered
             what kind of rights would be left to the minority—

FOOT: Well—

WFB: Already you are suggesting a repeal of some rights that
             have been considered sacred over the years.

FOOT: Well, I— Take Orwell, I happen to know him a bit. I don't
             know how well you knew him, but I certainly—

WFB: I didn't know him at all. I just read his books.

FOOT: —don't think he was writing about socialism in *this* coun-
             try. He was warning about the general trend of Western
             societies, whether they were Communist, capitalist, social-
             ist, or others. But you suggested that socialists were
             against freedom. I'm merely pointing out the historical
             fact that the socialists, trade unionists, and others in this
             country and in the United States—indeed, most of the
             great fighters for freedom—have been on the left. I don't
             say that all were, but most of them.

WFB: I absolutely deny this. To believe that requires a rather
             narrow definition of freedom. You talk rather valiantly
             about freedom of the working classes, and so on. But since
             socialism specializes in this macrocosmic rhetoric even for

the working classes—"let's all own the railroads"—my own observation is that you end up owning nothing at all of any substance. I want to understand you completely, if I may, Mr. Foot. Suppose—suppose somebody went to work, let's say at age eighteen, and ran a candy shop—a sweet shop, right?—and at age sixty having accumulated thirty-two hundred pounds decided that he simply wanted to take his family elsewhere for whatever reason. Maybe he didn't like the government, or maybe he fell in love with a Yugoslav or whatever. Do I understand that you would pass laws that would *forbid* him from taking his savings out of this country?

FOOT: I'm in favor of the right of people to move to other countries and take what belongings they've got, and I would like to see a world in which people could move freely across all these frontiers, and indeed I would like to see the frontiers abolished. But—I do not believe that you can do that *until* you have established a full employment society over many years in different parts of the world.

WFB: In other words, you wouldn't permit it.

FOOT: No, I wouldn't permit it at the present time. I would not permit a situation in which the capital of the society, which has been built up not merely by individuals but by people joining together in steelworks and coal mines, and the other factories where they produce the wealth—I would not allow the community's wealth which has been produced in this way to be used in a manner which damages and destroys the community, because we live in *one* community, and the idea that the few people can take a rake-off from it and use that wealth to injure that society is one that is offensive, I would have thought, to civilized world standards.

WFB: The reason I am always so surprised when I engage a socialist is there are so many paradoxes in their rhetoric. For instance, your hope is that socialism will weld the peoples of the world into one human family. Now, if Mr. Candyman takes his thirty-two hundred pounds to, let's say, Canada—or, if you like, let's take a better example:

India—in fact, the people in India *need* capital more than you do—

FOOT: Yes.

WFB: —and, therefore, he is making, is he not, a positive human contribution in those terms?

FOOT: That's right—

WFB: —therefore, there is an insularity here that you—

FOOT: Yes, well if—if your heart is bleeding for the people in India so much, the best way to ensure that the Indians get the assistance from the rich Western world which they require is to give it through instruments which are satisfying to the people of India themselves. That's if that's what you're *really* concerned with—and, indeed, of course that's the idea—

WFB: Well, of course I deny that—

FOOT: —of the United Nations—

WFB: When you say the *people* of India, you always mean the *government* of India, don't you?

FOOT: Well, I think it's absurd when this country is starved for the necessary capital to expand some of our industries, that we should say that it's quite okay that the capital should be transferred.

WFB: Mr. Foot, I can tell you how you can solve your problem tomorrow. And that is, simply cut your taxation down to the bone and permit people to have a higher rate of interest by investing in Great Britain and, according to your analysis, capital will flood in here and—there goes the problem. What's to keep you from doing *that*?

FOOT: I don't think it will solve it at all. In any case, if we were to cut down the taxes to the extent that you are suggesting, of course what we would have to knock out is all the assistance to the people who need it—the old-age pensioners who are required to be paid for out of taxes, or the health services run and paid for out of taxes. All this *squeal* about taxation—nobody likes being taxed, but if you're going to build a community in which you look after the people who need it most, you *have* to have some arrangement whereby everybody contributes into the community till in order that you have enough in the till to be able to distribute it to the people who want—

WFB: But, my dear Mr. Foot—you've got to—

FOOT: —it has not gone anything like far enough in that direction, in my opinion, yet.

Michael Foot, I think, demonstrated as clearly as anyone has done on *Firing Line* the subordination of individual rights to state purposes. I cannot imagine why I forgot to ask him to comment on his longtime socialist colleague's definition of freedom, when asked for it shortly after the war. Ernest Bevin said that freedom was his right to "go to Victoria Station and buy a ticket to anywhere I want to go." He did not qualify it by saying, ". . . on the understanding that I leave my savings behind in Britain."

What business ought the government to have a hand in? James Schlesinger is by profession an economist, and had been associated with Democratic and with Republican administrations. He came to *Firing Line* in 1978. When James Schlesinger was Secretary of Defense (I said, in introducing him), the good news is, there was no war. The bad news is that when he was Secretary of Energy, there was no energy; or at least not enough of it; or, more exactly, a looming world scarcity of it.

WFB: Secretary Schlesinger, how can the market mechanism fight its way through your bureaucracy? What is it that gives you the ahistorical sense of confidence that you can help individual investors to deploy wisely their investment money as between, for instance, plutonium, solar energy, oil, or gas?

SCHLESINGER: Well, we are leaving it up to the investors to make that choice. What is clear is, first, that the long-run prospects for oil and natural gas are such that it is unwise for industry now to invest, on the basis of current prices, in a capacity that will have a thirty- or thirty-five-year life-time. So through the oil and gas users' tax we are going to raise the prices *now* so that there is an inducement to turn to alternative technologies. As to other technologies, whether nuclear power, solar, and so forth, they are all made more attractive by this increase in oil and natural gas prices.

WFB: You mean to say that by artificially pegging the price up beyond what the market would normally sustain, you encourage the strategic investor? Now, why couldn't that argument be made in behalf of almost anything—public housing, for instance, or just plain housing?

SCHLESINGER: [As things stand,] there will not be the supplies of oil and natural gas that will permit the continued expansion of the American economy. The energy supplies for new plants coming in the future should be something other than oil and natural gas. That will permit us to retain oil for the transportation sector, increasing the share of natural gas for the household sector. I cannot conceive of such a mechanism with regard to public housing. What we are doing is to anticipate what we *know* will come, which are higher oil and natural gas prices in the future, as a way of inducing investment into all these alternative technologies.

That analysis was unfaithful—to the penetrative powers of the free market; and incorrect—as economic prediction. When the decontrol of oil and gas prices began fifteen months later, by President Carter, oil came flooding into the market, lowering prices. James Schlesinger did not succeed in doing any damage to the OPEC cartel. The free market did.

And at the broadest level, criticizing the whole constellation of conservative positions on domestic issues, the U.S.S. *John Kenneth Galbraith* in 1976. . . .

GALBRAITH: I suppose that the oldest of the conservative clichés is that assistance to people in caring for their health, and provid-

JOHN KENNETH GALBRAITH

ing them with better housing and jobs, and preventing inflation denies liberties to the people at large. I've always thought, Bill—although I've never myself experienced it—that one of the most constricting things that one can experience is to be without a job and without money. This must have an *enormously* adverse effect on liberty. And so your feeling that anybody who addresses himself to that problem is *limiting* liberty is something I confess I've never been able to understand. But there's so much in your point of view that I've never been able to understand that I don't want to single that out.

WFB: Well, a lot of people who are now without money would not be without money if the tax collector were to return some of what he took away. I think it's very hard to say to somebody from whom you take a couple of thousand dollars a year in taxes when he is heavily mortgaged that you are doing him any particular service in virtue of taking that money from him. It's all very well to say, "We will look after other people's schooling; we will look after other people's health; we will look after other people's psychological problems," but philosophical rigor requires you to say, "In order to do this, we shall *take* from other people."

GALBRAITH: I don't deny that for a moment. I don't deny that—

WFB: You don't stress it.

GALBRAITH: No, I *would* stress it. But I would say that one of the great
             civilizing influences of my lifetime and indeed of the whole
             period since 1913 has been the leveling effect of the pro-
             gressive income tax. If the progressive income tax had not
             been inaugurated—incidentally, by a Republican Presi-
             dent, President Taft—the extremes of income that would
             have developed would have been an enormously disturb-
             ing influence in the economy; and perhaps that tax is the
             single most important conserving and conservative force
             in the modern society. One of the things that best helps the
             poor and the deprived to bear life is to hear the occasional
             screams of the rich.

We have heard already from JKG, and will hear more later. But I take
advantage of my perch here, reminiscing on our encounters. I have
reflected, in thinking about J. K. Galbraith, that it is important to bear
in mind that he knows (sometimes uniquely) the secrets of every man's
heart. Above all, he knows that friends of the free market have in mind
primarily to make themselves richer. That, really, is why we all backed
the Kemp-Roth bill, in case you wondered. Mr. Galbraith has written:
"One yearns to hear someone admit that the added income will be
greatly relished by the rich. Or to have some Treasury official say this
before a congressional committee. But, except as an act of extreme
indiscretion, it will never happen. We like to think of ourselves as a
blunt, plainspoken people. But on some matters a careful social, economic or moral camouflage is clearly essential."

Now, there is a lot of simple, provocative, polemical fun in that
paragraph. However, it invites a mode of analysis the implications of
which are sobering.

"The real reason John Jones is backing that civil liberties bill is that
he desires to increase his civil liberties."

"The real reason John Jones is backing that defense bill is that he
wishes to be more secure."

"The real reason John Jones is backing the clean-air bill is that he
wants cleaner air."

Now we can, if our mind is given to such inclinations, go on to suspect
that John Jones wants that civil liberties bill because he wants to get on

with the production of pornography. That he wants the defense bill because he is loaded with airplane stocks. And that he is only interested in the clean-air bill because he suffers from asthma.

But the misanthropic view of human motives is not really reliable, not even in a sinful world. I can produce a Benedictine monk who has given away all his worldly goods—and is in favor of Kemp-Roth. And to desire that everyone should be relieved of the existing heavy burden of taxation is not to ask Congress for special benefits merely for oneself: No one overhearing a bargaining session between Mr. Galbraith and his publishers would justifiably conclude that Mr. Galbraith puts forward his claims with other motivations than those consistent with healthy appetites.

But I haven't needed to shoulder the burden of making all the extra-statist arguments. My guests have included George Gilder.

WFB: With the publication in 1980 of his book *Wealth and Poverty,* George Gilder emerged as arguably the leading *social* theorist of capitalism writing today. His book is extraordinary on a number of counts, not least of them that he challenged even the axiomatic assumption that capitalism is primarily animated by the desire for self-service. Even Adam Smith fares ill at the hands of George Gilder, whose book was hailed by Dr. Nathan Glazer of Harvard as demolishing "a host of pieties as to the causes of poverty and the conditions that overcome it." David Stockman said of it that "it shatters once and for all the Keynesian and welfare state illusions that burden the failed conventional wisdom of our era. It recovers," said Stockman, "the classic truths about the sources of prosperity and growth just in time." I should like to begin by asking Mr. Gilder to expand on his notion that capitalism has for two centuries been misunderstood as springing from human avarice.

GILDER: My central concern was how people get rich. It seemed to me to explain poverty, you first had to understand wealth; and as I was interviewing poor people, I repeatedly came upon the notion [they cling to] that wealth came from *taking*—that the source of wealth is really *taking*—and therefore the way to overcome poverty is to *take* it back and redistribute it. When I began to examine just how wealth is created, it seemed to me plain that it arises not from taking, but from *giving*. People get rich by giving rather than by taking, and this seemed to me to be a very important perception, because the reason for the crisis in capitalism today, it seems to me, is not its practical achievements, but rather the perception of its moral character.

I mean, I think it's perhaps more important that the Pope is a socialist than that the Taiwanese and the Japanese are capitalists. It's a fact that capitalism has difficulty defending itself as being in accord with Judeo-Christian values that underlie the good society. And the more I examined capitalism in anthropological terms, or even in its contemporary manifestations, the more it became clear to me that capitalists *give*. That is to say that they make investments without a predetermined return; and a gift is not something given necessarily without any return. Even in the Bible you often give alms, for example, in the hope of some form of return, perhaps a blessing.

WFB: Casting bread upon the waters in the expectation that it will be returned?

GILDER: Right.

WFB: But you ought to answer this question, because I think the audience is confused—I certainly am. I am determined to build a cheaper mousetrap in order to get your patronage and to line my pocket. But since in the course of creating a cheaper mousetrap I have made it possible for *you* to purchase one, I have committed an objectively altruistic act for selfish motives. Now, why do you assume there is an incompatibility between those two concepts?

GILDER: I don't. But I am focusing on the *essence* of capitalism. What is it that makes it succeed? What is it that makes it so *extraordinary* in creating wealth? Wealth is ubiquitous. But these acts of creativity are rare—relatively rare—and it's the acts of creativity that have to be explained.

All human motives are mixed in various ways. All
human beings sin; they're avaricious; they're evil in various ways. The question is, what is it about the capitalist
system that makes it so miraculous in the creation of
wealth? I don't think it's avarice. I think avarice is just as
prevalent in the Soviet Union as it is in Japan or in the
United States. I think what makes the system work is this
altruistic creativity, its moral foundation, combined with
faith in the future, which ordinarily expresses itself in faith
in God. I think this is what makes capitalism work.

It's interesting to me that the leading socialist—or at
least one of the leading socialists—in America today is
John Kenneth Galbraith. And he has virtually given up on
the development of the Third World because he has decided that the crucial problem of Third World poverty is
that the poor accommodate themselves to being poor.
They essentially resign themselves to poverty, and he says,
"Indeed, this is not an irrational response. It's a fully
rational response to the predicament of the poor." In other
words, according to Galbraith, the only way they can
escape poverty is to escape the countries in which they live
and move to successful capitalist countries. Yet, after all,
poverty once prevailed *everywhere* in the world. It prevailed in the United States in the early stages of our career
as a country, and in England, and in all the most successful industrial states, and yet he can't explain growth unless
it's already happening. The reason is, he can't understand
why somebody would risk his life to create something
without any assurance of return. He can't understand *giving,* and it's giving that—

WFB: Giving or risking?

GILDER: Risking. But it's giving yourself—

WFB: But that's different, isn't it?

GILDER: Well, it's giving of yourself without any assured return.
            It's giving—it's being willing to go out into the wilderness
            and cut down—

WFB: Look, if I go into a casino and turn in a hundred-dollar
            bill and get a chip and I stick it on three, I don't see that

I'm exhibiting any particular altruistic spirit by doing that.

GILDER: No, that's gambling, which is a zero-sum game. That's why it's not *risking*. You asked whether they were risking. I said they were giving without a predetermined return— giving of *themselves*—not just putting down some money and making no effort and having no moral engagement in activities that they're pursuing. That's the difference between gambling and capitalism. Unfortunately, a lot of people can't tell the difference.

Once again, reflections philosophical—but also personal.

I didn't walk away from the program convinced that George (I have known him for a very long time, hence the familiarity) had truly discovered a philanthropic base in capitalism.

But some time later, while I was vacationing with Milton Friedman at a ski lodge, we touched on the legend so widely attached to Friedman's name. It is, of course, *There is no such thing as a free lunch.* Friedman arrested my attention by telling me he would really like at this point to modify that. Because certain things are, he said, "free." The incremental benefit to each party of a free exchange confers a gift to the two parties.

If, let us say, you give me a sweater in exchange for a pair of shoes, you are left better off than you were before—by your own reckoning, which is the only relevant reckoning. That is so because you value the sweater more than the shoes. The difference between the value to you of the sweater and the value to you of the shoes is free.

By the same token, I am the beneficiary of the extra value I attach to the sweater, over against the shoes.

Viewed in this way, one finds a philanthropic base in capitalism provided the exchange of goods is voluntary. I find that analysis more seductive philosophically than the Gilder risk idea.

I cannot resist from remembering how, and why it was, George and I met. It was in 1966. He was working for the *New Leader* magazine, having graduated from Harvard a few years earlier. In dyspeptic protest against the Republican Party's nomination of Barry Goldwater, he and a friend had written a book called *The Party That Lost Its Head.* I.e., the GOP—by nominating Goldwater.

He had been assigned by *Playboy* magazine to do a profile of me, and we met together once, twice, a half-dozen times. The editor of *Playboy* wanted more of this and less of that, and this process went on endlessly. When in mid-January 1967 George called to tell me he would dearly like another couple of hours with me, I told him if so, he would need to board the American Airlines flight to Phoenix the next day, because I was going there with my wife and would go on from there to Saigon.

I told this to George as a joke. But he called me back a few minutes later to tell me that he had been authorized by *Playboy* to accompany me to Phoenix. He made his reservations at a local motel. My wife and I were staying with Senator Goldwater and his wife, as their guests.

When we arrived at the airport, Goldwater was there to greet us. We all piled into his station wagon, George Gilder absolutely silent and praying that Goldwater had not heard of, let alone read, *The Party That Lost Its Head.* When we came close to Goldwater's house George piped up from the backseat and asked might he please be let off at his motel.

"Why do you want to stay there?" Goldwater, who was driving, turned his head slightly. "Stay with *us.* Barry Jr.'s room is empty."

It was that way for two full days. "God, I'm glad I never met him before writing that book," George said when we parted. Perhaps he had run into the philanthropic lode in capitalism.

In practical politics, the economic views of Ronald Reagan were increasingly relevant. In 1980, I had asked candidate Reagan (as noted above):

WFB: What would you propose should be done to turn the economy back toward fuller employment?

REAGAN: Well, we would start an immediate program of cutting the income tax rates across the board.

And indeed, as President Reagan, he did.

Reagan was influenced by the steady advocacy of Congressman Jack Kemp, the former pro football player. Back in 1978, we heard from Kemp. I asked him to give us his understanding of the so-called Laffer curve. . . .

KEMP: The Laffer curve is based on one of Adam Smith's maxims on taxation: Don't discourage the industriousness of the people. That was [the insight] of what Professor Laffer drew on a napkin at the White House in 1971 or 1972. He just basically talked about that maxim—that taxes can get so high as to become counterproductive, not only lowering production, but *losing* revenue for government. So if this were the revenue line, and this were the tax line . . . [Mr. Kemp drew his lines so that the camera could pick them up.] Basically, it says that there are two points at which taxes yield no revenue—at zero taxation, obviously, but also at one hundred percent taxation. People cease to produce, or else they go into the barter economy or the black-market economy, so that as tax rates get *higher,* they can actually *reduce* government revenues by dampening economic activity.

WFB: Is it your position that tax rates in the United States today are so high as to be dampening economic activity?

KEMP: It is.

In 1981, the Kemp-Roth bill, of which Kemp was the principal author, became the principal vehicle for President Reagan's 1981 deep cuts in personal income tax rates. Congressman Kemp was delighted— but not satisfied. On *Firing Line,* in 1984, he argued with characteristic enthusiasm for still more tax cuts—specifically, the Kemp-Kasten bill, which would have provided for a substantially flat tax.

KEMP: Bill, imagine what this economy would be doing with a top tax rate of twenty-five percent on personal and corporate income, a lower capital gains rate, interest rates at single-digit levels, and, say, enterprise zones in every major urban area of America.* America would be an enterprise zone in and of itself. Now, I'm criticized for being too optimistic about the potential of the American economy to grow at sustainable rates of five or six percent without inflation.

WFB: Well, that's high.

KEMP: And that—well, it *is* high by historical standards, but it is *not* high when you think of the pent-up ability of this economy—

*The "enterprise zone" is the desolate urban area in which economic stimulation would be expedited, according to the Kemp plan, by tax relief.

WFB: Or by Japanese standards.

KEMP: —and the potential of the American people—and the
            technology that is now being applied to basic industry.
            It is incredible, as we shed our industrial skin, we're not
            entering a *post*industrial age, we're entering a *new* in-
            dustrial age where we're going to see a renaissance of
            the industrial manufacturing capacity of this country—
            if we allow industry a bond and equity market that's
            consistent with long-term investment, and a tax system
            and monetary policy that will allow them to export
            again. And not only that, it would finance recovery in
            the Third World, which is a part of the world we need
            to see recover so that they can be markets for our
            goods.

WFB: You believe that the manifest benefits to the society of
            such reforms as you propose would themselves guarantee
            their political success, or tend to?

KEMP: Well, yes. We would not [then] see the tax rates go up—
            because there would be so much objective and historical
            and empirical evidence to the contrary. No good politician
            would be talking about the redistribution of wealth. We
            would be talking about expanding opportunities to get
            access to wealth for people who heretofore have never had
            that opportunity. Egalitarianism is attractive only if
            there's no chance of people getting wealth. If you give the
            people *access* to wealth, the election of egalitarians falls off
            precipitously, as it has in the last six years.
               On this the Republican Party is split. One foot is in
            what I call the old guard—which sees a slow, steady three
            percent growth ad infinitum. That's boring to me, because
            I don't think it will ever get unemployment down fast
            enough. I don't think it really offers the poor a chance to
            work their way out of poverty. I don't think it really
            reaches out to blacks, which I think the Republican Party
            cannot, [must not,] fail to do. We can't continue this
            closed-door approach to minority Americans. It is going
            to split the country.

WFB: Who says it's closed-door?

KEMP: Well, it gives the impression of being closed-door, and the—

WFB: Well, it's a misimpression.

KEMP: We once were the party of minority equal opportunity and civil rights and human rights and economic growth and Abraham Lincoln, and we lost our way, I think, in the thirties. We need to stand for growth and opportunity again.

I gathered together some statistics, under the prodding of my guests.

Between 1921 and 1926, the top marginal tax rate was cut from 63 percent to 25 percent, and the bottom rate was cut from 9 percent to 4 percent. This obviously resulted in a great reduction in the taxes paid by the highest income earners, correct? Incorrect. Those who made more than $100,000 were, in 1926, paying 86 percent more income tax than in 1922 under the higher rate.

In 1964, we cut the top rate from 91 percent to 70 percent and other rates proportionately. It amounted, roughly, to a 20 percent reduction in each income bracket. The result? The top 5 percent of taxpayers in the United States paid 7.7 percent more income taxes after their rates were reduced. The bottom 50 percent of taxpayers paid 9.2 percent less in taxes in 1965 than they did in 1963.

Beginning in 1977, there has been a reduction in the top marginal tax rate to the current level. That reduction was from 70 percent to 28 percent. From which one imagines that the wealthier are paying less in taxes. But a study released in October 1987 reveals that the share of income taxes paid by the wealthiest 5 percent of American families will rise to 40.9 percent in 1988—up from 36.9 percent in 1977. That is a startling difference, a difference that sweeps away (or should do so) the demagogic din of the Reagan years about how the rich are benefiting from Reaganomics at the expense of the poor. In money terms it comes to this: If the wealthy had continued to pay the same percentage of taxes in 1988 as in 1977, tax revenue would have diminished by $16 billion.

After Reaganomics sets in, the wealthiest 1 percent of Americans will be paying 23.8 percent of all income taxes. That is up from 19.5 percent in 1977. The poorest 50 percent of families (income below $16,360) will pay 5.9 percent of the total tax. Before Reagan, they paid 6.4 percent.

As I reflect on two decades' controversy on tax policy and statism, I conclude that at least for the next policy generation (say ten, fifteen years) the temptation to set exorbitant tax rates has diminished. The utilitarian argument against them for the period prevails. It happened that I was visiting the Prime Minister of Portugal on the day the 1986 tax bill was passed. Mr. Anibal Cavaco Silva was clearly distracted. He finally turned to me and said, "Do you realize, Mr. Buckley, that after the new tax bill comes fully into play, our *lowest* tax will be higher than your *highest* tax?" I couldn't think what to say, except something vaguely pleasant about Magellan. But the impact of the benefits to be got from lowering the top marginal rate has affected the intelligentsia in Europe—and in Asia. No reform is permanent, but this reform will be long-lasting.

So will the indexation of tax brackets. The bracket creep, beloved of legislators because it permitted them to raise taxes without writing legislation to raise taxes, is not likely to be challenged by a future administration on the visible horizon.

The debate over the deficit and over the trade imbalance has raged for ten years without edging toward resolution. We do not know what lies ahead, though providence is capable of clearing its throat most resonantly, as it did on October 19, 1987. Professor Milton Friedman takes the position: *Do not raise taxes, whatever you do.* When one studies the surrounding arguments that crystallize his position, this conservative finds them persuasive.

16
POVERTY

MICHAEL HARRINGTON
CHARLES MURRAY
JESSE JACKSON
JAMES FARMER
THOMAS SOWELL

Not many people come out and say it in so many words. John Kenneth Galbraith does. He says that concern by American conservatives for the poor is phony. We are really interested in the rich and near-rich.

It is never possible absolutely to fix operative motives. The conservative case rests for the most part on empirical grounds. The question is: What works?

It isn't, to be sure, the only question. To take from John to give to James will help James; but society's attitude toward John is a congeries of commitments, and the commitment to respect his property, his acquisitions, his family's future acquisitions, oughtn't to be frivolously treated.

In any event, the subject occurs and recurs. The initial need is for the accumulation of data, and here Michael Harrington played a historic role.

In fact, although Norman Thomas was the first *Firing Line* guest aired, Michael Harrington was the first taped (in April 1966). He had published a book, *The Other America,* and would soon succeed Norman Thomas as president of the American Socialist Party. The book described a portion of the American population beset by tormenting poverty. It caught the attention of Professor Walter Heller, who brought its thesis to the attention of President Kennedy on November 19, 1963. The book sounded the tocsin for massive federal action to "make war" on poverty.

I had had a half-dozen public encounters with Michael Harrington, most of them public debates here and there. Some time after leaving Holy Cross College, Harrington joined the staff of *The Catholic Worker,* having first taken—or so the legend goes—a pledge of personal poverty. Murray Kempton some time later quipped to me that the foundations of America were going broke maintaining Michael Harrington in poverty. Michael Harrington lost his religious faith, even as his faith in socialism rose. He is a formidable polemicist—as here, over twenty years ago.

WFB: Mr. Harrington, there seem to be all kinds of definitions floating around. How do you define poverty for purposes of the Poverty Program?

HARRINGTON: Okay. My definition is the government's, because the official definition has become very precise. It says that the upper limits of poverty—the well-off poor—are a family in which the woman is presumed to be a good cook and shopper, and can spend twenty-two cents per person per meal. [We are talking 1966 dollars.] Or put another way, can spend for the big meal of the day, for all four members of the family, ninety-five cents. That's the top.

That meal, by the way, is a basic nutritional meal figured out by the Department of Agriculture. And the government's thesis, which I subscribe to, is that if you have an income under the amount necessary for this meal, you will be choosing between necessities. You will have to have less than enough food in order to have decent housing or clothing or medicine.

WFB: If you're making the point that people have to eat, I will concede it. But what disturbs me is that there are a number of professional students of the problem who raise questions and make points that, in your copious literature on the subject, you simply haven't disposed of. By the standard of three thousand dollars [the official poverty level, in 1966, for a family of four], for instance, over fifty percent of the United States was poor in 1929; and yet that is historically known as one of the exuberant years in American history.

Then, of course, it gets terribly confusing because, although you've been very well disciplined in your definition of poverty, in fact a lot of the literature on the poverty problem describes not only *material* poverty, but a poverty of a completely different order.

Paul Jacobs, whom you know and admire, has written that the poor in America are not so much physical as *psychological* paupers. And the economist Henry Warwicker said poverty seems to be primarily a social condition. They're talking about loneliness and alienation.

HARRINGTON: Let me not speak for Paul Jacobs or Warwicker, let me speak for myself. I talk about the fact that the rates of psychosis and neurosis as observed by the public authorities among poor people is two, three, four, and five times greater than among anyone else. Rich people have much less neurotic and psychotic lives than the poor people. Being kicked around and being pushed down, living in dense, miserable housing, and dealing with cockroaches and rats are not the kinds of things that make one a balanced, content, normal, and adjusted healthy personality.

WFB: I couldn't agree with you more. But I'm trying to raise the following question, namely: To what extent is a poverty program that is designed *materially* to dissipate such difficulties as you have elaborated—to what extent can we count on it to alleviate all these concomitant miseries?

Paul Jacobs, for instance, said that one of the things that afflict poor people is that they don't receive letters, they don't receive mail. And I think that he pinpoints a very poignant thing. Do you really think that the government, through a highly bureaucratized agency, can help a person of that kind?

You, after all, despise our social order. You don't believe there's such a thing as religion, and under the circumstances you are, in your active polemical life, doing very much what, in my judgment, has the effect of depriving people of some of the consolations (and some of the truths) that might make them more serene.

HARRINGTON: Well, there's so much that's been tossed at me—if I could have a second. To get to the basic point: Can a materially oriented public program affect the inner psychological torments of the poor? The answer, I think, is to a certain degree yes, to a certain degree no.

For example, in 1955, during the Montgomery bus boycott in Montgomery, Alabama, Martin Luther King and the leadership of the boycott did not make a single speech to the Negroes in Montgomery about stopping criminal behavior. But because the life of the Negro in Montgomery took on a dignity and meaning and purpose—without anybody ever mentioning crime—there was a decline of about twenty percent in the amount of crime among Negroes in Montgomery.

Similarly, this year the government has given us some figures that would indicate that if we would put more income into the slums, the incidence of broken families would drop, because one of the big reasons that families break up is that there's not enough money, because a man can't be an economic father, because many of our welfare programs literally penalize marriage by refusing any kind of welfare as long as there's an able-bodied although unemployed or poor male in the house. So, yes, by material federal action, we *can* change some of these circumstances and improve some of the psychological and spiritual life of the poor.

Twenty-two years later, some of the major assumptions of Michael Harrington and others who thought the war on poverty would be a conclusive engagement were challenged. The book *Losing Ground,* subtitled *American Social Policy, 1950–1980,* by Charles Murray had an effect on social thought comparable to Harrington's book in 1963. The book dealt with the effects on the poor of the policies generally associated with Lyndon Johnson and, it's fair to say, Michael Harrington.

What Murray said was that there was a correlation between the incidence of poverty and federal programs designed to reduce it, but that the correlation was inverse. After graduating from Harvard, Murray went to the Peace Corps in Thailand, where he lived and worked for six years. He returned, took his doctorate in political science from MIT, and then joined the American Institute for Research, which he served as chief scientist, taking responsibility for those of its research programs that inquired into urban education, welfare services, child nutrition, day care, adolescent pregnancy, and juvenile delinquency. His work there was widely publicized and applauded (by the Reverend Jesse Jackson, among others), and his first book, *Beyond Probation,* about juvenile offenders, was widely admired. Then came *Losing Ground.*

WFB: I should like to begin by asking Mr. Murray if we might take the three developments his book points to in order. First, what do you mean when you say that the government made it more attractive to be poor and dependent in 1970 than in 1960?

MURRAY: Between 1960 and 1970 we increased welfare benefits, and we also changed the rules of eligibility. So, for example, a young woman who had a child could live with a man in 1970 and receive benefits, whereas she could not do so in 1960. This is a major change in the attractiveness of her situation.

WFB: What about your second category, the breakdown of law and order? Now, there was something like a three hundred, four hundred percent rise in theft during this period we're talking about, right?

MURRAY: Right.

WFB: And do you think that the perpetual insecurity of physical belongings had a demoralizing effect on the desire for their accumulation?

MURRAY: That's pretty tenuous. I don't think I would make that argument. I do say that the major link that I see between

crime and the kinds of phenomena associated with the
increase in poverty, or with the end of the reduction in
poverty, was that it provided another way to get along
without joining and sticking with the labor market. This
had its most extreme effects, I would say, on young males.

WFB: Well, if crime *does* pay, then it becomes a market consid-
            eration.

MURRAY: That's quite correct, yes.

WFB: Okay, now a third factor singled out in your book has to
            do with what you call the withdrawal of status reinforce-
            ments for upward mobility, i.e., people are caused to de-
            sire less to improve. Now, this results from what?

MURRAY: Well, the main change that took place in the mid-1960s
            with regard to what I call status considerations is that we
            broke down the dividing line between being economically
            independent and being on welfare. Before the mid-1960s,
            if you had a job you really didn't qualify for anything. And
            more to the point, large numbers of poor people in this
            country, including, I know, my own parents and grand-
            parents, were brought up with the notion that we may
            have been poor but we never took a penny in charity from
            anyone and we pulled our own weight. As a result of that,
            you had status distinctions within poor communities. I
            mean, if you were holding a job and raising your children,
            even though you were poor, you were the backbone of the
            community, as compared to the trash out there.
                Then we put everybody on welfare in the low-income
            groups, in effect. I mean, we introduced what we called
            means-tested programs, the food stamps and the rest of it,
            so that we would not be unfair to the working poor. But
            we destroyed such useful boasts as "We never took a
            penny of charity." We also changed the nature of the
            respect that went along with simply paying your own way,
            so that we now have lots of middle-aged men who are
            taunted by their children for hanging on to lousy jobs as
            a foolish way to behave.

WFB: Yes, this is something that happens as a corollary, that
            certain kinds of work are disdained which would have

been gratefully and honorably executed a generation ago, right? Like domestic service, say, or even assembly-line work. Ken Galbraith says that a third of the people who occupy the assembly lines in Sweden are Turks, because the Swedes, after two generations, simply disdain assembly work. And we have this phenomenon in Detroit.

MURRAY: And we *encouraged* it in a way—by conveying the notion that some kinds of work are too demeaning to do. Or, if you do them, you should only do them under protest. These were subtle changes that were encouraged by all sorts of things, but the overall effect was pretty devastating.

WFB: So, how to restore the psychological ambition for self-improvement without restoring that part of it that produces pain is a part of the dilemma that you are trying to cope with, right?

MURRAY: Precisely. But I'm afraid that we've misconceived the nature of doing good, so that we only think, under the current policies, of "If I have x percent more food stamps, we're doing x percent more good," and we don't add up the pain-causing aspects of the policies at the same time.

One of the great undiscovered constituencies is that set of poor people who look around them and are appalled at what they see. I do see large numbers—and if you want to talk specifically about blacks—large numbers of blacks who feel themselves to be victims.

WFB: Are they looking for a leadership of a kind that understands these contributing causes that you outline in your book? Only a week or so ago the President met with one or two black leaders in Washington who are not associated with the Black Caucus and who therefore aren't burdened with the clichés on which they have depended for so long. And one of those leaders in particular made the point really that you're making now, I thought very eloquently. In fact he said, "Jesse Jackson would probably agree with me on this proposition: that even if we say that whitey victimized us, we're not entitled to say that whitey is going to pick us up off the floor, and therefore we're going to have to do it."

MURRAY: And I think that there are lots of people who are on the verge of going public with this, but more of them are caught in the same bind that Reverend Jackson is caught in. The Reverend Jackson had a program in the 1970s which was the Push for—

WFB: Push for Excellence, yes.

MURRAY: He would go out to public schools in the inner cities and talk to them as tough as I've ever heard anybody talk to anybody. It was superb.

            Then the government gave him some money to have a program. The program consisted of remedial efforts for kids who were at the very bottom of the class and who were having the most problems.

            I would say to some of his aides, somewhat timidly, "Wouldn't it be nice, in a Push for Excellence program, if you used some of this money to reinforce some of those youngsters who are trying for excellence?" The reaction was, "No, we can't do that because these others need the help more." So there is this bifurcation between rhetoric and practice which we've got to get over. We've got to get black leaders to make good on the rhetoric.

Black leaders: Let's have a look at three of them. The Reverend Jesse Jackson is a nimble man with a sense of humor and, of course, one of the most highly developed theatrical talents in town. Moreover, Mr. Jackson in recent years has aroused much support, as Charles Murray's comment attests, for his insistence that blacks press forward with the opportunities they have rather than sit back expecting to be endowed with professional skills. In his thunderous voice he will tell an audience of black students that if some of them can become great basketball players, so can they become great doctors, and engineers, and teachers.

    Then suddenly, in the late seventies, Jackson decided to turn his attention to the Middle East, and the next thing the public knew he was being carried on the shoulders of the Palestinians, who shouted out alternately, "Jackson! Arafat!" When, in 1979, he appeared again on *Firing Line,* he did so less as a spokesman for American blacks than as a spokesman for the interests of the PLO. But in 1982, as a feature of the annual PUSH convention, held that year in Charleston, South Carolina, at a large Baptist church, the discussion proceeded under the

heading "The Economy and the Blacks." Jackson was taking yet another tangent: pressure not via government, but on commercial enterprises by the black community. He began by saying that for a black, his
blackness is forever the supreme fact of life. In saying so, without
suggesting that he lamented this priority, he moved very far from Martin Luther King's Dream, in which color made no difference: color-
blindness isn't a desideratum for Jackson.

JACKSON: The black community is an identifiable community set
             aside by caste and color, and though there are variations
             in our community—various class distinctions sometimes
             born of color, sometimes born of education, sometimes
             born of economic mobility—the fact is our caste is the
             most dominant factor in our lives.

But he came quickly to the theme. The rubric that year of the PUSH
convention was "Black America: An Economic Common Market."

JACKSON: There is historic economic discrimination which pours
             over into today and will pour over into tomorrow unless
             we stop it. As we confront the beverage industry, for
             example, there are now twenty-two hundred soft drink
             franchises, zero black. Last year blacks bought fourteen
             billion dollars' worth of autos, and yet we find in
             Chrysler seven and a half billion in sales, less than
             twenty million worth of trade with black suppliers. It
             should have been a minimum of three hundred million in
             trade. Ford fifteen billion in procurement, less than
             ninety million in trade with blacks. It should have been
             a minimum of one and a half billion. General Motors,
             thirty billion in procurement. It should have been three
             billion minimum for blacks; it was less than three hun-
             dred million.
                 That five-billion-dollar trade deficit alone has left us
             either disproportionately on public aid or in desperation.
             But I might suggest to you that if in fact black talent and
             black money is allowed to be invested and that we are
             allowed to grow—to risk and reward—it will have the
             impact of *expanding* the economy and not *threatening* the
             economy.

I asked him to comment on the observation made in *Beyond the Melting Pot,* by Daniel Patrick Moynihan and Nathan Glazer, that blacks have not tended to patronize black enterprises, unlike, say, the Chinese-Americans. The result of this is that in the Chinese-American community, consumer spending was always stimulating and capitalizing Chinese-American enterprises; whereas the same thing was not going on in, say, Harlem. There, you would have a delicatessen store run by, let's say, Jewish-Americans, and a black-run store alongside, with no sense of preference shown to the black one.

JACKSON: One distinction, Bill, is that those groups who came as immigrants or refugees were able to keep their national identity and to keep their psyche intact, and thus were not subjected to brainwashing, the kind that would teach those of us who were black that blackness was inferior and white was superior. So they were not subjected to the same kind of psychological barrage, and so they used crossbreeding of their economy and inbreeding, and once they developed strength there, then they began to invest into the broader economy. Well, blacks who came as slaves and not as immigrants come from a very different tradition. . . . Blacks, of course, who are in a caste, distinguished by color, we have the double yoke of caste and class, and so even though we do some ingroup buying to begin to strengthen our economic class, we still have to move as a group to move into the broader economy. The same amount of energy that some people will get a mile out of, we can apply the same energy and it will have less effect because of this distinction.

I tried again, and he handled me deftly.

WFB: But if that is true, then does it not follow that your missionary work is primarily among your own people? And indeed, you have engaged in that kind of missionary work in Chicago, i.e., to dissipate that myth which works against what it is that you desire to accomplish. For instance, if you had here in Charleston, South Carolina—if you had a Ford dealer who was a black—is it your assumption that he would get a larger than normal share of black patronage in virtue of the fact that he is black? And if he doesn't, why wouldn't he?

JACKSON: His being black may be an immediate stimulus because there's a sense of self-esteem connected. But if in fact he gets cars later than the white Ford dealer and if in fact he cannot get the same financing from Ford's financial corporation as a white dealer can, then pretty soon the immediate stimulation gives way to economic realities that overwhelm him.

James Farmer dwelt entirely, in 1966, on the plight of blacks in America. As one of the earliest leaders of the civil rights movement, he provides historical perspective, touched with poignancy. At the time of his appearance James Farmer was probably the best-known Negro leader after Martin Luther King, Jr. Mr. Farmer, for all intents and purposes, founded CORE, the Congress for Racial Equality. He was generally classified as a militant whose public utterances and injunctions fell somewhere between those of the leaders of the relatively conservative National Association for the Advancement of Colored People and the (self-consciously) radical Student Nonviolent Coordinating Committee.

He is a man of extraordinary and varied talent. He earned a degree in chemistry and then a doctorate of divinity from Howard University. But he refused ordination in the Methodist Church on the grounds that the Methodists practiced racial segregation. He pioneered the sit-in, years before the practice became institutionalized. Mr. Farmer believed in protesting in all seasons. He flatly refused President Kennedy's request, in the summer of 1963, to call off the civil rights demonstrations pending debate on the civil rights bill (passed in the spring of 1964).

He spoke with the high moral passion one associates with the civil rights movement in its best moments.

WFB: Mr. Farmer, you have taken the civil rights movement and said that it has to go a step further, that Negroes must receive preferential treatment. Now by preferential treatment, I understand you to mean that, owing to the considerable privations of the Negroes during the past years, the society owes the Negro certain debts and that, under the circumstances, those debts have got to be redeemed by very special efforts, however costly, to give them these special rights. Is it possible to prefer a Negro without *dis*preferring a white?

FARMER: I would like to take exception to one point that you made. I do not ask for preferential treatment because of the debt that has to be paid for past abuses. All that I say is that the back wheels of a car can never catch the front wheels of a car while they are traveling at the same rate of speed. So we have to give the back wheels an additional push in order to help them to catch up. This is not for a past debt. This is to get us *even,* so we'll start off from the same line. This is precisely the tradition—speaking of tradition— that America accepts in dealing with GIs or veterans. We say that the veterans have been outside the mainstream of American economic life for one year, two years, three years, or however many, and therefore it's necessary to give them a little push back into that mainstream.

WFB: In return for services rendered.

FARMER: Of course. Services rendered—we've rendered services too—we've picked cotton, we've helped build buildings.

WFB: You know, that's not my favorite argument.

FARMER: May I continue my point, though?

WFB: Yes, go ahead.

FARMER: Let me continue my point. Now we have to give them an additional push. Civil Service even gives a veteran a five-point advantage. We don't ask for a five-point advantage. Nor do we ask that any unqualified Negroes be hired for jobs. Nor do we seek that any white person who has a job should be fired from his job so that a Negro may have the job. I would fight against that as vigorously as I fight for equal rights.

But what we *do* say is that if a company has discriminated for the hundred years of its existence, has hired no Negroes except janitors, and now it has an opening in a decent category, two persons apply, one black and one white, similarly qualified—since there's no such thing as equal qualification—now I say that the fact that the company has not hired any Negroes in the past and has no Negroes in its work force beyond the lowest category should be a factor weighing in favor of the Negro applicant.

President Kennedy, incidentally, adopted the same idea. It's said that he stepped off a plane in Washington. There was an honor guard there to meet him. He saw no Negroes. He called an officer, and said, "I see no Negroes here." The officer said, "Mr. President, no Negroes have applied." He said, "Go out and *find* some."

WFB: Well, one hopes he will find more productive jobs for Negroes than simply to make them stand parade for dignitaries.

FARMER: We want all kinds of jobs, even standing parade.

WFB: Well, let me agree with you at least insofar as you suggest that it is a heavy moral obligation on white employers to go out of their way to make opportunities for Negroes. I believe that that obligation is moral in nature, but also *voluntary* in nature. As you know, there are an awful lot of people tooling around, some of them in your own organizations, who are arguing in effect for a situation in which you go and get the personnel roster of a business and say, Well now, let me see, there are ten percent Negroes in this community. There are not ten percent Negroes in this particular firm; under the circumstances we find you are, *eo ipso,* guilty of segregation. And the involvement of the entire government mechanism here is something that means a great deal to me. I hope it means something to you.

FARMER: Well, CORE does *not* ask for a quota system. We do not ask that seventeen percent of the employees in any company in New York City should be Negroes, if Negroes are seventeen percent of the population.

WFB: And you, therefore, disavow those Negro leaders who *do* insist on this?

FARMER: I'm not aware of any substantial Negro leaders who do.
            We have been charged in the press with doing so, but what
            we say to an employer is "We see no Negroes working;
            you obviously have practiced some discrimination."

WFB: I don't deny that they do practice discrimination.

FARMER: Now wait. Let me finish.

WFB: I'm asking, What should be the *recourse*?

FARMER: All right. We say that he must take affirmative action to
            integrate the work force. And there must, therefore, be
            meaningful representation of the discriminated-against
            minorities in his work force.

WFB: So you *do* want to use the mechanism of the state to
            enforce integration.

FARMER: I'm not an anarchist. I believe it is the duty of the state
            to guarantee the rights of its citizens.

WFB: Now you're trying to steal a base. This has nothing to do
            with anarchy, because there hasn't been any anarchy in
            this country during the preceding one hundred and eighty
            years. These are, after all, revolutionary proposals, ac-
            cording to some people's lights—the idea that the govern-
            ment has a right to step in and inform a business how
            many Negroes and how many whites it has to hire.

They did not remain revolutionary proposals for very many years;
today, various forms of government coercion on behalf of affirmative
action are all but taken for granted. But black poverty remains acute;
and black family breakup has become worse.

James Farmer anticipated the argument that would crystallize ten
years later. On the one hand he wanted active intervention, enforced if
necessary by the law and the courts, to apply against discrimination. On
the other hand, his use of the term "affirmative action" specifically
denied the quota system as a fair means of achieving satisfactory black
representation in social and commercial enterprises. I remember thinking, after the program was over, that James Farmer had effectively
prevailed against any of the arguments I had used against his program.

.   .   .

Professor Thomas Sowell made his case on *Firing Line* with the passionate commitment I associated with James Farmer, but he was less the
moralist than the social scientist. Thomas Sowell is a prominent black
American, not a prominent black leader. He is not by character a man
who seeks to lead. He is rather more the rabbi who seeks to instruct.
He was born in North Carolina, and as a boy moved to New York. After
serving in the Marine Corps, he went to Harvard, where he took his first
degree in economics. He went then to Columbia, and took his Ph.D. at
the University of Chicago. He went on to teach at UCLA, at Amherst,
at Cornell. Since 1980 he has been a senior fellow at the Hoover Institution.

The subject of the program was the conclusions and insights he had
reached in his book *Markets and Minorities.* My enthusiasm for the
book and for his performance on *Firing Line* was undisguised. There are
very few racial clichés that survive his scrutiny. "Are you against labor
unions?" an indignant Harriet Pilpel, serving as the Examiner, asked
him on *Firing Line.*

"You asked what were some of the factors that stood in the way of
black economic progress and I said that one of them was the labor
union. That is a fact, and I'm simply reporting facts, not prejudices."
How do you handle such a man, if your political career is staked out
on the regnant clichés?

At one point, a few months before the program, journalist Carl
Rowan called his black brother Tom Sowell a "quisling." The charge
makes one smile. In the first place, the idea of Sowell being servile to
any regime, let alone one that sought accommodation with tyrants, is
laughable. But mostly one smiles because if you took from Carl Rowan
the planks which one by one the scholar Sowell turns into sawdust,
Rowan is left without anything whatever on which to rest his massive
frame. It is as if you removed from St. Paul the Resurrection *and*
original sin all in one afternoon. What then would happen to him?
(Rowan would be left, in an encounter with Sowell, only with his pistol.)

It isn't as if Sowell ignores racism. "People often say that I'm denying
that there's racism. On the contrary, racism exists everywhere around
the world, down through history. That's one of the reasons it's hard to
use it as an empirical explanation for anything. In the United States, for
example, Puerto Ricans have lower incomes than blacks. I don't know
of anyone who believes Puerto Ricans encounter more discrimination

than blacks. Obviously there must be something else involved besides discrimination."

And so the uncluttered mind of Sowell begins looking around. There is, for instance, the commonly accepted thesis that ever since the days of slavery, black families were dominated by mothers, the fathers having been shipped away to distant plantations.

The trouble with this, apparently, is that it isn't so. "The current large and rising numbers of female-headed families among blacks is a modern phenomenon stemming from the era of the welfare state—when the government began to subsidize desertion and teenage pregnancy."

Wait a minute, Professor, are you saying that the state is intentionally or unintentionally subsidizing discrimination? The answer to this will alarm not only statists, but the intellectual elite who consider themselves the primary opponents of discrimination. It is, once again, yes.

And so it goes. How account for the success of the (nonwhite) Chinese? They are discriminated against throughout Southeast Asia, but their income is five times as high as that of their neighbors. "Those who argue that the Chinese have gotten this by exploiting the natives could test this out by looking at places where there are only Chinese residents, such as, for example, Singapore or Hong Kong. In Hong Kong, ninety-eight percent of the population is Chinese. They have the highest standard of living in Southeast Asia. If they're getting it by exploitation, they must be exploiting those other two percent something awful—the other two percent being the British, who run the colony."

At least Professor Sowell would leave undisturbed the plain dumb fact that Anglo-Saxons are the privileged economic ethnic group in America? Mrs. Pilpel all but pleaded with him on the program. Yes, Professor? "No. Jews, Japanese, Poles, Chinese, and Italians make more money."

Fourteen percent of Americans are professionals, which is to say, lawyers, doctors, and teachers. Can anybody beat the Anglos on *that* scale? Well, yes. West Indians, 15 percent; Japanese, 18 percent; Filipinos, 23 percent; Chinese, 25 percent.

"How far have we come in removing discriminatory pay differences among individuals with the same qualifications and different racial or ethnic backgrounds? Among the younger generation?" Professor Sowell asks himself the question, and answers it: "We have come just about all the way."

It was suggested that Sowell's faith in the market was such as to make him its abject servant. To this his icy answer was: "I do not have faith in the market, I have evidence about the market."

But here is Sowell, extemporizing.

WFB: I think people read your book incorrectly who come to the following conclusion, but let me in any event state the conclusion they come to, namely that you oppose efforts—political efforts—to give equal opportunity, which in fact you do not. Correct?

SOWELL: Correct.

WFB: What you oppose, as I understand it and as your book very plainly states, is any preferential treatment that disguises objective standards. Is that correct?

SOWELL: Yes, and particularly since the net effect of the preferential treatment, which is preferential in intention more so than in results, is that those blacks who are particularly disadvantaged have fallen further behind under these policies. Such policies have typically benefited those blacks who were well off and then became better off. For example, blacks who have relatively less work experience, lower levels of education, black female-headed families, all these groups have fallen further behind during a decade or more of affirmative action. Black female-headed families have had an absolute decline in real income over this span and have fallen further *behind* white female-headed families.

            At the same time, black couples who are both college-educated earn higher incomes than white couples who are both college-educated. So that this whole program provides incentives to hire blacks who are safe; therefore, an employer will make some effort toward one's quota, but the employer will not take in people who might not progress enough for their promotions and discharge patterns to satisfy the government. So you make it risky to hire average blacks and more desirable to hire blacks who have privileges—not privileges, but advantages.

WFB: During the past ten years we've had affirmative action. We have also had a rise of between twenty-one and thirty-

PROFESSOR THOMAS SOWELL

seven percent of families—black families—that have a single parent—

SOWELL: Yes.

WFB: —i.e., there's been a desertion by the male—by the father.

SOWELL: Yes.

WFB: Now, is *that* owing to the welfare program, or is that entirely coincidental? To what extent is welfare the socially causative factor of the phenomenon you're describing?

SOWELL: Well, if I limit my description just to families that are female-headed, and I compare blacks and whites, then within that comparison I see that the blacks are falling further and further behind. Yet if I pick almost any measure of more advantaged families, I find the blacks not only catching up, but in some cases overtaking and passing the whites. And there are a number of ways you can look at it and you get the same result.

What that suggests to me is that those blacks who have the skills, the experience, the education, and so on are finding things much, much easier than ever before, whereas where there's a risk involved in hiring them, people aren't going to take it. I've heard it explained to me very explicitly in the case of women, and I suspect that they wanted me to draw the same conclusions with respect to blacks. Universities—people at universities— have said to me, "We will not hire a woman for assistant professor unless we are sure she's going to make associate professor because the cost of legal processes, in case she doesn't, is so high." I remember telling this to a woman who was a full professor to see what response I would get—

WFB: A black woman?

SOWELL: A black woman. —and her response was, "Yes, that's the way I hire, because I also have no time to waste at the EEOC and in the courtroom."

WFB: So therefore they don't get the same running chance as white scholars?

SOWELL: That's right. If you're going to hire someone mediocre, the employers are safer hiring mediocre whites who can be thrown out, if they don't work out, without any repercussions.

WFB: Okay. Now let me ask you this. Why, when we see on television and when we read the writings of the overwhelming number of acknowledged black leaders, is no thoughtful attention given to such analyses as your own? Is it because they are simply wedded to the notion that there is a political solution? Or is it because victimization is the easiest way for them to account for their plight? What is the dominant reason?

SOWELL: Well, both. Clearly if there is no political solution, then what is the use of political leaders? People often emphasize to me the enormous importance of leadership for any ethnic group to get ahead, and my response is often "Name me three Japanese-American leaders." And no one has yet been able to do it. So leadership itself—if you have the perspective that I have, then leadership itself becomes much less important, but for a leader to say that leadership isn't important is like, you know, Cadillac saying it doesn't matter what car you buy.

WFB: Well, all right. But suppose we take the word "leadership" away from its political context. Gandhi was both a political and a moral leader. Martin Luther King was both. Now, he had political objectives, no question about that, but having achieved those political objectives, on the basis of what you know about Martin Luther King, would he be saying the kind of thing you're saying?

SOWELL: It's impossible to know, obviously. Certainly I think that the declining quality of that leadership is a symptom rather than a cause. If we were in a situation where there were dire and important problems to be dealt with in the civil rights area, then that would attract the brightest and the best of the rising generation of blacks, and you would have a lot better people running organizations.

WFB: Let me put it another way. About two years ago Jesse Jackson made a lot of headlines by saying, "Look, my people are very good at baseball and basketball. I don't see why they shouldn't be very good at math." And then he lectured them about the necessity to spend hours on homework rather than hours on television and so on and so forth. He sounded very much like certain passages in your book about self-training. Now, he was, when he said those things, something of a leader—

SOWELL: Yes.

WFB: But he wasn't a *political* leader. Aren't you insisting on a rather narrow meaning for the word "leader"? He's got to be sort of an office seeker—

SOWELL: I see what you're saying.

WFB: Yes. Isn't he—*You* are a leader—

SOWELL: Oh, God help us.

WFB: —without being an office seeker. In that sense, Freud was a leader and Darwin was a leader—a man of great influence.

SOWELL: Well, I thank you for the compliment. I'm not sure how much I can endorse the accuracy of it, but that's for other people to say. Yes, that was a very statesmanlike thing [of Jesse Jackson] to say. However—once again, my study of other countries suggests that that is not what people *want* to hear. There was a politician in the Philippines in the thirties who pointed out that if the Filipinos were angry at the Chinese, who were dominant throughout the economy—remember, the Chinese were a minority—and wanted to take over their positions, they would have to work the way the Chinese worked: work as hard as they work, save as hard, live as frugally, et cetera. A storm of indignation fell upon this poor man, and no one else wanted to be in his position again. From there on out people referred to the dominance of the Chinese as showing exploitation, because that, really, is much easier to deal with politically. So the political incentives are really toward saying what people *want* to hear.

But I haven't been able to find a single country in the world where the policies that are being advocated for blacks in the United States have lifted any people out of poverty. I've seen many examples around the world of people who began in poverty and ended in affluence. Not one of them has followed any of the patterns being advocated for blacks in the United States. Many groups have remained in poverty for a very long time trying to follow those patterns.

One ruminates on the analysis, the idealism, the inventiveness, the disillusion, the demoralization expressed here; and the thought and research of Thomas Sowell strike one as overwhelmingly cogent. But as he tells us, to suggest that politics is not the solution is to endanger political careers. It is not a subject directly addressed by Jean-François Revel—the difficulty in achieving the desired circulation of thought, for the purpose of ameliorating such problems as race relations in such a country as the United States. But we can add this difficulty to the heavy difficulties of democracy suggested in Revel's thesis. How many blacks are inspired and instructed—and heartened by—Tom Sowell?

CHINA

GUESTS:
YEHUDI MENUHIN
FOX BUTTERFIELD
CHIANG CHING-KUO

AFRICA

GUESTS:
ELSPETH HUXLEY
ANTHONY LEWIS
ARNAUD DE
  BORCHGRAVE
ALAN PATON
ERNEST URBAN
  TREVOR
  HUDDLESTON
PAUL JOHNSON

LATIN AMERICA

GUESTS:
CARLOS LACERDA
LAWRENCE BIRNS
NENA OSSA

THE PACIFIC RIM

GUESTS:
FERDINAND MARCOS
LEE KWAN YEW

China has figured over the years in *Firing Line*'s focus, pre–Nixon's trip, post–Nixon's trip, and post–Chiang's death. Much work has been done, some of it searingly eloquent (one thinks of Simon Leys' *Chinese Shadows,* and of course Fox Butterfield's masterful *China: Alive in the Bitter Sea*). Here is a brief tribute to the transideological endurance of music from (Sir) Yehudi Menuhin, who had just come back from China.

MENUHIN: As far as I know, there has never been a society without its music, from the most ancient or primitive. There is no question that music, much more than words, moves us to tears and to joy, whether it's Schubert's *Winterreise* or, in a patriotic way during the war, the national anthem, or a chorale. And in Bach, the *Passion* was transmuted into music which moved the souls of the congregation. I don't think there can be any doubt of that.

WFB: I'm not here to contend that music doesn't affect people, but since you have spoken and written about large social themes, I was wondering whether you had established a nexus there. For instance, we both know that in his late, crazy days, as distinguished from his early crazy days, Mao Tse-tung decided that Mozart and Beethoven were great public enemies of the revolution and sought to extirpate them and—I suppose—others from the inventory of music the Chinese were permitted to listen to. Now, granted that he was a madman, as, in a sense, Lenin was—Lenin refused to listen to music on the grounds that it softened those hard bones he wanted to develop. Was there detectable any after-trace in China of that awful effort?

MENUHIN: Mao's effort simply pushed music underground. It was touching to see, walking in the parks early in the morning—the parks are the only place where the people have the space and the freedom to express themselves—housing is very tight, very limited—and to hear these young Chinese everywhere, in bushes and next to trees, declaiming and singing opera arias, violinists practicing the Vivaldi concerti. It was quite extraordinary. The human spirit cannot be suppressed.

But a very good try at it can be made. *The New York Times'* superjournalist Fox Butterfield became infatuated with China while a sophomore at Harvard. He mastered the language in Taiwan, earned a Ph.D., turned to journalism as a career, and in 1979 arrived in Peking as the first correspondent in thirty years to represent *The New York Times.*

He appeared on *Firing Line* in 1982, after the publication of his epochal book, written just after the end of the Cultural Revolution and some time before the reforms of Deng Xiaoping had taken effective hold. Now Fox Butterfield, as we will see, had to do a little struggling. He had written the most comprehensive indictment ever published in America of Mao Tse-tung. And yet Butterfield was a protégé of John K. Fairbank of Harvard, a leading apologist for Mao for years and years. He needed, as we will see, to give such credit as he thought he could responsibly give to the early Mao. And he had to explain, without being obvious about it, how the Communist movement attracted in its early days the enthusiasm of many non-Communists. The same point, viewed in a different and more abrasive way, was made during the mid-fifties by Senators McCarren and McCarthy, the former in his prodigious study of the Institute of Pacific Relations. Obviously Mr. Butterfield wanted to stay out of the way of the conventional controversies.

I began by asking the tamest question of all: How does one apportion credit for progress to Communist-run regimes? For instance, does the present Chinese leadership seek an improvement in living standards to the extent even of being willing to forsake some of the ideological rigidities?

BUTTERFIELD: I think people in China today are *less* willing to forsake these things than they were before. I think that in the 1950s—

WFB: To forsake what?

BUTTERFIELD: To forsake freedom of speech, or the right to choose the place where they live. In the early 1950s people *were* willing to sacrifice. There was a moment, or a period of several years, maybe a decade, of *genuine* enthusiasm about the Communists. Finally here was a group who were going to get China going again after a hundred years of humiliation by the foreign imperialists. No more foreign gunboats; inflation was stopped; no more warlords. Things looked pretty good, and the Communists, for five or ten years, *did* get the economy going. There was great growth.

But then they began asking for too much. The series of political campaigns took a terrible toll and led to cynicism. The economy slowed down, and from the mid-1960s through the late 1970s there was really very little growth. In fact, real wages fell. We now know that income in the countryside, in real terms, was not much greater than it was many years ago; that in fact the food consumption per capita in China was no better in the late 1970s than it had been in the early 1930s.

WFB: Well now, Professor [Donald] Zagoria [of Hunter College] confirms everything you have said, but seems to be saying

that that early rise in productive energy may very easily
have issued simply from energies that had been choked up
by thirty years of civil war plus fighting the Japanese, and
that it is very difficult to attribute any growth to an *élan
vital* for which Mao claims credit.

BUTTERFIELD: I think *both* things were at work. Obviously there was
tremendous stored-up energy, and people were delighted
by whoever would come and provide order and get the
economy going again in the fifties. But I think there were
a lot of people who genuinely thought the Communists
represented the great tradition of Chinese nationalism and
were working for something good. Even [some] people
who weren't Communists themselves [thought that]. I met
men—a Harvard-trained doctor, for example—who had
gone back to China in 1950. He was not a Communist, but
he wanted to take part in the rebuilding of the motherland.

WFB: And ended up in jail?

BUTTERFIELD: He was willing to give Communism a chance. And yes, he
did end up in jail.

WFB: Well, on this matter of the economic improvement of the
average Chinese life, may I ask, Have you found that there
is a considerable tendency to prescind from the passage of
time improvements in literacy or in health or in food
consumption? I find it happening, for instance, when people compare, let's say, calories available to the average
Russian in 1960 over against calories available in 1917.
Actually that's not a very good example to use, because
there were probably more calories [available] in 1917. But
they always do it to [mitigate] Castro, and I see you doing
it a little bit. You talk about the rise in literacy. Shouldn't
we expect that *any* country, given the widespread knowledge revolution that the twentieth century gives us, in
forty years, should have come through with considerable
improvement somewhere along the line? What leads us to
believe that there wouldn't have been a comparable rise in
literacy had Mao Zedong *not* been the head of a revolution? Had it gone some other way? The way of Taiwan,
for instance? Or the way of Japan or whatever? Another
way of putting this is: Why do you say, "For all that we

criticize Mao Zedong, we have at least to grant that under Mao Zedong there was a tremendous spread in literacy"?

BUTTERFIELD: I think you certainly have made a good point, that *if* the Chinese Nationalists had stayed in power on the mainland, *if* there hadn't been a World War II with the Japanese invasion, and *if* there hadn't been the rise of the Communist Party, the Nationalists *might* have done many of these same things too. They *have* done them on Taiwan, I absolutely agree. But it was the *Communists* who were there after 1949, and it was the *Communists* who have pulled off some of those advances, and I think we have to give them credit for it.

WFB: I would put it differently: We have to acknowledge that *it happened while they were there.* But that doesn't mean we have to give them credit for it, does it? Unless they had taken a sort of Cambodian Khmer Rouge antiliteracy position where they started to shoot anybody for the sin of learning how to read. That they did not do, that is correct. But beyond that it's extremely hard, I think, to make any [claims] based on the attitudes of Mao Zedong, especially when you consider what he did to university life, to the life of the mind.

BUTTERFIELD: This gets us into the heart of the matter. We have to acknowledge that the Communists did achieve many of these things—that the rate of literacy greatly improved, that there are now two hundred and ten million Chinese children in school. The Communists *did* build a lot of schools, they *did* train a lot of teachers.

But then, if you look further, we can now see that the Communists have *not* gone as far in carrying out these reforms as they had claimed or as we had thought a few years ago.

WFB: Now, was that because they were very good at fooling us or because we were easy to fool?

BUTTERFIELD: It's some of both. It's also because they made claims that were greater than what they had achieved.

WFB: But Zagoria saw through them.

BUTTERFIELD: I think there are a number of foreigners who saw through them.

WFB: Yes?

BUTTERFIELD: But I think a lot of us were—there was an infatuation with China. This has historical roots. You go back to American missionaries in the nineteenth century who believed that they could convert the heathen Chinese to Christianity in a single generation; American businessmen who have long dreamed of that fabulous China market—hundreds of millions of customers, if they'd all only buy a single widget, American companies would prosper. In World War II, when we were fighting against the Japanese, we envisioned Chiang Kai-shek as a valiant democrat upholding the same ideals as we. These were projections of our own myths, rather than a hard look at Chinese reality.

WFB: Yes. Don't you think that a lot of Americans forget that we really had very little grounds for knowing how Chiang Kai-shek would evolutionize, inasmuch as he never had, during the whole of his supervision of Chinese affairs, a nonturbulent situation? He had a civil war, then he had the warlords, then he had the occupation of Japan, then he had the Chinese Communists. So it's very difficult to say, up until he reached Taiwan, how in fact he might have behaved had he had a little bit of serenity.

BUTTERFIELD: One of those great historical ifs that we can't really answer. We do—I think the historical record now shows that the Chinese Nationalists accomplished more positive, constructive [things] than we gave them credit for at the time. That literacy was spreading, that roads and railroads were being built, that industry was being constructed. We missed some of that, what with the war and with the Communists, with terrible inflation and corruption.

WFB: Their [the Kuomintang's, in Taiwan] anxiety for literacy extended even to cutting down on the cost of books by not paying royalties to the authors. [*Laughter*] [The aside referred to the commonplace book piracy in Taiwan.]

A statement was made four or five years ago as follows, in *The New York Times:* "In a country where misery and want were the foundation of the social structure, famine was endemic, death from starvation common, death pervasive, thievery normal, and corruption taken for granted, the elimination of these conditions in China"—i.e., under Mao—"is so striking that negative aspects of the new rule fade in relative importance." I don't want this to be an ambush; that was Barbara Tuchman writing. Barbara Tuchman now endorses *your* book and calls it—a marvelously chosen word—sobering. She might have said "self-sobering." Now, do you find that somebody who spoke as positively as she did, dismissing what you revealed here, which is about as hideous as anything we have known in the twentieth century, as "negative aspects"—is that an example of that anxiety to romanticize the revolution against which you are now contending?

BUTTERFIELD: I think there's a very complicated process going on in how Americans have perceived China. There was this romantic period. It started with Edgar Snow going to the caves of Yenan in the late 1930s, and coming out—

WFB: Yes, and you acknowledge Edgar Snow in your book—

BUTTERFIELD: Certainly, I think he—

WFB: —as having been a very important figure.

BUTTERFIELD: It's a very exciting account for us to read. It was [exciting] for the Chinese too. It was a very important book in China. It was the first account many Chinese had of what the Communists were like. We sometimes forget that. But, you know, I think we in the United States tend to forget how good the Chinese are at what I refer to as "hostmanship," that is, a very practiced art of entertaining and persuading foreigners. It really goes back to Confucius. In fact, the opening lines of Confucius are: "Is it not a pleasure to have guests come from afar?" When a foreign delegation goes to China, they are met at the airport by a group of smiling schoolchildren with their cheeks rouged and bouquets of flowers, and then they're whisked off in limousines with lace curtains and taken to a banquet at the Great Hall of the People where they have twelve- or fifteen-course epicurean meals and their libations of mai-pais, and people are dazed or dazzled or whatever by this performance.

WFB: Some people are.

Fox Butterfield's extraordinary book had a shorter run than it deserved. The reason for it was that by the time the full horror of Mao Tse-tung transpired—and Butterfield was an important instrument in getting the truth out—China was embarked on a different course. The Gang of Four had been prosecuted and convicted, and, under Deng, considerable liberalization went forward. It is too early to predict that China will be liberated from its thralldom to Communism, but it is headed in the right direction. And the tidal wave of enthusiasm for Mao turns now into a tidal wave of enthusiasm for Mao's successors to the extent that they repudiate Mao in deed, if not in word. Scholarship published in the trough of these historical tidal waves is not given the attention it merits.

American conservatives were much taken with Chiang Kai-shek ever since he was displaced in 1949 by Mao Tse-tung, left only with the island of Taiwan to administer. The independence of Taiwan, which continues to call itself the Republic of China, has been a cause militant of conservatives for years. I remember the dramatic day in which Taiwan was kicked out of the United Nations, pursuant to a resolution introduced by the Democratic Republic of Albania, indignant at the imposture of Little China, pretending to be the legitimate ruler of Great China. Shortly before the vote expelling Taiwan, a presidential airplane landed in Los Angeles carrying Governor Ronald Reagan, who had been sent by President Nixon to do an Asiatic tour for the primary purpose of reassuring our old allies that our new interest in China (this was four months before Nixon's trip to China in February 1972) did not herald any diminished interest by the U.S. in the independence of Taiwan. The phone rang at nearly midnight, and it was Reagan to ask if I had any inside knowledge of what he thought to be a great diplomatic betrayal. "Last week I was in Taiwan telling them that they had nothing to worry about in the UN. Right after I get back here, they've been thrown out!" The following day, I discussed the whole matter, on *Firing Line,* with Ambassador George Bush, who had unsuccessfully attempted to prevent the rout in the General Assembly.

We can only guess what Chiang might have accomplished if he had remained on the mainland; but we *know* what he accomplished on Taiwan. In 1977, his son President Chiang Ching-kuo appeared on *Firing Line.*

CCK, as he was universally referred to (at least by foreigners), was a large, corpulent man, with a fixed smile on his weathered face. By negotiation with his aides it had been agreed that our program would be taped in a highly unorthodox way, never attempted before or since.

Firing Line is a nuanced program, and a thorough knowledge of English is required to do justice to subtle thought. For that reason I have tried to have foreign guests only if they speak excellent English. (My most conspicuous failure was the Dalai Lama. I was assured that he spoke excellent English. After a few minutes I was driven to speaking to him in child-talk—"Me-too-likee-peace.") CCK advised us, through his staff, that he could understand English well enough to do without an interpreter but that he could not *speak* English well enough to do without an interpreter. Accordingly, I would speak to him in English, he would reply in Chinese; and an interpreter would perform his function, paragraph by paragraph. Then *Firing Line*'s producer would edit out the Chinese segments and transpose the English into these slots. It worked just fine.

CCK joined the Communist Party at age sixteen and went to the Soviet Union to study. He was there for twelve years, three of them spent in a labor camp, as punishment for "antiparty activity" (Stalin time). He served as a common laborer, as a white-collar worker, as an assistant engineer, and as a military student, finally getting permission, in the late thirties, to return to China to join his estranged father and combine efforts against the Japanese. Thirty years later, after serving the Kuomintang in myriad roles, he emerged as the logical successor to Chiang Kai-shek.

I asked him whether there was any possibility that Taiwan might make an alliance with the Soviet Union at some point in the future, if necessary to substitute for vitiating Western support (President Carter had recently booted CCK's ambassador out of Washington, replacing him with China's).

No, he said. To contemplate even a transideological alliance with the Soviet Union would destroy the spiritual claims of the Chinese in Taiwan.

Well, what about continuing links between Taiwan and the mainland? Hadn't his government's claim to be the legitimate government of all of

China become largely fancy? What widely goes by the name of "the Taiwan question"?

CHIANG: Everyone talks about this question as "the Taiwan question." As a matter of fact, it is the *China* question. *We* are the government of the Republic of China. We have the responsibility to give back to the Chinese people of the mainland their freedom. In order to accomplish this, we do not have to rely on military means. Rather, we rely on political means. We have often said that in solving this problem we should rely seventy percent on political means and only thirty percent on military means. The Chinese people on the mainland have been suffering from oppression without uprising. When the uprising takes place on the Chinese mainland, we would give appropriate support. Only then can the *China question* be solved.

Concerning the future of China, he had this to say: "I predict that before too long there will be a deep malcontent in the Chinese Communist regime, just [as, in Russia, after] the de-Stalinization campaign. . . . After Mao's death [September 9, 1976], the Chinese Communist regime cannot [gain] firm control in all parts of China. Not Hua Guofeng. Not Deng Xiaoping. Not any of the other leaders has [Mao's] ability. In the future, the Chinese mainland will disintegrate. There will be different power groups appearing on the mainland, some of them having contact with us. This is the scenario I foresee for our recovery of the mainland."

"This" did not (will never?) happen. On the other hand, neither has happened to Taiwan what was so widely predicted would happen to it after the United States severed its formal ties.

It was widely predicted that the diplomatic boycott of Taiwan for affecting to be the true government of China that followed would have a terminal effect on its role as an independent state. The big airlines began to boycott it. Foreign embassies were closed. Taiwan was even denied its athletes' participation in the Olympics in Canada, a seizure of diplomatic rectitude that did not affect Prime Minister Pierre Trudeau at the expense of any Soviet satellite, though Russia's de facto rule over the Baltic states is at least as questionable—or at least as offensive—as Taiwan's dream of ruling over China. Objectively, it seemed as though diplomatic, economic, and cultural isolation would topple the regime.

That did not happen. The United States stumbled upon a functional deception that gave us what, after all, served our interests. While formally going along with Peking in its insistence of sovereignty, we maintained, in effect, diplomatic representation in Taiwan. Meanwhile, the graduated liberal reforms of CCK combined with the industry and energy of the people of Taiwan to nurture an evolutionized super-minipower. And direct irredentist pressure from the mainland . . . lessened. Far from demanding with increasing truculence the diplomatic reincorporation of Taiwan, the government of Deng simply let the phlogistonic question . . . cool. Although there was never any suggestion from Peking that Taiwan is other than a province of the mainland, the matter is not nowadays pressed to the point of increasing hostilities between the mainland and Taiwan; as CCK might have put it, Not military, Not economic, Not rhetorical.

With the death of CCK, I have thought the myth over. It was in 1895 that the Japanese occupied Taiwan. It was liberated in 1945. For only four years it was restored to China—the China ruled by Chiang Kai-shek. Its resident population is 84 percent Taiwanese; its president (named by CCK) is Taiwanese in origin. "You mentioned," CCK said, "the possibility of Taiwan being a separate political entity. The residents—the Chinese people in Taiwan—know very well that this alternative would mean self-destruction for them. They would not accept this course of action."

They will resist it. But it is overdue to blow the cobwebs of the One China mystique away. Acclaim Taiwanese independence. Legitimize its government, formalize our own relations with it, and hope that someday in the future, what Chiang Kai-shek and CCK did for Taiwan, the successors to Deng will do for the mainland.

When talking about Africa with Elspeth Huxley I thought to raise rather directly the bugaboo of colonialism. The atrocities committed in Africa in the postcolonial period had narcotized American interest in African affairs—one more coup, one more gruesome story of savagery, loot, and depradation. Mrs. Huxley was raised in Kenya and had written about Africa all her life. We spoke in 1970. She explained, even if she did not entirely justify, the one-party tradition in Africa. In doing so she reminded us that "democracy," which we accept automatically as the *ne plus ultra* in government, is simply not the traditional way of getting on in many societies.

WFB: I should like to begin by asking Mrs. Huxley whether she thinks it quite responsible for England to have liquidated her empire at quite the speed she did?

HUXLEY: Whether it was responsible? I think there was no alternative. There comes a point when events collect their own momentum.

WFB: What I am trying to explore is whether two dogmas are reconcilable. The one is that a nation ought not irresponsibly to retreat from a position in which it enjoys a certain prestige and maintains a certain stability; the second that colonialism is always, under all circumstances, wrong.

For instance, it would have been an act of statesmanship, would it not, to have prevented such losses of life as took place in Nigeria and Biafra during a period of eighteen months? Will history speak kindly of England's precipitate withdrawal? Or will history say—in effect—that because England found it an easier thing to do, the English cloaked their withdrawal in anticolonial and humanitarian rhetoric—and simply got out while the going was good?

HUXLEY: I don't think they did cloak it with that; I think they tried to delay it as much as they could—with conferences of every kind, you know—constitutions were as thick as—

WFB: But surely they could have delayed more. After all, the resources of England are at least equal to those of Portugal [which has not withdrawn from Africa].

HUXLEY: Only by using a massive force in a great many different countries—

WFB: Portugal didn't use massive force—

HUXLEY: They are still doing so. There are four years' compulsory national service in Portugal for every man over eighteen. I believe they spent forty percent of their budget on mili-

tary—defense, whatever it is called—I mean, this would
have been a crippling burden, financially.

But also, the heart of the British people was not in it.
I don't think we'd ever wish to suppress people by force
in our country in large numbers. We perhaps had an
illusion that we were doing good—I don't think it was an
illusion. I think we *were* doing good. I think we left more
hurriedly than would have been desirable—but I don't
think as hurriedly as all that. You talk about precipitate:
I don't think it was precipitate—it was going on, well, ever
since 1947, when India became independent. It was
known it was going on, I think. The Sudan was the first,
then there was Ghana—which was sometime in the late
fifties [1959]. Nigeria in about 1960. It *wasn't* very precipitate.

WFB: Well, forty-two new countries in eight years is generally
            thought of as quite fast.

HUXLEY: Yes, but I think you can't compare it with the situation
            in the Belgian Congo, where it *was* precipitate. But there
            does come a point when you've got to choose. Either you
            say, We'll wait for an ideal situation, when more people
            have had time to graduate from universities and there are
            more skilled people equipped to take over the reins of
            government. You can do this. Or you can say, That is
            worse—because it involves shooting a lot of people. Then
            there is the question of any kind of future based on good-
            will. If you leave in an atmosphere of bloodshed and vio-
            lence, you can't expect to attain what you hope to be a
            commonwealth.

WFB: You say now, and perhaps you thought then, "They can-
            not possibly have democratic government," from which I
            understand you to be saying it simply isn't in the cards,
            considering the—

HUXLEY: Did I say it just like that?

WFB: Your elaboration was: "I've never thought that parlia-
            mentary democracy would work in Africa, or that the
            Africans wanted it. It isn't the kind of system that they
            like."

HUXLEY: No. This is the in-and-out system that they *don't* like. The two-party system in which the opposition is just waiting—you have a changeover—you blow a whistle because it's halftime and decide to change. This is the thing—they haven't really been brought up on football and cricket and so on.

WFB: But, Mrs. Huxley, it was part of the dream of decolonization that one *should* be self-ruling. Now, "self-rule" surely [depends on] whether the individuals' preferences count—whether they are *tabulated.* So for you to say that they are going to have one-party systems because they don't believe in parliamentary democracy but, on the other hand, they are going to have the blessings of self-rule strikes me as making a rather abstract point.

HUXLEY: I don't think an African would say that. You see, their traditional method was to have their arguments—their dialogue to straighten things out—but at a preliminary stage. And they will now say that in a one-party state there can be a number of candidates [and one will be selected]. This comes down from the traditional tribal government. In that way you could have conferences in which people would talk; but they didn't end by taking votes. At the end, the chief would more or less sum up and say, Well, this is what is going to happen. And then it *happened,* and the argument was over. At that point it became more or less treasonable to question the word of the chief. If this particular chief, who was your traditional head, was overthrown by another chief, this was anarchy—this was civil war. That's why I think parliamentary democracy to be very often the wrong thing for them.

WFB: [I think I commented rather priggishly.] I don't doubt people's infinite ingenuity in justifying one-party government—for that matter, one-man government. What I am wondering is whether or not it is a form of Western paternalism simply to accept such a mockery of political freedom in that part of the world.

·   ·   ·

And South Africa. Discussions on Angola become, almost inevitably, discussions on South Africa.

The question before the house, in January 1986, specifically, was whether to give help to Jonas Savimbi, who was fighting the Angola government, a satellite of the Soviet Union maintained in power by Cuban troops. Savimbi was taking aid from South Africa, illegitimizing, in the opinion of some, his entire venture and our participation in it. Two forceful journalists were guests, Anthony Lewis of *The New York Times,* and Arnaud de Borchgrave, the conservative and anti-Communist editor of the *Washington Times.* Anthony Lewis offered an explanation for why the government of Angola was so dependent on the Soviet Union.

ANTHONY LEWIS

LEWIS: The MPLA [Popular Movement for the Liberation of Angola] government of Angola has become increasingly dependent because of South African pressure and armed incursions over the last half-dozen years. South African forces have been in and out of that country a dozen times. They are there now.

Wait a minute, I said. Five years before Savimbi even approached the South Africans, Fidel Castro's Cuban soldiers were maintaining in power the government of Angola.

LEWIS: I am entirely against the Cuban troops there, and if we want to have a fight about our ardor for that proposition, I am confident that I will be at least as strong as you are. The question is how to get them out. I find it hard to believe that we can get them out by becoming involved one way or another, either by covert aid or overt aid or some kind of aid, in the war against the Angolan government. Your position means, as a practical matter, that the United States is going to become deeply involved as an ally of South Africa, a country whose government—minority white government—is hated by everybody else in southern Africa.

Representative Kemp [the sponsor of the aid-Savimbi bill] says, "Oh, no, we will *replace* South Africa, so that we won't be entangled with them anymore." Now, that would mean that we would be replacing military activity [by South Africa] that includes air force bombing runs, close support, troops on the ground—are [you proposing that we] send American troops into Africa?

DE BORCHGRAVE: No, we're not. That's not—

LEWIS: Then what is it all about? Are you going to win with monetary aid?

DE BORCHGRAVE: Fifteen million dollars in aid is all that's being discussed right now.

LEWIS: Fifteen million? You'd be up to two, three, four, five billions if you are really going to fight that war. And you *know* it. Why not be honest about it?

DE BORCHGRAVE: Tony, Jonas Savimbi is the first to tell you that he has indeed accepted South African aid. He denounces apartheid just as vehemently as you do—

LEWIS: Oh, I don't disagree with that. He does, that's true.

DE BORCHGRAVE: He is *not* an ally of apartheid. He is *not* an ally of
                 P. W. Botha.

WFB: God knows Savimbi was not an ally of Portugal. He went
                 all the way to Mao Zedong to learn how to fight them.

DE BORCHGRAVE: He is no more grateful to South Africa for its aid than
                 Joseph Stalin was grateful to us in World War II for
                 lend-lease aid. It didn't mean that Stalin was genuflecting
                 in front of pluralistic democratic principles.

I asked why there should be any division of opinion among whites and
blacks in resenting the colonization of Angola by the Soviet Union.

LEWIS: May I answer that question?

DE BORCHGRAVE: I don't see how aiding Savimbi makes us an *ally* of
                 South Africa.

LEWIS: Well, I want to just tell you gentlemen both something
                 with the utmost sincerity. And that is: Try to think of it
                 not from your point of view, but from the point of view
                 of the black majority in South Africa. What you have to
                 understand is that those people have been brutalized for
                 a couple of hundred years. They are not allowed to vote.
                 They can't live with their families. They are the majority
                 of the country and they have *no* say in its running. They
                 of course feel very oppressed by all that, and hence when
                 they see the government that does that to them helping
                 Mr. Savimbi, they don't make sophisticated judgments
                 on what a nice charismatic fellow he is or whether he is
                 good, bad, or indifferent. From their point of view he is
                 an ally of their oppressor. And that's all they are going
                 to see.

And so the points of reference go back to South Africa, again and
again. It is probably true that the average black South African does not
distinguish between an internal aggressor (the South African government, aggressor against the natural rights of South African blacks) and
an international aggressor (the Soviet Union). Understanding the difference between the two is understanding why the United States picks

on the one species rather than the other. If many South Africans do not understand the difference, Anthony Lewis should.

It was in 1948 that a book was published with a bewildering title, by an unknown author, on a theme alien at the time to American concerns. The book became a central cultural document of South Africa, where it has sold more copies than any other book save the Bible. *Cry, the Beloved Country* is free of bitterness, telling the story of a fraternal bond between a black minister tormented by the sins of his son and his sister, and a white man.

I thought back to a conversation years earlier with a well-known publisher. I asked him how many books he published that came into his house over the transom, i.e., unescorted by literary agents. He replied that he had felt it a professional obligation to read unsolicited manuscripts, to which end he always retained on the staff two bright college graduates. "That began in 1932," he said to me in 1965. "Since then we have published exactly two unsolicited manuscripts. But one"—he lowered his head devoutly—"was *Cry, the Beloved Country.*"

In later years Alan Paton, the book's white author, became if not bitter, at least harsh in his criticisms of the policies of his government. Until the party was proscribed, he was the president of the Liberal Party, which called for the universal franchise in South Africa.

Economic sanctions were being heatedly debated in 1977, so I took particular care in eliciting Mr. Paton's economic views on the subject.

PATON: I distrust words like "capitalism" and "socialism." I distrust even a word like "liberalism," as a matter of fact, because it's a label and it immediately fixes a pattern from which there are so many exceptions and so many divergences that I don't really like these labels at all. I certainly would be much more inclined toward a socialist system than I would toward a rigid capitalist system, but I would never say that I was a socialist. I would say that I was socialistically inclined, certainly.

I asked him if he thought that racial progress in South Africa could be made only by a socialist government.

PATON: I can see a point when political action would take no account of the economic situation at all. But if there's to be any kind of *evolutionary* progress, there will have to be a very great closing of the gap, because the disparity between white wealth and positions and black wealth and positions is very great indeed. In other words it would be quite impossible to build any kind of a common society so long as that disparity exists.

WFB: Well, it seems to be acknowledged even by some of the most persistent critics of South African society that there is considerable relative economic progress by blacks in that country. Is your point the same as de Tocqueville's, that the more progress you make the more dissatisfied you are with the insufficient rate of that progress?

PATON: Well, that's quite possible, I think, but I think that's a danger that has to be faced. Much worse would be the resentment and the hatred if *no* progress was made at all.

On the matter of sanctions, Mr. Paton was as adamant as a man can be.

PATON: There is only one firm statement that I can make on disinvestment—I will have nothing to do with it. I will not, by any written or spoken word, give it any support whatsoever.

In 1986 the same debate over sanctions raged in Great Britain. Mrs. Thatcher was opposed to sanctions, but there was division within her own government. Worse, at the last meeting of the Commonwealth ministers, some threatened to withdraw from the Commonwealth unless Great Britain changed its policy. What emerged was a compromise: mild sanctions, accompanied by the threat to make them more severe unless the South African government moved faster toward the elimination of apartheid.

The president of the antiapartheid movement in Great Britain was an Anglican bishop. The Most Reverend Ernest Urban Trevor Huddleston was born in England in 1913, and his diocese for many years was Johannesburg. The archbishop finally left South Africa and published the book *Naught for Your Comfort,* a description of the impact of apartheid on the African people. He was now retired, but continued to be active in the antiapartheid and other causes. He arrived at the makeshift studio at the nave of St. James's Church in Piccadilly in full episcopal regalia, and in very high dudgeon.

Paul Johnson is the author of the spectacularly ambitious *Modern Times,* subtitled *The World from the Twenties to the Eighties.* Mr. Johnson was for some years the editor of the left-wing *New Statesman.* He left it following an epiphany that took him away from socialism and agnosticism to the free market and Christianity. He is a prodigious scholar, the author of over a dozen books on a wide range of subjects. His essay opposing sanctions, published in *Commentary* magazine in 1985, was said to have influenced the position taken by President Reagan in opposing sanctions.

I relay the transcript very substantially because all the relevant inflections of the South Africa argument are touched on here by able advocates of conflicting positions.

WFB: I should like to begin by asking Bishop Huddleston whether he would alter his views on sanctions if he were persuaded that their imposition would hurt primarily the black people of South Africa.

HUDDLESTON: I've been involved in that argument for seventy years, and there is no question *whatever* of my changing my view, because I think it is a specious argument. It has no foundation and it is simply used as an excuse for doing nothing— talking, but doing *nothing.*

WFB: Well, would that include Alan Paton, for instance?

HUDDLESTON: Yes, absolutely. He's a great friend of mine, Alan Paton, but I totally disagree with him. I was the figure in one of his books, and I have kept in touch with him, but he knows what I think about him, and on that issue I am absolutely and totally opposed to him.

WFB: But I asked you a rather concrete question, namely, If it were documented that the harm done by sanctions would harm primarily the black people, would that affect your thinking? Or would you say, "Even so, I would be in favor of them"?

HUDDLESTON: I would say it, because that is what the black people say. I am not saying anything from *my* point of view. It is not *my* job to tell the African people how they should meet the challenge of apartheid. That's for them. And the struggle that they are fighting is *their* struggle. I am here simply to try to represent what I believe to be the true view of the majority population in South Africa, the black population. And I have no evidence whatsoever to make me change my mind.

WFB: Well, let me try this out on you [I turned to our other guest], Mr. Johnson. There are those who say that the black people in South Africa are in favor of sanctions, and there are others who say they are not. Now, do you happen to have a position on whether or not a plebiscite of black South Africans would reveal that they were *for* or *against* this kind of economic activity?

JOHNSON: Frankly, I have no idea what the answer to that question is. It would be very difficult to organize a plebiscite in present circumstances because there is an atmosphere of terror among the black communities, created by the African National Congress. The people who come out against sanctions are liable to be murdered or burnt alive, in fact.

The trouble with the whole sanctions debate is that people on both sides are very clear about what's going to happen, and I find that there is no basis for this clarity and certainty about it. It seems to me that once you interfere in a free-market economic situation, you set up unpredictable consequences, and nobody can be sure what they are going to be or which section of the population is going to be hurt. All you can be sure of is that you are setting in motion a train of events which you can't foresee.

For instance, the mere *threat* of sanctions—the first actual real consequence has been to send up the price of gold, which has gone over the four-hundred-dollar mark again, and that, of course, has been of enormous financial benefit to the South Africans as a whole and to the South African government in particular, and it has helped to build up their morale. So that is the one consequence of the threat of sanctions we *can* see.

I tend to look at this problem from a historian's point of view and ask myself what happened before. Again, there were unpredictable effects. When arms to South

Africa were banned [by the U.S.]—that was an early form of sanctions—the main consequence was to create a South African arms industry. They were able to use their particular expertise in high explosives (because they've got this huge mining industry) to challenge the two leading powers, Sweden and the United States, in that particular field. They now sell high explosives all over the world.

They also used it to create an armored-vehicle industry, which is very important from the police point of view, and they now export armored vehicles all over the world, including particularly to black African states—they are sort of under-the-counter deals. So that is one example of where sanctions, far from weakening the regime, have actually strengthened it. And another example, of course, is the oil sanctions, which led to the creation of an indigenous South African oil substitution industry and, more important, enormously increased their coal industry.

So what I am saying is that sanctions may have the effect that its supporters claim it will have or—I don't know. I suspect that on balance sanctions will probably *strengthen* the regime.

WFB: Well, Archbishop, what I am trying to probe is the question whether people who are for sanctions understand themselves to be dominated primarily by the imperative of making a *moral* statement, or whether they think they are also making a *utilitarian* point.

HUDDLESTON: Well, for myself, it's *always* a moral issue. It is a moral issue in the sense that the *purpose* of sanctions is perfectly clear. Whether they work or whether they do not work, the purpose of sanctions is to isolate a regime which is based on institutionalized racism, which is a form of slavery. In fact, the struggle parallels the struggle for the abolition of slavery. The abolition of slavery, as Lincoln knew only too well, deprived the South of over four billion dollars of capital, because slaves were worth a lot of money. That didn't mean you didn't fight for the abolition of slavery. The whole issue of sanctions is a moral issue, because the purpose of them is to isolate South Africa from the civilized community until it dismantles apartheid absolutely.

You cannot *reform* apartheid. There is no *evolutionary* solution to this problem. Apartheid is intrinsically evil, and if this country or West Germany or Israel or any other country really regards the economic aspect of sanctions as being paramount, then they are the people who are [truly immoral]. And I regret to state my own country is the worst offender because of its long history.

Incidentally, I must correct one statement that Mr. Johnson made on the terrorism of the African National Congress. He must be a very bad historian if he thinks that, because the African National Congress has been in existence longer than any other political party in South Africa, and for sixty years—until the Sharpeville Massacre—it was a totally nonviolent organization, and is still prepared to be a nonviolent organization once the violence of the state is stopped. We are fighting terror in South Africa, against the terrorist *government.*

JOHNSON: One would concede that there is terror on both sides. As a historian, I have to look and see what is likely to happen, [judging] from previous precedents. The ANC is not now wholly committed to violence, but it is *using* violence on a very large and increasing scale. That violence is directed against the moderates.

Unfortunately, we have seen this happen before. For instance, in the 1920s, when the first big rush of settlers to Israel took place, many of the Arabs were then prepared to cooperate with the Jews, as indeed were the Jews with the Arabs. Unfortunately, what we saw developing then was the destruction—the physical *murder*—of the moderates by the Arab extremists, and therein lie the seeds of the present situation in the Middle East. It was a takeover by the extremists.

I myself saw it happen again in Algeria in the 1950s, where most of the original representatives of the Arabs were prepared to work with the French. They were gradually eliminated. They were either driven out by terror or murdered by the extremists, and the result was that the entire country really has been wrecked. The old, moderate servants of the French government, who were perfectly decent people—they were used as human mine detectors on the minefields at the end.

That sort of thing is happening in South Africa now. And what I am terrified of is if the ANC continues to move toward violence—and it is being encouraged to do so by a lot of people in the West who, I fear, *like* violence—then of course the moderates will be completely eliminated and there will be a chasm between the races. And *that* is what is going to produce not only civil war, but entirely destroy the economy of the country.

WFB: Well, I am very discouraged to hear the archbishop say that there is no evolutionary way out. Certainly Abraham Lincoln thought there would be an evolutionary way out.

HUDDLESTON: He didn't succeed in getting one, did he?

WFB: No, he did not.

HUDDLESTON: Your civil war was one of the bloodiest civil wars.

WFB: I was going to say, he succeeded in presiding over a war in which a million people were killed.

HUDDLESTON: Yes. Exactly.

WFB: But he did write to Horace Greeley, even after the war had begun, to say that he would tolerate slavery in part, and for a while, for so long as it was necessary to preserve the Union. And of course the idea was that the Kansas-Nebraska bill *would* lead to evolutionary emancipation. Now, to take the position that there is no evolutionary end possible here seems to me to commit one to the position that civil war is welcomed. And I'd be surprised to hear you take that position.

HUDDLESTON: I would never suggest civil war is *welcome.* I say it is *inevitable.* How much longer do you suppose the black African majority is going to wait for its human rights in their own country, when they are a majority population? For seventy-five years—in fact for longer, ever since the Act of Union—they have tried; they have beaten on that door for all those years. Do you really think—is it conceivably fair to say—that the casualties inflicted by the ANC

are more than minuscule, compared to what the South
African government is doing the whole time?

WFB: Well, the Catholics in England waited three hundred years
            for the right to vote.

HUDDLESTON: They may have done that—

WFB: I am not saying that they should have waited three hun-
            dred years. Maybe they should have become revolution-
            ary. But in fact it seems to me that a study of history
            instructs one that one has to be patient simply because
            that's the way the world works. Presumably we would
            welcome civil war in the Soviet Union, right?

HUDDLESTON: I would not welcome civil war in the Soviet Union at all,
            but I think we won't get onto *that* subject. I want to
            continue on this subject of the right of people to justice,
            and the church, the Catholic Church, has always main-
            tained the principles of a just rebellion, and if there isn't
            a just rebellion in the world like this one, I don't know
            where it is.

WFB: But in a just war, are we not admonished that the ends that
            are to be achieved have to be harmonious with the efforts
            taken to achieve them? You can't, for instance, automati-
            cally say, "Well, let's have a million people killed," and
            then end up with a state in which you have as much
            freedom as you have, say, in Tanzania.

HUDDLESTON: Well, I lived in Tanzania, and there is a great deal of
            freedom in Tanzania, but we won't get into that subject
            either, because you are sliding away from the main issue
            here.

JOHNSON: Can I get back to what seems to be one of the main issues:
            the inevitability of civil war. The archbishop says that civil
            war is inevitable. I don't believe that, and I think it is very
            wicked to say so, if I may put it that way, because I think
            these tend to become self-fulfilling prophecies. One cannot
            say what is going to happen in South Africa. Certainly no
            historian would dream of predicting a civil war, because
            everyone has got a great deal to lose there.
            South Africa is the one really modern economy in the

whole of Africa. Africa is just a very, very poor continent. It is going through—it is just entering the really critical phase of—the population explosion, which will presumably last for about twenty years. There are going to be scores of million more mouths to be fed, and it is vital for the future of the whole continent that that powerful and growing economy should continue to work and should produce the goods and services that all those new mouths are going to need.

Take the case of the mining industry. I know a bit about it, because I have been working on a book involving the South African mining industry. This is the largest mining industry in the world, and certainly the most efficient. It employs seven hundred thousand people, of whom five hundred thousand or more are blacks. Now those are the best-paid workers—black workers—in the whole of Africa. Their real incomes, their real wages, have gone up three times in the last ten years. That is a very, very big improvement. Whereas in most of Africa—for instance in Zaire—the per capita incomes are only ten percent of what they were twenty years ago. So here we have a country where the black population is to a very great extent *benefiting* from huge improvements in their living standards.

WFB: Would you say there was any evolutionary progress in the acquisition of *rights* that has come with this newfound wealth?

JOHNSON: It depends on what you mean by rights. I mean, for instance, mobility. A lot of blacks have now got cars. There are more private owners of cars in the South African republic than there are in the whole of the Soviet Union. That is a fact which sometimes astonishes people when they are told—

HUDDLESTON: But what percentage of those are black?

JOHNSON: I am saying that there are more *black* owners of cars in South Africa than in the whole of the Soviet Union—

HUDDLESTON: Than in the whole of the Soviet Union? I don't believe it for a moment.

JOHNSON: Private cars. Private cars.

HUDDLESTON: Are you including the homeland?

JOHNSON: I am including the whole lot. But I think on this sanctions thing, which I repeat is the key to the present argument, the difficulty there is that I have not met *anyone* involved in business in South Africa—and as the archbishop rightly says, that includes a lot of Afrikaners—who would now defend apartheid in any shape or form. The *entire* business community as far as I can see is opposed to it.

Unfortunately, the base of the strength of the Afrikaner element and of the regime, the government there, is more from farmers who are descended from the Boers who came there in the early seventeenth century. They have been there as long as the Americans have been in America, apart from the Indians. It's a very long time, three or four hundred years. And these people are *not* affected by sanctions. They don't care about big business. They *hate* big business. They regard it as the work of the devil. They are Christian fundamentalists. If we put pressure on them, they will dig their heels in. And, basically, they are the core of the regime. Herein lies the complexity of it.

HUDDLESTON: I would agree, they *would* dig their heels in. They have done it for three hundred and fifty years and they will go on doing it.

The old Afrikaners I have the greatest respect for, far more than I have for the English-speaking South Africans who went there and still go there to make money. Britain invests in South Africa more than any other country because it *wants* to sustain apartheid. Mrs. Thatcher has every intention of sustaining apartheid in South Africa.

WFB: Oh, come off it.

HUDDLESTON: I do believe—I have heard Mrs. Thatcher on this subject. I am not saying anything that I wouldn't say to her.

WFB: Yes, I concede that you've met everybody. But—

JOHNSON: Can't we just get back to the point here—

WFB: —there is no reason to suppose that Mrs. Thatcher desires to sustain apartheid—

HUDDLESTON: But she *does* say it. That's all I can say. She refuses any attempt to— [I have not found any evidence that Mrs. Thatcher has ever supported apartheid.]

JOHNSON: You've just made the point that Britain invests a lot in South Africa, as though the only consequence of that investment is to make money for *us*. But if you actually look at it on the ground, it may seem different. For instance, when I was out there, I learnt that to sink the main shaft of a new gold mine there—and they have the biggest and deepest and richest gold mines in the world—just to sink the main shaft of one gold mine now costs one billion dollars—

WFB: One *billion* dollars?

JOHNSON: One billion dollars. And that money has to come mainly from Western investors, including a lot over here in Britain. And that shaft goes down miles and miles and miles. They're absolutely enormous, these mines. However, that one mine will employ twenty thousand people for at least a century. And of those twenty thousand people, about seventeen or eighteen thousand will be Africans earning the highest wages in Africa. So that is the actual *physical* consequence of investment from Britain and the United States—that Africans get well-paid jobs. And I think Africans ought to have well-paid jobs, and this is the best way we can give them such jobs. *That* is the function of our investment. If you are going to wreck the economy, if you are going to stop investment, then of course those Africans and their families will starve.

HUDDLESTON: It's very touching of you to think so much about these Africans when you know perfectly well that the average wage of the whites in South Africa is seven or eight times that of every African and continues to be so.

JOHNSON: But what difference does *that* make? If African black miners are getting three times in real terms what they were getting ten years ago? Isn't that *progress*? Isn't that a *good* thing? Don't you *want* them and their families to be happy?

HUDDLESTON: You know very well that I do, and *I* know them and their families a great deal better than *you* do.

JOHNSON: Then why are you trying to stop a process which is in fact increasing their real wealth and their real standard of living?

HUDDLESTON: Why should that process stop because there is an African government in control? Do you imagine that that is going to be happening?

JOHNSON: Obviously if you stop investment that shaft will not be sunk, will it?

HUDDLESTON: No, and we *will* stop investment if we can. Of course there is no chance of that with the present government in Great Britain, because investment is everything. We live in a consumer society here and we model everything on that one concept.

But of course the purpose of sanctions is not an end in itself. It is the bringing to an end of apartheid. And my quarrel, not only with Mrs. Thatcher's government but with previous governments of different political persuasion, is that nothing has happened except words and words and words, and no action whatsoever has been taken by the West to end apartheid. Even now as we're speaking to you, West Germany, which has the biggest trade relationship with South Africa, has blocked a rule in the European Economic Community to impose a sanction on the export of coal.

JOHNSON: But what would happen if you *got* coal sanctions? Those two thousand African workers, plus their families, will no longer have jobs. How are you going to *feed* them, Archbishop?

HUDDLESTON: Well, I am *not* going to feed them. What I am going to say is just this: Obviously sanctions has a price and the price ought to be *paid*—

JOHNSON: It's a price *you* are not going to pay. It's a price that Western liberals who are screaming for sanctions are not going to have to pay. The price is going to have to be paid by *blacks* and their—

HUDDLESTON: Why?

JOHNSON: —families in South Africa. Why are you insisting *they* pay the price?

HUDDLESTON: Well, because the people who *ought* to pay the price are those companies in the West that have made billions and billions out of slave labor in South Africa. If you are going to impose sanctions, you've got to guarantee the frontline states that whatever South Africa does they will not be—

WFB: Why do you use the term "slave labor"—

HUDDLESTON: Because that's what it is.

WFB: —when you have just heard from Mr. Johnson that they earn ten times as much as they do in Zimbabwe—

HUDDLESTON: I am not talking about economics. I am talking about *human rights,* and the majority population of South Africa are totally denied human rights on the basis of the color of their skin.

WFB: Now, wait a minute. I want to know when you are using metaphors and when you are not. When you use "slave labor," are you suggesting that these people are conscripted and forced to work in the mine?

HUDDLESTON: Yes, basically that is what happens, because they—

WFB: That is not my understanding.

HUDDLESTON: Well, my understanding is different from yours, then. Lesotho couldn't live without the wages of the black miners because they've got nothing to live on, and that is why they go to the coal mines—

WFB: That's true of everybody in the world as far as I know. They've got to earn their keep unless they are going to call on others to earn it for them.

HUDDLESTON: Yes, but the conditions under which they earn their keep in South Africa are intolerable conditions.

WFB: But however intolerable they are by your standards and mine, they are nevertheless conditions that attract a lot of people from other parts of Africa because they consider them relatively tolerable—

HUDDLESTON: Yes, well, Uncle Tom thought that about slavery, didn't he?

WFB: And he might have been right.

HUDDLESTON: He might have been right, but he *wasn't* right. He was morally wrong.

WFB: Now, wait a minute. Wait a *minute*. A lot of Christians living life in the catacombs thought it a life that was better than the life they could have led in luxury in Rome.

HUDDLESTON: Are you suggesting that it would have been a good idea to reform slavery and keep it?

WFB: No, I am saying that I would much have preferred slavery to have disappeared from the South without a civil war, without a million deaths.

HUDDLESTON: Yes, well, you ought to be on my side over sanctions in that case, because although it is very, very late in the day and I wouldn't say that sanctions can do what we hope they might do, but morally there is absolutely no alternative. If you abhor apartheid as Mrs. Thatcher says she does, if you abhor apartheid, then you have *got* to do something to remove it, and that something is not words. It's *action*.

JOHNSON: One thing I don't know about the whole South African problem is whether it is better for the outside world to interfere or not. I have a hunch—and I have no doubt that the archbishop will say I am completely wrong about this—I have a hunch that among the white community on the whole, the penny has dropped, not only about apartheid, but about white supremacy, and that most people there, particularly the people of goodwill, are prepared to move quite rapidly toward a multiracial society. But the more the outside world attacks them—

WFB: The dream of Bantustans is dead. [I.e., of separate, black-run states within South Africa, the much-touted "solution" to the African problem in the fifties and sixties.]

JOHNSON: —the less likely this is to happen.

HUDDLESTON: Why do you say the Bantustan is dead, when there are
            three and a half million people who have been removed
            from their homes? As it happens, my parish was one of
            those first places to fall under the removal scheme and
            dumped into the Bantustans. How can you say they're
            dead?

WFB: I say the *dream* of Bantustans is dead. The notion that a
            separate development is going to solve the racial problems
            in South Africa is intellectually and empirically dead. I am
            agreeing with Mr. Johnson that white people don't believe
            it anymore. Under the circumstances they know they have
            to move.

JOHNSON: It's now very rare in South Africa to come across anyone
            who is prepared to defend apartheid. I'm not saying there
            aren't such people.

WFB: Even government officials?

JOHNSON: Yes, that's right.

WFB: The question is *how* to get from here to there, not whether
            they *ought* to go in that direction. And how to get from
            here to there *without* a civil war.

JOHNSON: One thing I *am* sure of. The more violence, the less real
            progress that will be made. That is the only thing I am
            really sure of about South Africa.

Democracy simply isn't a live issue in mainland China, and not much
of an issue in Africa. But it *is* an issue, very much so, in Latin America
and in parts of Asia.

   One of my guests in 1967 was Carlos Lacerda, the governor of Brazil's
Guanabara Province. In the course of his career he had opposed the
landowning plutocrats who for so long dominated Brazil. Then Getulio
Vargas, the semifascist dictator. Subsequently, Kubitschek, Quadros,
Castello Goulart, Branco, and then Costa e Silva. He served as the
Governor of Guanabara Province and was credited with a near-miracu-
lous recovery of Rio, which as governor he administered. But mostly he

had been known in his own country as an orator, a disputatious editor, a relentless enemy. When President Vargas was accosted with the evidence that one of his own bodyguards, in collusion with one of his own children, had attempted, after one of Mr. Lacerda's inflammatory broadcasts, to assassinate Mr. Lacerda, President Vargas withdrew upstairs and shot himself.

It was 1967 when Lacerda appeared on *Firing Line*. He had withdrawn his support from the military who then dominated Brazil, protesting the regime's undemocratic character.

WFB: Those of us who are familiar with your career know that you have very consistently supported freedom. But in the course of supporting freedom, you are sometimes in favor, and sometimes not in favor, of people who have been democratically elected. So the question arises, What are the theoretical circumstances under which you pull away from democracy?

LACERDA: But in Latin America, you cannot speak of freedom in an abstract sense. Freedom is connected with lots of things such as food, such as education. And such is real freedom for all—not only for those who are in power. In other words, we are a little tired of just the juridical aspects of democracy.

Lacerda was saying, in effect, that one should free oneself of formalisms in respect of democracy because that, in the real situation, is what they are. And it is probably true, in evaluating his tempestuous career, that he was attracted to whatever movement he thought maximized freedom. Which was not necessarily democracy.

In 1977, four years after General Pinochet overthrew Salvador Allende, there was a passionate exchange respecting the two despots. Lawrence Birns, a Latin American scholar, edited the book *The End of Chilean Democracy*. Nena Ossa is a Chilean, born in Santiago and educated there as a journalist. She works now for the cultural department of the Chilean government and writes for *El Mercurio*.

WFB: I should like to begin by asking Mr. Birns why he supposes that Chilean democracy has ended.

BIRNS: Certainly one of the factors would be the errors, mistakes, incapacities, inexperience, and innocence of the coalition government that came in with Allende. Secondly, it ended because the opposition did not abide by the definition of what a loyal opposition is. At the very end, when conditions rapidly deteriorated, it was prepared to sacrifice the system in order to bring down the government. What happened, of course, was the incorporation of perhaps the most systematic totalitarian society—government—that has existed in Latin America since the close of the nineteenth century.

WFB: By the way, I assume that you intended to exclude Cuba from the term "Latin America"—is that correct?

BIRNS: I would say that perhaps Cuba is more totalitarian in terms of all institutions affected. But certainly in terms of the brutality and level of repression that now exists in both countries, I would say that Chile, by a scale of twenty to one, is more repressive than Cuba.

WFB: Well, that's a rather provocative statement. I'd like to hear Mrs. Ossa comment on it. You've been back just a few days from Chile. What are the freedoms that are exercisable in Chile under Pinochet?

OSSA: Well, practically everything, really, in the sense that we can move within the country, wherever we want.

WFB: Okay, that's number one, right? Now, you can't do that in Cuba, correct? Okay, next.

OSSA: We can leave the country whenever we want, with no red tape of any kind. During Allende, we had to fill in a lot of papers we don't fill in anymore.

WFB: The purpose of filling in those papers was what?

OSSA: Trying to keep people from leaving, asking questions from the tax reports and all kinds of things. And you got so demoralized with it, in fact, sometimes you didn't even travel.

WFB: Can you criticize the government?

OSSA: We all do in some ways. We may be for the government, as I am, intensely, but we do criticize it if we want to. We can go to the authorities and say things.

WFB: You can't do that in Cuba. So there's another. What about *El Mercurio*?

OSSA: It's the leading paper, and it does criticize constantly, in editorials and in person if they have to.

WFB: Can you attend church?

OSSA: We can go to any church we wish.

WFB: But you can't in Cuba. What else can you do? Can you invite Milton Friedman [as a Santiago group recently had] to go down and lecture and say what he wants to and to deplore [as Friedman did] tyrannical systems? Can you do that in Cuba? No. Well, Mr. Birns, how are we doing?

Mr. Birns directed the discussion to future prospects for bettering conditions all over Latin America.

In 1977, in Manila, we did a program with President Ferdinand Marcos. I don't think it is anywhere disputed that Ferdinand Marcos was identified, during the early days of his political career, as a fierce defender of human rights and civil liberties. Then, having been twice elected President, with a year left before his term of office ran out, he declared martial law. That was five years before our program, and although elections of sorts were scheduled, there was considerable skepticism in Manila that they would bring in democracy on the Western model. I brought up the subject. And it troubled Ferdinand Marcos not at all that there should be such skepticism.

MARCOS: You came [he referred to the U.S. occupation of the Philippines from 1898 to 1946] and tried to plant your kind of democracy with us. It didn't work. It would require more than fifty years to adapt an American apple tree to grow in Philippine soil. Why should it surprise anyone that American democracy didn't take root?

My own judgment in 1977—as I recorded in my columns—was that Marcos would be judged, finally, by his respect for human rights, on the understanding that political liberty is a rare thing and, in any case, of purely instrumental significance: Dr. Johnson reminded us that the "end of political liberty is personal liberty." If the latter had been achieved by Marcos even without the former, I thought, he would have served his country. In the end, of course, he did not succeed. But it is not yet safe to say that in overthrowing Marcos, democracy took apple-deep root in the Philippines.

In 1978, *Firing Line* did an hour in Singapore with the legendary Lee Kuan Yew.

There is no political freedom in Singapore. There is only the single party. Lee's will prevailed. All the same, Lee has not, by thoughtful observers, been dismissed merely as a classical despot. Senator Moynihan has written that, while ambassador to India in 1976, he reflected on the three great metropolises of the Bay of Bengal: Calcutta, Rangoon, and Singapore. Calcutta, he wrote, was a "city of the dead and dying. Vast, putrefying, forsaken." Rangoon was "rapidly reverting to the village it had once been, its rulers surrounded with barbed wire."

And then, "of liberty, Singapore had not nearly enough; but Rangoon had none at all, and what there was in Calcutta was less and less real as the mob grew. Something had made the difference. And what was it if not a rational liberalism in economic affairs? Singapore [with] very possibly the highest urban standard of living in the world had committed itself to the creation of wealth rather than to its redistribution."

Singapore is the showcase of a fabled intersection of values. At the UN, you regularly hear the totalitarians proclaim that genuine freedom is social and economic security. For that reason, there is "freedom" in East Germany, but not in West Germany. The argument is philosophically an imposture—just to begin with—because "freedom" is properly defined as an absence of constraint from man-made impediments.

The Great Lie, in my judgment, has always been that the totalitarian countries furnish freedom defined in *any* way. There has been more pain—from hunger, exposure, ill health—in the totalitarian countries than in countries that are genuinely free. But genuinely free countries aren't merely countries where people are free to march to the polls at regular intervals. Which is why Senator Moynihan talks about economic liberalism. Singapore is the showplace of freedom in the sense in which the term is falsely used philosophically and empirically. It is a social success only because it is economically free. Carlos Rómulo, at the time foreign minister of the Philippines and early on, and for generations, an idol of U.S. liberals, cut short a discussion of the subject by saying that, "freedom from want" takes priority over "freedom of expression" in developing countries.

That was the point that Lee stressed. "Human rights in a Third World situation has more important facets than freedom of the press. There's freedom from hunger, from want, from ignorance, from disease. . . ." Individual observers had to pass judgment on his sincerity. More power tends to corrupt, and he accumulated something very nearly like absolute power. There is freedom in Singapore—except to oppose the government. And Lee, trained at Oxford, where he achieved a double first, brilliantly defended the proposition that in a world of apocalyptic alternatives, subscription to political freedom is no more the first value for the Oriental than it was for Abraham Lincoln or Winston Churchill at the moment of our great Western crises.

In brief, during the life of *Firing Line,* democracy has had its ups and its downs, as has freedom. Political democracy made a substantial comeback in Latin America during the eighties. But the great polarities continue to govern the thought of much of the thinking public. Singapore is surrounded by Communist countries. Chile was for a period in the hands of a President who most admired Fidel Castro. Central America is face to face with Communism. South Africa's most highly organized opposition is in league with Communism. And the great question, for those in the Third World, continues to be the pathetic one: Can we eke out a tolerable life, with such freedom as we can wrest from our governments?

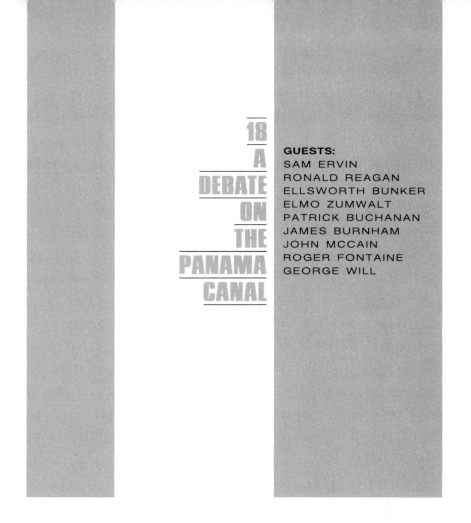

GUESTS:
SAM ERVIN
RONALD REAGAN
ELLSWORTH BUNKER
ELMO ZUMWALT
PATRICK BUCHANAN
JAMES BURNHAM
JOHN MCCAIN
ROGER FONTAINE
GEORGE WILL

President Carter's signing of the Panama Canal treaties in 1977 was vigorously opposed by most conservatives. (The most visible exceptions, from highly perched conservative figures, were one sometime presidential candidate, and one actor with a mass following: Barry Goldwater and John Wayne.) Ronald Reagan, campaigning for the presidential nomination in 1976, lost narrowly in New Hampshire and then again in Florida against the incumbent President Gerald Ford. But in North Carolina, Reagan thought to make his opposition to the treaty the center of his campaign—and he won. This propelled a heavy political movement toward him. It proved too late to wrest the nomination from President Ford. But Reagan did not forget the impact, especially among conservatives, of his stand on the Panama Canal.

My own opposition to the proposed treaty (for convenience's sake, I combine from now on the two treaties dealing with the transfer of authority and with neutrality) changed after a five-day visit to Panama in 1976. From that moment on, after I had recorded my change of mind in a series of columns, and in *National Review,* Ronald Reagan and I would from time to time genially disagree on the subject, in public and in private. Late in 1977, I thought to ask him, in a telephone conversation, whether he would debate the subject on a special two-hour *Firing Line.* At first he was reluctant ("Why should I want to debate with you?"). But a few days later, after he had contemplated my proposed format, he said yes.

Others (e.g., John Judis in his biography of me*) have assigned to this debate something of historical significance. Whether this is to inflate its consequence I do not know. Certainly it was of major consequence in my own career as a conservative—I received much disparaging mail for having deserted first principles, and the stand I took is still here and there cited as evidence of my unreliability as a conservative.

But one objection cited bitterly by many of my friends is that the public departure from orthodoxy by a conservative, even though assisted by other important conservatives (see below), shattered the notion that opposition to the Panama treaty was a position that bound all conservatives with the anomalous exceptions of John Wayne and Barry Goldwater, who were excused on the grounds of eccentricity. I happen to believe, as I wrote elsewhere, that Reagan's conspicuous position on the treaty, combined with the treaty's passage, combined to make possible his election as President four years later. My thesis is that if he had favored the treaty, he'd have lost his hard conservative support (Howard Baker suffered crucially for his support of the treaty). But—I speculated—if the treaty had not passed the Senate, which it might not have done if the conservative opposition had been hegemonic, uprisings in Central America during the 1980 campaign might have frustrated Reagan's presidential campaign.

I had suggested to Reagan that each one of us bring along two debating partners, and also one military expert, and that the principal treaty negotiator, Ambassador Ellsworth Bunker, be present to answer technical questions concerning the treaty put to him from either side. And that former Senator, former Judge, Samuel Ervin, recently retired

---

William F. Buckley, Jr.: Patron Saint of the Conservatives (New York: Simon & Schuster, 1988).

from the Senate, where he presided over the liquidation of Richard Nixon, should act as moderator.

I picked my team, and Reagan picked his.

It was after I stared at the roster of names signed up for the debate that I recalled something the late Herman Kahn, futurist and theoretician, and founder of the Hudson Institute, had once told me. It was what I came to call Kahn's Theory of Contiguous Dialogue.

You cannot, Kahn said, argue effectively with anyone whose position is removed from your own by more than one dialectical unit. He gave me as an example:

A. —Who believes in preemptive war against the Soviet Union.

B. —Who believes in tough, inventive opposition to the Soviet Union, short of war.

C. —Who believes in restricting any action against the Soviet Union to diplomatic initiatives.

D. —Who believes in generous gestures of conciliation toward the Soviet Union, attempting always to forge détente.

E. —Who believes in unilateral nuclear disarmament.

F. —Who believes that the use of any military force, in any circumstance, is wrong.

Kahn's declaration was that A could argue with B, and possibly stretch over to argue with C. Similarly, F can argue with E, and perhaps with D. The implicit challenge is to the cozy rationalist superstition that dialectical exchanges are profitable even between positions totally removed from each other.

In going over the names of Mr. Reagan's allies and my own it struck me that, to use Clare Boothe Luce's phrase, "you couldn't slide a piece of Kleenex between any two of them"—as regards our antipathy to Communism and our wholehearted belief that the United States was, and should continue to be, the principal engine by which to oppose world Communism.

And yet there was not only a division on the tactical question before the house, it was a division so deeply felt as to approach emotional intensity.

It ought to be, I thought, a perfect debate, given Kahn's Theory of Contiguous Dialogue. And its participants were very bright people.

On my side was my colleague, the late James Burnham, the foremost (in my judgment) anti-Communist strategist in the free world. And George Will, a sometime colleague at *National Review,* one of the nation's premier polemicists, a journalist of high style and learning. My

military expert was Admiral Elmo Zumwalt, former Chief of Naval
Operations, and a stalwart and resourceful anti-Communist.

On Ronald Reagan's side was Patrick Buchanan, the hugely talented
columnist and polemicist, former assistant to Richard Nixon; and Professor Roger Fontaine of Georgetown, a highly informed anti-Soviet
expert whose field is Latin America. Reagan's military expert was Admiral John McCain, Jr., former CINCPAC, the (theoretical) supreme
commander of our military forces during much of the Vietnam War.

All the participants, excepting Fontaine, whom I hadn't known, were
personal friends, many of them colleagues in one or another enterprise.

The question before the house: "Resolved, That the Senate should
ratify the proposed Panama Canal treaties."

Reagan was the first speaker. He performed eloquently for fifteen
minutes. I followed for fifteen minutes. Each one of our seconders made
a briefer statement. Came time for the cross-interrogation.

ERVIN: At this time . . . the chair will recognize Governor Reagan
            and give him the privilege of questioning William Buck-
            ley.

REAGAN: Well, Bill, my first question is why haven't you already
            rushed across the room here to tell me that you've seen the
            light? [*Laughter and applause*]

WFB: I'm afraid that if I came any closer to you the force of my
            illumination would blind you. [*Laughter and applause*]

REAGAN: Well, all right. The United States has run the Canal at no
            profit. We have maintained its neutrality throughout the
            history of the Canal. We have certainly vastly benefited
            Panama. What do we gain by making this change?

WFB: Well, what we gain by making this change, to quote my-
            self, is increased security and increased self-esteem. I un-
            derstand the arguments you use in opposition to the
            treaty, but I do think that some of them are based on
            factual misconceptions. It would be useful to ask Ambas-
            sador Bunker to straighten you out—if I may put it thus
            bluntly.

BUNKER: The question which Mr. Buckley addressed, and which
            you mentioned, Governor Reagan, had to do with the

question of our [continuing] right to take any action necessary to protect the Canal, and to protect the neutrality of
the Canal, and the question of our rights of passage for our
ships. Now, as you'll recall, the Declaration of Understanding agreed to by President Carter and General Torrijos in October [1977] specifically spells out the
right—*our* right—to take *any* action against any threat to
the Canal or *any* action against [attempts to affect] the
neutrality of the Canal, and [specifies] that we [alone] are
the judge of that. It does not include the right of [U.S.]
intervention in the internal affairs of Panama, and that *we*
made clear because [any such right] is against the United
Nations Charter. With regard to expeditious passage of
ships, the declaration stipulates that our ships are entitled
to expeditious passage and, in case of emergency, to go to
the head of the line, which lets them move in ahead of *any*
of the other ships.

WFB: So, Governor, put *that* in your pipe and smoke it! [*Laugh-
           ter*]

REAGAN: To simply sign a statement between the current two Presi-
           dents, outside the treaty, I think, has no bearing whatso-
           ever. It has no legal weight, and what's to happen when
           there are two different Presidents, and someone is running
           Panama who never was a party to all of this?

BUNKER: Our legal opinion is that they do have weight in the inter-
           pretation of the treaties.

REAGAN: Okay, we're in disagreement on that. Am I still asking
           questions? Thank you, Mr. Ambassador.

ERVIN: You have about two more minutes.

REAGAN: Bill, the next question is, If the Canal is so unimportant
           to us commercially, defense-wise, or whatever, why don't
           we just *give* it to them? Why do we *pay* them to take it
           off our hands? And if it *is* important to us, why don't we
           keep it?

WFB: You have outlined nonexclusive alternatives. In the first
           place, under the projected treaty there would be a net

income to the United States for the next twenty-two years. In the second place, under the projected treaty, there would be a period of orderly transition during which power gradually accumulates in the Panamanian government. I would like to, if I may, supplement my answer to your question by reasserting that there *is* an importance to the Canal, but that its importance is precisely *protected* by that treaty, and let me ask Admiral Zumwalt to give the military reasons why this is so.

ZUMWALT: The military reasons why . . . ?

WFB: Why it is so that our security is *enhanced* by this treaty.

ZUMWALT: The situation, in thumbnail, is the following. The United States has surrendered strategic nuclear superiority to the Soviet Union. This means that *conventional* military war is likelier. It means that, as both you and Governor Reagan have said, the need for the Panama Canal is *vital*. We *must* be able to deploy ships from one ocean to another in choosing which of our allies we will save, because we can't save them all. The best security—the best certainty—the likeliest probability of being able to use that canal is to have a friendly regime in support of the operation rather than a hostile regime. Those of us who have had to deal with insurgencies—as I did in Vietnam—can tell you that it is impossible to defend that canal, as all the Joint Chiefs have agreed, against a hostile insurgency and that the odds are greatly increased that that insurgency would occur if the United States fails to ratify these treaties.

Ronald Reagan had so far focused his fire on two general points. The first, that the Canal historically and legally belonged to the United States (on this I think he was indisputably correct). The second was a series of tactical objections to deficiencies in the treaty, among them what he thought was the preeminent right of the United States, acting unilaterally, to move to protect the Canal against abuse. Although Ambassador Bunker dented his second argument, Reagan profited by clinging closely to his first.

ERVIN: The chair now extends to Mr. Buckley the right to interrogate Governor Reagan for seven minutes.

WFB: Governor, do I understand you to say that you are considerably influenced in your opposition to this treaty because of your dislike of Torrijos? [Omar Torrijos was the left-leaning strongman, undisputed boss of Panama.]

REAGAN: No, but I think we have to recognize that we're talking about the thing that our country has always deplored. We're talking about a dictator, and we have no assurance that he represents the thinking of the people of Panama.

WFB: Well, let me ask you to give me the answer to a question which you cannot document, but in which I permit you to consult only your insight. Would you guess that the Panamanian people would prefer, or not prefer, to exercise sovereignty over their own territory? Take as long as you want to answer that. [*Laughter and applause*]

REAGAN: I was just sitting here wishing that I had with me the transcript of the impassioned plea that was made to United States senators at a meeting of the Civic Council a week or so ago in Panama. The Civic Council is made up of representatives of all the towns in the Canal Zone. The speaker was a black—a Panamanian, not an American. His father, a West Indian, worked on the Canal, in building the Canal. The speaker had worked all his life on the Canal, and his impassioned plea was, even though he was a Panamanian, "Don't! Don't do this! Don't ratify those treaties!"

I could quote the *Chicago Tribune* reporter who did a man-on-the-street thing in Panama with many Panamanians—some refused to give their names, but they answered. But many of them were so outraged that they didn't care. They gave their names even though relatives and friends were pulling at their sleeves and saying, "Don't answer! You'll go to jail!"

WFB: If what you're saying, Governor, is that Torrijos has *enemies,* it seems to me that you do not need to say that at any length because I concede that he does. Among his enemies are yourself and myself and anybody who has any respect for human freedom. But it is a worldwide phenomenon that irrespective of the ugly character of the ruler, people do desire independence. They do desire sovereignty. There were Russians who fought even under Stalin and fought to the death to defend their territory. Why is it that those impulses which you so liberally recognize as beating in the breasts of people all over the world should suddenly stop beating in Panama because of Torrijos?

REAGAN: Well, I have to ask, Bill, whether this [urge for independence] is all that strong on the part of the people. As I've said before, we deal with a government that does not represent the will of the people. The people never had a chance to express their will, and—

WFB: But it was before Torrijos became the dictator that the initial riots took place demanding an assertion of that sovereignty. How do you account for that?

REAGAN: I think the first time that it was expressed was in 1932 in the charter of the new Communist Party of Panama. They put as one of their top objectives the taking over of the Canal.

WFB: Are you saying that the Communists invented patriotism in Panama?

REAGAN: No, no.

WFB: Yes. Well, you really tried to say that.

REAGAN: No. [Laughter and applause] No, Bill, I really didn't, but I also have to point out something else about this. The Canal and Panama are Siamese twins. Neither one could have been born without the other, and ninety percent of all of the industry and the population of Panama is on one side of that Canal. We have the right to sovereignty, as we say, by that treaty. Panama had the worst riots of all in 1964. More than a score of people were killed. Yet not one move was made to attempt to sabotage the Canal. Business didn't stop for one second, and a statement was made about those riots that said, "Led by persons trained in Communist countries for political action." The government of Panama, instead of attempting to restore order, was, through a controlled press, TV, and radio, inciting the people to attack and to violence.

WFB: Who was it who taught the people who did the Boston Tea Party how to exercise violence?

REAGAN: Well, the gentleman who [recounted what was done] is Mr. Bunker, and I think it's a very eloquent statement and description of what took place in 1964. [*Applause*]

WFB: In making that statement Mr. Bunker was reiterating a statement made at some length by Professor James Burnham in his book *The Struggle for the World,* showing exactly how the Soviet Union would attempt to take over patriotic movements. But to attempt to take them over does not mean necessarily to *contaminate* them, and the notion that someone who wants freedom for Panama wants freedom for Panama because he is being manipulated by the Communists is the kind of talk that belongs in Belmont, Massachusetts [home of the John Birch Society, renowned at the time for imputing pro-Communist motivation to liberal movements], not at the University of South Carolina [whose facilities we were using]. [*Applause*]

REAGAN: But I think—to answer your question, Bill—I think that there are alternatives which would benefit the people of Panama, at the same time that we preserved our right to protect the Canal for our own national security—and the security of the hemisphere. And so far no one has suggested any way that this can be done unless we retain the right of sovereignty that we have in the Canal Zone.

        I recognize that there are irritation points. I was going to suggest that I think long before now the Americans should have offered the people of Panama who are arrested for crimes in the Panama Canal Zone the choice of whether they wanted to be tried in our courts or be returned to their own country for trial in their own. I think it would be offensive to us to have our people tried in Panamanian courts, which they will be as soon as the treaties are ratified.

WFB: Well, Governor, the Status of Forces Treaty—

ERVIN: The chair hates to interrupt, but the chair will now be compelled by the compunction of time to recognize Patrick Buchanan to interrogate William Buckley.

REAGAN: Thank you, Mr. Chairman. [*Laughter*]

BUCHANAN: Mr. Buckley, you've spoken eloquently, as usual, about Panamanian pride and Panamanian patriotism. Now I'd like to ask you about American pride and American patriotism. As you've suggested, those treaty negotiations were begun in 1964 by virtue of Panamanian riots which were or were not Communist-inspired. They've been concluded under a threat of sabotage and guerrilla warfare which has been discussed [earlier] this evening. Now, is it realistic to suggest that American prestige will rise if, *under these conditions,* the United States walks away from that Canal, surrenders money, territory, military bases, the Canal Zone, and the Canal itself? Secondly, is it realistic—

WFB: No, no. One at a time, please.

BUCHANAN: All right.

WFB: The answer to the first is that if *you* were the President of the United States and concluded the treaty—handed over the instrument of ratification to General Torrijos with such a statement as you just finished making—the answer is, No, American prestige would not rise. On the other hand, if *I* were President and I handed over the identical treaty, my answer is, Yes. The prestige of the United States is increased, in my judgment, when we show by our acts that we believe in our own rhetoric.

BUCHANAN: Was the prestige of Great Britain enhanced after it turned over the Suez Canal to Egypt?

WFB: It didn't turn it over. One of the confusions of Governor Reagan has to do with that. What happened was that the Suez Company was an Egyptian corporation whose shareholders were Englishmen and French. It was nationalized. There is a general understanding that you can nationalize a corporation registered under the laws of your own country. What we're talking about is not a corporation. It's a

United States agency. The Panamanians would no more have the right to nationalize the Panama Commission, as specified under this treaty, than they would the Statue of Liberty.

BUCHANAN: One final comment—or question, rather. Given the conditions under which we're departing—the threat of sabotage and the like—is it realistic to think that the United States would send the marines into the Panama Canal Zone after Panama takes control of the Zone in 1980 if, for example, Panama then closed the Canal, or blacklisted vessels going to and from such pariah states as South Africa, Chile, and Taiwan?

WFB: It would if we had a self-respecting President. If you ask will we have a self-respecting President in 1980, the answer—

BUCHANAN: Do we?

WFB: —is I don't know.

BUCHANAN: Do you *know* who will be in the office in 1980?

WFB: Do you mean, Would President Carter, as commander in chief—

BUCHANAN: And would the Senate support him?

WFB: —would he assert American rights in the Panama Canal? In my judgment he would. Yes, sir.

BUCHANAN: With regard to South Africa and Chile?

WFB: Excuse me?

BUCHANAN: With regard to South African and Chilean vessels, or vessels going to and from those two pariah countries?

WFB: We have a guarantee that antedates this treaty to see to it that nondiscriminatory passage is guaranteed. It's the Hay-Pauncefote Treaty.

BUCHANAN: Right, but do you think American marines would *go in* to guarantee passage to vessels headed for South Africa?

WFB: You're asking me a question that has nothing to do with the language of the treaty.

BUCHANAN: It has to do with Panamanian control of its own—

WFB: Because whether they would or they wouldn't has nothing to do with what we're discussing tonight. If we *don't* pass the treaty, we have identical obligations in respect of the question you ask as if we *do* pass the treaty. Am I correct, Mr. Bunker?

BUNKER: That's correct.

BUCHANAN: In 1980 Panama will have full control, as I understand it, of both sides of the Canal Zone. Is that correct, Ambassador? In 1980—if the treaty is passed, in thirty months Panama gets full control of both sides of the Canal Zone?

BUNKER: Full jurisdiction.

BUCHANAN: Jurisdiction, right.

BUNKER: Yes.

BUCHANAN: Suppose they say—in response to a call of the General Assembly—that this Canal is to be closed to all vessels that travel to and from South Africa. Do you think the United States would really *act* under those circumstances, having left Panama under the circumstances under which we're leaving right now, which is in response to riots in '64, to threats of sabotage and threats of guerrilla warfare?

BUNKER: Panama will have jurisdiction over the Zone, but we will have rights to use the lands and waters necessary to protect the Canal.

BUCHANAN: Do you think we would—again, in response to my question—do you think the United States *would* send in the marines under those conditions, given the conditions under which we've departed?

BUNKER: I think they would, yes.

BUCHANAN: Do you think *Carter* would send in the marines?

Buchanan had a pretty good point there. It would be easier, in the future, for any President to assert operational control over an area he

already commanded than to send down the marines to do it afresh. A
legitimate objection, I thought.

ERVIN: The chair will now recognize Mr. Burnham.

BURNHAM: I'd like to try to single out one specific question and
                put it as just a single actual event—not in terms of ab-
                straction. Now, we've said a good deal about this matter
                of the priority of our vessels under an emergency, so
                let's try to see what might happen. Suppose that a red
                alert or ultimate emergency was declared and the naval
                forces in the Caribbean were ordered to transit the
                Canal immediately, and let's say that Ronald Reagan is
                the commanding admiral. Now, how would he pro-
                ceed?
                    Will he send a message to the Port Authority and say,
                "Well, I'd like authorization to send my ships through
                on the double," and sort of get to the head of the line?
                And then if he hears in reply, "Well, I'm very sorry, but
                under my interpretation of the treaty that was signed in
                1978, I don't interpret it to give you that right, and I'm
                afraid we've got eighty-three shrimp boats and we've got
                nineteen tankers and we've got a number of ships and
                we've got three canoes that are ahead of you, and if
                you'd just sign the list, then you'll be in line here, and
                it'll take about sixty-four hours." Now, is the reply of
                the commanding admiral going to be "Oh, yes, sir.
                Thanks very much. I am following your instructions;
                please let me know a couple of hours ahead of time when
                our turn will come"?

REAGAN: Well, Mr. Burnham, I think you're ignoring a physical
                fact that those other ships aren't sitting on a shelf waiting
                to go through. They're in the *way* of those American
                ships. A captain is going to have to pull up an anchor and
                move to get out of the way, and how does an American
                naval officer— And incidentally, thank you for the promo-
                tion. I was a captain of cavalry—horse cavalry. There is
                a very physical fact that ships will be in the water, in the
                roadway, off the entrance of the Canal, in the Canal itself,
                in the locks going through—and what do we *do* about
                them? We can't blow them up.

BURNHAM: If I may ask, then, what does the treaty have to do with
             it one way or another?

REAGAN: Well, no, no. If the American ships had the right, then
             those ships that were there in the way would *have* to turn,
             reverse course, and get out of the way to let us through.
             But if the American ships don't have the right, the captain
             may order it, but I'm quite sure the captain's not going to
             fire on an unarmed merchant vessel or tanker.

BURNHAM: Well, I've known admirals who sometimes give those or-
             ders, too.

   Burnham, I thought, had also scored. It usually doesn't matter, in the
chaos associated with an emergency, whether there is or isn't a treaty.

ERVIN: The chair will have to interrupt and recognize Dr. Fon-
             taine for a question.

FONTAINE: Thank you, Senator. Mr. Buckley, let me see if you share
             a worry—another worry—that I have. I know you are, in
             fact, worried about the character of public enterprise in
             Panama, but another worry—and that's this. Under the
             treaty, we will have a gradual phasing out of American
             technicians and managers. Within thirty months they will
             fall under the jurisdiction of Panamanian courts and po-
             lice—perhaps I could say "fall into the clutches of," be-
             cause that's how the American workers view it. Now, at
             this point, some twenty-five or thirty percent of the work
             force in the Canal Zone are Americans. They're also the
             top managers and the most skilled technicians, dredge
             operators, Canal pilots, and that sort of thing. According
             to reliable polls, some seventy percent of that American
             work force will leave on treaty day. Are you concerned,
             as I am and some others in the Senate, that the guarantees
             to the American work force provided under the present
             treaty are not very adequate and that perhaps radical
             surgery of the present treaty would be wise?

WFB: Mr. Fontaine, I was asked tonight whether I would vote
             for the treaty or against it, and my answer is I would
             vote for it. If you say "Are there ways in which it

might be improved?" my answer is, Obviously there are certain ways in which it might be improved. For instance, rather than give the Panamanians ten million dollars, I would rather give them nine million. Rather than give them nine million, I'd give them eight million. The fact of the matter is that we have come out of a *negotiation.* We have not come out of a situation in which Mr. Bunker went down there and said, "I am going to vouchsafe you the following." If you are suggesting that Mr. Bunker acted unreasonably, then you are required to say that the Status of Forces Treaties under which our men overseas have operated for thirty years is unreasonable, and you also have to say that it is unreasonable for Ambassador Bunker to have worked into the treaty a provision that allows Americans convicted of crimes under Guatemalan law to serve out their sentences in United States jails.

FONTAINE: But you're not saying that the possibility or even the probability of—well, let's not even say seventy percent, let's say fifty percent—is a detail like the difference between one or two million dollars. For example, if fifty percent of the highly skilled technicians and managers left, there would be *no* functioning and operating Canal.

WFB: Well, may I set your mind at ease? Seventy percent of Americans are not going to quit, and one of the reasons they're not going to quit is because they did something very smart down there—something that as of October of last year they hadn't thought to do. The [U.S.] guaranteed the American working force permanent employment for the rest of their working lives under similar, if not exact, conditions. That is what the people in [the] Panama [Canal Zone] primarily wanted. That's what they told me they wanted when I went to several meetings down there last October.

FONTAINE: Who arranged the meetings?

WFB: People who are violently opposed to any change in the status quo. [*Applause*]

I found throughout the debate this resistance to recognizing that
although we had the decisive chips, we had been in *negotiation* with the
Panamanians.

ERVIN: The chair recognizes George Will.

WILL: Governor, I think we're all struck by how narrow, really,
                  are our differences here and that we all accept that the
                  world is dangerous and the Canal is essential, and both are
                  apt to remain the same. But in that regard, I'd like you to
                  address yourself to a statement made earlier by Admiral
                  Zumwalt which is—if I can embroider it just a bit—that
                  there's a sense in which, given the widespread technology
                  for freelance violence in the world and the ideology of
                  terrorism, isn't it the case that it's easier for the United
                  States to protect Europe than it is to protect this Canal—
                  to keep it functioning? That is, of all the crucial water-
                  ways, the choke points, as it were, that Admiral McCain
                  mentioned, only the locks on the Panama Canal make it
                  so terribly vulnerable. Therefore, is it not conservative,
                  reasoned, hardheaded prudence to rewrite the treaties, as
                  Mr. Bunker and others have done, to give the Panamani-
                  ans a greater psychic and economic stake in maintaining
                  and defending those canals?

REAGAN: Well, no, and I don't think it's all that difficult. The Pan-
                  ama Canal is not something—as one of the advocates of
                  the treaty said—that a man with a stick of dynamite stuck
                  in his belt can disable. There *are* some vulnerable points.
                  The locks, of course, and the dams for the lakes that
                  provide the water, the tens of millions of gallons of water
                  that it takes to put a ship through the locks, but you're
                  talking about something—a lock gate is made of steel. It's
                  about seven feet thick. They've survived an earthquake, a
                  very severe earthquake, virtually right after they were
                  installed.

ERVIN: The chair is going to have to interrupt. Personally, I wish
                  this debate could go on till the last lingering echo of Ga-
                  briel's horn trembled into ultimate silence, but we are
                  prisoners of time, and at this time, the chair is going to call

on Governor Ronald Reagan for his rebuttal and going to give the very sad advice that it has to end at strictly 10:44.

REAGAN: I have how long?

ERVIN: It's about ten minutes.

REAGAN: Oh, for heaven's sake. I don't know if I've got that much to say, Mr. Chairman.

Well, Mr. Chairman and ladies and gentlemen: I think, again, we come back to the original premise that I was making here, and I would start, I think, with the question that I was unable to answer just now—the defensibility of the Canal. If we're talking nuclear defense of the Panama Canal—if a missile is to come in aimed at the Panama Canal—then no, [you can't defend it]. But you have to ask yourself, in the event of a nuclear war, who's going to waste a missile on the Canal? They'll be dropping missiles on New York, Chicago, San Francisco, Los Angeles, and so forth, and it would be a waste of time to use that. So we come down to conventional warfare and we come down to sabotage.

I claim that the United States, with a military force trained on the ground, which has defended the Canal against any attempt at sabotage through four wars, recognizing the fact that it's going to take more than a single saboteur slipping in in the night with a hand grenade or an explosive charge—it's going to take a trained demolition team, with plenty of time to work and no interruption, to do something to disable the gates, the locks, and so forth. Or the other means of sabotage would be to assault the dams that hold back the lakes—a two-hundred-square-mile lake, for one; there're three lakes—that provide the water that, through gravity flow, floods these locks. Now, I submit that with an American armed force on hand guarding those vulnerable points, they are far safer than if the Panamanians are in charge and the Americans are not there, and the sabotage we could expect would come from people within the ranks of the Panamanians. I don't know who else it would be.

We do also know that there are elements in Panama

who have said that these treaties are unsatisfactory to
them because they take twenty years [before Panama gets
full sovereignty]. They want the Canal *now,* and that
they're going to riot and cause trouble unless they're given
the Canal now. But I think we come back to the point that
is at issue. Yes, there is a problem—sensitivity to the
Panamanian people, to what they want, to their pride. I
agree with that, but also, on our side, is a responsibility we
cannot abdicate—to protect and make sure that the Canal
remains open to all shipping and that it is there for the
defense of this hemisphere and of our own nation.

Now, we have to face the Panamanians in a negotiation,
not because we've been threatened that they're going to
cause trouble—I say that this is one of the first things that
should have called off the negotiations. When they threatened violence, I believe the United States should have said
to them, "We don't negotiate with anyone under threats.
If you want to sit down and talk in a spirit of goodwill,
we'll do it." [*Applause*] But we go back now and say, "If
we can find a way that ensures our right to the security
the Canal must have, we'll do everything we can to find
a way to erase the friction points"—some of which I
pointed out and was pointing out there in my previous
remarks. The Canal is not a natural resource of Panama
that has been exploited by the United States. We haven't
taken minerals out of the Canal Zone. We haven't plun-
dered it. We've gone in for one purpose and one only—the
one the treaty called for—to build and operate a canal,
and I don't know of anyone who has benefited more than
the people of Panama. Their ships even have an advantage
in the tolls that they must pay, as do the ships of Co-
lombia.

We're dealing with a government that, as I've said repeatedly here, has not been elected, and with a dictatorship that has accumulated the highest per capita debt in
nine years of any nation in the world. Thirty-nine percent
of the Panamanian budget goes to service that debt. If our
debt was comparably that size, it would have to be five
times as big as it is right now, and it's already seven
hundred million dollars—seven hundred billion. That was
a big slip. [*Laughter*]

(A.D. 1988, a *very* big slip! U.S. debt in 1987 was over three times our debt in 1977.)

REAGAN: I don't believe that in Latin America we would do any-
          thing to strengthen our position by, again, yielding to this
          unpleasantness in this treaty. I think, if anything, we
          would become a laughingstock by surrendering to unrea-
          sonable demands, and by doing so, I think we cloak weak-
          ness in the suit of virtue. This has to be treated in the
          whole area of the international situation. The Panama
          Canal is just one facet of our foreign policy, and with this
          treaty, what do we do to ourselves in the eyes of the world,
          and to our allies? Will they, as Mr. Buckley says, see that
          as the magnanimous gesture of a great and powerful na-
          tion? I don't think so, not in view of our recent history,
          not in view of our bug-out in Vietnam, not in view of an
          administration that is hinting that we're going to throw
          aside an ally named Taiwan. I think that the world would
          see it as, once again, Uncle Sam putting his tail between
          his legs and creeping away rather than face trouble. [*Ap-
          plause*]
             I think that Professor Fontaine was right to question
          the ability of the Panamanians to run this. This particular
          administration of Panama has started three sugar mills, a
          hydroelectric project, an airport, a public transportation
          system, a resort island, an agriculture development pro-
          gram, and an exploration for natural resources, and has
          failed in every one of them.
             But, again, I come down to the basic argument of
          whether we, as a great nation, return to Panama and
          say, "We cannot forsake this one responsibility. Now
          here are the things that we are prepared to do, and if
          you have any other suggestions do them in negotiation."
          But I submit, with all due respect to those who nego-
          tiated, I think they were put in an untenable position. I
          think our negotiators did the best they could under a
          circumstance in which they were sent there not to nego-
          tiate, but literally to concede as little as they had to in
          order to pacify the demands of the dictator and to avoid
          violence. [*Applause*]

ERVIN: The chair recognizes William Buckley, and he has to do like he did to Governor Reagan. He's got to give you a warning. You've got to stop at exactly 10:54.

WFB: Mr. Chairman, Governor Reagan. James Thurber once said, "You know, women are ruling the world, and the reason they're ruling the world is because they have so insecure a knowledge of history." He said, "I found myself sitting next to a lady on an airplane the other day who all of a sudden turned to me, and she said, 'Why did we have to pay for Louisiana when we got all the other states free?' " So he said, "I explained it to her." He said, "Louisiana was owned by two sisters called Louisa and Anna Wilmot, and they offered to give it to the United States, provided it was named after them. That was the Wilmot Proviso. But President Winfield Scott refused to do that. That was the Dred Scott Decision." She said, "Well, that's all very well, but I still don't understand why we had to pay for Louisiana." [*Laughter*]

Now, intending no slur on my friend Ronald Reagan, the politician in America I admire most, his rendition of recent history and his generalities remind me a little bit of that explanation of how the state of Louisiana was incorporated into this country.

He says we, in fact, don't negotiate under threats, and everybody here bursts out in applause. The trouble with *that* is that it's not true. We *do* negotiate under threats. Ninety-nine percent of all the negotiations that have gone on from the beginning of this world have gone on as a result of threats, as the result of somebody saying, "If you don't give me a raise, I threaten to leave my job." That's a threat, isn't it? What do you call what we did to George III? It was a most convincing threat. The fact of the matter is that there are people in Panama who don't accept the notion of Governor Reagan about the undisputed, unambiguous sovereignty that the United States exercises over that territory.

In 1948, the Supreme Court of the United States, in one of its decisions—*Vermilya-Brown Co.* v. *Connell*—made the following reference. "Admittedly, Panama is territory over which we do not have sovereignty." 1948. In 1928,

in the Luckenback Steam Company Case, the Canal Zone
was referred to by the Supreme Court as a place in which
there were no foreign ports. William Howard Taft said to
Panama that we had "not the slightest interest in coloniz-
ing." Dulles said to the United Nations in 1946, "Panama
is sovereign." In 1936, we reaffirmed the titular sovereignty of Panama. Children born of foreign parents in
Panama don't become Americans. We do have there the
absolute right, which I do not deny and which my colleagues do not deny, to stay there as long as we want. But
to say that we have sovereignty, as Governor Reagan has
said, is to belie the intention of the people who supervised
our diplomacy in the early part of the century, and it is
also to urge people to believe that we harbor an appetite
for colonialism which we shrink from, having ourselves
declared in the Declaration of Independence principles
that were not only applicable to people fortunate enough
to be born in Massachusetts or in Connecticut or in New
York or in Virginia, but people born everywhere.

And all of a sudden we find that we resent it when
people say that they're willing to fight for *their* freedom.
There was fighting done within a hundred yards of where
we're standing here because the people of the South felt
that they wanted their freedom from the Union. We
fought back, and it continues to be an open question
whether there was successful diplomacy in the course of
resisting that insurrection. But who is to doubt that the
people who backed up their demands for freedom by saying they were willing to die for them are people for whom
we should feel contempt? I don't feel that contempt, Mr.
Chairman, and I don't think the American people feel that
contempt either.

I think that Governor Reagan put his finger on it when
he said the reason this treaty is unpopular is because we're
tired of being pushed around. We were pushed out of
Vietnam because we didn't have the guts to go in there and
do it right, just as Admiral McCain said. [*Applause*] We're
prepared, as it was said, to desert Taiwan because three
and a half Harvard professors think that we ought to
normalize our relations with Red China. [*Applause*] We
are prepared to allow sixteen semisavage countries to car-

telize the oil that is indispensable to the entire industrial might of the West because we don't have a diplomacy that's firm enough to do something about it, and, therefore, how do we get our kicks? How do we get our kicks? By saying no to the people of Panama. [*Laughter and applause*]

I say—when I am in a mood to say no, representing the United States—I want to be looking the Soviet Union in the face and say no to the Soviet Union, next time it wants to send its tanks running over students who want a little freedom in Czechoslovakia. I want to say no to China when it subsidizes genocide in Cambodia on a scale that has not been known in this century, rather than simply forget that it exists. I don't want to feel that the United States has to affirm its independence by throwing away its powers—by saying we must not distinguish between the intrinsic merits of rewriting the treaty in Panama and pulling out of Taiwan because it is all a part of the same syndrome.

Who in this room doubts that if the President of the United States weren't Jimmy Carter but, let us say, Douglas MacArthur, and if the chairman of the Joint Chiefs of Staff were Curtis LeMay, and if the Secretary of State were Theodore Roosevelt, and this instrument was recommended to the Senate—who doubts that the conservative community of America would endorse it?

We are allowing ourselves to be beguiled not by those ideals to which we profess allegiance every time we meditate on the Declaration of Independence. We are allowing ourselves to be pushed around because we express a quite understandable bitterness at the way we have been kicked around. We ought to be mad not at the Panamanian students who are asking for nothing more than what our great-great-grandparents asked for. We ought to be mad at our own leaders—for screwing up the peace during the last twenty-five years.

But do we want to go down and take it out on people who simply want to recover the Canal Zone? What we have done to Panama is the equivalent of taking the falls away from Niagara. Is it the kind of satisfaction we really feel we are entitled to, to proceed on that basis in order to assert a sovereignty which is, in any case, not a part of the historical tradition on the basis of which the Panama Canal was opened?

No. Let's listen to reason. Let's recognize, as Admiral Zumwalt has so effectively said, that we are so impoverished militarily as a result of so many lamentable decisions that we need the Panama Canal and that we need the Panama Canal with a people who are residents of Panama, who understand themselves as joined with us in a common enterprise, because when they look at the leaders of the United States they can recognize that, not as a result of our attempt to curry favor with anybody, but as a result of our concern for our own self-esteem, we were big enough to grant little people what we ourselves fought for two hundred years ago. [*Applause*]

ERVIN: Tonight we have had the privilege of hearing a great debate between two great Americans, and I would just like to say this. As long as this can go on in America, America will remain free, and I would like to give all Americans the admonition that Daniel Webster gave us. He said, "God grants liberty only to those who love it and are always ready to guard and defend it." And I trust that the American people will remember that and also remember what John Philpot Curran said—that "the condition upon which God grants liberty to mankind is eternal vigilance." I thank you very much. [*Applause*]

The postdebate reception was chilled by (a) our host the governor's teetotalism, and (b) the sad news (everyone had known for weeks that it would not be long delayed) that Hubert Humphrey had died.

I write ten years after the debate, during almost eight of which the main speaker in opposition to the Panama Canal treaties has served as President. History plays its ironies. What is not threatened at this writing is the security of the Canal, notwithstanding that the dictator of Panama is another strongman who, unlike Torrijos, is rather specially depraved. The mishandling of our diplomacy in Panama cannot, at this point, be laid on the shoulders of Jimmy Carter.

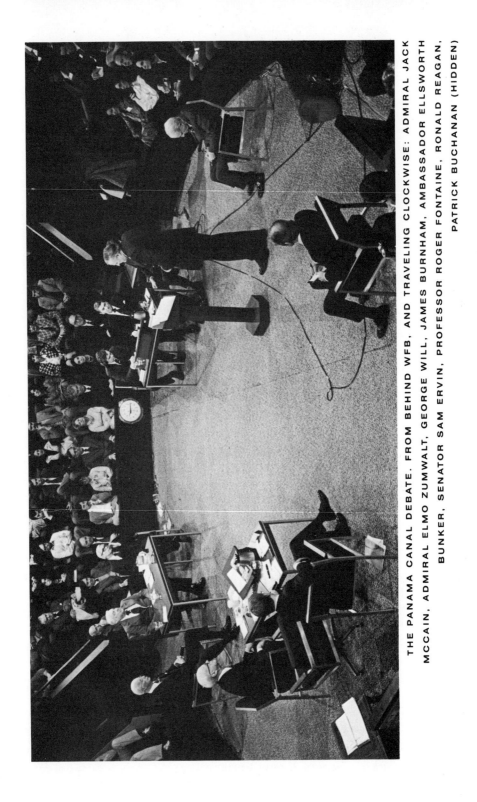

THE PANAMA CANAL DEBATE. FROM BEHIND WFB, AND TRAVELING CLOCKWISE: ADMIRAL JACK MCCAIN, ADMIRAL ELMO ZUMWALT, GEORGE WILL, JAMES BURNHAM, AMBASSADOR ELLSWORTH BUNKER, SENATOR SAM ERVIN, PROFESSOR ROGER FONTAINE, RONALD REAGAN, PATRICK BUCHANAN (HIDDEN)

19
THE STRUGGLE FOR THE WORLD

GUESTS:
PAUL JOHNSON
VLADIMIR BUKOVSKY
LEE KUAN YEW
HENRY KISSINGER
JEANE KIRKPATRICK
JAMES MICHENER

I t is commonly acknowledged that the relative success with which we dealt with the missile crisis of 1962 had the effect on the Soviet Union of a silent declaration, "Never again." Its military buildup during the sixties (and on into the seventies and eighties) was on a scale unparalleled in human history. Our absorption during the sixties was with Vietnam abroad, and civil rights at home. The prophetic volume *No Exit from Vietnam* (1969), by Robert Thompson, foretold the consequences of losing that war, not merely for Indochina but elsewhere.

And, indeed, the Soviet Union was everywhere aggressive. As Secretary of State, Henry Kissinger endeavored, in quiet collusion with Valéry Giscard d'Estaing, to devise a French military operation, backed by the United States, to oust the Cuban Communist mercenaries from southern Africa: to no effect. Nixon, in his waning days of political power, endeavored to do something about the military thrust, in violation of the 1972 agreement, of the North Vietnamese into South Vietnam. He was stopped by the Case-Church Amendment. The conclusion of the SALT I and ABM treaties, designed to arrest the huge expansion of nuclear weapons, had the opposite effect. Ten years later, 80 percent of existing Soviet nuclear bombs had been built since SALT I's pious declarations about the need to reduce nuclear armament. The ABM Treaty put a quietus on U.S. defensive technology: We even dismantled a protective ring of antinuclear defense missiles planted in the area of Wyoming, and did not trouble to avail ourselves of the option to construct a ring of defensive weapons around Washington, D.C.— while the Soviet Union worked hard to protect Moscow and, in anticipation of a nuclear defense, constructed a radar station at Krasnoyarsk and the beginnings of seven others in critical parts of Russia. The Soviet naval buildup continued exuberantly, and our most valuable secrets were conveyed to the Soviet Union by an American spy, a transaction done for private profit.

Ronald Reagan emphasized, in his 1980 presidential campaign, the need to rearm, much as John F. Kennedy had done, emphasizing the "missile gap" (which proved fictitious) in 1960. Rearmament came; but the convivialities of 1972 (Nixon's affectionate démarche in China in 1972, at which he spoke of the "long march together" faced by the United States and Mao's China, and the warm circumstances behind Nixon's and Brezhnev's Moscow meeting in 1972) affected the public mood unalterably, and led, notwithstanding the hiatus which historians will perhaps refer to as the "evil empire" period of Ronald Reagan, to the ardor of the Soviet-U.S. embrace in Moscow in the spring of 1988. Under Gorbachev, we all hoped, and continue to do so at this writing, the Soviet Union will never again be the same. There remained the difficulty. After exhibitionistic denunciations of war and aggression, Gorbachev, though the cautious retreat from Afghanistan had begun, had done nothing conclusive by way of dismantling his aggressive nuclear conventional arsenals, nor to call back his legions from Latin America, Africa, and Asia.

I raised these and allied questions with historian Paul Johnson, already introduced above. It was he who had remarked, "The evils of the twentieth century do not have any historical precedent."

. . .

JOHNSON: Previous absolutist systems in world history have always
             been anchored in an absolute morality. They were, for the
             most part, religiously orientated—virtually all of them, in
             fact. And any religion based upon absolute belief is almost
             by necessity a system of absolute value. That is, certain
             things are wrong, and certain things are right, and there's
             no way in which those things can be changed. In the West
             we have the Christian-Judaic system, which is an absolute
             value based ultimately on the Ten Commandments, and
             that gives one a solid anchor in the world of value.
                 Now what happened, early in the twentieth century,
             was something very sinister, I believe. Just after the First
             World War, Einstein's General Theory of Relativity was
             popularized. Now, Einstein was someone who believed in
             absolute values very strongly, and he was very disturbed
             by the way in which people interpreted his theory to prop-
             agate relativistic ideas about morals. But, of course, the
             Marxist system of morality is a relative system, and the
             system which Hitler elaborated in Germany is, again, a
             relative system. Hitler called it the "higher morality of the
             party." Lenin called it the "revolutionary conscience."
             They're both basically the same thing. In other words, you
             say, "Anything is right which it is convenient for the party
             to consider right at a particular time, and anything is
             wrong which we find convenient to consider wrong." So
             you write your morality as you proceed, and that is what
             both these two great totalitarian systems did.

WFB: The terminological licentiousness of the day is very strik-
             ing, isn't it? In your book you quote Castro as saying, "Of
             course we're a democratic society. We have a democracy
             every day, inasmuch as we're expressing the will of the
             people." It's that kind of wordplay which is the essence,
             as Orwell told us in another connection, of totalitarianism.

JOHNSON: I think one of the sources of evil in the modern world is
             the devaluation of language and the way in which it can
             be manipulated by those who seek power. Language is a
             very delicate plant. It's something which goes very deeply
             into our system. I mean, when the Bible says, "In the
             beginning was the Word," in a sense that is manifestly true

because words form images in our minds. So if you can
tamper with the language, you get at people's psyche; you
get inside their minds in a way you can't do with bayonets.
And this is one of the things, of course, that Lenin was
terribly good at. Lenin was a very, very clever man. He
was a man devoted to his profession, which was the pursuit of power, almost more completely than any other
individual in the whole of history. He gave up chess, he
gave up music, he gave up all his pleasures in order to
concentrate entirely on politics, and he grasped right from
the beginning that if you can alter the terminology in your
own favor, then you have a tremendously powerful
weapon for controlling men's minds.

On December 18, 1976, a Soviet prisoner was advised he would be sent
to a different jail. He was handcuffed and led to a chartered Aeroflot jet.
Only after the airplane had left Soviet airspace did his guard release the
handcuffs (made, ironically, in the U.S.A.). At that point, Vladimir
Bukovsky, an internationally famous dissident, was told what it was all
about. He was being released from jail in response to an initiative of
General Pinochet of Chile. The Soviets had asked that he release the
Chilean Communist Party leader Luis Corvalán. All right, Pinochet
said, but in exchange, you release Bukovsky. A few weeks later, Bu-
kovsky visited with the President of the United States, in the White
House.

Vladimir Bukovsky was born in 1942 in East Russia. He was expelled
from Moscow University, where he was studying biophysics, for the
offense of publishing a satirical journal. Two years later he was arrested
for distributing copies of *The New Class* by Yugoslav dissident Milovan
Djilas. While at the famous Lubyanka Prison he read English grammar
books. During the next fourteen years he was mostly in Soviet insane
asylums, which is where the densest collection of Soviet heroes is nowadays herded. There are four hundred thousand berths in Russia's insane
asylums, twenty-seven square feet per person. Mr. Bukovsky endured
the years of hell, and his name came gradually into prominence in the
West. His meeting with President Carter was a milestone—not, one
hopes, the highwater mark—in the Western crusade for human rights.

I asked Mr. Bukovsky why the Soviets used psychiatric hospitals to
incarcerate political prisoners.

BUKOVSKY: According to Marxist or Communist doctrine, people's minds, people's consciences, are created, are shaped, by conditioning. That's why they can't explain the appearance of people who fight *against* the system; why they can't explain, for example, religious people. In a country where for sixty years on end they sponsored tremendous atheist propaganda and tortured and destroyed religion there's no explanation in Marxist ways as to why people still believe in God or are opposed to socialism or Communism. And there were only two explanations: one of them, external influence; the other, subversive activity by international imperialists. But when they cannot prove either one, as it was with me—a very young man who never *saw* a capitalist society, who had Communist parents, who was never exposed to any external influence—then what? Then the only explanation is that such a person is mentally ill.

I asked Lee Kuan Yew, Prime Minister of Singapore, about *his* dissenters. Here was a despot, almost universally, in 1978, acknowledged as benign, who faced not democratic dissenters but Communist dissenters.

He told me that there were fewer than a hundred dissenters in Singapore jails and that 95 percent of them were Communists consecrated to terror and disruption. He was morally untroubled about the absence of political freedom in the Singapore he ruled over. He explained: "When *we* win, our foes live comfortably even in prison, with butter and eggs and meat according to special rations which the rules of the game lay down upon us. This is in part an unequal conflict; because on the one side is terror that is absolute, on the other side terror which is not really terror. It is just a deterrent, and often no more than a soporific. You put a man in, you feed him, he studies, he writes memoirs, he comes out, and he resumes fighting. If *his* side wins, he pulls your fingernails out and you are dead."

And, on the subject, Henry Kissinger:

KISSINGER: The younger establishment, or at least a significant part of the establishment, believes that the Soviet Union is not really geopolitically aggressive and that most, or many,

SECRETARY OF STATE HENRY KISSINGER

Soviet actions are in response to *our* initiatives. Therefore, to the extent that we rearm we bring about more aggressive Soviet tendencies rather than the opposite. The younger establishment also believes that sooner or later the Soviet Union is going to change by its own inward tensions.

WFB: Which is not inconceivable, is it?

KISSINGER: It is not inconceivable.

WFB: But must not be counted on.

KISSINGER: No. It is, in fact, highly probable—provided the international environment does not supply the Soviet Union with the substitute for the domestic achievements they will never have. I would be very confident that if the Soviet Union is deprived of major foreign policy successes, internal strains in the Soviet system will be very severe.

WFB: So that either you have attrition there, or else you get the opposite of it, namely extravagant efforts at successful imperialism?

KISSINGER: I believe that the Soviet Union is in no position to conduct consistent imperialism against a determined enemy. All the Soviet adventures have occurred in areas where there were *no* Western troops, where there were *no* Western nuclear weapons, quite the opposite of what so many of the demonstrators are implying [when they speak of provocative U.S. presences]. All the pressures were in Vietnam, in Angola, in Ethiopia, in Korea, in places where there was [then] a [U.S.] vacuum and where the risk seemed relatively low.

WFB: Is the operative word in what you just said "consistent"? Might they be disposed to apply sudden, deathstroke-type actions? In which case, is there a potential threat of a strike against Europe? Or only if there were such a vacuum?

KISSINGER: If the inequality of power becomes too great, then there is such a danger. On the other hand, I believe that while the Soviet Union is militarily very strong, it is also a system with massive inefficiencies. Every time one discovers the truth about the various Communist systems— when there is a revolution or some sort of upheaval—one finds how inefficient they are. So for the Soviet Union to launch itself into a vast adventure in which they cannot calculate the outcome with high certainty strikes me as improbable. However, if they could calculate a high probability of success, then Communist theory really gives them no [alternative than] to use their advantage.

WFB: For instance, if they thought they could have taken Berlin in '61, they'd have done so?

KISSINGER: Yes, they would have had a *duty* to do so.

WFB: Does that ideological imperative, in your judgment, continue to govern?

KISSINGER: I believe that the Soviet Union—that a Marxist society, especially a Leninist society—tends to believe very strongly in what they call the correlation of forces. If the correlation of forces is favorable to them, then they *must* exploit it, and they do not even consider such moves as aggressive action. They consider that a ratification of reality. Similarly, if the correlation of forces is unfavorable to them, they must adjust to *that,* and they don't consider that a defeat—they consider that a tactical move. Of course, one cannot carry this to the extreme of saying that if, based on [an] overwhelming superiority, we demanded tomorrow that they abandon their system, [we could not predict] that they would not fight to the death. But within the margins in which the conflicts have heretofore been conducted, I think a military advantage will give the Soviet Union the temptation to exploit it.

In 1987, Jeane Kirkpatrick appeared on *Firing Line* on returning from a visit to Managua. It was she, while at the United Nations, who did so much to popularize the case against the Sandinistas. In recognition of this, she was greeted by the resistance in Managua as a liberator.

She opined that it was *just possible* that the Sandinista government would abide by the terms of the cease-fire scheduled to begin on November 7. Pressed to account for admitting a possibility never before experienced in any Marxist-Leninist dictatorship (the toleration of political freedom), Mrs. K. said that the pressures on the Sandinista government were very great. There was, to begin with, the pressure from the signatories to the Arias cease-fire plan for which the President of Costa Rica received the Nobel Peace Prize, probably the fastest Nobel gestation in history. Then there were the economic pressures. Inflation was at 700 percent, she reported, and per capita earnings were down to 40 percent of what they were in 1981.

Above all, there was the pressure from the Contras. "There are fifteen or sixteen thousand of them, and they are growing in number."

Question: If the Contras lose support from the U.S. government, would the chances of a cease-fire with political freedom simply evaporate?

Always the scholar, Mrs. Kirkpatrick avoids facile answers. But to this question she replied, simply, "Yes."

She reminded the audience that the Soviet Union, in 1985, had sent $1 billion worth of armaments to Nicaragua. The same sum in 1986. And $1 billion had already been sent when she visited Managua in October 1987. Meanwhile, Congress was caviling over $200-odd million, and only one of the Democrats then running for President (Gore)

EXAMINER MICHAEL KINSLEY, JEANE KIRKPATRICK

favored aid of any sort. Senator Albert Gore was in favor of "humanitarian aid," one of the emptiest concepts in political history. (What is it one is supposed to do with humanitarian aid for a resistance movement?)

I asked her: Did she think there would be elections? Yes, she did—but probably they would be rigged. Then the subtle question: Would they be rigged in such a way as to be tolerable to us? Mexico, I observed, rigs *its* elections, and nobody much cared until the summer of 1988. The ruling party (Partido Revolucionario Institucional) had been at it since 1929, and the techniques are refined: You permit just enough of the opposition to give the impression that there is political liberty, but stick-and-carrot are used, as required, and the dynastic tradition—one president selecting his successor, after a single term—continues. But it cannot safely be predicted that the sham will endure another political generation.

The government of Nicaragua could imitate the Mexican model and tranquilize the opposition, Mrs. Kirkpatrick said.

KIRKPATRICK: The Sandinistas are very enthusiastic and very orthodox Communists.

WFB: Yes.

KIRKPATRICK: However, they also are under very heavy pressure. Like most Marxist-Leninist leaders, they have made a shambles of the economy. Inflation last year was at about seven hundred and fifty percent. The dollarization of the economy is now complete, because the value of the Nicaraguan currency declines so fast that you cannot hold the price steady from one day to the next.

WFB: Weimar Republic stuff.

KIRKPATRICK: That's right. Exactly. Even the government—the government is paying most of its professionals now in dollars even. It's a terrible, terrible mess. Real wages are less than half of what they were in 1979, and production continues to decline in all spheres, in fact. Beyond that, of course, there are about fifteen, sixteen thousand Contras fighting inside Nicaragua today, and they are in all parts of Nicaragua, north, south, east, west. And they're making themselves felt.

WFB: We're about to immobilize them, aren't we?

KIRKPATRICK: Frankly, I believe that the worst thing that the United States government could do with regard to encouraging democracy in Nicaragua would be to demobilize and dismantle the Contras. That's the *worst* thing surely that we could do. The government of Nicaragua must be brought to see that democracy is the only alternative to defeat. I think it's possible with very heavy pressure.

If the Communist regime in Nicaragua could contrive to seal off its program, maintaining borders secure against centrifugal imperialist pressures, then we would indeed see something never before seen in the twentieth century. All the Maryknoll missionaries could then rejoice over the undisturbed pace of liberation theology confined within Nicaragua.

KIRKPATRICK: There are ways in which Nicaragua is very different than all the other Marxist regimes we've talked about—you know, Hungary, Czechoslovakia, Poland—where the people have manifested their clear unhappiness with their Communist governments. It's finally been Soviet troops and Soviet tanks that have held those governments in place. There aren't any Soviet troops and Soviet tanks in Central America yet.

But it is the logic of Communism to imperialize, and the peace of El Salvador and Honduras and Guatemala and Costa Rica—and, yes, Panama and Mexico—depends on containing a dynamo that, in order to breathe, needs to breathe the fetid air that comes from the corpses of free institutions and human beings. The kind of power needed to bring about a Communist state on the East European or Cuban model, even if limited by its own borders, absolutely excludes such liberties as are enjoyed by Mexicans. What happens in Mexico is despotism, not totalitarianism, to revive an important distinction.

A summary of Mrs. Kirkpatrick's findings? There was no hope for substantial change in Nicaragua unless we continued to arm the Contras. Four months later—as I began work on this book, it happens—the House of Representatives voted on the final request of the Reagan administration for aid to the Contras. It voted no.

I recall the very first *Firing Line,* featuring Norman Thomas, in April 1966. In arguing against our role in Vietnam, Thomas asserted that if we were to win the military struggle, securing a free Vietnam, we would be left with an impossible burden. "We would have to support Vietnam as a colony halfway around the world, on the very borders of China, which can no more be done peacefully than China can do the same thing to a colony in Mexico." Well, such a thing was done, not by China, granted, but by the Soviet Union, also.

"The question of pessimism or optimism," Revel said dismissively, "those are mere psychological moods." Well, yes; but the objective situation is far from encouraging. And there are times when the pessimism simply overwhelms one. I had an experience the night before doing that *Firing Line* with James Michener. And I let my gloom hang out after the hour on *Firing Line* in a syndicated column:

> I have just read James Michener's book *Poland.* It tells of a nation whose very life as an independent country was obliterated for 125 years before World War I and even now continues to face a deterioration—yes, a deterioration—in its standard of living.
>
> "No, life has not improved," *New York Times* Executive Editor A. M. Rosenthal wrote, revisiting Poland a few months ago, after fifteen years' absence (he was booted out for writing the truth in 1959,

landing on the showcase of the Pulitzer Prize awards). The first day
Rosenthal was in Poland, he joined spontaneously a funeral proces-
sion for a nineteen-year-old boy who had been beaten to death by the
police more or less for the fun of it, there being no other explanation
for it than that some people actually amuse themselves by torturing
other people.

Arriving in Austin, Texas, with mechanical paperwork in hand that
required no concentration, I turned on the television and found myself
listening to a man lecturing, uninterrupted, to an enthusiastic Texan
audience. He was talking about how in 1954 the leaders of the United
States conspired to take from the people of Guatemala and their
elected leader Colonel Arbenz the small power they had painfully
amassed.

All that the Arbenz government wanted to do, the speaker explained, was to take from the United Fruit Company that much of its
land that remained unused, so that the peasants might have land of
their own. The Guatemalans had offered a few dollars per acre, the
United Fruit Company had held out for twenty times that amount,
and before you knew it, prospects for reform had evaporated—along
with the government of Colonel Arbenz. The speaker said that it
gradually transpired that the principal actors in this antidemocratic
coup were Henry Cabot Lodge, John Foster Dulles, and Allen
Dulles—all of whom had commercial interests in the United Fruit
Company.

A half-hour later, in his televised course on contemporary history
featuring the exploitative hunger of acquisitive American imperialists,
the speaker got to the Korean Airline 007. "That was a dastardly
deed," he said. Pause. "The question is: who are the dastards?"
Laughter. Applause.

"There's almost nothing an American on welfare or a Briton on
the dole would buy in Warsaw's main department store," Rosenthal
writes. It isn't that Poles are kept unaware that such luxuries exist
as electric coffee makers, or watches, or pens, or toasters, or canned
food, or color television. These can be seen in store windows—of
establishments opened only for those who have dollars to spend.
Fifteen years ago in Poland these commercial luxury resorts were
secreted away from casual public perception, behind windowless
walls, in locations known only to tourists and Poles with dollars
sent by relatives abroad. Now the Polish government simply does
not care about the acuteness of the public sense of deprivation. The
big shopping day is on Saturdays from nine to twelve and what
appears to be all of Poland gathers for the feast. I came close to
tears in the marketplace, spread out over acres and acres, in piles on

the ground or in small stalls: it was junk, acres and acres of pitiful, secondhand junk."

James Michener sighs, in contemplating Poland. How old are its problems? "Whenever the people of Poland enjoy a better life than those in Russia, we are in mortal danger." The quote is from Catherine the Great, 1792.

Dare one hope? "Hope for Poland," writes Rosenthal, "belongs to the Poles; only they pay the price. The realization of the strength and pervasiveness of hope—hope for Soviet change of heart, hope for a miracle, hope in themselves, hope undefined—did affect me. Not dramatically; it just opened my mind a bit, made me see a little more clearly."

What one comes to see a little more clearly is that everywhere in America—not alone in the revolutionary cafés of Greenwich Village or in centers of anomie like Haight-Ashbury—there is moral rot at work. Pray God their ministers' audience will continue small, late at night, confined to public access channels.

When gloom descends I remind myself of what I was told by a Viennese colleague when I was still in my twenties. The only way for modern man, he said, is objective pessimism, and subjective optimism. (The data are discouraging, the data be damned.) Since my visit to Austin, Texas, to talk with Michener, and since Rosenthal's visit to Poland, the Poles have shown that they are very much alive. They were beaten one more time; but who knows—and they can dream, along with Martin Luther King. The data be damned.

20

THE

ROLE

OF

INTELLIGENCE

GUESTS:
NADIA ULANOVSKAYA
CLAIRE STERLING
ROY COHN
VERNON WALTERS
ALLEN DULLES
REBECCA WEST
PAUL JOHNSON
CONSTANTINE
 FITZGIBBON

I t does not surprise that much attention, over the years, has been given to the Soviet threat. More generically, to the Communist threat. I have always found it unbalancing that the same people who invest much time looking for an opportunity to criticize "obsessive" anti-Communism spend so little time contemplating either existing excesses of Communism (the Soviet empire comprehends much of Eastern Europe) or the potential threat of further aggressions. (There is no other explanation, I have held, for the design of Soviet nuclear resources. Just as the logic of the wheel is to turn, the logic of twelve thousand nuclear warheads is to threaten—or to fire.)

It is hard to know, really, the implications of this designation "obses-sive." President Jimmy Carter used a similar word when he spoke, at commencement at Notre Dame (1977), about our "inordinate fear of

Communism." It can't reasonably be said that, say, Poland's Lech Walesa suffers from an "inordinate" fear of Communism. It is like saying about a man who has pneumonia that he suffers from an inordinate fear of pneumonia. In the matter of "obsessive," the word suggests a preoccupation to the exclusion of virtually all other concerns. On whatever plane this question is asked, it seems unlikely that a successful case could be made against America as being "obsessively" anti-Communist. Defense expenditures use up only about 25 percent of the national budget. As for time, it can't be persuasively held that our politicians, when watching a football game or turning the spit at a barbecue, are actually engaged in counting Russian tanks.

It is true that I was in the CIA. I was a "deep cover" agent, which meant that not even my family (exception: my wife, after she was cleared, which took three months) could know that the reason I was in Mexico had nothing to do with the ostensible reason I was there (to inquire into, with the view possibly of resurrecting, commercial interests once owned by my father). I kept my secret rigorously, never mentioning the CIA to anyone after my resignation and return to the United States in 1952.

And then—in 1973—I found myself on the telephone with the Rev. William Sloane Coffin, Jr., about whom it was widely known that he had been in the CIA. The day before, Egil Krogh, one of the Watergate "plumbers," had pleaded guilty to however many counts of perjury. *The New York Times* had run a biography of Krogh which included the news that he had studied ethics under the Rev. William Sloane Coffin, Jr., at Williams. I found this too good to resist, and so I twitted Coffin on his impact as an ethics teacher. Then—suddenly—I found myself saying: "But don't feel too bad about this, Bill; my boss in the Agency was Howard Hunt."

I shouldn't have said this, but comforted myself after my slip with the knowledge that it had been told to a fellow former covert agent. Ah, but Bill Coffin promptly told someone else about my past and—it quickly became a part of the public record. People continue to ask me what I did in the CIA, and I continue to say that what I did is a secret. I have volunteered only that (a) the training I received was exactly the training received by my fictional protagonist, Blackford Oakes, in *Saving the Queen;* (b) I didn't kill anybody or do anything exciting; and (c) if I had been captured and tortured, I would not have been able to give out the name of a single fellow CIA operative other than that of my boss, Howard Hunt.

It can all be made to sound very carefree, the intelligence and counterintelligence business. It is nothing of the sort. Consider Nadia Ulanovskaya.

She was once a spy in America for the Soviet Union. As had her husband been. Before the revolution, he had at one point occupied the same prison cell with two other anti-Czarists. One of them, Jacob Sverdlov, a few years later presided over the execution of the Czar, the Czarina, and their daughters and son. This act was committed in Ekaterinburg, renamed Sverdlov after the killings, to memorialize the killer.

The other prisoner was Josef Stalin.

When Mrs. Ulanovskaya's husband was dispatched to set up shop in the Far East, he recruited a Russo-German called Richard Sorge, the most notorious spy of World War II. It was he who informed Stalin of the exact day in 1941 when Adolf Hitler would launch the war to the east. Shortly before the war's end, Sorge was caught and hanged in Tokyo.

While in America, one of Mrs. Ulanovskaya's agents was Whittaker Chambers. During the war, the Ulanovskayas were called back to Moscow. There Nadia did translation work and came to know a number of American journalists, including C. L. Sulzberger, Walter Kerr, Larry LeSuer, and Drew Middleton. Unhappily, she also came to know the Australian journalist Godfrey Blunden, to whom she confided her progressive disenchantment with the world created by her husband's former jailmate, Josef Stalin. Blunden wrote a novel called *A Room on the Route,* based in substantial part on the disguised experiences of Nadia Ulanovskaya. But that didn't fool the KGB. Mrs. Ulanovskaya was arrested, kept in solitary confinement at the Lubyanka for a year, then sentenced to fifteen years of hard labor in concentration camps in various parts of the Gulag Empire. Her husband wrote a personal plea to Josef Stalin, in return for which he was picked up and sentenced to ten years in a workcamp. Their daughter Maya, then fifteen years old, was arrested two years later for associating with dissident students, and she was sentenced, at age eighteen, to twenty-five years in Siberian labor camps.

Many years later, after Khrushchev's denunciation of Stalin, they were let out of concentration camps. And in the little reconstituted apartment at Moscow, Solzhenitsyn would visit with them. Nadia devoted herself to translating books, among them Robert Conquest's *The Great Terror* and Koestler's *Darkness at Noon.* Yevtushenko first read it there. The high point of their social season was always March 5, when they and their friends would drink a glass of vodka in celebration of the day that Stalin died.

At the prodding of her grandson, Mrs. Ulanovskaya, now widowed, moved to Israel in 1975 with her daughter and son-in-law. She came to London in 1977 to participate in *Firing Line*. Her English was rusty, but she made herself understood.

WFB: You left the United States in what year?

ULANOVSKAYA: It was 1934, or the end of 1933. I can't remember exactly.

WFB: Which was before Whittaker Chambers met Alger Hiss?

ULANOVSKAYA: Oh yes.

WFB: So, therefore, you had no direct knowledge of Alger Hiss when you were in the espionage apparatus in America?

ULANOVSKAYA: None at all.

WFB: How long did you know Whittaker Chambers?

ULANOVSKAYA: We knew him from 1931 until we left.

WFB: What was the nature of your activities during that period?

ULANOVSKAYA: Well, you know, my husband was what I called a resident, and my role was very unimportant. I was just doing technical work. They were more interested in technical— you see, the word "espionage" sounds a bit—

WFB: Well, whatever the word is for stealing other countries' documents. That was certainly your assignment, wasn't it?

ULANOVSKAYA: Yes. They were mostly interested in technical—I remember my role was—well, I photographed them. By the way, Whittaker Chambers—

WFB: You mean you photographed material that Chambers brought to you?

ULANOVSKAYA: Not only Chambers. Well, just materials that were brought to us.

WFB: You knew Chambers as what?

ULANOVSKAYA: I met Chambers as soon as he was assigned to my party.

WFB: But you didn't know his name, did you?

ULANOVSKAYA: Well, we were not supposed to know each other's names, but I happened to know him because he was a bit unusual.

WFB: In what sense?

ULANOVSKAYA: He was more intelligent than the ordinary—

WFB: Spy?

ULANOVSKAYA: —people that the Communist Party sent to us for that work. And as a matter of fact my husband said that it was a waste on the part of the Party to send him for that kind of work—a waste because he was more intelligent, and he was at that time an editor of *New Masses*. And [my husband] said he could be more useful in some other capacity whereas here we didn't need such an intelligent man for that kind of work.

WFB: So during that period you and your husband were amassing information of any kind that might prove useful in Moscow?

ULANOVSKAYA: Yes. . . . I remember all kinds of plans about Sikorsky, De Seversky—something like that. I remember those names from that time.

WFB: Well, one was the helicopter man—

ULANOVSKAYA: Yes, yes.

WFB: How many Americans did you come into contact with who were part of the apparatus?

ULANOVSKAYA: Not many. Well, all of those Whittaker mentions in his book. I found old, familiar names in his book—all the names that I knew and—

WFB: You knew most of them?

ULANOVSKAYA: Yes, and I knew what happened to some of them afterward, when they came to Russia. They all perished in the purges.

WFB: Was there anything in Whittaker Chambers' book that was inaccurate insofar as you had personal knowledge of the events?

ULANOVSKAYA: You mean in his book?

WFB: Yes.

ULANOVSKAYA: Some dates. Very minor mistakes, minor errors. Well, maybe my memory's not so good, but in general he gives a quite clear picture and a very accurate picture of it.

When Mrs. Ulanovskaya said on the program that she and her husband thought it a waste of time to use men with the skills of Chambers in such unexacting capacity I thought back to a late summer evening—I think the year was 1956—when I was driving Whittaker Chambers from the offices of *National Review* in New York, where he had joined me, to Stamford, Connecticut, where he would weekend with my wife and me. We talked about everything, as we had done since we became friends in 1954, and now I asked him the identical question: How could it be that someone of his manifest talents had been used so extensively by the Party, in those years, as a mere courier? He replied with his deep chuckle, "You have obviously never worked for Soviet intelligence." Sometimes Chambers was enigmatic, and one felt that to ask for details was to get in the way of his exposition as he wished to plot that exposition. But he did not go on. I was left to infer that while serving as a courier, he was proving to his case officer his utter reliability (subject, of course, to apostasy from the Communist movement). There is so very much in the spy business that *is* routine, and those who do it need to be trusted.

Senator Joe McCarthy, Chambers told me in the heyday of McCarthyism, had violated a sacred tacit understanding. In the beginning, Chambers had been friendly to McCarthy, as all anti-Communists had been. But then one day Senator McCarthy, cornered by the press to ask what documentation he had against one of the men he was publicly pursuing, had said, "No comment"—and then had leaked to the press that that afternoon he was driving to Westminster, Maryland, to visit with Whittaker Chambers. The impression was unmistakable that Chambers was McCarthy's source. After that, Chambers gave McCarthy a wide berth.

In retrospect, it is clear that McCarthy's indiscretions and exaggerations had the practical effect of lowering the nation's guard against Soviet agents, indeed the West's. It was after McCarthy was dead that British intelligence came close to promoting Kim Philby to the highest position within MI-6, in charge of anti-Soviet operations and counterintelligence. No general charge ever leveled by McCarthy about the penetration of U.S. intelligence exceeded the specific gravity of the British situation at the time. And the lax security procedures that permitted to pass into top-sensitive positions the spies who, in the mid-eighties, gave the Soviet Union, among other things, our top submarine secrets were happy survivors of security systems assailed by McCarthy, whose personal excesses, however, had the effect of undermining his own purposes.

But the intelligence and counterintelligence struggle went on—and continues.

Claire Sterling graduated from Brooklyn College and from the Journalism School at Columbia. As a schoolgirl, she was a Communist (she still considers herself a member of the moderate left). For more than thirty years she lived in Europe, primarily in Rome, as a journalist. Her 1981 book *The Terror Network: The Secret War of International Terrorism* grew out of an investigation into the killing of Premier Aldo Moro of Italy. On *Firing Line* she made the arresting point that among those who resisted seeing Soviet activity for what it was were—the CIA. I asked her at what the critics of her startling book had taken greatest offense.

STERLING: I must say I haven't found yet a single reviewer who has said my book is *inaccurate.* They just don't *like* what I conclude. And I'm not in the political business. I'm a *reporter,* and I did not set out to prove a thesis. I set out, as an investigative reporter, to look for a pattern, and, in the end, I believe I found one. It was very convincing to me and it's backed by a mass of facts. My conclusion is that the Soviet Union *does* have primary responsibility for creating terrorist groups. Not for orchestrating them, and certainly not for masterminding them. That's a comic-book concept—to think that there is a phantom mastermind in a subterranean map room who presses buttons and tells them what to do—but in providing the *wherewithal* for these terrorist groups to become extremely efficient at their craft and therefore to become effective destabilizing influences in democratic societies.

It's a form of warfare in which, largely through surrogates—mainly through Cuba and the Palestine Liberation Front—the Russians have . . . put a loaded gun on the table and said to these terrorist groups [that they should go forward with their destabilization efforts]. These men and women are not necessarily the Soviets' ideological companions. They might be Trotskyites, anarchists, nihilists, Maoists, [people who] often criticize the Soviet Union's policies but still accept it as [the supreme] socialist state and concentrate their hostility against the West. They do not attack Soviet objectives. Their job is to destabilize, to undermine authority, to humiliate officials in Western democratic countries—

WFB: But you haven't made it plain why it is that—

STERLING: And that is what my critics don't like.

WFB: —this disturbs your critics. You yourself have gone so far as to accuse the CIA of *cowardly* behavior—

STERLING: Yes, I have.

WFB: —and you had specific reference to its failure to acknowledge the directional role of the Soviet Union in world terrorism?

STERLING: I found there was a draft report some weeks ago issued by the CIA at the request of Secretary of State Haig on the CIA's findings so far—what evidence existed—to indicate Soviet responsibility for terrorist activity. This report took the smoking-gun theory. If you couldn't find a Russian there with a smoking gun and the bloody corpse on the floor, you could not say that the Russians were responsible for these acts of terrorism.

At the time Miss Sterling appeared, William J. Casey was head of the CIA.

If she was correct, one thinks again of Jean-François Revel and his indictment—the proclivity of democracies to dissipate energies out of a sense of guilt. And, granted, American intelligence-gathering agencies have not always behaved well, a point I took up with Roy Cohn, the most adamant McCarthyite in the whole, wide world.

I asked him whether the director of the FBI might be justified in going to Good Judge A, rather than Uncooperative Judge B, if the director sought permission to bug a target or otherwise keep eyes on him.

COHN: The answer is a certain amount of discretion should be vested in the director of the FBI to trust absolutely *no one* not working *directly* on the matter—

WFB: How would you put that into law? What would you say?

He elected to answer not by reference to the friendly judge, but by appeals to what he assumed was common practice.

COHN: . . . If you give the FBI the authority in national security cases to engage in surreptitious entries with the approval of the Attorney General, and with the approval of the director of the FBI on certain showings, to me, as an American, that is sufficiently protective. Looking at a fifty-year record, the FBI has *not* abused this right nor abused this privilege, and the instances—

WFB: Oh, come *on.*

COHN: I don't think it has.

WFB: You mean finding out about the sex life of Martin Luther King was not an abuse?

COHN: Well, I don't know if finding out about the sex life of Martin Luther King was an abuse, or how they happened to find out about it, whether that was part of something else, but a very liberal Attorney General, Robert F. Kennedy, authorized the interception of Martin Luther King's wires—

WFB: It was certainly an abuse.

COHN: Now, you might raise this question: Why has the congressional committee that investigated the matter not released any portions of the fifty-five-page report on Dr. Martin Luther King?—which, I understand, would have shed a great deal of light on certain activities of his which might have fully justified Attorney General Robert Kennedy and the Bureau in doing what they did. That report has been locked up by the committee, [in deference to] the memory of Dr. Martin Luther King.

            But the committee has not extended a similar courtesy

to the memory of John Edgar Hoover and has permitted all sorts of rank hearsay, abusive attacks on him, leaks to the papers, and everything else. And the result of it has been? How can they get new FBI agents? How can they restore the morale? Look, these people take care of bank robberies; they take care of kidnappings, hijackings; they have done a *fantastic* job for this country. Why anyone would want to be an FBI agent today, with a salary that's about equal to that of an elevator operator here in New York, with this kind of indiscriminate abuse being heaped on all of them because of a possible few *mistakes*—

The excerpt is a fine cross section of Roy Cohn at bat. He shows his adamant loyalty to the FBI, well-sheltered contempt for the character of M. L. King, and scorn for hypocritical comparative judgments, he accuses the accuser, and he ends with a mom-and-pop defense of a favorite government agency. I say this, by the way, invidiously. I cherish Roy Cohn's partner Tom Bolan's unforgettable quotation. It was the manager of Sonny Liston, the gargantuan prizefighter, who said to Bolan at a moment when Liston was being accused of a half-dozen or so felonies and misdemeanors, "You know, Sonny has a lot of good points. It's his bad points that aren't so good."

I talked with Vernon Walters about intelligence and ethical criteria governing its practices. General Walters was U.S. ambassador to the United Nations, and had served as deputy director of the CIA for four years. He had written a book (*Silent Missions*) describing high doings and misdoings in the international world of diplomacy and intrigue in which General Walters had played a role, sometimes as assistant architect, sometimes as technician. It is easier to enumerate those international conferences and midnight sessions at which he was not present than those at which he was. His principal merchandisable commodity has been an uncanny memory and proficiency in languages. He speaks fluently French, Spanish, Italian, German, Portuguese, Dutch, Greek, and Russian. He has difficulty with Japanese, but he can manage. Accordingly, before he went to the CIA—and even while he was at the CIA—he served as confidential translator for Presidents Truman, Eisenhower, Kennedy, and Nixon; for Henry Kissinger and Averell Harriman; in Paris, China, South America, Italy, wherever the action was.

AMBASSADOR VERNON WALTERS

WALTERS: We have a great ambivalence toward intelligence. The
average American thinks it's something that isn't very
clean, it isn't very American and the Founding Fathers
wouldn't like it. Well, I have news for them. George
Washington was one of the most prolific readers of other
people's mail. Benjamin Franklin was assistant postmaster
of British North America before the Revolution, when we
were all loyal subjects of George III. He was busily opening all the British mail. They caught him. They sent him
to London to stand trial before the Privy Council. They
found him guilty. Before they could sentence him he

skipped off to France to conduct the covert operation that was to bring France into the war on the side of the Revolution. Now this was a remarkable achievement, seeing that Anthony Eden's great-great-great-grandfather had fully penetrated Benjamin Franklin's office. Franklin's valet was a British agent, his secretary was a British agent, and we have some doubts about one of the three commissioners.

WFB: But a dozen generations after Franklin, the Secretary of State of the United States said, "Gentlemen don't read other people's mail."

WALTERS: That was Mr. [Henry] Stimson in 1932.

WFB: That's right.

WALTERS: Mr. Stimson, in 1941, was so busy reading other people's mail that he didn't have much time to do anything else.

I pause to record that Vernon Walters was the most effective apologist for the United Nations who has ever appeared on *Firing Line*. He is a fine and trained advocate, especially when one pauses to reflect that he really has very little use for the United Nations.

Allen Dulles was, of course, the head of the second-largest intelligence operation in the world, the Central Intelligence Agency, for nine years, until November 1961. During that period, and as a matter of fact since then, he and the CIA are criticized more or less coterminously: Allen Dulles was the CIA incarnate. When we spoke, in 1967, it was obvious that he found it difficult, now and again, to defend his policies, or the CIA's, as convincingly as he might have done—he gave the impression—if he had been free to reveal The Secrets.

Allen Dulles served eight Presidents of the United States in various capacities. He was at the Versailles Conference as a very young man. President Harry Truman asked him to organize the CIA. President Eisenhower asked him to head the organization. And President Kennedy asked him (tactfully) to stay on as Director of Central Intelligence until his retirement—a discreet interval after the colossal failure of, among other things, intelligence at the Bay of Pigs. When Nikita Khrushchev was here in 1959 he twitted Dulles. Why not, asked Khrushchev, economize by merging the CIA and the KGB? After all, Khrushchev said, winking broadly, the Soviet Union knows all U.S. secrets anyway. . . .

WFB: What is your opinion of the reasons for the continued derogation of the intelligence function? Why should the CIA be made a—a sort of a general laughing stock? People in the CIA aren't *dumb;* they've all got Ph.D.s and are pretty flashy intellectually. What is it that gave the CIA its bad name? Is it the fact that you have to lie?

DULLES: No, I don't think—Let me say as to that, how do you mean lie? Do you mean if you are asked if you are a member of the CIA, you don't have to admit it? You don't lie about the facts you're trying to get hold of. That's the last thing you would do.

WFB: Well, for instance, the President of the United States *lied* about the U-2 plane, and he was thought to have done so at the suggestion of the CIA, i.e., presumably, the CIA asked the President of the United States, who, let us suppose, did not come by lying naturally, to *lie.* [*Laughter*]

DULLES: Well, that was a decision made at a very high level, by the President himself. And I don't think the mere fact you don't *admit* everything, that doesn't mean you're *lying* all the time. You can keep quiet about a great many things.

WFB: Or you can act evasively, which Mr. Eisenhower found it easy to do. [*Laughter*] But he actually said—referring to our U-2 spy plane—he said, "No, this is not a surveillance operation, this was a *weather* plane." A weather plane, because we were [presumably] concerned about the snows in Afghanistan. [*Laughter*] "Lie" is a blunt word, but that *was* a lie, wasn't it? And do you suppose it's because of incidents like that that people tend to believe that the CIA is, you know, a sort of underworld operation?

DULLES: Well, the British have followed that principle for a great many many years, and they don't seem to have had the same difficulty.

WFB: They're much more *worldly* than Americans.

DULLES: Are they? Well . . .

WFB: Don't you agree?

DULLES: Maybe they feel they've had a longer period of experience,
           but still, I—I think that now, in intelligence, we're as good
           as they are. And they've had more difficulty with penetra-
           tions than we've had.

There was no quarreling with that point, not in the decade of Philby,
Burgess, and McLean. It was deft of Mr. Dulles to shift the line of
questioning over to the British experiences, thereby easing American
ethical doubts.

We moved to other questions, but the residual impression left, by
stout Presbyterian Allen Dulles, was of serenity, in an upset world not
of his making.

Speaking of British intelligence, Rebecca West appeared on *Firing Line*
in 1969 to discuss the spectacular defection from Britain to the Soviet
Union of Kim Philby (1912–1988).

She was a formidable woman, hailed by many critics as the finest
woman prose writer alive. She had been a socialist, but always anti-
Communist. And one of her more recent books had been *The New
Meaning of Treason,* in which she examined the implications of the
activities of assorted British and American spies. In 1969 her reputation
was as a historian, a novelist, and a critic. I remarked (our exchange was
filmed in a London hotel) that "here in England" there seemed to be
more popular interest in the techniques of spying than in the moral
questions. I asked, "Is it becoming sort of chic, in some quarters, to be
a traitor?"

WEST: Well, I think it is in a way, because it's a form of dissent;
           but in any case, I think the real feelings that people get out
           of reading the Philby books are of annoyance at the Estab-
           lishment.

WFB: Is that true? I have heard it said that in England there is
           this great establishmentarian *loyalty,* and that so long as
           one is a member of your ruling class, one finds it very
           difficult to get into trouble. Do you think that it made a

difference that Mr. Philby went to Cambridge, had a public school education, and so on?

WEST: I think it *must* have, because, you see, it is historically interesting that he wasn't really of a very important family. He was of a very *charming* family. But he wasn't of a very *important* family.

WFB: If he had been important, he wouldn't have been discovered yet, do you mean?

WEST: No. What I mean is that Philby had all the slight thrill that his father gave people. You see, his father was pro-Arab. And the British Establishment, the British upper class, has always been pro-Arab—I think because the British upper class has always been very fond of horses—

WFB: No, come *on*. [*Laughter*]

WEST: —and it all works together. Yes, that's quite true.

WFB: Do I understand that he was not identified as a loyalty risk because the Arabs love horses?

WEST: Yes. [*Laughter*] Because—

WFB: There's no better reason, come to think of it. [*Laughter*]

WEST: No, no. If you'll listen to me, really. Think of how the British in the nineteenth century—the British always backed the Turks in the east of Europe because they were very good horsemen. Well, it's the same thing, there's a kind of sporting-life atmosphere about the Arabs—

WFB: Uh-hmm.

WEST: A great many of the English upper-class people approved of Philby because he was on the right side with those Bedouin chaps.

Rebecca West made it all sound like a *jeu d'esprit,* but this, you see, was British upper-lip time, a defense against questioning by ex-colonial Americans. I knew something about her habits and her train of mind, and later we became close friends. But several years earlier, before meeting her, I had attempted to get her to cover, for *National Review,* the first post-prison appearance of Alger Hiss, at Princeton. It was in the late fifties, and she had been lecturing, on *Hamlet,* at Yale. I learned much later that, at the same time, she had been telephoned by William Shawn of *The New Yorker* with the suggestion that she cover the trial in the Midwest of a young man who blew up a commercial airliner, causing several dozen deaths, with the design of killing his mother, a passenger on the airplane, and collecting insurance. This happened only a few months after *The New Yorker* had published a "short story" written by Anthony West, natural son of Rebecca and H. G. Wells, which dealt severely with his mother. Rebecca's alleged answer to Mr. Shawn: "Oh? I didn't know you disapproved of matricide."

In fact she was deadly serious on the subject of treason, and her thoughts on Kim Philby, far from permissive, most closely resembled those of Lord Birkenhead, whose review of Philby's book in the *Daily Telegraph* closed with one of those Biblical excoriations that linger in the memory: "We shall never know how many agents were killed or tortured as a result of Philby's work as a double agent, and how many operations failed. He is now safe in Russia, and we must, alas, abandon any wistful dream of seeing this little carrion gibbeted."

It all becomes very serious. Again, Vernon Walters.

WALTERS: The greatest defense against a nuclear Pearl Harbor is the existence of an effective intelligence community that will make it quite clear to anybody that preparations for such an operation *will* be picked up.

WFB: The trouble with that statement is that everybody agrees with it, but when you go on to ask certain questions that you consider derivative, you will find considerable disagreement. Let's take a hard one, shall we?

WALTERS: Right.

WFB: Assassination. Both of us know that it has been widely charged recently, for instance, that the CIA assassinated Lumumba, assassinated Diem, tried to assassinate Castro, so on and so forth. I guess we both know that, in fact, the CIA didn't do—

WALTERS: That's right.

WFB: —at least the first two of those things.

WALTERS: If they had, Senator Church would have brought it out
             quite plainly.

WFB: Sure. Now, let me ask you this. If the first responsibility
             of a country is to protect itself, then can't you *ex hypothesi*
             come up with a situation in which an assassination *would*
             be sanctioned by the Walters Rule just mentioned, protec-
             tion against a nuclear attack?

WALTERS: Well, let me—

WFB: And yet it's something we wouldn't quite want to discuss,
             would we?

WALTERS: Let me just amplify a little bit on that. My own position
             on assassination is I'm against it for three reasons: It's
             against the law of God; it's against the law of man; and
             it generally doesn't work. Now—

WFB: Which shows that God was prudent? [*Laughter*]

WALTERS: Very. We know that. Now, if you go into something like,
             for instance, the Bay of Pigs—now, two U.S. govern-
             ments—Eisenhower's and Kennedy's—sanctioned that.
             I'm not in favor of assassination, I want to make this clear,
             but they knew that a lot of young men were going to be
             killed if that operation went forward. Why do you spread
             an umbrella over one person [for example, Castro] and not
             over the others [for example, the young men who died
             trying to invade Castro's Cuba]?
                 Having said that, I say, I don't believe that assassination
             works. I think if you do it you get another fanatic who is
             even worse.

WFB: You're well into a metaphysical paradox, aren't you?

WALTERS: Yes.

WFB: You keep saying, "You understand, I don't believe in as-
             sassination," however the intellectual arguments favor it.

WALTERS: But I have religious feelings that oppose it. Rationally, I
             would agree.

WFB: All right, let's bring this out then. Assuming that you
             didn't feel the negative religious sanction and you were

guided only by juridical arguments, let me ask you this question: Suppose Idi Amin were reported by Israeli intelligence as on his way with an atomic bomb that he had managed to filch from some arsenal to bomb Tel Aviv. Now, we acknowledge the right of self-defense, do we not?

WALTERS: Yes.

WFB: Suppose that—

WALTERS: It's the limits of it that are the problem.

WFB: Correct, and to what extent can you preempt a strike of that sort via assassination? Or must you go through a juridical ritual? For instance a declaration of war, in order to justify it?

WALTERS: I would say the latter is correct, except that declaratory war has gone out of fashion since 1945. We've had large numbers of conflicts, nearly all of them undeclared. You know, you heard a lot of people say, "Oh, you could do that in wartime, but you couldn't do it during the Vietnam War." But what *was* the Vietnam War? It wasn't a declared war, but the Congress was voting the money to keep the war going, thereby sanctioning it.

WFB: Does it follow that because you have a de facto war you inherit de jure rights that a normal war confers on you? For instance, we certainly tried very hard to assassinate individual Japanese leaders, and in some cases, we succeeded.

WALTERS: We did. Yamamoto.

WFB: Yamamoto, yes. We succeeded. Now, would we have been justified in searching out Ho Chi Minh during the Vietnam War and assassinating him?

WALTERS: Well, whether you say assassinate him or whether you say killing the commander in chief of the enemy army, I would certainly say we had the right to do the latter.

WFB: And you don't call it assassination because the juridical protections of a de facto war give you the right moral cover?

WALTERS: Well, the whole problem is that all of these questions of
                division between assassination and killing an enemy de-
                pend on who writes the history books. And the victors
                usually write the history books.

The plot, as they say, thickens. I have written eight novels featuring
CIA activity. In them I have attempted to probe the ethical mysteries
of the spy and espionage worlds. When I began work on the first of these
novels, I thought to attempt to write a book in which it was never left
in doubt that the CIA, for all the complaints about its performance, is,
when all is said and done, not persuasively compared with the KGB.
My own admiration for the mission of the CIA has never been confused
with any evaluation of its overall effectiveness. A few years after leaving
the CIA, I published in *National Review* an editorial paragraph that
read, "The attempted assassination of Sukarno in Jakarta last week had
all the earmarks of a CIA operation. Everyone in the room was killed
except Sukarno."

The point I have sought to make in these novels is that the CIA,
whatever its failures, has sought to advance the honorable alternative
in the struggle for the world. In the novels of the past—novels by
Graham Greene, and John Le Carré, and Len Deighton, for instance—
the point, really, is that there is little to choose from in a contest between
the KGB and the CIA. Both organizations, it is fashionable to believe,
are defined by their practices. I said to a television host on a network
program, after he raised the question, that to say that the CIA and the
KGB engage in similar practices is the equivalent of saying that the man
who pushes an old lady into the path of a hurtling bus is not to be
distinguished from the man who pushes an old lady out of the way of
a hurtling bus, on the grounds that, after all, in both cases someone is
pushing an old lady around.

The novelistic urge of the great ideological egalitarians who write
books with such titles as *The Ugly American* has been to invest in their
protagonist in the CIA—or in his counterpart in the British MI-5—
appropriately disfiguring personal characteristics. So that the American
(or British) spy had become, typically, late-middle-aged, paunchy, alcoholic, a cuckold—moreover, an agent who, late at night when well along
in booze, ruminates to the effect that, after all, who really is to judge
so indecipherable a question as whether the United States is all that
much better than the Soviet Union? The KGB and the CIA, when all

is said and done, really engage in the same kind of thing, and what they do defines them, not why they do it, right?

So that when, having no preset idea of where I was going, I sat down to write that first novel it suddenly occurred to me that it would need a protagonist, and so by the end of the day, I had created Blackford Oakes, the principal character in a book called *Saving the Queen.*

A year later, the editor of *Vogue* magazine wrote to me to say that many reviewers had denominated Blackford Oakes as being "quintessentially" American. She invited me to explain, explicitly, the "American look." I thought to reject the invitation, because I reject the very notion of quintessence as here applied. It is a concept, really, that runs into its inherent incredibility. You will remember that F. P. Adams once said that the average American is a little above average.

The reason you cannot have the quintessential American is the very same reason you cannot have a quintessential apple pie, or indeed anything that is composed of ingredients. In all composites there has got to be an arrangement of attributes, and no such arrangement can project one quality to the point of distorting others. This is true even in the matter of physical beauty. An absolutely perfect nose has the effect of satellizing the other features of a human face, and a beautiful face is a comprehensive achievement.

So anyway, Blackford Oakes is not the quintessential American, but I have fancied that he is *distinctively* American, and the first feature of the distinctively American male is, I think, spontaneity. A kind of freshness born of curiosity—and enterprise—and native wit.

Blackford Oakes is physically handsome. Here I took something of a chance. I decided not only to make him routinely good-looking, but to make him startlingly so. When I decided that Blackford Oakes should be startlingly handsome, it was required that he be that in a distinctively American way, and what does that mean? The American look, in the Startlingly Handsome Man, requires: animation, but tempered by a certain . . . reserve.

I thought, when pondering the question, of Billy Budd. I have long since forgotten just how Melville actually described him, but Melville communicated that Billy Budd was startlingly handsome. But looks aside, his distinctiveness was not that of Blackford Oakes. Billy Budd is practically an eponym for—innocence; purity. Oakes, though far removed from jadedness, is worldly. And then, and then . . .

Billy Budd, alas, is humorless. Correction: not *alas.* "Do not go about as a demagogue, urging a triangle to break out of the prison of its three sides," G. K. Chesterton warned us—"because if you succeed, its life will come to a lamentable end." Give Billy Budd a sense of humor and he shatters in front of you into thousands of little pieces, which you can never reconstruct.

The American look here is a leavened sarcasm. But careful, now: Escalate sarcasm and you break through the clouds into the ice-cold of nihilism, and that, in this interpolation on U.S.-Soviet intelligence and counterintelligence, is my last word on the American look.

The American must—*believe.* However discreetly, or understatedly. Blackford Oakes believes. He tends to divulge his beliefs in a kind of slouchy, oblique way. But at the margin he is, well, an American, with Judeo-Christian predilections; and he knows, as with the clothes he wears so casually, that he is snug as such; that, like his easygoing sweater and trousers, they—fit him. As do the ideals, and even most of the practices, of his country.

I remember with delight reading a review of that first novel, published in the *Kansas City Star,* written by a professor of English from the University of Missouri, I think it was. I had never heard of the gentleman, but he made it quite clear that he had spent a considerable part of his adult life abominating me and my works and my opinions. He was manifestly distressed at not quite disliking my first novel, which he proceeded to describe. He saved his conscience by concluding, "The hero of *Saving the Queen,* Mr. Blackford Oakes, is tall, handsome, witty, agreeable, compassionate and likable, from which at least we can take comfort from knowing that the book is not autobiographical."

Blackford Oakes lives in an age when what matters most is the survival of basic distinctions. That difference, between Us and Them, is the difference that matters. And any failure, I have contended, by beneficiaries of the free world to recognize what it is that we have here, over against what it is that they would impose upon us, amounts to a moral and intellectual nihilism: far more incriminating of our culture than any transgression against eristic scruples of the kind that preoccupy so many of our moralists, as Vernon Walters and others suggest, concerning the moral protocols that properly bind the CIA.

I may not have succeeded, but at least I have labored hard, in my Blackford Oakes novels, to document the reality, which is that espionage is a moral art.

And on the point at issue—which is, really, the need to know the intentions (as well as the strength) of the enemy—I quote from three

guests, two of them already introduced. One hears the sepulchral organ
tones as they speak of America's vulnerability.

JOHNSON: You see, it is very interesting what has happened to the
                United States. If you take the United States as it was in
                the early 1930s, it was still, as I call it, the last Arcadia.
                It was this huge, rich country defended by enormous
                oceans on both sides, apparently something which could
                not be assailed by the evil societies of the Old World or
                the ancient societies of Asia because it was so remote and
                protected by its watery barriers. At that stage, when
                [Franklin] Roosevelt, for instance, first became President,
                America had one of the smallest armies in the world. It
                had an army of about one hundred and fifty thousand
                people. It had a fairly respectable navy, but an out-of-date
                navy, and really a very small air force.
                    Nowadays the United States is often accused of being
                a militaristic power with a military-industrial complex
                and so on—huge armed forces and all that. But, of course,
                America did not *wish* to be this. America wanted to *pre-
                serve* its Arcadia. It found itself—simply because modern
                technology assassinated distance and turned us all into
                one world—it found itself *obliged* to defend itself, and
                obliged to defend other societies which were similar to its
                own; and thus it was *thrust* into the position of a heavily
                armed power.
                    Now, you see, that illustrates the dilemma. America
                didn't want to become a great armed power. It wanted to
                be a great industrial and agricultural nation with its own
                traditions, and to preserve them. It was thrust into this
                position, and there is always a danger; and that is one of
                the themes of my book, *Modern Times,* that one kind of
                regime corrupts another. Just as Hitler's regime was cor-
                rupted by Leninism, and Hitler, in turn, helped to further
                corrupt Stalinism, so the totalitarian regimes can corrupt
                the free regimes simply by forcing them to defend them-
                selves.

WALTERS: The United States, and this isn't popular to say right now,
                is more threatened than it has been in any time in its

history. We have never, since the American Revolution, faced a global power. Germany, at the height of its power, was a basically European regional power. Japan, at the height of its power, was basically a western Pacific, Southeast Asian power. Recent events in Angola, in the Horn of Africa, have shown that the Soviet Union is not only capable but willing to project its power thousands of miles from the boundaries of the Soviet Union. It has never in the past been possible to destroy the sovereignty of a nation in a matter of hours. That is possible now.

We survived a conventional Pearl Harbor. Who could survive a *nuclear* Pearl Harbor?

And the late Constantine Fitzgibbon, author, most appropriately, of the novel *When the Kissing Had to Stop,* also a critic, a historian, and a veteran of the undercover war against Hitler:

FITZGIBBON: In 1939, we had five years of seeing the causes of the war building up. Today—well, you would probably have only a few hours.

That is the thought that makes the nightmare. We have lived forty years in the nuclear age. Perhaps, in historians' terms, we can speak proudly of having gone that long without a world war. But the strategic balance, and the apocalyptic nuclear thunderclouds, gravely affect the thought of serious men. And women, I suppose we must, nowadays, add—in the nuclear age.

21
TWO
REGULAR
GUESTS

ALLARD LOWENSTEIN,
R.I.P.
CLARE BOOTHE LUCE,
R.I.P.

*ast Thursday, the day before he died, he was writing a
speech he wanted me to give. His last words in that speech
read, "Do we want four more years of what we have experienced to
date?" It was the wonder and the glory of Al Lowenstein that he never
wanted more years of what we have experienced to date.*

That excerpt is from the eulogy by Senator Edward Kennedy, one of
six pronounced on Tuesday, March 18, 1980, at the funeral of Allard
Lowenstein.

It is within the loose design of this volume to publish in this chapter
two modest character portraits. Selected are two public figures I have
known well, one of them a charismatic liberal, the other a charismatic
conservative. The first, Allard Lowenstein, was shot and killed in March

1980, while working in his office in New York, by a former colleague
presumably deranged. The second, Clare Boothe Luce, was a figure of
spectacular dimensions, as we will see. She died on October 9, 1987,
from brain cancer, at age eighty-four. I knew them both well, in and out
of *Firing Line*.

It is probable that history will portray Lowenstein as the most consistently active liberal, in the years 1950–1980, on the liberal-cultural-
political scene. As a student at the University of North Carolina, he was
committed to all liberal causes. There he was deeply influenced by its
president, Dr. Frank Graham. He went from Chapel Hill to the law
school at Yale, where he labored for causes he loved (World Federalism,
the National Students Association), and against causes he loathed (loyalty oaths, the Mundt-Nixon bill, Eisenhowerism more or less in gen-

ALLARD LOWENSTEIN, PRODUCER WARREN STEIBEL

eral). On one matter, Lowenstein was not typical: His opposition to the
Soviet Union was always explicit and unbending, and in later years this
got him into some difficulty when he was serving as an ambassador (in
rank) within the United Nations, on the staff of Andrew Young. In
between, he had run for Congress three times (winning once), taught at
the law school at Stanford University, launched the anti-LBJ campaign
for the presidency with Senator Eugene McCarthy, and joined the staff
of Bobby Kennedy. He was a roving political-missionary institution,

lecturing everywhere, everywhere surrounded by young people to whom
he was always the soul of courtesy and passion. We became good
friends.

Allard Lowenstein's hectic life is, in odd little fragments, chronicled
in his frequent appearances on *Firing Line.* The first appearance was in
the late summer of 1968, immediately after the stormy convention in
Chicago that handed the Democratic nomination to Senator Humphrey.
I introduced him, that first time on *Firing Line,* as follows:

WFB: Mr. Al Lowenstein is generally regarded as the proximate
          agent of the whole [Eugene] McCarthy phenomenon. At-
          tempting to recruit somebody to run against President
          Lyndon Johnson he went first to Senator Robert Kennedy,
          but was turned down; then to Senator McGovern, ditto;
          finally, to Senator Eugene McCarthy whom he persuaded
          to challenge Lyndon Johnson in the Democratic prima-
          ries. The rest, as they say, is history.

          He has had many victories, too, since he strove at
          Chapel Hill as an undergraduate to integrate the Student
          Council and served, fresh out of Yale Law School, as
          president of the National Students Association. He re-
          vered and was revered by Eleanor Roosevelt; Norman
          Thomas thinks him the hope of his generation, ditto Rich-
          ard Goodwin; John Kenneth Galbraith wants him elected
          to Congress. Mr. Galbraith says that he "can't think of
          anyone who could possibly be such a force for liberal
          policy in Congress," which certainly would suggest that
          Mr. Lowenstein should go to Congress or that Mr. Gal-
          braith can't think. [*Laughter*]

          I should like to begin by asking Mr. Lowenstein
          whether he approves of Senator [Eugene] McCarthy's re-
          fusal to back the ticket.

LOWENSTEIN: Well, I've not backed the ticket myself, so I don't know
          that I could disapprove of someone else taking the same
          position. I would say that I approve of [party indepen-
          dence] more as a *principle* than as a political tactic. I
          suppose that on balance what I believe has to be done this
          year is for people across the country to say what they feel
          is right and attempt to survive doing that.

Lowenstein's opposition to the Vietnam War was so comprehensive he could not tolerate Hubert Humphrey's relative ambiguity on the matter. Lowenstein wished always to be known for his positions, rather than for his affiliations. But three years had now gone by. Lowenstein was a member of Congress. It was one year before Watergate. I reminded him of his disloyalty to his party in 1968, and asked him to define "desirable party loyalty." Or ought one to be loyal only to those other voters, of whatever party, to whom one felt bound by a common cause? There was, initially, a little uncomfortable friskiness in his reply.

LOWENSTEIN: Now, first I will answer what I was trying to answer before you tried to get me to answer something I'm not trying to answer. Then I'll answer—

WFB: Which you will *then* not answer.

LOWENSTEIN: Well, I'll answer both in due course. What my feelings are—and I think you would agree with this—that people, regardless of party labels, ought to work together on issues they agree about. We happen to agree about the draft [I had come out against the draft, proposing that only volunteers be sent to Vietnam]. I don't think that my agreeing with you about the draft means that I am committed necessarily to supporting you if you run for President. If so, it would be an awful decision for me to make, because I'd like to continue to work with you. [*Laughter*] I would like to continue working with you against the draft without feeling that that obliged me to support your ambitions.

WFB: You are being very sly, Al. [*Laughter*] [I was clearly trying to get a yes or no to the question of party loyalty.]

LOWENSTEIN: I can't keep up with you in the department of being sly. [Bad stuff. *Tu quoque* in debate—so's-your-old-man—is almost always to be avoided.]

It was toward the end of President Nixon's presidency, and there were quarrels over jurisdiction: executive vs. legislative vs. judicial.

LOWENSTEIN: If the only problem were the balance of powers between three branches I'd be much less troubled. But it's my sense of the present difficulty—

WFB: You'd lose your persona if you appeared untroubled. [*Laughter*] I *like* you troubled.

LOWENSTEIN: I'll try to stay troubled. Although my rabbi used to tell me I must not engage in *Schadenfreude,* which is the process of enjoying the suffering of others. But I must admit that every time I think of the latest involvement of the White House—when I think of—

WFB: You're tempted to enjoyment.

LOWENSTEIN: I'm tempted! [*Laughter*] There's something about people who have most preached at you engaged in the process of redemptive suffering themselves that makes one feel it's perhaps a little less wicked to enjoy their suffering, given what they have previously done to other people. You think of Miss Glueshoes, the contortionist [he refers here to Rosemary Woods, Nixon's secretary], sitting there trying to explain how she managed to erase all that tape [the famous 18 ½-minute gap], and you remember back to the haranguing you had to endure from people when you said that this administration was not honest. But I wander a bit.

WFB: Yes. [*Laughter*] But not necessarily aimlessly.

LOWENSTEIN: But if I could take one second, I'd like to say that, curiously, out of our long history of basic disagreement on many questions, I find now, I think, from reading your writings extensively, that there is a greater overlap in what we feel the country needs to do than probably there's ever been before. [Al was always straining to find common denominators. This was in part technique, in part his nature. Everyone—almost—was to some extent *good* and *rational,* and therefore agreed *to some extent* with Al.] And I've tried to figure out why that is. Is it that our disagreements are less? I think not. Is it that our sense of America has come to be the same? I think maybe that's part of it. I think that there is now an opportunity to agree on priorities that *transcend* ideological differences, although those remain, and at some point in the future will have to be battled over again.

But the first thing I think we share is the feeling that *integrity* is the basis of democracy, that you can't have consent of the governed if they don't know what they're consenting to. And any administration that misleads the people and misuses its powers—I admired your column on [Nixon's] Enemies List especially, possibly because I'm 007 on the list. And so, as a beneficiary of the attentions of federal agencies that were improperly visited on me, I found it very important that, in your words, you called this the most "hideous" document—the most proto-fascist document—to come out of an American administration in a long time.

But Lowenstein, for all the pleasure he took from fraternal partisanship, did not conceal his concern for the distracting symbols by which his own confederates were being misguided.

LOWENSTEIN: I favored recognizing China for a long time when you didn't. But I *never* favored what we call détente now— what Nixon calls détente now—when it turns out that détente consists, for instance, of subsidizing the Soviet Union, or of abandoning policies we ought to follow in India and Pakistan, in order to appease the Chinese Communists.

In January 1977, Allard Lowenstein was made the American delegate to the Human Rights Commission of the United Nations, which meets every year in Geneva. For the first time in the twenty-five-year history of that commission—thanks to Allard Lowenstein—there was public U.S. criticism of the suppression of human rights in the Soviet Union; specifically, of persecution of dissidents. Visiting me in nearby Rougemont, where I spend a part of the winter every year, Lowenstein confided to me that the State Department (under Cyrus Vance) was not pleased by his direct attacks on the Soviet Union and that he had been given one very strict order: *Under no circumstances* was Lowenstein to so much as *mention* the name of Vladimir Bukovsky (see Chapter 19). After President Carter's greeting, the Kremlin had roared, threatening flood, fire, and famine. Evidently the State Department decided that one go-round with Bukovsky was quite enough.

Allard did as he was told. His dissent, in administrative situations, was strictly private, confided only to his friends. He could, and, notwithstanding his devotion to principle, did engage in collegiate enterprises.

He came, a few weeks after this incident, to London to do a *Firing Line* on the general subject of human rights. Al was uncomfortable, I thought, looking at my old friend. But he was enough the professional advocate to defend the United Nations; which, privately, he had pretty well given up on.

LOWENSTEIN: I made this comment at the Human Rights Commission during the discussion on self-determination. You know, we have this sort of drill we go through every year, denouncing colonialization and all of that.

I said, "One thing we ought to congratulate ourselves on is that if you look at the map, it's in different colors now. There isn't this great set of empires which used to dominate the map of the world. A lot of that came out of the impetus of the developing countries and out of the United Nations' emphasis on decolonialization."

But, I said, "It's also true that self-determination has to mean more than not having a foreign army occupy your country. It has to mean that people can *choose* their own form of government. And if you are denied that *right* in your own country, by your own armed forces—" [Al Lowenstein was here contending with the thesis of Elspeth Huxley, that "democracy" is differently understood, and differently practiced, in different countries.]

WFB: You're not really decolonized.

LOWENSTEIN: You don't *have* self-determination. Now, that doesn't mean that we're trying to tell countries what form of government they should select. But we do have an obligation to be concerned. Concerned as John Quincy Adams once described it, "through prayers and benedictions," I believe he said. We have the right to be concerned that people have a chance to select their *own* form of government.

Now, in that context, let's understand something that ought to be very clear. It is perfectly true that if you don't have food, you're not terribly concerned about what form

of government you have. When other people *are* concerned about what kind of government they want, we
ought to be sympathetic. And if they're denied the right
to express their choice—by their own colonels or whatever—then any support by us for those colonels or whatever would be a form of imperialism because *we* would be
inflicting that government upon those people.

Allard was saying (a) people need to eat before they need their choice
of government; (b) people governed by the few or by forms not of their
own choosing resent it if foreign governments (e.g., the U.S.) support
those people, or forms, on the mistaken assumption that they are the
forms desired by the people. In doing so, such governments are guilty
of a kind of imperialism.

His principal point here was that the United Nations gave such
"oppressed" people a better forum than they had before. We never
entirely unscrambled the question: If a Third World country is dominated by a military junta or a tribal chieftain, are its citizens qualita-
tively better off because the same despot who rules them at home can
also represent them in the UN?

We ended the hour by questioning the usefulness of the United Nations as an agent of idealistic diplomatic behavior. Lowenstein confessed
his misgivings but stressed, as ever, the need for reform.

The question before the house was this. Although a delegate to the
United Nations cannot go to the podium with a speech that has not been
cleared by the State Department, he can at any time, provided he does
so on the spot, use his Right of Reply to go to the podium to answer
an attack from an unfriendly delegate from another nation. When I was
a delegate (1973) I did this once or twice and, in remarks about the
Soviet Union and its empire, wandered a little bit off the reservation.
Ambassador Moynihan did this as a matter of practice. He later admitted, on *Firing Line,* that time after time he would go to the podium,
exercising his Right of Reply, and launch into accusations against Iron
Curtain countries which would never have been cleared ahead of time
by the antiassassin division of the State Department, had he paused to
solicit their permission. Al Lowenstein was talking about this device.

LOWENSTEIN: I was very active for Anatoly Shcharansky [the prominent
             Soviet dissident] while I was an American official, and
             sometimes said things that went beyond what was being
             said by higher officials. Was I, in your view, acting im-

properly in expressing those views while I was a person in the government service?

WFB: The United Nations treaty specifies in crystal-clear language that delegates to the United Nations shall take positions that represent the views of the President of the United States, whose Secretary of State shall routinely communicate his views. [I researched the question before writing my book *United Nations Journal,* and the historical circumstances of the language were interesting. Mrs. Eleanor Roosevelt was firmly situated as the head of the Human Rights Delegation of the U.S. President Harry Truman had no appetite to have Mrs. Roosevelt in effect conduct her own foreign policy. Accordingly, the word was given that the treaty ratified by the Senate should specify that all voices in the United Nations representing the United States should represent the views of the President, as transmitted by the Secretary of State.] Therefore, when Andrew Young says something as harrowing as his recent imputation that the massacre of the missionaries was a plot by [Rhodesia's then Prime Minister] Ian Smith, or that the United States is hardly to be distinguished from the Soviet Union in respect of political prisoners, it is extremely embarrassing to the President of the United States and violates the law. [I should have said "violates legal arrangements."]

    You ask me, What kind of a reform ought we to have that permits the kind of license you exercised and Moynihan exercised? I acknowledge that I took a few liberties, but I don't think any I took would have embarrassed the President under whom I served. I didn't make *preposterous* statements. My own proposal is one that would detach those emissaries in the United Nations [who talk about human rights] from the formal diplomatic establishment and give them a sort of a judgelike tenure. What we want in our Human Rights Commissions are Roger Baldwins [I referred to the principal historical figure of the ACLU, an incorruptible human-rights advocate, after he got over his brief enthusiasm for the Soviet Union], not people who aren't even permitted to raise the subject of Cambodia because we are seeking détente with China.

LOWENSTEIN: I was fishing, over the past year and a half, for a formulation that would satisfy both my feeling—which your book
states [to my satisfaction]—about having delegates sent to
the UN who are not supposed to be robots, and the dilemma we're put into when statements are made by delegates which in fact are statements that do not represent
U.S. policy. Just how that line is drawn seems to me to
carry implications far beyond the immediate situation in
the United States with Shcharansky.

WFB: I agree. [Al had fingered a dilemma. As ever, he was
uncomfortable acting out a role that didn't exactly represent his own views.]

The last program, aired in January of 1980, reflected on the principal
events of 1979. He meditated on the public dialogue, the course of the
presidential elections, and, as he put it, "the nature of the civilization
we're trying to build."

LOWENSTEIN: The question I really wanted to get to, if I can just take
a second, is that we've tottered on toward the question of
politicians saying very little as they run, no matter who
they are. That's an indictment that applies to most politicians in most campaigns. It is compounded by the fact that
everybody now spends ninety percent of their money on
television—where it's very difficult to say anything in
thirty seconds or one minute that *means* anything. I think
that's true of every candidate for President right now, and
I think it's sad. That's a terrible problem in a society faced
with great crises.
  Fifty-two percent of the people in this country now
receive assistance from the government. How far is that
going to go? What are we going to do about energy? Why
don't we put a dollar tax on gas so we can begin to con-
serve instead of waste? I mean, these topics are not being
discussed by any candidates.

WFB: Are you saying that nobody who's running for President
has taken positions on any of these subjects?

LOWENSTEIN: Well, I say that most of them in the end sound like a *blur.*
It's part of the process we seem to have arrived at of

everything getting homogenized. How do we get a country which is capable of magnificent conduct out of the terrible sloth that seems to have seized us—sloth that's led us to the position where we are now, where everybody is more parochial, more self-seeking? Not just the politicians, but the public and all the communities that constitute that mosaic? What is it we should do to raise the level of that discussion? So that we discuss not only individuals for President, but the nature of the civilization we're trying to build?

I had seen Allard Lowenstein for the last time. Eight weeks later, I was asked by his family to be one of the eulogists at a ceremony before a packed synagogue. I spoke about an old friend I admired, and loved.

Possibly, as a dissenter, my own experience with him was unique, in that we conservatives did not generally endorse his political prescriptions. So that we were, presumptively, opponents of Al Lowenstein, in those straitened chambers in which we spend and misspend so much of our lives. It was his genius that so many of those of us he touched discovered intuitively the underlying communion. He was, in our time, the *original* activist, such was his impatience with the sluggishness of justice, so that his rhythms were more often than not disharmonious with those that govern the practical, banausic councils of this world. His habits were appropriately disarrayed. He was late to breakfast, to all his appointments; late in announcing his sequential availability for public service. He was punctual only in registering for service in any army that conceived itself bound in righteousness.

How did he live such a life, so hectic with public concern, while preoccupying himself so fully with the individual human being, whose torments, never mind their singularity, he adopted as his own with the passion that some give only to the universal? Eleanor Roosevelt, James Burnham once mused, looked on all the world as her personal slum project. Although at home with collectivist formulations, one had the impression of Allard Lowenstein that he might be late in aborting a Third World War because of his absorption with the problems of one sophomore. Oh, they followed him everywhere, because they experienced in him the essence of an entirely personal dedication. Of all the partisans I have known, from the furthest steppes of the spectrum, his was the most undistracted concern, not for humanity but for human beings.

Those of us who dealt with him—often in those narrow passages constrained by time clocks and fire laws and deadlines—think back

ruefully on the happy blend of purpose and carelessness with which
he arranged his own career and his own schedule. A poet might be
tempted to say, "If only the Lord had granted us that Allard should
also have arrived late at his own assassination!"

But all his life he was felled by mysteries, dominant among them
those most readily understood by more worldly men—namely, that
his rhythms were not of this world. His days, foreshortened, lived out
the secular dissonances. "Behold, Thou has made my days as it were
a span long: and mine age is even as nothing in respect of Thee; and
verily every man living is altogether vanity." The psalmist spoke to
Al on Friday last—"I became dumb, and opened not my mouth, for
it was Thy doing." To those of us not yet dumb, the psalmist also
spoke, saying, "The Lord is close to the brokenhearted; and those who
are crushed in spirit, He saves." Who was the wit who said that
Nature abhors a vacuum? Let Nature then fill this vacuum. That is
the challenge which, bereft, the friends of Allard Lowenstein hurl up
to Nature and to Nature's God, prayerfully, demandingly, because
today, Lord, our loneliness is great.

CLARE BOOTHE LUCE

On October 9, 1987, Clare Boothe Luce, from whom we heard in
Chapter 9, died. In no time at all, she was being referred to as "The
Woman of the Century." She had earned that title.

Books have been written about her, and more books are being written about her right now. What follows does not seek to be biographical, or even comprehensive in noting her achievements. What is intended here, as with Allard Lowenstein, is to present Clare Boothe Luce in mosaic, on four or five different occasions, appearing on *Firing Line.*

But a few formal details should be given. She grew up in Connecticut and New York, the daughter of a musician (who had abandoned his wife), and an ambitious mother who cared mostly for the upbringing of her daughter.

She did not attend college but soon married a wealthy and dissolute young man by whom she had a daughter, Ann. There was a divorce, and she went to the flourishing monthly *Vanity Fair,* of which in due course she became the managing editor.

Those were high and stylish days, notwithstanding the Depression. And then one day she met the formidable Henry R. Luce, editor of *Time* magazine and already the most influential journalist in America. She married him and set out to write hit plays, most notably *The Women.*

They were the most prominent professional married couple in New York City, and soon Clare Luce insisted on working the world war as a journalist. From this came a highly successful book, followed by her run for Congress. She was elected from Fairfield County and became a kind of tourist attraction in the House of Representatives in Washington.

She quit to have a hand in the campaign of General Eisenhower for President. He named her ambassador to Italy. There she flourished, and was in one poll named the best-known woman in Europe.

When her daughter, Ann, died as an undergraduate at Stanford University in a motor accident, Clare Luce became briefly a recluse, and emerged from it as a Roman Catholic convert. She devoted herself to bringing together a life of the saints, and to miscellaneous civic and cultural duties, retiring to Arizona to live with her semiretired husband until he died.

After that she went to Hawaii for ten years, returning regularly to Washington to serve with the President's Foreign Intelligence board. It was there that she was struck with her final illness, coincidentally a tumor of the identical kind that had brought down her close friend and associate William Casey a few months earlier. At no point did she lose the hard analytical apparatus or the tart tongue that made her victims so eager to depreciate her. But then neither did she ever lose her magnetic and unmistakably feminine allure.

It was said of her, in the obituary in *Time* magazine, that many powerful men, on conferring with Mrs. Luce, felt that they had been "dynamited by an angel cake."

In an earlier chapter, we have heard her on politics, discussing the future of the Republican Party, in 1966, when the party was still reeling from the defeat of Barry Goldwater. In the last chapter we will hear from her again, on religious faith. In this one case she spoke as something of a skeptic, in the other, as a profound believer. In the lively segment that follows, she speaks, above all, as a woman.

It becomes relevant here to bear in mind that she was always, necessarily, ineffaceably, a very *attractive* woman, no matter how hard she strove to make a theoretical cultural case forbidding any distinction between men and women, except those that were necessary for biological reasons.

She was capable, in discussing feminism, of extreme analytical severity, and her host was here a victim of this. Perhaps for the first time he showed his masochistic reserves: because I had a very good time. The scene here is Hawaii.

WFB: [I went on about her, ending with this sentence:] The Equal Rights Amendment, which for a while appeared to be on the verge of adoption, appears once again to be stalled, suggesting a subliminal resistance to formal equality for women, which surprises not at all Mrs. Clare Boothe Luce, who throughout her life has given her time equally to pleading the cause of female equality and demonstrating the fact of female superiority.

LUCE: Bill, you will be pleased to know that in the entire introduction, which is flattering to say the least, there was only one masculine put-down. [*Laughter*]

WFB: Which is less than you're used to?

LUCE: Oh, infinitely, yes.

WFB: What would be a characteristic introduction of you that would show more traces of male chauvinism?

LUCE: Well—

WFB: "Although Mrs. Luce is a woman"—that kind of thing? [*Laughter*]

LUCE: No, the sort of thing that happens to a woman. I remember my maiden speech, my first speech on the floor of the Congress.

WFB: Is a man's maiden speech also a maiden speech?

LUCE: Yes. But as I came down from the rostrum, a congressman walked up to me, and he said, "Mrs. Luce, it's true what they say. You have a very good-looking pair of legs." I said to him, and this was my motto straight through Congress, "It's the other end of me you'd better begin to pay some attention to." But imagine how you would have felt had you— Let's call it brother Jim. If your brother Jim had made his maiden speech on the floor of the Senate and a woman congressman came up to him and said, "Oh, Senator, that suit fits you beautifully around the hips."

WFB: Well, if somebody said that to me in the Senate, I should think it would suggest some improvement in the normal quality of Senate dialogue. [*Laughter*]

LUCE: Yes, I agree with you there.

WFB: But it's one thing to say "You have beautiful legs" when you have just delivered the *Areopagitica*. It is another thing to say that it is always wrong under any circumstances to say that such-and-such behavior by such-and-such person is typically feminine. Are you saying that there is no such thing as that which is typically feminine?

LUCE: Oh, yes.

WFB: You are saying that.

LUCE: I am not saying it. I agree there is.

WFB: You agree—

LUCE: Having a baby is typically feminine.

WFB: Well—

LUCE: Not having a baby—

WFB: No, I'm *not* talking about biological functions.

LUCE: Oh.

WFB: I am talking about modes of thought or modes of expression.

LUCE: Well, I don't think there are typically feminine— Modes of expression, yes, but not modes of thought.

WFB: Well, suppose—would you say that any novelist who used in his book, let's say, the phrase "quintessentially feminine" was primarily a male chauvinist or that he was a poor observer, a bad sociologist—

LUCE: Isn't that the German *ewigweibliche,* "eternally feminine"? Yes, I would like to get at the heart of a rather interesting question. Do you think it's possible for a man to be a Christian and not a feminist?

I note that she takes charge of the interview, posing her own questions.

WFB: And not a *what?*

LUCE: Not a feminist. Christian man has got to be a feminist. Jesus Christ was the first feminist.

WFB: I think before you get any more tantalizing, you should define your meaning of feminism.

LUCE: I will define mine, but if you don't accept it, you will have to reach a definition that we can agree on.

WFB: Well, I can gallantly concede.

LUCE: A feminist— That's a put-down. [*Laughter*]

WFB: You mean I can't use the word "gallant"?

LUCE: You can say "I concede," as you would to another man, but what you're doing is putting a little rose on you for being so nice and not ticking me off or even for taking the trouble to agree. "I gallantly agree." Why not "I agree"?

WFB: Why couldn't you say that to a man?

LUCE: Ah, well, I think you would look like a proper *fool* if you did. Imagine your saying to a man sitting in this chair, "I gallantly agree."

WFB: I could—

LUCE: He'd think you were an idiot.

WFB: Well, you're precommitted on that point of view.

LUCE: But to go back—

WFB: On the definition of feminism.

LUCE: If you will permit me—

WFB: You were going to define feminism.

LUCE: Oh, I was going to define feminism. I simply use the definition—there's one in the dictionary—which is equal rights and opportunities for women in the legislative and social field. That's a good enough definition for me. I think you may find in the dictionary "the advancement of women's rights."

        But I wish to go back to the heart of the question. The Old Testament myth of the Garden of Eden has aroused the ire of women feminists for generations. The legend creates—God creates heaven and earth in this legend in Genesis. He then creates man; man shares in the spirit of God.

WFB: Man the male or man the synecdoche for human beings?

LUCE: No, God created Adam. The first man. I am talking about this legend. He then more or less leaves Adam to his own devices and Adam gets rather bored, and as an afterthought, God creates woman, but he doesn't even create her, boom, like that. He lets Adam give birth to Eve, thus denying to woman in the first few chapters of the Bible, the Old Testament, the right to be the first mother. She's not even the first mother. Adam is her mother. Then as the legend goes along, the end of it—the rather cruel and dreadful end—is that Eve bears the burden of having brought sin and death into the world. Adam, in a most ungallant fashion, tries to blame the whole thing on Eve. "The woman tempted me." Oh, he streaks to the bushes, gets himself in the bushes and hides from God. And then when God hauls him forth, he blames it on the woman.

There's your typical male chauvinist right from the beginning.

WFB: Are you saying there is Biblical sanction to male chauvinism but that it is anti-Christian?

LUCE: Yes, I say there is an Old Testament sanction for the hierarchy which makes God the master of man, man the master of women and his children, and also of nature.

WFB: Well, it seems to me that if you are going to take legendary auspices for current attitudes, you will find ten animadversions on man for every one on woman in literature.

LUCE: Oh, so you will. The Old Testament, which is a very lively legend, has profoundly conditioned human attitudes and the New Testament, but the Old Testament teaches the superiority of man. There is no doubt that the old Jews believed it.

           But in the New Testament, there is the most extraordinary amount of evidence in the Gospel that Jesus had a most unusual mission to women. If you read the Gospels you will be startled by how many of the miracles are performed at the request of women and on women. I love the one of the twelve-year-old child, and Jesus takes her hand and says, "Little girl, arise." I think that was a nice feminist phrase, by the way. But he announced his coming first to a woman who says that God has looked on the low estate of his handmaiden and is raising her up.

           His first miracle is a submission, in a sense, to a woman because—

WFB: She ran out of wine.

LUCE: She ran out of wine for a wedding, an integrated occasion, you see. There were very few occasions of a holy nature where there was any integration in the old Jewish world. The women sat upstairs, they were separated in the synagogue, they were not allowed to speak, and they weren't even required to go to church because the salvation of a woman didn't matter much to them.

           But Jesus performs innumerable miracles for women, and then he announces, which is really marvelous, I think,

"I am the Resurrection and the Life"—he announces to a Samarian woman who is plainly a harlot. And the New Testament notes that his disciples, seeing him talk to a woman, talk to a Samarian, talking to a harlot, marvel at him.

Now another gesture toward women—when Mary Magdalene brought the ointment to put on, in one Gospel she puts it on his feet and in another she anoints his head. In any case she anoints his body, as he says, against the hour of his burial. And when Judas protests that he allows her to touch him and to waste money in this fashion that might be given to the poor for the purchase of food, then Jesus says, "What this woman has done for me will be remembered. She will be remembered as long as the Gospel is preached in the world." This is what made Judas so angry in this episode between Jesus and a woman, and he forthwith went out to betray him.

WFB: Well, now, are you saying that there is a remarkable reversal in the New Testament of the attitude—

LUCE: Of the Old Testament about women.

WFB: About women. Well, you've still got St. Paul to cope with. [For obvious reasons, I was here correcting the point that Paul was something of a misogynist.]

LUCE: Not so much as people think, because if St. Paul contradicts Jesus, then we really have a problem about Paul, don't we?

But to finish about Jesus, when he spoke from the cross, it was to a woman. The Gospels record that many women followed him from Galilee to be there and stand at the crucifixion. All his male disciples left him and only the women stood by.

Now the whole evidence as you read the New Testament is that he had some extraordinary mission to women, because otherwise you cannot account for their love and their loyalty and their devotion. You cannot find one word in the New Testament from the mouth of our Lord that is unkind or harsh or critical of women.

. . .

After that program there was a long hiatus, and not as many words from
the mouth of Clare. And then in 1987 it was agreed that she would
appear again in February, almost exactly ten years later. But she called
two weeks before to say that her duties to her stepdaughter, who was
dying of cancer, made it impossible to accept any fixed engagements. So
we agreed to a brief postponement. Then she herself became ill. She was
alternately reclusive and gregarious in the six months that were left. She
happily scheduled one day a social dinner in New York for the last day
in September with a few old friends, and refused to cancel it even when
it was plain that she would not be permitted to leave her apartment, let
alone leave Washington: Her friends simply knew not to come. A fort-
night later, on the ninth of October, she died. We go now to St. Patrick's
Cathedral in New York City to a portion of the High Mass said in her
memory, Cardinal John O'Connor officiating.

O'CONNOR: We offer this Mass with a great sense of joy in the hope
                 that we are truly celebrating Clare's own resurrection. We
                 offer the Mass in the hope that she may at this moment
                 be facing Almighty God in happiness for all eternity, but
                 we offer it also, if need be, that there be a cessation of any
                 suffering that might be due and that soon she will be in the
                 arms of Almighty God. If you will join me then, we will
                 begin. Mr. Buckley is the first eulogist.

WFB: I first laid eyes on her in 1948. She was delivering the
                 Keynote Address to the Republican Convention, and she
                 said of Henry Wallace, who was running for President on
                 the Progressive ticket, that he was "Joe Stalin's Mortimer
                 Snerd." They all rocked with laughter, and the critics, of
                 course, bit her again.
                    I first met her at her quarters, on Fifth Avenue. She had
                 telephoned and asked if I could come by to discuss the
                 worsening crisis under President Diem in South Vietnam.
                 I was there at four and she opened the door with paint-
                 brushes in one hand. I told her by all means to finish what
                 she was doing before we got down to the problems of
                 Southeast Asia, and so she led me happily to her atelier,
                 but instead of herself painting, she undertook to teach me

there and then how to use acrylics, launching me in a mute
inglorious career. Two months later there came in the mail
at my office a big manuscript pulsating with scorn and
indignation over the treatment of President Diem by
Washington, with special focus on Diem's sister-in-law,
Madame Nhu. She called it "The Lady's Not for Burning." I put the article on the cover of the next issue of
National Review and had a startled call from the press
editor of *Newsweek.* He wished to know how it came
about that . . . Clare Boothe Luce . . . was writing for
National Review. I told him solemnly (I could manage a
hidden smile, since we were speaking by telephone): *"Tous
les beaux esprits se rencontrent"*—roughly translated, that
beautiful spirits seek each other out. The following day,
President Diem and his brother, the Dragon Lady's husband, were murdered. The only happy result of that Byz-
antine mess, for me, was that I was never again out of
touch with Clare Boothe Luce, for whom, months ago, my
wife and I scheduled a dinner—at her request—to be held
here, in New York, on September twenty-ninth, two
weeks before she died.

I have thought a lot about her in the past few days and
weeks. The last time we stayed with her in Honolulu we
were met at the airport by her gardener, Tom. There were
twelve of us for dinner. We were seated in her lanai, being
served cocktails, while Tom was quietly lighting the out-
door gas lamps. Suddenly he fell. In minutes the ambu-
lance arrived. Surrounded by Clare's anxious, silent
guests, Tom was given artificial respiration. Clare gripped
my hand and whispered to me: *"Tom is going to die."*
There was dumb grief in her voice; and absolute finality.
Two hours later, the hospital confirmed that Tom was
dead. Clare said goodnight to her guests, and departed to
keep the widow company.

Clare knew when an act was done. In so many respects,
she was a woman resigned.

I think back on her career. . . . Look, you are a young,
beautiful woman. Pearl Harbor was only yesterday, and
you have spent several months poking about disconsolate
Allied fronts in Asia and the Mideast. You have written

a long analysis, cruelly objective about Allied disorder, infinitely embarrassing to the Allies and correspondingly useful to the Axis powers. On the last leg of your journey, a sharp-eyed British customs officer in Trinidad insists on examining your papers. His eyes pass over your journal, he reads in it, snaps it shut, and calls in British security which packs you off under house arrest. What do you do?

Well, if you are Clare Boothe Luce, you get in touch with the American consulate, and the American consulate gets a message through to your husband, Henry Luce. Mr. Luce calls General Donovan, the head of U.S. intelligence. General Donovan arranges to appoint you *retroactively* an intelligence official of the United States government. The British agree to let you fly to New York, and there they turn your report over to the British ambassador. He is so shaken by it that he instantly advises Winston Churchill of its contents. Churchill pauses from the war effort to cable back his regards to Clare, who meanwhile has been asked by the Joint Chiefs of Staff to brief them on her analyses, which, suitably bowdlerized, appear in successive issues of *Life* magazine and are a journalistic sensation.

Thus passeth a week in the life of the deceased.

The excitement and the glamor, the distinctions and the awards, a range of successes unequaled by any other American woman. But ten years later she was writing not about tanks and planes, but about the saints. She began coquettishly by quoting Ambrose Bierce, who had defined a saint as a "dead sinner, revised and edited."

But, quickly, Clare Luce's tone of voice altered. She wrote that perspectives are very changed now. "Augustine," she said, "came into a pagan world turning to Christianity, as we have come into a Christian world turning towards paganism."

St. Augustine fascinated her. She wrote that "he explored his interior sufferings with the same passionate zeal with which he had explored exterior pleasures, and he quailed to the depths of his being at the [projected] cost of reforming himself. 'These petty toys of toys,' "—she quoted him—" 'these vanities of vanities, my longtime fascinations, still held me. They plucked at the garment of my flesh, and murmured caressingly: Does thou cast us off? From this moment on shall this delight or that be no more lawful for thee forever?' Habit," Clare Luce commented, "whispered insistently in his ear: 'Dost thou think that thou canst live without these things?' And Augustine, haunted by Truth, hounded by Love, harried by Grace, 'had nothing at all to answer but those dull and dreary words: Anon, Anon; or Presently, or, Leave me alone but a little while. . . .' "

Clare Luce knew that it was truly miserable to fail to enjoy some of life's pleasures. When asked which priest she wished to confess to on entering the Catholic Church, she had said, "Just bring me someone who has seen the rise and fall of empires." But some years later, told by someone how utterly admirable were the characters of Clare's play *The Women,* she replied in writing, "The women who inspired this play deserved to be smacked across the head with a meat axe and that, I flatter myself, is exactly what I smacked them with. They are vulgar and dirty-minded and alien to grace, and I would not, if I could, which I hasten to say I cannot, cross their obscenities with a wit which is foreign to them or gild their futilities with the glamour which by birth and breeding and performance they do not possess." So much for the beautiful people.

"Stooping a dozen times a day quietly"—Clare Luce was writing now about another saint, St. Thérèse of Lisieux—"she picked up and carried the splinters of the cross that strewed her path as they strew ours. And when she had gathered them all up, she had the material of a cross of no inconsiderable weight. The 'little way of the Cross' is not the 'way of a little cross.' "

Last Wednesday, in Washington, Clare's doctor confided to the White House that Clare would not live out the week, and that no doubt she would be pleased by a telephone call. The President called that night. Her attendant announced to her who it was who was calling. Clare Boothe Luce shook her head. You see, she would not speak to anyone she could not simultaneously entertain, and she could no longer do this. The call was diplomatically turned aside. The performer knew she had given her last performance, but at least she had never failed.

And then last Sunday, her tombstone at Mepkin no longer sat over an empty grave. She is there with Harry. Over the grave is—"a shady tree sculpted above the names, and to either side her mother, Ann Clare, and her daughter, Ann Clare, in a grove of oak and cypress and Spanish moss running down to the Cooper River."

When Bill Sheed wrote those lines, visiting Mepkin with Clare five years ago, he quoted Abbot Anthony telling him quietly as they walked away, "She's taking it—the graves of husband and daughter—pretty well this year. She's usually very disturbed by this."

Clare Luce, now at Mepkin finally, is no longer disturbed. It is only we who are disturbed, Hank Luce above all, and her friends; disconsolate, and sad, so sad without her, yet happy for her, embarked finally, after stooping so many times to pick up so many splinters, on her way to the Cross.

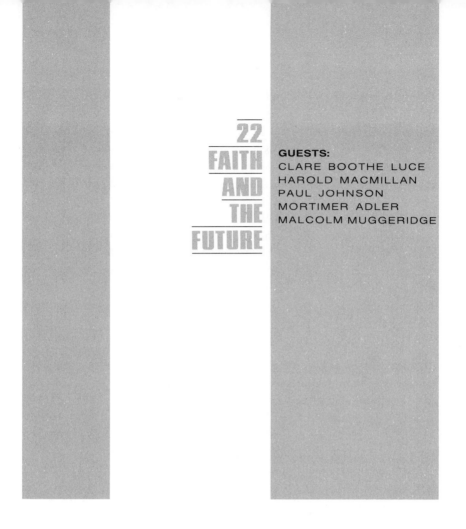

22 FAITH AND THE FUTURE

GUESTS:
CLARE BOOTHE LUCE
HAROLD MACMILLAN
PAUL JOHNSON
MORTIMER ADLER
MALCOLM MUGGERIDGE

One is entitled to ask, What are the causes of subjective optimism? Well, there is enough romance in almost everyone to believe that evil cannot triumph. In order to wrest historical confirmation from such a statement, it becomes necessary to take a very long view of history. Too many dictators have died peacefully as old men in their beds. So that although it is true that dreadful people, doing dreadful things, can for dreadfully long periods hold sway, still there is a secure enough sense of poetic justice to lead much of mankind to believe that if the tyrant does not receive his just deserts in this life, he will in a successive life.

And then, too, there are those cracks of hope. Whittaker Chambers once wrote to me, "Pasternak inspired Ilya Ehrenburg to make what seems to me one of the memorable utterances of the time. I have long disliked Ehrenburg to the point where I would simply turn away from anything he had said. . . . So it was astonishing, when Pasternak was under official fire before the Zhivago business, to hear that old time-server, Ehrenburg, rise to Pasternak's defense. This is what Ehrenburg said, inter alia: *'If the whole world were to be covered with asphalt, one day a crack would appear in the asphalt; and in that crack grass would grow.'* " (My italics.)

But hope, thus expressed, is very different from the utopianism we hear condemned by Paul Johnson, as we shall be seeing.

Discussions of religion as it bears on (illuminates?) government policy and as it does not, of religion, even qua religion, have engaged our attention on *Firing Line,* perhaps subconsciously in search of the causes of that subjective optimism. Here are samples from some in which I have taken great delight. Have a look.

Clare Boothe Luce was discussing what we would think of as anomalous human behavior, seeking an explanation for it.

LUCE: Consider what happens in a crowded theater when the cry goes up, "Fire!" Panic and fear will seize five hundred people, perhaps not one of whom would slap a child, even in anger. But they will nevertheless trample on babies and knock down women in order to get out.

WFB: Is this an aspect of evil?

LUCE: It is an aspect of the seizure of the spirit. It is an aspect of self-idolatry.

I put to her a line from Whittaker Chambers that had always puzzled me. Why had Chambers written that faith, specifically the Christian church, represented the only truly conservative force in the world?

LUCE: Perhaps what he meant was that the church has succeeded in preserving for millions of people, for two thousand years, a true view of the nature of man: a creature who is capable of being a saint and who is most of the time a sinner.

Harold Macmillan, at eighty-six, was asked what would be his valedictory statement on the prospects for the survival of the West. He stared for a while and said that he couldn't understand why it was that so many people who believe so firmly in the brotherhood of man have so much difficulty believing in the fatherhood of God.

MACMILLAN: If you don't believe in God, all you have left is decency. Decency is very good. Better decent than indecent. But I don't think it's enough.

Paul Johnson took the question directly to the political consequences of certain blends of idealism and atheism.

JOHNSON: Broadly speaking, in our society there are two types of people. One is the person who believes in God and in an afterlife. He is prepared to accept that human nature is very fallible and that life on earth is very, very imperfect and likely to remain so indefinitely and that there is something better to come. That is a reasonably rational approach to things. Now, there is the other type, who says, "I don't believe in God. I don't believe in an afterlife. It's all nonsense. This life is the *only* one we've got, and we have to try and improve it, and I don't believe that human—"

WFB: The millenarian?

JOHNSON: Yes. "—I don't accept that human nature is permanently imperfect. It can be perfected." And of course once you conceive that a utopia is possible, you create within yourself a very, very powerful drive to bring it about, and that is how one gets to totalitarianism. You create a race of people who say, "Yes, we can improve human nature, we can perfect human society, and we *must* do it; and, if possible, within our own lifetime, and anything that stands in the way must be brushed aside."

Now, when you come to look at society, you find in a free society, where people are left, on the whole, to do things for themselves, many, many imperfections and many evils. Therefore, such people who believe in utopia, who have no God, who believe in the perfectibility of mankind—they say, "We can't allow people to run things for themselves because they make a mess of it."

WFB: They're a social distraction—

JOHNSON: "Let's have the state do it." So they start to create the state. And as the state (they find in practice) doesn't work, they then increase the degree of compulsion, to *make* it work. So one point I make in the book [*Modern Times*] is that when you drive toward a utopian state, there is no point of balance; there is no stasis there; there is no point at which you can rest. You have to drive onwards or else you go backward—and relapse into capitalism. You have to drive onward, and onward, until you create boat people, and put men like Vladimir Bukovsky in psychiatric asylums.

And so Paul Johnson invites a direct inquiry into the nature of religious reasoning. Mortimer Adler (who has appeared more frequently than any other featured guest on *Firing Line*) is surely a great many things, but indisputably the world's most dogged philosopher and probably that discipline's most exuberant practitioner.

He took his doctorate in psychology from Columbia University, notwithstanding that he never earned an undergraduate degree (he refused to learn to swim). He graduated from law school, but soon joined with Robert Hutchins to devote himself to curriculum reform in the University of Chicago, to editing the Britannica's Great Books with its famous *Syntopicon,* which is correctly described as a Baedeker through the world of thought.

In 1980 we met to discuss his most recent book, *How to Think About God: A Guide for the 20th Century Pagan.* He gives the unthinking agnostic a rough time. As a matter of fact, he gives the thinking agnostic a rough time. And, on reconsideration, I find Adler even better transcribed than listened to, notwithstanding his extraordinary extemporaneous fluency, as the following generous excerpts prove.

WFB: Now, while recognizing St. Thomas and the theologians of several religions, you point out to the reader that you are going to start on the premise that, in effect, nothing is known, but things are knowable.

ADLER: That's correct.

WFB: You begin by reaching a very interesting conclusion which I would like to hear you dilate on, namely that it doesn't really matter whether there was a prime mover [i.e., a force that created the first earthly thing].

ADLER: That, it seems to me, is terribly important. That is, if one begins by assuming that the world started at some time—there was a time when there was nothing and the world began—

WFB: You're making a temporal point.

ADLER: That's right. A temporal point. Then one has begged the question because one has *assumed* God's existence.

WFB: Why?

ADLER: Because if anything comes into existence out of nothing it needs a cause, and that cause has to be the—my word for that cause—

WFB: Exnihilation. [The creation of something from nothing.]

ADLER: —is exnihilation. And the word "creation" *means* exnihilation. Hence—and St. Thomas is very clear about this—

WFB: Why can't that cause be chemical?

ADLER: Because all of our natural science, which I think is reliable, teaches us that the causes in nature do nothing but cause *change.* No, there is no natural cause that is the cause of *existence* or *being.*

One of the great— I think I learned the fundamental truth that helped me write this book in one sentence in St. Thomas. St. Thomas says, "God is the proper cause of being." Only God causes being—not motion, not change, not the pattern of things. The only thing that God is exclusively the cause of is—existence; or being.

There are, in the sacred theology of St. Thomas, two great insights. One is this point about God being the exclusive cause of being. The other, as St. Thomas himself argues, is that only by faith does one hold that the world began. Obviously, it takes faith to accept the opening sentence of Genesis: "In the beginning, God created heaven and earth." Reason can neither prove that the world began nor that it didn't begin. I mean, with respect to the question—the cosmological question—of the world's having a beginning, St. Thomas is completely agnostic, and I think quite rightly so.

WFB: You are saying that reason is not entitled to prefer one position over the other?

ADLER: Correct.

WFB: But you also say [elsewhere] that science is tending to the Big Bang—

ADLER: Well, the Big Bang theory is not a theory of the world's exnihilation [i.e., making something out of nothing]. After all, *something* exploded. "Something" therefore *existed* before the Big Bang happened. All that the Big Bang accounts for is the present *shape* of the universe, not its origin. So that I think the scientist is very loose in saying that was the *beginning.* That's not a beginning in any real sense of "beginning." That's merely the emergence of the present shape of the cosmos. So that one must—in order to *prove* God's existence without begging any questions— one must prove God's existence in terms of a world that is everlasting, without beginning and end—

WFB: Prove or deduce?

ADLER: I would prefer to say—I guess the word "prove" is too strong. I think it is really a more modest claim than that. To establish the *reasonableness* of the belief in God's existence—

WFB: And the converse: the unreasonableness of disbelief?

ADLER: Yes, the opposite. And to do it with, in a sense, the jury's verdict of "beyond a reasonable doubt"—not beyond the shadow of a doubt, but beyond *reasonable* doubt.

WFB: Well now, develop if you will, Dr. Adler, the importance in your analysis of leaving in abeyance the question of whether there *was* a beginning.

ADLER: The importance of it is to avoid doing something which is a logical error and would be begging the question. If one assumes, without proof, that the world had a beginning, one is in effect assuming God's existence. Therefore, in order not to make that illicit assumption, one must assume the contrary—make the problem hard for oneself by assuming an everlasting universe, a cosmos that had no beginning or end. And then ask, Given that cosmos, can we prove?—can we infer?—can we show the reasonableness of believing in God?

WFB: So in other words, what you do is take the more difficult of the two alternatives.

ADLER: That's right. The one against yourself.

WFB: That's right. And then proceed to argue from there.

ADLER: Precisely.

So, Mortimer Adler concludes that to reason to God's existence requires accepting the most difficult metaphysical alternative: namely that matter always existed. In doing so, one removes the (pro-God) argument of the need for a prime mover. Instead, ask: How did matter become transmuted into the universe with which we are familiar, which includes atom bombs and daffodils, Hitler and St. Francis of Assisi?

WFB: Okay. Now, having done that, you take us on into the uniqueness of the word "God," and I wonder whether in that particular section of your book you might be accused of a formal subjectivity.

ADLER: I think not. Here, by the way, I am most greatly indebted to that marvelous, extraordinary eleventh-century archbishop of Canterbury St. Anselm. Anselm said, If you're going to think about God, your mind obliges you to think about a being than which no greater can be thought of. That's binding on the mind.

WFB: The ontological. [I.e., the argument from being, the essence.]

ADLER: No—we're not here arguing for God's existence. This is an argument about what you must think *when* you think about God. And yes, it's called the ontological argument. What is fallacious is when we suppose that it *proves* God's existence. What Anselm is saying is, You must think of God as that than which nothing greater can be thought of, namely the Supreme Being. And if you are thinking of a Supreme Being, you *must* think of that being as really existing. For if that being you're thinking of is only in your mind, then it is not the Supreme Being, because a Supreme Being is a more and a greater being that exists in reality as well as in the mind. Therefore, you must think of God as really existing. Furthermore, you must think of God as having an everlasting or enduring existence, not a transient existence—it doesn't come into being and pass away.

WFB: Are we talking about an attribute now, or something that's—

ADLER: Not an attribute. We are saying how we must think about God. If you think about God as the Supreme Being—as that than which nothing greater can be thought of—you must think of God as really existing, permanently or everlastingly in existence, and also as having an independent and unconditioned existence depending on nothing else for his existence and unconditioned by anything else. When you've done that, you've thought about the Supreme Being who is omnipotent and omniscient, unconditioned and independent. That is the notion of God that—

WFB: Now, could two people's notions of God, if they followed your specifications, differ, or must they, by definition, be identical?

ADLER: I think—that is, what I take Anselm to be saying—if one uses one's reason in thinking about God, one is obliged—one is necessitated—to affirm in one's notion of God these attributes: omnipotence, omniscience, real existence, everlasting existence, unconditioned existence, independent existence.

WFB: Now—

ADLER: May I say, the error—you mentioned the ontological argument. Anselm himself—I think he made an extraordinary discovery when he did that—[but] then he made the mistake of saying that because I must think of God as really existing, *therefore* God exists. That does *not* follow. But the ontological—so-called ontological—argument, which is not a reasonable basis for believing in God's existence, *is* absolutely controlling in how one must think about God's nature. And I think this reverses the order of sacred theology, because in sacred theology, St. Thomas proceeds from God's existence to God's nature, whereas in philosophical theology, one proceeds from one's understanding of God's nature, as Anselm has done it, to the questions of God's existence. Unless one has this clear notion of God's nature—or a sufficiently clear notion—one can't even begin to ask whether in the world of reality there exists something that corresponds to that notion.

WFB: Well, but is the skeptic, even after reading Anselm, not left with the suspicion that the perception of such a creature as God—

ADLER: I have to stop you.

WFB: Yes, I can't use "creature." [*Laughter*] You don't like the word "creature."

ADLER: Well, the creator can't be a creature.

WFB: That's right, sorry. The *perception* of such an *idea* as God is an act of philosophical exertion that simply attempts to deal with infinity without defining it?

ADLER: Well, I'm glad you mentioned infinity because an unconditioned and independent existence is an unlimited existence and an infinite existence. I would again—I did mention—if one thinks about God as the Supreme Being than which nothing greater can be thought of, one must think of an infinite being. But this is simply saying—you see what Anselm did by that extraordinary phrase!—it's one of the most extraordinary acts of mind: "God is that than which nothing greater can be thought of." When you say that, what follows—an infinite existence, real existence, everlasting existence, omnipotence, omniscience, independent existence, unconditioned existence—*that* is the notion of God. Now the question remains, Is there in reality a being

corresponding to that notion? That's where the crux—
where the argument begins.

WFB: Yes, and the ontological argument doesn't necessarily fol-
            low from the insight of Anselm.

ADLER: No.

WFB: There is no nexus. So this is your criticism of sacred
            theology: Reasoning from Anselm's insight on over to the
            ontological existence—

ADLER: Aquinas criticizes Anselm for doing the invalid thing of
            saying, Because I must think of God as really and neces-
            sarily existing, God does exist that way. Curiously
            enough, Aquinas was acquainted with Anselm's argument
            as an argument for God's existence and rejected it as
            invalid, but he didn't do what I've just done. He didn't see
            what a remarkable contribution Anselm made to the ne-
            cessity of God's existence. And with that notion in mind,
            then the [truly interesting] question opens up.
                And the next step is a very simple one. Ask yourself,
            What question is there to which there is only one answer,
            namely, God? What question can you ask to which no
            other answer can be given, except God? For example,
            Why does the world—the cosmos—have the shape it has
            at present? God is not the answer to that question because
            there are other answers possible. Maybe God *is* [the an-
            swer]—but not *necessarily*. Why do things happen as they
            do? God is not the answer to that question, though God
            may be the answer, but not *necessarily*. Why do some men
            in life reap rich rewards and others suffer calamity? God
            is not the answer to that question.

WFB: Not *necessarily*.

ADLER: Not *necessarily*. There is only *one* question to which *no*
            other answer is possible, and that is, Why is there *some-
            thing* rather than *nothing*? Why? Now, that at first looks
            simple, but—

WFB: Because someone is capable of exnihilation?

ADLER: The answer is, If the present world—the cosmos as it
            exists now, right now—is merely a *possible* cosmos, and

everyone—I don't think anyone would say that the world could not be otherwise than it is. And what can be otherwise than it is also is capable of not being at all. And if the present cosmos, being capable of being otherwise than it is, is also capable of not being at all, then *at this very moment,* unless *something* caused its existence in the sense of preventing it from being reduced to nothingness, nothingness would take its place. And so at this very instant, and at every instant in time in which the cosmos exists, without beginning or end, an exnihilating cause is operative. The act of God is that required cause, not in the sense of *initiating* the existence of the world, but in *preserving* it in existence. I think I learned more from Question 104 of the *Summa Theologica* than any other, in which Thomas explains that God's preservation of the cosmos is *creative.*

WFB: Well now, explain why? Inasmuch as it is a workaday piece of scientific knowledge that matter cannot be destroyed; it merely changes its form.

ADLER: That's right.

WFB: So under the circumstances, annihilation is as difficult as exnihilation?

ADLER: Precisely. In that—

WFB: You can have entropy, but you still have matter?

ADLER: Right. Again, the third-most-remarkable sentence in the whole of the *Summa:* One was that God is the proper cause of being, the only cause of being. Two, that there is no way of proving that the world had either beginning or end. The third is—I was stunned by it when I first read it—God annihilates nothing.

WFB: Because He cannot?

ADLER: No. No. That's an act of *will.* That's free will. But the point is that in the whole of our science we've never seen anything annihilated. All change, I mean, is transformation. We talk about destruction. We talk about things being—we use the word "annihilated" loosely. We say,

"That city was annihilated by a war." Not at all. It was just reduced to rubble and ashes and dust. *Nothing* is annihilated. And so since we have no experience of annihilation, we have no experience of exnihilation either. But at this very moment, since what is *could* be not—or not be—it needs a cause for its existence that it doesn't have in itself—

WFB: In other words, there *has* to be an agent of its being—

ADLER: Yes.

    The appreciative sigh is mine. But I yearn, exnihilatively, to create it with others.

Malcolm Muggeridge would probably win the one poll I would never conduct, namely: Who is your favorite *Firing Line* guest? It became a tradition, under the creative sponsorship of my beloved Jewish-agnostic-liberal producer, Warren Steibel, to run an hour with Muggeridge during Christmas week. The practice continues.

    Muggeridge desired, this time around (September 1980), to talk on "Why I Am Not a Catholic." We proceeded to do so, though this show went as "On Religion."

WFB: You once called yourself an imperfect Christian. Is your refusal to join the Catholic Church a sign of pride?

MUGGERIDGE: I don't think so, because I would have no troubles if I felt that I could go as a sinner into the church. I'm sure many people have done so. It's a feeling instead that I would go there in some degree under false pretenses. I don't know. There was an incident which, trivial in itself, played quite a part in my decision not to become a Catholic. The time when I was nearest to joining and asking to be instructed—and I'd planned that I would go to Father [Martin] D'Arcy because I had a great love for him—it was when I was rector at Edinburgh University, and I ran into a row there which you might have heard of when I was asked, as rector, by the students—

WFB: To supply contraceptives.

MALCOLM MUGGERIDGE

MUGGERIDGE: That's right—to recommend that the students should be given, unquestioningly, free supplies of contraceptives by the university medical unit. I refused to do this and there was a hullabaloo. And I thought to myself, you see, "Well, there are a thousand Catholics in the university, and they'll be on my side anyway. I've got a thousand men on my side." What happened was that the first big blast against me was a letter in *The Scotsman* by the Roman Catholic chaplain at the university, saying what a monstrous thing this was that I had done.

WFB: Excuse me, but why was it monstrous?

MUGGERIDGE: It was monstrous, according to him, because it accused the students of wanting to be promiscuous. But in a letter I wrote in answer to it, I said I wondered what the Reverend Father thought they wanted the contraceptives for. Was it to save up for their wedding day? He offered no answer to that. But then I thought that somebody would give him a very big reprimand. No such thing happened. Then I thought he'd almost certainly become a bishop. But that didn't happen either. What *has* happened is the perfect payoff of the whole episode: He's now rector of Edinburgh University. [*Laughter*]

WFB: Well, I'm, to put it lightly, stupefied that you would make a decision whether or not to extend your loyalty to an institution based on the behavior of some of its communicants. I can't imagine any time in history when anybody would have become a Catholic if he had been so easily put off.

MUGGERIDGE: That's true. That obviously wasn't a *major* thing, Bill, but what it did was, it kind of *crystallized* certain feelings I had, that the very things in the church that hold my admiration are the very things that it's turning its back on—that if I joined, I would be involved in endless controversies connected with them.

WFB: Well, you would be the millionth Catholic who was.

MUGGERIDGE: Yes, I suppose so. But can't you see that—perhaps it's an excuse I've invented myself. It's quite possible.

WFB: You have no problem then, I take it, with the Apostles' Creed?

MUGGERIDGE: None at all. I assent to it with—

WFB: Or with apostolicity?

MUGGERIDGE: Not at all. I assent to it. Or the infallibility of the Pope; that doesn't worry me at all. I can see the purpose of all those things, and I see the context of people that I so admire—like St. Augustine and St. Francis—who were ready to accept all that. None of that has ever presented any difficulty. On the contrary, it's the feeling that the church *itself* is moving away from these basic beliefs that is distressing.

WFB: I'm not here to try to convert you. I'm just exploring.

MUGGERIDGE: No, no, no. I know.

WFB: Well, then, why are you a Christian?

MUGGERIDGE: Why did this longing for faith assail me? Insofar as I can point to anything it has to do with this profession which both you and I have followed of observing what's going on in the world and attempting to report and comment thereon, because that particular occupation gives one a very heightened sense of the sheer fantasy of human affairs—the sheer fantasy of power and of the structures that men construct out of power—and therefore gives one an intense, overwhelming longing to be in contact with reality. And so you look for reality and you try this and try that, and ultimately you arrive at the conclusion (great oversimplification) that reality is a mystery. The heart of reality is a mystery.

WFB: Even if that were so, why should that mystery lead you to Christian belief?

MUGGERIDGE: Because it leads you to God. The mystery—and I think the best expression for it I've ever read is in a book I'm very fond of and I'm sure you know, called *The Cloud of Unknowing* [a fourteenth-century treatise on mystical prayer]. And it's when you are aware of the cloud of unknowing that you begin to know, and what you know— to simplify and put it very simply—is God. That's the beginning of faith for me.

WFB: Christian belief requires grace, but you seem to have described a purely deductive process.

MUGGERIDGE: No, because without— The deductive process is the means, but faith is the motive force that takes you there.

WFB: In other words, if as an observer you cease to observe, then you don't have that motive force that grace contributes?

MUGGERIDGE: Absolutely right. That is the grace. It's exactly like—Bill, it's exactly like falling in love. You see another human being and for some extraordinary reason you're in a state of joy and ecstasy over that person, but the driving force which enables you to express that and to bring it into your life is love. Without love, it's nothing; it passes. It's the same with seeking reality, and there the driving force we call faith. It's a very difficult thing to define, actually.

WFB: Well, why is it that scientists, who devote themselves at least as avidly as journalists to seeking out the truth,

why is it that so many of them don't stumble on this
mystery?

MUGGERIDGE: The greatest ones do, incidentally: Einstein, Whitehead,
people like that. The very highest names in science do
stumble on it and for precisely the same reason: because
the knowledge that they have through their researches is
so limited, so fragile, and so inadequate that they, too, are
forced to find some absolute.

WFB: Now, the use of the word "mystery" has been much dis-
dained by skeptics as too easy a way to account for some
of the hideous anomalies of history: the Holocaust, to take
something on a macrocosmic scale; the six-year-old girl
who dies of leukemia, on another scale. Isn't it probably
the case that such anomalies as these do more to encourage skepticism than anything in the divine order?

MUGGERIDGE: I don't think they encourage skepticism. On the contrary,
I would say that they encourage *belief,* as a matter of fact.
What they do is they present a dilemma to which reason
provides no answer.

WFB: Yes?

MUGGERIDGE: And you can only find that answer through what is called
mysticism, or indeed through what Blake called the Imagination, which is art.

WFB: What did Blake mean by Imagination?

MUGGERIDGE: He meant—putting it in one of my very favorite sayings
of his—he said, "They ever must believe a lie who see
with, not thro', the eye." He meant by Imagination seeing
through the eye—seeing into the *meaning* of things rather
than seeing things.

WFB: How would Blake have seen through to the meaning of
such a phenomenon as I mentioned—the death of a six-
year-old child?

MUGGERIDGE: Because he would see in it—there are some lines of his
which I can't quote exactly from memory, but: "Joy and
woe are woven fine, A clothing for the soul divine." In
other words, suffering, affliction, disappointment, fail-

ure—all these things are an *integral* part of the drama of our human existence, and without them there'd be no drama.

Let me tell you what will be a simple parable which I've often thought of. Some very humane, rather simple-minded old lady sees the play *King Lear* performed and she is outraged that a poor old man should be so humiliated, made to suffer so. And in the eternal shade she meets Shakespeare, and she says to him, "What a monstrous thing to make that poor old man go through all that." And Shakespeare says, "Yes, I quite agree. It was very painful, and I could have arranged for him to take a sedative at the end of Act I, but then, ma'am, there would have been no play." See my point?

WFB: Yes, I see your point. On the other hand, I'm not sure that King Lear wouldn't have preferred that there should not have been a play than that he should have lived through Acts II and III.

MUGGERIDGE: But then he would have been a cowardly man, and, of course, he did in fact have to go through that suffering in order to understand why there had to be a play; and, of course, in that marvelous speech of his—one of my favorite things in all Shakespeare—when he, to Cordelia, says, "Come, let's away to prison"—you know—"and take upon 's the mystery of things." It's a beautiful phrase, isn't it? It expresses exactly what I mean. This affliction *has* to be, and that of course is why one is drawn irresistibly as a West European to the Christian faith and to Christ, because this is the central point: the Cross.

There's another parable I've often thought of. When St. Paul starts off on his journeys, he consults with an eminent public relations man: "I've got this campaign and I want to promote this gospel." And the man would say, "Well, you've got to have some sort of symbol. You've got to have an image. You've got to have some sign of your faith." And then Paul would say, "Well, I have got one. I've got this cross." The public relations man would have laughed his head off: "You can't popularize a thing like that. . . . It's absolutely mad!"

But it wasn't mad. It worked for centuries and centuries, bringing out all the creativity in people, all the love and disinterestedness in people; this symbol of suffering, *that's* the heart of the thing. As an old man, Bill, looking back on one's life, it's one of the things that strikes you most forcibly—that the only thing that's taught one anything is *suffering.* Not success, not happiness, not anything like that. The only thing that *really* teaches one what life's about—the joy of understanding, the joy of coming in contact with what life *really* signifies—is suffering, affliction.

WFB: Well, you may recall the closing passages in *The Life of St. Francis,* in which Chesterton remarks that whatever tortures he suffered, as his life came to an end, it was a happy man dying.

MUGGERIDGE: Certainly. We live to work out a drama which is God's drama, and therefore anything that happens to us is in some degree God's will. We are *participating* in the unfolding of God's will. Supposing it's true, for instance, at this moment—which I think it probably is—that what we call Western civilization is guttering out to collapse. If you take that in purely human historical terms this is an unmitigated catastrophe. You and I must beat our breast and say that we lived to see the end of everything, what we love is coming to an end.

WFB: Christendom.

MUGGERIDGE: Christendom is finished.

WFB: It probably *has* finished.

MUGGERIDGE: Why, certainly. But the point is, that is a catastrophe only to the extent that you don't see it as part of the realization of God's purposes.

I tell you, a thing I often think of, as I beat my breast over what's going on in the world, is St. Augustine receiving the news in Carthage that Rome has been sacked. Well, I mean, that's an appalling thing. He was a very civilized Roman, and it was a dreadful thing that the barbarians should have come in there and have burned the place down.

WFB: And he had lived there for ten years.

MUGGERIDGE: Absolutely. Now, what did he say to his flock? He said, "This is grievous news, but let us remember if it's happened, then God has willed it; that men build cities and men destroy cities; that there's also the City of God, and that's where we belong." To me, that's the perfect expression, and I think—

WFB: Well, he said that's where we belong, but this is what we will never achieve.

MUGGERIDGE: Right, but it's only insofar as we're citizens of the City of God that we can be Christians in the City of Man.

WFB: That we can bear it.

MUGGERIDGE: That we can bear it. You remember St. Teresa of Avila, Bill, who said life in this world is like a night in a second-class hotel. I think that's very good. You know, you can get sort of sick of a second-class hotel and look elsewhere.
                But I think that the denigration of this world implicit in the Christian faith is not what it seems to be in materialist terms. In fact, I would say without any hesitation that it's in realizing that life in this world could be suitably compared to life in a second-class hotel that I suddenly realize how incredibly beautiful and wonderful this life is, because it contains all these extraordinary hints and intimations of what it's related to.
                In other words, the earthly city of St. Augustine is a grubby place, but once you see the City of God, its grubbiness somehow seems much less, much more bearable, because you know that every single thing in it, even the grubbiness, is related to this other City of God.

A biographical note. A year or two later, Malcolm Muggeridge and his wife, Kitty, went to the local church, and joined the Catholic Church.

I suspect that the great force of Muggeridge has much to do with his reputation as a polemical killer. I remember—it was perhaps in the early seventies—that he was brought in as substitute for the principal luncheon speaker at the annual meeting of the American Society of Newspaper Editors. If memory serves, the listed speaker was President Richard Nixon, then embroiled in Watergate. I was away at noon, but that night the editors were aflame from the luncheon experience with Malcolm Muggeridge. And the end of his talk, which I read that evening, announced that his own crowning discovery, in a lifetime's searching, was of the star that shone one night over Bethlehem.

Not the kind of thing you can hope to get away with saying to salty cosmopolites. But to hear it *from* the saltiest cosmopolite in the room, well, if you can imagine Einstein serving as an altar boy . . .

Envoi: I am a younger man than Malcolm Muggeridge (though not by much), and I cannot reasonably aspire to his eloquence or learning. But I feel for him, as for a few other men and women I have known, a sense of gratitude that I have always felt inexplicable, save through language that transcends the vernacular in which favors are recorded, and obligations acknowledged. As a schoolboy in England, all our essays were introduced with the initials A.M.D.G. *(Ad Maiorem Dei Gloriam):* To the greater glory of God. I close this book on the day that *Firing Line* begins its twenty-third season, with the exchanges continuing, and I pray that the considerable effort that went into this volume's production will be seen, by those who care, as a token of the gratitude I feel for the experiences I have had, and the wisdom to which I have been exposed, far beyond my powers fully to absorb, let alone requite. Like Our Lady's juggler, I can proffer only such skills as I have, a working, workaday juggler, in pursuit of a little learning, and of the means by which I can repay that which has come to me.

TWENTIETH-ANNIVERSARY ROAST. FROM THE LEFT: HENRY KISSINGER, EUGENE McCARTHY, HARRIET PILPEL, JOHN KENNETH GALBRAITH, JEFF GREENFIELD, TOM WOLFE

AN ALPHABETICAL LIST OF GUESTS ON FIRING LINE 1966-1988

NAME	TAPING DATE	TOPIC
A		
Abassi, Mahmoud	1/24/72	Inside Israel
Abell, Richard	6/23/79	Young Republicans on '80 Election
Abram, Morris	6/23/82	Odyssey of a Southern Liberal
Abram, Morris	7/20/83	Civil Rights and Affirmative Action
Abrams, Elliott	6/6/84	U.S. Policy and Human Rights
Abrams, Elliott	8/19/87	At Stake in Nicaragua
Abrams, Floyd	1/15/79	Boundaries of the Press
Abrams, Floyd	9/18/87	Re. MacDonald vs. McGinniss
Ackerman, Mike	9/26/85	Three Approaches to Terrorists
Adelman, M. A.	4/11/79	Breaking up OPEC
Adelman, Morris	9/13/73	Energy Crisis and Energy Policy
Adler, Mortimer	1/27/86	Continuing to Learn
Adler, Mortimer	1/27/86	Revising Our Teaching
Adler, Mortimer	10/11/84	Adler's Great Ideas (I)
Adler, Mortimer	10/11/84	Adler's Great Ideas (II)
Adler, Mortimer	10/27/82	The Paideia Proposal
Adler, Mortimer	2/15/80	How to Think About God
Adler, Mortimer	3/1/82	How Are Human Beings Angelic?
Adler, Mortimer	3/13/70	The Idea of *The Great Ideas*
Adler, Mortimer	4/14/83	How to Speak, How to Listen
Adler, Mortimer	4/6/87	Adler on the Constitution (I and II)
Adler, Mortimer	2/25/81	Mortimer Adler and His Great Ideas
Adler, Mortimer	5/8/85	Ten Philosophical Mistakes (I and II)
Adler, Mortimer	5/6/88	Adler and the Closing of the American Mind
Agnew, Spiro T.	12/8/70	The Vice President's Speeches

B

Bennett, John	1/15/70	The My Lai Massacre
Bennett, William J.	1/5/83	Federal Government and Humanities
Bennett, William J.	8/31/83	Re. the Mess in the Schools
Berger, Peter L.	10/1/87	Capitalism Viewed Historically
Berger, Raoul	10/5/77	Government by Judiciary
Berkson, Larry	5/21/79	Merit System for Judges
Berle, Adolph	1/26/70	*Power*
Berman, Ronald	6/3/74	Government and the Arts
Berns, Walter	5/19/69	Cornell and the Conflict of Generations
Bernstein, Carl	7/9/74	Journalistic Investigation
Berry, Mary Frances	1/7/85	Black–Jewish Coalition
Berry, Mary Frances	10/13/83	Debate on Affirmative Action
Bethe, Hans	6/2/69	ABM
Beyea, Jan	5/4/79	Crisis of Nuclear Energy
Biden, Joseph	7/1/87	SPECIAL—Democratic Presidential Candidates
Bierman, Arthur	4/2/70	R.O.T.C.
Bierman, John	3/15/79	Mideast Foreign Correspondents
Bikel, Theodore	6/27/66	Unrest on the Campus
Birch, John	12/3/87	Re. Soviets and Afghanistan
Birns, Laurence	4/25/77	Looking Back on Allende
Birns, Laurence	12/10/81	The Enemy in Central America
Blakely, G. Robert	9/10/81	Does Warren Report Hold Up?
Bleiberg, Robert	4/22/80	Is Big Business Out of Hand?
Bleiberg, Robert	1/7/82	Debate re. the Economy
Bloom, Allan	4/15/87	Higher Education Has Failed Democracy
Bloomfield, George	3/13/70	The New Realism in Movies
Bloomstein, Charles	8/19/87	Re. South Africa
Blount, Winston	9/9/69	Post Office Reform
Blumenthal, Sidney	11/20/86	Rise of Conservative Establishment
Blumer, Dietrich	10/18/73	Psychosurgery/Brain Control
Boles, Alan	6/20/68	Student Unrest—Harvard, Yale, Michigan
Bond, Julian	1/23/74	Politics and Black Progress
Bonilla, Ruben	11/1/85	The Hispanic Rumble
Boorstin, Daniel	1/6/70	Dissent and Society
Borges, Jorge Luis	2/1/77	Borges: South America's Titan
Bork, Robert	1/3/80	Is the Supreme Court Out of Hand?
Bork, Robert	5/11/81	Can Congress Create People?
Bork, Robert	7/10/85	The Trouble with Lawyers
Boutelle, Paul	7/10/68	The Old Left
Bovard, James	2/26/85	Are We Coddling the Farmers?
Boyson, Rhodes	2/13/79	Three MP's Question WFB
Bradley, Thomas	7/24/73	What Now for the Ghetto?
Braestrup, Peter	3/16/78	How the U.S. Press Handled Tet

Braine, John	5/9/70	The Road Back
Braley, Russ	11/13/84	Bias in the Press
Breilenfeld, Frederick	11/13/79	Whither TV?
Brennan, Dr. Donald	6/2/69	ABM
Breslin, Jimmy	11/26/75	Problems of New York City
Brickner, Balfour	1/7/85	Black–Jewish Coalition
Brito, J. T. Gonzales	10/1/87	Young Latin Americans
Broder, David	7/6/68	The Washington Press
Brookhiser, Richard	10/29/87	Debates and Politics
Brookhiser, Richard	7/10/85	A Look Back at Watergate
Brookhiser, Richard	10/5/82	Debate Re. Education
Brookhiser, Richard	6/20/84	Ahead for the Democrats? (I)
Brookhiser, Richard	6/20/84	Ahead for the Democrats? (II)
Brophy, Brigid	7/24/69	Is There a Place for the Old Order?
Brown, Edmund G.	12/9/69	The Future of the Democratic Party
Brown, Edmund G.	10/3/75	Limits of Liberalism
Brown, John Y.	11/20/81	The Mountain States' View of Washington
Brown, Michael	1/14/74	WFB Defends *Four Reforms*
Browne, Harry	9/3/70	How Does It Look for the Dollar?
Browne, Noel	2/12/74	Irish Socialism
Brudnoy, David	6/2/69	Black Studies
Bryant, Thomas	12/21/72	Marijuana Laws
Brzezinski, Zbigniew	3/31/83	Re. the Carter Years
Brzezinski, Zbigniew	7/23/86	On U.S. Strategy
Brzezinski, Zbigniew	9/23/68	The Cold War
Brzezinski, Zbigniew	10/8/70	America's Role in Technetronic Era
Brzezinski, Zbigniew	9/9/76	Foreign Policy: Democratic Dissent (II)
Buchanan, Patrick	8/15/75	The Third Party
Buchanan, Patrick	12/20/73	Views of a Nixonite
Buchanan, Patrick	4/28/69	Problems of a Chief Executive
Buchanan, Patrick	5/18/77	Nixon Revisited
Buchanan, Patrick	5/22/80	Who Should Reagan Pick as VP?
Bucher, Lloyd	9/10/70	The *Pueblo* Story
Buckley, James L.	1/2/79	Conservative Panel
Buckley, James L.	9/15/83	On Radio Free Europe
Buckley, James L.	9/4/74	Nixon and U.S. Conservatives
Buckley, James L.	7/15/71	Re. Conservative Legislators
Buckley, James L.	1/5/72	SPECIAL—Conservatives Confront 1972
Buckley, John	7/21/80	Re. Gun Control
Bugliosi, Vincent	10/3/75	The Manson Case
Bukovsky, Vladimir	7/25/77	Human Rights and the U.S.S.R.
Bundy, McGeorge	7/20/83	Sakharov and the Freeze Movement
Bundy, William	6/15/77	Council on Foreign Relations
Bundy, William	2/25/81	Reagan's Foreign Policy

C

Carter, Hodding	9/20/76	The Claims of Jimmy Carter
Carter, Hodding	4/15/68	Robert F. Kennedy
Carter, Hodding	12/12/72	The Civil Rights Law
Carter, Jimmy	4/23/73	Proposals for Welfare
Carver, George	5/31/85	Yale: Class of 1950
Castillo, Leonel	1/15/79	The Problem of Illegal Aliens
Caute, David	6/26/78	The 1950s Communist Purge
Chace, James	6/12/81	Debate on American Security
Chafee, John	9/15/66	Do Liberals Make Good Republicans?
Chalfont, Lord	3/8/77	Disarmament and Jimmy Carter
Champlin, Joseph	4/22/80	The Catholic Controversy
Chang, Parris	11/4/76	What's Going on in China?
Chapin, Schuyler	7/17/85	Re. Musical Performances
Chapman, Guillermo	9/30/76	Panama Canal Problems
Charney, Maurice	12/11/84	Re. William Shakespeare
Chase, James	6/12/81	Debate on American Security
Chavez, Linda	7/20/83	Civil Rights and Affirmative Action
Cheney, Lynne	9/18/87	Problems in Our High Schools
Cherne, Leo	1/19/68	Army–McCarthy Hearings (I and II)
Cherne, Leo	1/6/71	Amnesty and Counterrevolution
Cherne, Leo	12/3/87	Re. Soviets and Afghanistan
Cherne, Leo	5/16/66	McCarthyism
Cherne, Leo	7/20/78	Cambodia and the Refugee Problem
Cheshire, William	4/2/70	*National Review*
Chettle, John	4/1/85	The Challenge of South Africa
Cheveille, Richard	9/30/76	Panama Canal Problems
Chevigny, Paul	2/2/69	Police Power
Chevrillon, Oliver	2/24/84	Re. French–U.S. Relations
Ching-Kuo, Chiang	11/15/77	Taiwan
Chirac, Jacques	2/23/84	Conservative Dissent in France
Chomsky, Noam	4/3/69	Vietnam and the Intellectuals
Church, Frank	7/9/72	The SALT Agreements
Clark, Colin	6/23/69	The Population Explosion
Clark, Eugene	11/20/86	The Catholic Controversy
Clark, Joseph	5/15/67	The Poverty Problem
Clark, Kenneth	8/28/67	The Ghetto
Clark, Ramsey	6/3/74	Amnesty
Clark, Robert	5/16/73	Correspondents Question WFB
Clay, Cassius	12/12/68	Muhammad Ali and the Negro Movement
Cleaver, Eldridge	11/13/68	The Black Panthers
Cleaver, Eldridge	1/14/77	Education of Eldridge Cleaver
Clements, Richard	3/9/76	WFB on an English Firing Line
Cleveland, Harlan	12/6/69	Vietnam
Cline, Ray S.	1/18/79	Recognition of China
Cline, William	1/24/83	Do Banks Know What They're Doing?

Cloud, Stan	1/18/72	Vietnam—Looking Back
Clurman, Richard	11/3/83	Was It Censorship in Grenada?
Clurman, Richard	12/11/86	Re. Reagan—Damage from Iranscam
Cobb, James	11/11/82	Is the South Changing?
Coffin, William Sloane	12/10/87	Morality and Disarmament
Coffin, William Sloane	6/27/66	Role of the Church Militant
Coffin, William Sloane	12/9/80	Time for Civil Defense?
Cohalan, Florence	2/22/83	Confidentiality and Betrayal
Cohen, Bernard	5/4/79	Crisis of Nuclear Energy
Cohen, Jerome	1/18/79	Recognition of China
Cohen, Samuel T.	4/24/78	The Neutron Bomb
Cohen, Wilbur J.	9/25/67	Medicare
Cohn, Roy	9/20/76	Subversion and the Law
Cohn, Roy	1/19/68	Army–McCarthy Hearings (I and II)
Coleman, Kate	1/14/74	WFB Defends *Four Reforms*
Colson, Charles	1/18/84	The Prison Problem
Colson, Charles	4/15/82	Where to Go on Prison Reform
Commoner, Barry	5/1/73	The Environment
Conant, James	4/23/70	*My Several Lives*
Connally, John	1/8/76	Are Major Parties Stalemated?
Conquest, Robert	2/8/72	Genocide
Conquest, Robert	9/4/86	SPECIAL—*Harvest of Despair*
Conrad, Alfred	2/25/69	Restructuring the University
Conrad, Barnaby	12/12/68	The Uses of Animals
Conrad, John P.	9/29/83	Re. Capital Punishment
Conway, Jill	11/23/76	Future of the Private College
Conyers, John	10/7/69	Race and Conservatism
Cooke, Alistair	11/4/68	Influence of TV on American Politics
Cope, Karin	5/31/85	Yale: Class of 1985
Copeland, Miles	3/9/76	What Is Their CIA Up To?
Corddry, Charles	1/11/78	Journalists Question WFB
Costello, John	1/23/76	The Concorde Conspiracy
Coughlin, Thomas A.	1/18/84	The Prison Problem
Courter, James	10/19/87	Drive for Disarmament
Courter, James	2/23/87	Re. Arms Control
Courtney, C. C.	11/4/69	Salvation, Rock Music and the New Iconoclasm
Courtright, Steven	11/16/71	Eighteen-Year-Old Vote
Cousins, Norman	7/30/73	World Federalism
Cox, Robert	2/1/77	Terrorism in Latin America
Coxe, Donald	1/9/86	Is Canada's Mulroney a Disappointment?
Coyne, John	2/26/69	Black Student Power—Five Campuses
Crane, Philip	1/3/80	Presidential Hopeful

Cranston, Alan	7/13/81	Plight of the Democratic Party
Crosby, Emeral	9/18/80	Crisis in Education
Crossman, Richard	10/21/70	In Defense of Practical Socialism
Crozier, Brian	3/8/77	Disarmament and Jimmy Carter
Cuddihy, John M.	12/2/74	Jews in American Politics
Curran, Charles E.	11/20/86	The Catholic Controversy
Cutler, Lloyd N.	7/27/87	The Bork Controversy

D

Dalai Lama	9/27/84	The Dalai Lama Looks Back
Daly, Mary	6/24/68	The Rib Uncaged: Women and the Church
Davidson, James	1/13/87	Conservatives and Reagan's State of Union
Davidson, James	2/24/81	WFB Faces the Firing Line
Davidson, James	3/24/86	Preliminary Talk About 1988
Davidson, James	1/24/83	Do Banks Know What They're Doing
Davidson, James	2/24/81	Reagan's Economic Policy
Davidson, James	6/15/82	A Budget Balancing Amendment?
Davidson, James	3/31/80	Government by Plebiscite?
Davidson, James	4/11/79	Constitutional Convention for Balanced Budget?
Davies, Michael	4/22/80	The Catholic Controversy
Davis, Lanny J.	11/8/74	Election Rhetoric—1974
de Antonio, Emile	1/19/68	Army–McCarthy Hearings (I and II)
de Borchgrave, Arnaud	1/13/86	Who to Back in Angola
de Borchgrave, Arnaud	12/11/86	Re. Reagan—Damage from Iranscam
de Borchgrave, Arnaud	5/9/80	Soviet Disinformation
de Borchgrave, Arnaud	6/9/83	Inside the KGB
de Borchgrave, Arnaud	6/17/81	Angola and Southern Africa
de Hoz, Martinez	1/31/77	Argentina After Perón
de Kemoularia, Claude	5/30/86	Terrorism: Viewed from Abroad
de Onis, Juan	2/1/77	Terrorism in Latin America
de Toledano, Ralph	1/27/69	Unfinished Odyssey of Robert Kennedy
Decter, Midge	11/13/84	Bias in the Press
Dellinger, David	4/25/68	The New Left
Dellums, Ronald	6/15/71	The Black Caucus
Denton, Jeremiah	6/5/81	What to Do About Terrorism
Deressa, Dereje	2/14/80	Ethiopia
Derian, Patricia	1/22/81	Human Rights and Foreign Policy
Dershowitz, Alan	12/2/85	AIDS—Patient Rights/Public Rights
Dershowitz, Alan	4/12/76	The Hearst Trial

Dershowitz, Alan	7/20/78	What Rights Do Nazis Have?
Dershowitz, Alan	7/9/86	Re. Jailing Murderers
Dershowitz, Alan	12/13/76	*Deep Throat* and First Amendment
De Sapio, Carmine	5/1/67	The Regular in Politics
Devlin, Bernadette	3/25/72	The Irish Problem
Diamond, Larry	11/16/71	Eighteen-Year-Old Vote
Dickey, James	11/30/82	Debate Re. Women vs. Men
Dickey, James	4/22/71	What's Happened to American Spirit?
Dodd, Thomas	7/15/66	Senator Dodd and General Klein
Doi, Nelson	11/21/77	Asian Policy: From Hawaii
Dole, Robert	10/28/87	SPECIAL—GOP Presidential Candidates
Dole, Robert	6/15/79	Presidential Hopeful
Dole, Robert	3/28/77	The Future of the GOP
Donoghue, Denis	7/22/69	The Irish Problem
Dornan, Robert	10/28/85	The Crisis in Congress
Douglas-Home, Alec	9/28/73	The Security of Europe
Dow, Steven	5/31/85	Yale: Class of 1985
Down, A. Graham	4/14/83	How to Read, How to Figure
Down, A. Graham	9/18/80	Crisis in Education
Draskovich, Slobodan M.	1/8/68	The John Birch Society
DuBois, Larry	4/2/70	*National Review*
Dubos, Rene	1/7/71	Ecology
DuBrul, Paul	8/29/77	Abuse of Power
Duffey, Joseph D.	12/12/78	Federal Aid to the Humanities?
Dugger, Ronnie	1/23/73	Texas Politics
Dugger, Ronnie	5/4/82	Looking Back on LBJ
Duignan, Peter	1/17/80	U.S. in the Eighties: Foreign Policy
Dukakis, Michael	11/23/76	Problems of Massachusetts
Dukakis, Michael	7/1/87	SPECIAL—Democratic Presidential Candidates
Dulles, Allen	12/14/67	Is There a Need for Intelligence?
du Pont, Pete	1/23/87	Why I Should Be President
du Pont, Pete	10/28/87	SPECIAL—GOP Presidential Candidates
Dworkin, Andrea	2/25/85	Women Against Pornography
Dyk, Timothy B.	10/10/86	Tennessee Textbook Controversy
Dystel, Oscar	5/22/80	Controversy over Book Awards

E

Eagleburger, Lawrence	2/23/87	Pull Out of NATO?
Eagleburger, Lawrence	7/31/85	Diplomats: Polite or Truthful?
Eban, Abba	9/28/70	The Middle East

Eberstadt, Fernanda	7/17/85	Re. Young Novelists
Edwards, Harry	7/12/84	Re. The Olympics
Edwards, James	4/11/75	Wallace and the GOP
Efron, Edith	9/1/71	The News Twisters
Elegant, Robert S.	9/26/77	Normalization
Ellis, Bret Easton	7/17/85	Re. Young Novelists
Ellsberg, Daniel	7/25/72	The Pentagon Papers
Ennis, Bruce	1/3/80	Is the Supreme Court Out of Hand?
Ervin, Sam	4/17/78	The Aftermath of Watergate
Etzioni, Amitai	9/29/83	Should America Be Bilingual?
Etzioni, Amitai	5/9/84	Re. Federal Election Campaign Act
Evans, Roger	6/27/78	*Firing Line*'s British Correspondents
Evans, Roger	2/8/72	Inquiry into American Conservatism
Evans, Rowland, Jr.	10/3/66	LBJ: The Exercise of Power
Evans, Rowland, Jr.	11/22/71	Nixon in the White House
Evans, M. Stanton	8/15/75	The Third Party

F

Fairbank, John K.	4/2/82	Relations with Mainland China
Falwell, Jerry	1/22/81	Menaced by the Moral Majority?
Farenthold, Frances	1/23/73	Texas Politics
Farmer, James	4/18/66	Non-Violence
Farris, Michael	10/10/86	Tennessee Textbook Controversy
Faud, Kim	10/4/76	Venezuela and the U.S.
Faulk, John Henry	4/21/66	HUAC
Fein, Leonard	7/21/80	Is Camp David Falling Apart?
Felder, John	2/26/69	Black Student Power—Five Campuses
Feldstein, Martin	5/6/76	Unemployment
Fellman, David	9/10/70	Supreme Court/Rule of Law/Academic Freedom
Felt, W. Mark	9/20/76	Subversion and the Law
Ferris, Charles	12/13/79	The Changing Media
Ferris, William R.	11/11/82	Is the South Changing?
Festinger, Leon	10/16/73	Mechanism of Moral Development
Fiedler, Leslie	11/15/74	Democratic Culture
Finch, Robert	5/5/72	Electoral Reform
Findlay, Paul	7/13/81	Mr. Begin's Preemptive Strike
Fine, Max	6/10/74	National Health Insurance
Fischer, Lee A.	3/31/88	Will Doctors Have to Go Out of Business?
Fitzgerald, Frances	5/22/80	Controversy over Book Awards
Fitzgibbon, Constantine	7/22/69	Decline of Anti-Communism
Fitzgibbon, Constantine	1/14/77	Re. Secret Intelligence

Fontaine, André	10/27/72	U.S. Election Viewed from Abroad
Foot, Michael	10/7/67	Is Socialism the Answer?
Foot, Michael	8/20/73	Democracy and Political Scandals
Forbes, Malcolm	1/7/88	Do Capitalists Go Too Far?
Ford, Gerald R.	6/28/74	Problems of a Vice President
Ford, Gerald R.	7/8/68	What the Republican Party Has to Offer
Fort, Joel	10/3/72	Sex Education
Fort, Joel	4/12/76	Implications of the Hearst Trial
Fossedal, Gregory	4/25/85	Debate re. SDI
Fox, Muriel	11/30/82	Debate re. Women vs. Men
Fraga, Manuel Iribarne	2/23/76	The Future of Spain
Frank, Victor	11/12/85	What About Corporate Profits?
Frankel, Charles	1/15/70	The My Lai Massacre
Frankel, Marvin E.	6/25/86	Clemency, Parole and Sentencing
Fraser, Malcolm	10/25/78	Australia
Frederick, Pauline	9/4/74	WFB as UN Delegate
Freeman, Erika	11/30/82	Debate re. Women vs. Men
Friedan, Betty	1/11/71	Women's Lib
Friedman, Milton	1/8/68	The Economic Crisis
Friedman, Milton	4/10/86	Debate re. Privatization (I and II)
Friedman, Milton	1/5/72	SPECIAL—Conservatives Confront 1972
Friendly, Fred	10/5/82	Debate re. Education
Friendly, Fred	5/15/81	The Press and the Law
Friendly, Fred	7/8/76	The Fairness Doctrine
Fritchey, Clayton	3/8/67	U.S. Policy in Southeast Asia
Froomkin, Daniel	5/31/85	Yale: Class of 1985
Frost, David	3/11/70	English and American Audiences
Fuerbringer, Otto	5/28/68	Journals of News and Opinions
Fuldheim, Dorothy	6/29/79	The Television Machine
Fumento, Michael	3/31/88	Scare Tactics and AIDS
Futrell, Mary	8/31/83	Re. the Mess in the Schools

G

Gabler, Mel	1/11/82	Local Control of Reading Material
Gabler, Norma	1/11/82	Local Control of Reading Material
Galamison, Milton	2/25/69	Black Anti-Semitism
Galbraith, Evan	10/27/72	The Free Market and America
Galbraith, Evan	12/9/68	The American Challenge
Galbraith, Evan	2/24/84	Re. French–U.S. Relations
Galbraith, Evan	5/31/85	Yale: Class of 1950
Galbraith, Evan	7/31/85	Diplomats: Polite or Truthful?
Galbraith, James	7/9/72	The McGovern Phenomenon
Galbraith, John Kenneth	6/5/81	John Kenneth Galbraith Looks Back

Galbraith, John Kenneth	1/7/82	Debate re. Economy
Galbraith, John Kenneth	12/18/69	The Kennedy Years
Galbraith, John Kenneth	3/30/78	Debate re. Oil/Gas Prices
Galbraith, John Kenneth	7/15/76	Re. the Democratic Convention
Galbraith, John Kenneth	7/9/72	The McGovern Phenomenon
Galbraith, Peter	7/9/72	The McGovern Phenomenon
Galebach, Stephen	5/11/81	Can Congress Create People?
Garcia, Gilbert	5/31/85	Yale: Class of 1985
Gardner, Richard	3/2/82	Is Italy Falling Apart?
Garment, Leonard	7/17/80	The Republican Vice-Presidency
Garreau, Joel	10/15/81	Myth of American Homogeneity
Garry, Charles	4/10/70	Order and the Law
Gaspari, Elio	10/5/80	What's Happening in Brazil?
Gephardt, Richard	7/1/87	SPECIAL—Democratic Presidential Candidates
Gerber, Dave	11/16/71	Eighteen-Year-Old Vote
Germino, Dante	4/2/70	R.O.T.C.
Geyelin, Philip	1/11/78	Journalists Question WFB
Geyer, Georgie Anne	4/25/77	Looking Back on Allende
Geyer, Georgie Anne	10/8/70	Chile and the Future of South America
Giamatti, A. Bartlett	10/5/82	Debate re. Education
Giamatti, A. Bartlett	10/30/79	Re. Private Colleges
Gibson, Christopher	5/8/70	English Youth
Gilder, George	1/5/81	Fresh Views on Capitalism
Gilkey, Langdon	9/27/84	Christianity and Other Faiths
Gingrich, Newt	12/6/84	Where Is the GOP Headed?
Ginsberg, Allen	5/7/68	The Avant-Garde
Giscard d'Estaing, Valéry	10/27/72	Free Market and America
Glasser, Ira	3/24/86	Let's Legalize Those Drugs
Glasser, Ira	2/29/88	Should We Legalize Drugs?
Glazer, Nathan	10/3/72	The Jewish Vote
Glazer, Nathan	1/7/85	Black–Jewish Coalition
Gold, Victor	12/13/83	Re. *The Day After* (ABC-TV)
Golden, Harry	5/23/66	States Rights
Goldman, Eric	1/13/69	The Tragedy of Lyndon Johnson
Goldschmidt, Neil	5/15/80	U.S. Transportation Policy
Goldwater, Barry	6/9/66	Future of Conservatism
Goldwater, Barry	9/9/69	Where Should the Nixon Administration Go?
Goodell, Charles E.	9/23/68	Problems of Freshman Senators
Goodman, Paul	9/12/66	Public School Education
Goodpastor, Andrew	9/6/78	Military Morale Crisis
Goodwin, Richard	5/6/66	The Great Society
Gordey, Michel	10/27/72	U.S. Election Viewed from Abroad
Gore, Albert	4/28/69	The ABM Conflict
Gore, Albert	6/9/66	Public Power vs. Private Power

Gore, Albert, Jr.	7/1/87	SPECIAL—Democratic Presidential Candidates
Gotbaum, Victor H.	6/15/71	Strikes in Defiance of Law?
Gottfried, Kurt	10/3/85	Reflections on Star Wars (I and II)
Gottfried, Richard	6/15/77	Marijuana and New York State
Grace, J. Peter	9/6/84	How to Reduce the Deficit
Graffe, William	11/14/75	The Right to Die
Graham, Billy	6/12/69	The Decline of Christianity
Graham, Daniel O.	7/26/82	A Defense Beyond ABM?
Graham, Daniel O.	4/25/85	Debate re. SDI
Graham, Hugh Davis	6/23/69	Violence in America
Graham, William	7/26/82	A Defense Beyond ABM?
Greeley, Andrew	6/8/79	Modern Role of Catholic Church
Green, Bill	12/6/84	Where Is the GOP Headed?
Green, Mark	1/24/83	WFB's Turn to Explain Himself
Green, Mark	7/7/82	Young Liberal vs. Young Conservative
Green, Mark	11/12/81	WFB on the Firing Line
Green, Mark	11/12/85	What About Corporate Profits?
Green, Mark	2/24/87	WFB on the Firing Line
Green, Mark	4/22/80	Is Big Business Out of Hand?
Green, Mark	6/20/84	Ahead for the Democrats? (I)
Green, Mark	6/20/84	Ahead for the Democrats? (II)
Green, Mark	7/31/85	Three Against One (WFB Questioned)
Green, Mark	7/7/83	Re. Future of Democrats
Green, Mark	9/18/84	Politics American Style
Green, Mark	12/30/87	How Do Conservatives View 1988?
Green, Ronald M.	3/30/81	How Much Loyalty to the Boss?
Greenberg, Jack	10/13/83	Debate on Affirmative Action
Greenfield, Jeff	12/13/79	That Was the Year That Was
Greenfield, Jeff	2/24/87	WFB on the Firing Line
Greenfield, Jeff	2/25/85	What Should We Be Worrying About?
Greenfield, Jeff	3/3/71	Some Reflections on TV Programming
Greenfield, Jeff	5/15/72	A Populist Manifesto
Greenfield, Jeff	7/7/83	Re. Future of Democrats
Greenway, H.D.S.	5/29/85	The Fall of Saigon
Greenway, John	12/21/72	Marijuana Laws
Greer, Germaine	2/27/73	Women's Liberation Movement
Gregory, Dick	5/16/66	Civil Disobedience
Grenier, Richard	6/9/83	Was Gandhi for Real?
Grinspoon, Lester	6/30/71	Marijuana Reconsidered
Gross, Martin	5/13/78	*The Psychological Society*
Gross, Richard	3/15/79	Mideast Foreign Correspondents
Grossman, Allen	2/25/69	Restructuring the University

Guggenheim, Martin	12/1/83	Children and the Law
Gurr, Ted Robert	6/23/69	Violence in America
Guttmacher, Alan	10/24/69	Abortion

H

Hadley, Arthur T.	7/23/86	Problems with America's Military
Haig, Alexander	10/28/87	SPECIAL—GOP Presidential Candidates
Haig, Alexander	5/29/84	General Haig Looks Back
Haig, Alexander	6/24/87	What Makes Al Haig Run?
Haig, Alexander	2/12/79	NATO and European Security
Halberstam, David	12/1/86	Has America Lost Industrial Know-how?
Halberstam, David	1/27/69	Unfinished Odyssey of Robert Kennedy
Halbert, John	6/12/81	El Salvador/Christianity/Marxism
Halleck, Seymour	12/1/83	Psychiatrists and Criminal Law
Halpernin, Morton	7/22/75	Public's Right to Know
Halstead, Fred	7/10/68	The Old Left
Hamilton, Willie	3/10/76	Re. British Royalty
Harrington, Donald	2/24/81	WFB Faces the Firing Line
Harrington, Michael	11/13/84	Re. Poverty in America
Harrington, Michael	4/4/66	Poverty: Hopeful or Hopeless
Harrington, Michael	10/13/77	Debate re. Public Sector Growth
Harrington, Michael	3/3/71	AFTRA: Compulsory Unionism and Civil Liberties
Harris, Albert	7/22/74	George Jackson
Harris, Fred	9/14/71	The Politics of Fred Harris
Harris, Richard	1/3/77	*Freedom Spent*
Harroff, Mark	6/16/72	Nixon and Young Conservatives
Hart, Gary	3/28/77	Break Up the Oil Companies?
Hart, Jeffrey	2/25/69	Restructuring the University
Hart, Jeffrey	5/4/87	Uses of the Past
Hart, Jeffrey	7/26/82	Have We Misread the Fifties?
Hartke, Vance	3/6/67	LBJ and Vietnam
Harvey, William	3/31/83	Reagan and Legal Services
Hatch, Orrin	1/2/79	Conservative Panel
Hatfield, Mark	12/14/67	Was Goldwater a Mistake?
Hawke, Robert	2/7/86	*Firing Line* '66–'86 World Leaders
Hawke, Robert	10/25/78	Australia
Hawley, Willis	11/20/81	How Stands It with Busing?
Healey, Denis	6/26/78	The Sinking Dollar
Heard, Alexander	11/11/82	Views on the Election
Heath, Edward	9/10/74	England at the Brink
Heckler, Margaret	2/21/86	*Firing Line* '66–'86 Persuaders

Heckler, Margaret	7/17/80	GOP Platform and ERA
Heffernan, John J.	2/2/69	Police Power
Hefner, Hugh	9/27/66	The Playboy Philosophy
Heifetz, Milton	11/14/75	The Right to Die
Heilbroner, Robert	2/24/81	Reagan's Economic Policy
Heilbroner, Robert	6/15/82	A Budget Balancing Amendment?
Heller, Walter	9/9/75	The Economic Mess
Helms, Jesse	7/7/82	Voting Rights and the Southern Legacy
Henry, Milton	11/18/68	The Republic of New Africa
Hentoff, Margot	3/31/75	Abortion
Hentoff, Nat	3/7/67	Black Power
Hentoff, Nat	7/8/76	Journalists Question WFB
Hentoff, Nat	7/30/86	WFB on the Firing Line
Heren, Louis	8/22/73	WFB Questioned About America
Herendeen, Warren	1/18/84	No Title
Herman, Dick	4/18/84	Prospects for Democrats
Herrnstein, Richard	10/16/73	Heredity/I.Q./Social Issues
Hersh, Seymour	7/7/71	War Crimes
Hersh, Seymour	1/14/77	Re. Secret Intelligence
Hesburgh, Theodore	1/6/84	Crisis in Catholic Church?
Hesburgh, Theodore	12/12/74	Christian Conference/Food
Hess, Karl	1/6/71	The Karl Hess Phenomenon
Hess, Wolf	5/8/70	The Hess Story
Hewitt, Tim	10/25/78	Australian Journalists and WFB
Hickel, Walter J.	11/16/71	*Who Owns America?*
Hill, Robert	1/31/77	Should the U.S. Pressure Argentina?
Hines, Cragg	10/29/87	Day After GOP Debate
Hirsh, Joseph	5/15/72	Alcoholism
Hitchcock, James	1/10/77	The Latin Liturgy
Hitchens, Christopher	12/11/84	The Liberal Crack-up
Hitchens, Christopher	9/4/86	SPECIAL—*Harvest of Despair*
Hoffa, James	9/22/72	Jimmy Hoffa
Holbrooke, Richard	1/18/82	How to Deal with Taiwan
Holbrooke, Richard	3/25/87	The Role of South Korea
Hollander, Paul	12/3/81	Why Are Intellectuals Dumb?
Hollings, Ernest	9/20/79	SALT II and the U.S. Senate
Hollings, Ernest	4/23/73	Re. the Post Office
Honig, Bill	4/10/86	Debate re. Privatization (I and II)
Hook, Sidney	6/1/87	Hook Evaluates Liberalism
Hook, Sidney	3/9/67	What to Fear from Socialism?
Horne, Alistair	4/17/78	Algeria: A Savage War of Peace
Houser, George	11/4/68	Is South Africa Everybody's Business?
Howard, Anthony	3/9/76	WFB on an English Firing Line
Howard, Anthony	8/22/73	WFB Questioned About America
Huddleston, Trevor	9/15/86	British Views on South Africa

Hukari, Harvey	12/9/69	Why Don't Conservatives Understand?
Hukari, Harvey	6/16/72	Nixon and Young Conservatives
Hume, John	2/12/74	The Irish Problem—1974
Humphrey, Hubert	5/24/73	Limitations of Presidential Power
Hunt, E. Howard	1/18/73	The CIA and U.S. Foreign Policy
Hunt, E. Howard	5/20/74	Hush Money
Hunt, Guy	3/25/87	Republicanize the South?
Hunter, David R.	4/29/82	Future of Philanthropy
Hutchinson, John	11/7/85	*Cry, the Beloved Country*
Hutchinson, Kay Bailie	11/10/83	Re. Texas
Huxley, Elspeth	10/20/70	Africa and Colonialism
Huxtable, Ada Louise	11/2/71	Good Buildings Being Built?
Hyde, Henry	10/28/85	Problems in the Philippines
Hyde, Henry	10/5/77	Abortion and the Law
Hyland, William	5/4/87	Re. the Moscow Talks
Hyland, William	7/8/87	Sovietology
Hyland, William	1/7/88	Coming Up: The INF Hearings

I

Ikle, Fred C.	8/6/75	Disarmament
Innis, Roy	4/3/69	Separate Development
Irvin, Morenike	5/31/85	Yale: Class of 1985
Isaacs, Stephen	12/2/74	Jews in American Politics

J

Jackson, Henry	5/29/75	Détente
Jackson, Henry	7/9/72	The SALT Agreements
Jackson, Jesse	7/1/87	SPECIAL—Democratic Presidential Candidates
Jackson, Jesse	7/12/82	Reagan and Blacks
Jackson, Jesse	11/28/79	Debate on PLO
Jackson, Jesse	10/2/71	Is America Hospitable to Negroes?
Jacobs, Jo	11/28/79	Re. HEW and Colleges (Title IX)
Jacobs, Paul	4/10/70	The Uses of Radicalism
Janeway, Eliot	9/3/70	How Does It Look for the Dollar?
Janitschek, Hans	3/8/77	How Much Liberty?
Jastrow, Robert	10/3/85	Reflections on Star Wars (I and II)
Javits, Jacob	10/24/69	Conservatism vs. Progressive Republicanism
Jenkins, Brian	9/26/85	Three Approaches to Terrorists
Jenkins, Clive	10/7/67	The Union in Modern Society

Jenkins, Peter	4/28/75	U.S. Prestige in Europe
Jenkins, Roy	7/3/72	*Afternoon on the Potomac*
Jenrette, Levitas	11/15/74	Post-Election South
Jimenez-Leal, Orlando	6/13/84	The Real Cuba (I)
Johnson, Gerry	2/27/68	English Youth and Vietnam
Johnson, Nicholas	1/26/70	Broadcasting and the Public
Johnson, Paul	2/22/84	The World View of Paul Johnson
Johnson, Paul	9/15/86	British Views on South Africa
Jordan, Hamilton	11/4/82	Re. the Hostage Crisis
Jordan, June	8/26/76	Censorship in Libraries
Jordan, Vernon	11/7/77	Has President Carter Let Down Blacks?
Jordan, Vernon	1/8/75	Future Direction of Equality
Jorge, Antonio	3/26/80	What to Do About Cuba
Joseph, Keith	2/12/79	Reason and Politics
Joseph, Keith	9/4/80	How to Unscramble an Egg
Judd, Walter	1/18/82	How to Deal with Taiwan

K

Kahn, Alfred	1/7/85	Deregulation: Good or Bad?
Kahn, Alfred	10/13/80	Carter Administration and Inflation
Kahn, Alfred	8/22/78	Federal Regulation and Travel Explosion
Kahn, Herman	5/7/68	Can We Win in Vietnam?
Kaiser, Robert	1/8/76	The Russians
Kaiser, Robert	6/6/84	The Russians and Reagan
Kalangula, Peter T.	7/17/81	Question of Namibia
Kaplan, John	9/3/70	Marijuana and the Law
Kassebaum, Nancy	4/19/84	Budget Deficit and the GOP
Kastle, Leonard	3/13/70	The New Realism in Movies
Katz, Samuel	3/16/79	Peace in the Middle East?
Kaufman, Ben	1/3/77	The Moon Movement
Kaufman, Murray the K	11/14/66	Re. American Teenagers
Kavanagh, Michael	6/25/86	McGivern, Cuomo—Politics of Crime
Kearns, Doris	5/14/76	The Intimate Lyndon Johnson
Keiser, Robert	8/15/80	Re. the Democratic Convention
Kelly, J. B.	9/5/80	Arabia, the Gulf and the West
Kelman, Steven	6/9/70	The Escalation of Student Power
Kemp, Jack	1/2/79	Conservative Panel
Kemp, Jack	10/28/87	SPECIAL—GOP Presidential Candidates
Kemp, Jack	11/15/84	Reagan's Economic Program
Kemp, Jack	4/24/78	The Tax Mess
Kempton, Murray	6/20/84	Ahead for the Democrats? (I)

Kempton, Murray	6/20/84	Ahead for the Democrats? (II)
Kempton, Murray	6/6/66	Robert F. Kennedy
Kempton, Murray	7/9/74	Leadership in America
Kendall, Henry	10/3/85	Reflections on Star Wars (I and II)
Kenner, Hugh	6/26/74	Political Responsibility of Artists
Kerouac, Jack	9/3/68	The Hippies
Kerrey, Robert	4/18/84	Re. Middle America
Kerry, John	11/2/71	Re. Treaties in International Affairs
Keyes, Alan L.	8/19/87	Re. South Africa
Keyworth, George	4/25/85	Debate re. SDI
Keyworth, George	5/29/84	The High Frontier Concept
Kheel, Theodore	10/7/66	Civilian Review Board: Yes or No?
Kilpatrick, James J.	7/21/82	A Prayer Amendment?
Kinnock, Neil	2/13/79	Three MP's Question WFB
Kinnock, Neil	2/21/84	Re. Socialists in England
Kinnock, Neil	2/4/75	Three MP's Against WFB
Kinsley, Michael	1/13/86	What's Wrong with Political Parties?
Kinsley, Michael	1/24/83	WFB's Turn to Explain Himself
Kinsley, Michael	1/5/83	Nuclear Hysteria
Kinsley, Michael	7/31/85	Three Against One (WFB Questioned)
Kinsley, Michael	9/3/85	Do We Have a Foreign Policy?
Kinsley, Michael	12/30/87	How Do Conservatives View 1988?
Kirkpatrick, Jeane	1/28/85	Can an American Dominate the UN?
Kirkpatrick, Jeane	10/14/87	New Republican Looks at the Party
Kirkpatrick, Jeane	5/11/81	What Can Be Done with the UN?
Kissinger, Henry	1/13/87	Afterthoughts on Reykjavik
Kissinger, Henry	7/15/82	Statesmen Writing About History
Kissinger, Henry	8/31/84	Is Bipartisanism Dead?
Kissinger, Henry	9/10/75	Politics of Henry Kissinger
Klein, Alexander	6/9/70	The Escalation of Student Power
Klein, Herbert	1/6/70	Agnew and the Media
Kleindienst, Richard	7/10/85	A Look Back at Watergate
Kleindienst, Richard	9/3/70	Marijuana and the Law
Kliment, Nicholas M.	2/26/85	Role of Song at School (Whiffenpoofs)
Knight, Andrew	2/21/84	How Is Mrs. Thatcher Doing?
Knight, Andrew	3/9/76	WFB on an English Firing Line
Knight, Andrew	4/28/75	The Economic Quandary
Knight, Andrew	9/15/86	What's Wrong with the U.S.?
Knight, Hans	12/6/71	The Edgar Smith Story (II)
Kobin, William	11/13/79	Whither TV?
Koch, Edward I.	10/16/86	The Drug Problem
Koch, Edward I.	10/30/79	Can New York City Govern Itself?
Koch, Edward I.	10/7/69	Race and Conservatism

Koch, Edward I.	5/4/82	What's Left of the Idea of Federalism?
Koch, Edward I.	8/31/84	New York's View of the Election
Koch, Edward I.	8/31/83	Plight of Democratic Moderates
Koch, Edward I.	4/28/88	Problems of Mayor Koch, Democrat
Kollek, Teddy	11/18/68	Jerusalem and the Middle East
Koltypin, Peter	3/2/71	John Birch Society and the American Right
Kondracke, Morton	1/24/83	WFB's Turn to Explain Himself
Kondracke, Morton	11/24/80	The New Political Outlook
Kondracke, Morton	7/30/86	WFB on the Firing Line
Kondracke, Morton	8/15/80	Re. the Democratic Convention
Korry, Edward	9/20/74	Chile and the CIA
Kort, Fred	9/10/70	Supreme Court/Rule of Law/Academic Freedom
Kraft, Joseph	11/4/76	The Electoral Verdict
Kraft, Joseph	2/15/80	WFB/Others View America
Kramer, Joel	6/20/68	Student Unrest—Harvard, Yale, Michigan
Kramer, Larry	3/13/70	The New Realism in Movies
Kramer, Michael	11/24/80	The New Political Outlook
Kramer, Michael	3/25/81	Should Press Rights Be Limited?
Kramer, Michael	7/30/86	WFB on the Firing Line
Kramer, Michael	8/15/80	Re. the Democratic Convention
Kraslow, David	7/6/68	The Washington Press
Krauss, Melvyn	2/23/87	Pull Out of NATO?
Kriegisch, Franz	11/3/83	Are Young Europeans Suicidal?
Kuh, Richard H.	6/24/68	Obscenity and the Supreme Court
Kukla, Robert	1/10/77	Gun Control
Kunstler, William	6/24/71	The Lawyer's Role
Kuper, Charles	2/27/73	Corporal Punishment
Ky, Nguyen Cao	9/14/75	How Vietnam War Was Lost

L

Lacerda, Carlos	11/13/67	Struggle for Democracy in Brazil
Laffer, Arthur	1/7/82	Debate re. the Economy
Lakas, Demitrio	9/30/76	Panama and the U.S.
Lamont, Norman	2/4/75	Three MPs Against WFB
Lane, Mark	12/1/66	The Warren Commission: Fact or Fiction?
Lansman, Harry A.	6/16/72	No-Fault Insurance
LaRocque, Gene	10/19/87	Drive for Disarmament
Lasky, Melvin	2/27/68	The Anti-Communist Left
Lazo, Mario	1/18/73	The CIA and U.S. Foreign Policy
Leach, Jim	9/6/84	The GOP and the Moderates
Leary, Timothy	4/10/67	The World of LSD

Ledeen, Michael	9/3/85	Do We Have a Foreign Policy?
Lee, Dennis	10/21/68	Why Do So Many Canadians Hate America?
Lee, Robert E.	7/15/82	Looking Back at Senator McCarthy
Lehman, John	9/18/81	The Draft and Politics
Lehrman, Lewis	1/9/86	Monetary Reform
Lehrman, Lewis	12/10/81	Gold and Current Economic Impasse
Lejeune, Anthony	2/14/74	The British Crisis
Lekachman, Robert	6/1/87	Two Dissenters
Lekachman, Robert	1/5/81	Fresh Views on Capitalism
Lekachman, Robert	1/7/82	Debate re. the Economy
Lekachman, Robert	10/1/79	Is Socialism Dead?
Lelyveld, Joseph	11/7/85	*Cry, the Beloved Country*
Leonard, Jerris	11/30/70	Desegregation: How Far Should Government Go?
Leonard, John	12/13/83	Re. *The Day After* (ABC-TV)
Leonard, John	4/2/70	*National Review*
Leonard, John	5/22/80	Controversy over Book Awards
Leonard, John	7/26/82	Have We Misread the Fifties?
Lerner, Max	9/19/66	Red China
Lerner, Max	12/30/87	Max Lerner's America
Lestor, Joan	3/9/77	Is There a Solution for Rhodesia?
Leubsdorf, Carl P.	10/29/87	Day After GOP Debate
Levin, Bernard	2/14/74	The British Crisis
Levin, Bernard	3/10/76	Vision of Solzhenitsyn
Levin, Bernard	4/28/75	U.S. Prestige in Europe
Levy, Leon	7/1/70	The Stock Market—Ups and Downs
Lewis, Anthony	1/13/86	Who to Back in Angola
Lewis, Anthony	2/25/85	What Should We Be Worrying About?
Lewis, Anthony	7/24/69	American Popularity Abroad
Lewis, Anthony	11/3/83	Was It Censorship in Grenada?
Lewis, Anthony	12/11/86	Re. Reagan—Damage from Iranscam
Lewis, Anthony	3/10/75	U.S. Role in Indochina
Lewis, Anthony	3/30/81	Reagan: A Preliminary Evaluation
Lewis, Drew	7/17/80	The Republican Vice Presidency
Lewis, John	1/23/74	Politics and Black Progress
Lewis, Marvin E.	6/16/72	No-Fault Insurance
Lichtman, Judith	10/13/83	Debate on Affirmative Action
Liddy, G. Gordon	1/11/78	Gordon Liddy and Penal Reform
Lilienthal, Alfred	11/26/75	The Zionist Vote
Lilienthal, Alfred	6/29/67	The Mideast Crisis
Lincoln, C. Eric	6/2/69	Black Studies
Lind, William	7/23/86	Problems with America's Military
Link, Peter	11/4/69	Salvation, Rock Music and the New Iconoclasm

Lipski, Sam	10/25/78	Australian Journalists and WFB
Livingston, Ken	9/16/86	A British Socialist Speaks Up
Livingston, Robert G.	5/13/83	Re. Modern Europe
Loebel, Eugen	6/27/77	Euro-Communism
Lofton, John	6/24/87	WFB Quizzed by Dissatisfied Right
Loh, I-cheng	10/29/71	Meaning of the China Vote
Long, Edward	1/24/68	Wiretapping—Electronic Bugging
Lopez, Donald	9/27/84	Christianity and Other Faiths
Lopez, Valencia	11/17/77	Martial Law in Philippines
Lord, Winston	3/1/82	The CFR and Its Critics
Lott, Trent	11/15/74	Post-Election South
Lowenstein, Allard	4/22/80	Lowenstein Retrospective
Lowenstein, Allard	12/13/79	That Was the Year That Was
Lowenstein, Allard	3/9/77	Human Rights
Lowenstein, Allard	4/11/75	RFK and the Second Gun
Lowenstein, Allard	5/26/71	Dump Nixon?
Lowenstein, Allard	7/21/78	Three vs. WFB
Lowenstein, Allard	9/9/68	The McCarthy Phenomenon
Lowenstein, Allard	12/7/73	Learned from Watergate?
Lowenstein, Allard	6/15/79	Lifting Trade Ban on Rhodesia
Lowenstein, Allard	8/2/76	Aid to Church-Related Schools
Lowenstein, Hubertus	5/13/83	Re. Modern Europe
Lubell, Samuel	9/28/73	The Nixon Presidency
Lucas, J. Anthony	10/29/71	Conservatives and Nixon
Lucas, Roy	7/25/72	Abortion: Yes or No?
Luce, Clare Boothe	12/6/69	Reflections on the Current Scene
Luce, Clare Boothe	3/31/75	Feminism
Luce, Clare Boothe	5/26/66	Future of the Republican Party
Luce, Clare Boothe	1/5/72	Special—Conservatives Confront 1972
Luce, Clare Boothe	11/21/77	GOP and American Leadership
Luce, Clare Boothe	3/4/88	In Memory of—Retrospective
Lugar, Richard	2/14/80	Government Bailout (Chrysler)
Lukacs, John	1/18/82	The Polish Challenge
Lukacs, John	7/12/84	Threat from the Third World
Lunn, Arnold	11/28/66	Sports, Persecution and Christians
Luxenburg, Norman	6/13/84	The Real Cuba (II)
Lyman, Richard	4/29/82	Future of Philanthropy
Lynd, Staughton	5/23/66	Vietnam—What Next?

M

MacBride, Roger	6/28/76	Would Anarchy Work?
MacCallum, Mungo	10/25/78	Australian Journalists and WFB
MacDonald, Dwight	5/1/67	How to Protest

Machan, Tibor	4/2/82	The Libertarian Credo
MacInnes, Helen	1/6/69	The Plight of the American Novelist
MacKay, Donald M.	10/2/71	The Case Against Freedom
Macmillan, Harold	11/1/72	Harold Macmillan
Macmillan, Harold	11/24/80	Harold Macmillan Revisited
MacNeil, Robert	11/4/68	Influence of TV on American Politics
Maddy, Kenneth L.	9/14/77	The Case Against Jerry Brown
Mahoney, J. Daniel	5/22/80	Whom Should Reagan Pick as VP?
Mahoney, J. Daniel	6/15/77	Marijuana and New York State
Mahoney, J. Daniel	9/18/84	Politics American Style
Mahoney, J. Daniel	7/7/69	Conservative Party and Future of the GOP
Mahoney, J. Daniel	1/5/72	SPECIAL—Conservatives Confront 1972
Mahoney, J. Daniel	7/7/83	Re. Future of Democrats
Mailer, Norman	12/2/85	What Does P.E.N. Have to Offer?
Mailer, Norman	5/28/68	*Armies of the Night*
Mailer, Norman	10/11/79	Capital Punishment—Gary Gilmore
Malania, Leo	1/13/75	Book of Common Prayer
Malarky, Thomas	6/2/83	Can the Well-Qualified Find Jobs?
Malcolm, Derrick	10/21/70	British Journalists Question WFB
Malkiel, Burton	3/31/80	Approaches to Inflation
Mandy, S. Nigel	9/26/85	Capitalism and Apartheid
Mangakis, Lambrias	5/10/75	U.S.–Greek Relations
Mankiewicz, Frank	9/22/72	The McGovern Phenomenon
Mann, Joseph, Jr.	10/4/76	Venezuela and the U.S.
Mannes, Marya	7/10/68	Liberalism and the Intellectuals
Manning, Bayliss	6/15/77	Council on Foreign Relations
Mannix, Arthur	5/3/83	Medical Malpractice
Marcos, Ferdinand	11/17/77	The Philippines
Marreco, Anthony	5/8/70	The Hess Story
Martin, Ian	2/27/68	English Youth and Vietnam
Martin, James	3/25/87	Republicanize the South?
Martin, Malachi	12/7/73	The Jesus Movement
Martin, Malachi	9/6/78	The Mission of the Pope
Martin, Marcia	11/16/71	Eighteen-Year-Old Vote
Martin, Preston	1/9/86	Monetary Reform
Martin, Preston	4/11/85	Should the Fed Be Tamed?
Marx, Groucho	7/7/67	Is the World Funny?
Massie, Robert	5/31/85	Yale: Class of 1950
Mathias, Charles, Jr.	3/16/78	Liberals in GOP
Mathias, Charles, Jr.	9/18/81	Liberal Republicanism
Mating, Leeda P.	4/29/82	Future of Philanthropy
Matthews, Bob	2/27/68	English Youth and Vietnam
Maurro, Garry	11/10/83	Re. Texas
Mayobre, José Antonio	10/4/76	Venezuela and the U.S.

McArthur, George	1/18/72	Vietnam—Looking Back
McBrien, Richard	2/29/88	The Pope's New Encyclical
McCarthy, Eugene	5/9/84	Re. Federal Election Campaign Act
McCarthy, Eugene	5/9/74	The Presidency: How Strong?
McCarthy, Mary	6/30/71	Is America a Terrible Letdown?
McCloskey, Pete	2/29/72	The New Hampshire Primary
McCloskey, Paul	5/26/71	Dump Nixon?
McCormack, Elizabeth	11/30/70	Future of Catholic Education
McElroy, Michael	7/9/75	Ozone Controversy
McGinniss, Joe	11/10/69	The Selling of the President 1968
McGinniss, Joe	12/1/83	Psychiatrists and Criminal Law
McGinniss, Joe	7/9/74	Leadership in America
McGinniss, Joe	9/18/87	Re. MacDonald vs. McGinniss
McGovern, George	1/19/84	Debate re. President Reagan
McGovern, George	9/19/78	SALT Debate
McGovern, George	5/5/70	Hunger and the Government
McGrath, Marco	9/30/76	Panama Canal Problems
McInerny, Ralph	1/6/84	Is There a Natural Law?
McKeithen, John J.	4/23/70	The New South
McKinney, Laurence	6/30/71	Marijuana Reconsidered
McKissick, Floyd	8/22/66	Civil Rights and Foreign Policy
McManus, Charles	1/10/77	The Latin Liturgy
McWilliams, Wilson Carey	10/29/71	Conservatives and Nixon
Means, Marianne	7/6/68	The Washington Press
Mehdi, Mohammad	11/4/82	Reagan's Mideast Peace Proposal
Mehdi, Mohammed	1/8/75	Problems for the PLO
Mehling, Alice	11/7/85	The Right to Die
Melcher, Thomas A.	2/26/85	Role of Song at School (Whiffenpoofs)
Melman, Seymour	10/3/66	S.A.N.E.
Mendel, Meta	11/16/71	Eighteen-Year-Old Vote
Menninger, Walter	4/19/84	Crime and Insanity
Menuhin, Yehudi	4/2/86	What's on Yehudi Menuhin's Mind?
Merari, Ariel	9/26/85	Three Approaches to Terrorists
Merrick, David	6/6/66	Future of the American Theatre
Metzenbaum, Howard	6/29/79	U.S. Oil Policy
Meyer, Cord	12/4/80	Are Freedom and the CIA Compatible?
Michener, James	11/10/83	Poland and Europe; Poland and the U.S.
Middleweek, Helene	6/27/78	*Firing Line*'s British Correspondents
Middleweek, Helene	2/21/84	How Is Mrs. Thatcher Doing?
Middleweek, Helene	2/8/72	Inquiry re. American Conservatism
Middleweek, Helene	2/4/75	Three MPs Against WFB
Mikva, Abner	1/10/77	Gun Control
Milburn, Beryl Buckley	1/23/73	Texas Politics
Miller, Arthur	11/22/71	The Assault on Privacy

Miller, Howard	9/10/81	How to Win Arguments
Millner, Steven	11/11/82	Is the South Changing?
Mills, Wilbur	7/7/71	Revenue Sharing
Minogue, Kenneth	4/11/85	Is There a Conservative Ideology?
Mitchell, Edgar	5/18/77	The Space Program
Mitford, Jessica	1/14/74	Penal Reform
Modlin, Herbert	4/19/84	Crime and Insanity
Montgomery, Robert M.	3/31/88	Will Doctors Have to Go Out of Business?
Moosa, Spencer	11/16/77	Three Journalists on Taiwan
Morgan, Steve	11/16/71	Eighteen-Year-Old Vote
Morgenthau, Hans	11/12/73	Mideast and American Détente
Morgenthau, Hans	1/12/67	LBJ and the Intellectuals
Morrison, Stephen	11/3/83	Are Young Europeans Suicidal?
Morse, Robert S.	1/18/79	Ecumenism and Schism
Morsell, John	11/7/66	Open Housing
Morton, Thurston	9/25/67	Vietnam and the GOP
Moses, Robert	3/11/70	*Public Works*
Moskin, Robert	11/10/69	Negotiating for Peace
Moskowitz, Richard	5/3/83	Medical Malpractice
Mosley, Oswald	3/25/72	*My Life*
Moss, John	10/7/69	Race and Conservatism
Moss, Robert	3/8/77	How Much Liberty?
Moss, Robert	5/9/80	Soviet Disinformation
Moynihan, Daniel P.	1/26/76	Uses of the UN
Moynihan, Daniel P.	10/7/69	Welfare Reform Proposal
Moynihan, Daniel P.	8/15/80	Defense and the Democrats
Moynihan, Daniel P.	1/18/73	Conservative Values
Moynihan, Daniel P.	9/23/77	Welfare (I and II)
Mozingo, David	5/5/72	Implications of the China Trip
Mroczyk, Peter	7/8/87	What's with Solidarity?
Muggeridge, Malcolm	2/19/84	What's on Muggeridge's Mind?
Muggeridge, Malcolm	2/26/68	The Culture of the Left
Muggeridge, Malcolm	2/5/75	WFB, Malcolm Muggeridge and the World
Muggeridge, Malcolm	6/27/78	Muggeridge Revisited
Muggeridge, Malcolm	8/22/73	Has America Had It?
Muggeridge, Malcolm	3/10/76	Vision of Solzhenitsyn
Muggeridge, Malcolm	5/21/79	Attitudes re. Life and Death
Muggeridge, Malcolm	9/5/80	How Does One Find Faith?
Muggeridge, Malcolm	9/5/80	On Religion
Muggeridge, Malcolm	9/14/86	The Prospect of Death
Mullins, Robert J.	2/26/85	Are We Coddling the Farmers?
Murphy, Reg	5/16/73	Correspondents Question WFB
Murphy, Reg	5/15/74	Kidnaper, Victim and Society
Murray, Charles	1/28/85	The Poverty Problem
Murray, Linda	3/31/88	Scare Tactics and AIDS

Musgrove, Martha	3/31/88	Will Doctors Have to Go Out of Business?
Muskie, Edmund	1/21/74	Government and Public Confidence
Muzorewa, Abel	7/21/78	The Rhodesian Dilemma
Myrdal, Gunnar	11/4/69	What Have We Learned from Socialism?

N

Nahas, Gabriel	5/22/85	Case for Legalizing Drugs
Navarro, Antonio	6/13/84	The Real Cuba (I)
Navarro, Antonio	7/15/81	A Strategy for Cuba
Navasky, Victor	12/4/80	Cooperation of Ex-Communists
Navin, Hank	6/2/83	Can the Well-Qualified Find Jobs?
Neese, Knut	11/3/83	Are Young Europeans Suicidal?
Netanyahu, Benjamin	5/30/86	Terrorism: Viewed from Abroad
Neuhaus, Richard John	12/10/87	Problems of Catholic Church
Neuhaus, Richard John	9/18/84	Church and State
Neuhaus, Richard John	9/26/85	Capitalism and Apartheid
Neusner, Jacob	5/12/78	The Holocaust Controversy
Newell, Peter	2/27/73	Corporal Punishment
Newfield, Jack	5/15/72	A Populist Manifesto
Newfield, Jack	8/29/77	Abuse of Power
Newton, Huey P.	1/23/73	Re. the Black Movement
Ney, Richard	12/10/75	Is the Stock Market Honest?
Neyer, Arieh	11/7/66	The Supreme Court and the Criminal
Neyer, Arieh	7/20/78	What Rights Do Nazis Have?
Neyer, Arieh	3/3/71	AFTRA: Compulsory Unionism and Civil Liberties
Nichols, Mary Perot	1/10/73	Conservative Challenges in '73
Niemeyer, Gerhart	1/6/84	Is There a Natural Law?
Niemeyer, Gerhart	6/24/71	Is St. Augustine Relevant?
Nisker, Wes	12/9/69	Why Don't Conservatives Understand?
Nitze, Paul	6/12/81	Debate on American Security
Nitze, Paul	7/22/74	SALT II
Nixon, Richard	9/14/67	The Future of the GOP
Noonan, John T., Jr.	5/1/73	Abortion: Legal Aspects
Noonan, John T., Jr.	7/25/72	Abortion: Yes or No?
Norman, Geoffrey	12/6/71	The Edgar Smith Story (II)
North, James	4/1/85	The Challenge of South Africa
North, Oliver	7/7/71	War Crimes (II)
Norton, Howard	7/8/76	Journalists Question WFB
Novak, Michael	5/27/87	Crisis in the Catholic Church
Novak, Michael	6/12/81	El Salvador/Christianity/Marxism

O

P

Perle, Richard	12/13/83	Re. *The Day After* (ABC-TV)
Perle, Richard	12/13/83	The U.S. and Her Alliance
Perle, Richard	1/7/88	Coming Up: The INF Hearings
Perlmutter, Amos	11/4/82	Reagan's Mideast Peace Proposal
Perlmutter, Nathan	10/3/72	The Jewish Vote
Perlmutter, Nathan	2/25/69	Black Anti-Semitism
Perlmutter, Nathan	7/21/80	Is Camp David Falling Apart?
Peterson, Peter	12/9/82	Re. Social Security
Peterson, Peter	6/17/81	Can America Compete?
Peterson, Russell	7/9/75	Ozone Controversy
Petri, Thomas E.	2/24/69	The Ripon Society
Pfeffer, Leo	8/2/76	State Aid to Church-Related Schools
Pfister, Edward J.	11/13/79	Whither TV?
Phillips, Howard	6/24/87	WFB Quizzed by Dissatisfied Right
Phillips, Kevin	7/7/82	Young Liberals vs. Young Conservatives
Pifer, Alan	4/2/86	Challenges of Medical Care
Pike, Douglas	12/17/70	Vietnamization
Pike, James	4/6/66	Prayer Amendment
Pike, John	4/25/85	Debate re. SDI
Pike, Otis	10/28/85	The Crisis in Congress
Pike, Otis	12/4/75	Security and Intelligence
Pilpel, Harriet	10/5/77	Abortion and the Law
Pilpel, Harriet	11/12/81	WFB on the Firing Line
Pilpel, Harriet	11/29/84	Book Burning and Moral Majority
Pilpel, Harriet	11/30/82	Debate re. Women vs. Men
Pilpel, Harriet	12/1/83	Children and the Law
Pilpel, Harriet	12/11/86	Does Sex Education Work?
Pilpel, Harriet	12/13/79	That Was the Year That Was
Pilpel, Harriet	12/2/74	Kids, Sex and Doctors
Pilpel, Harriet	2/22/83	Confidentiality and Betrayal
Pilpel, Harriet	2/24/81	WFB Faces the Firing Line
Pilpel, Harriet	2/24/87	WFB on the Firing Line
Pilpel, Harriet	2/25/85	Women Against Pornography
Pilpel, Harriet	4/15/87	Future of Feminist Movement
Pilpel, Harriet	5/1/73	Abortion: Legal Aspects
Pilpel, Harriet	7/10/85	The Trouble with Lawyers
Pilpel, Harriet	7/21/78	Three vs. WFB
Pilpel, Harriet	7/31/85	Three Against One (WFB Questioned)
Pilpel, Harriet	7/9/86	Pornography and the State
Pilpel, Harriet	8/26/76	Censorship in Libraries
Pilpel, Harriet	9/18/84	Politics American Style
Pilpel, Harriet	12/30/87	How Do Conservatives View 1988?
Piñera, José	4/28/88	Chile and a Novel Approach to Social Security
Pipes, Richard	12/10/87	Morality and Disarmament

Pipes, Richard	12/9/82	Is Communism Evolving?
Pipes, Richard	7/8/87	Sovietology
Pitts, Frank	1/11/82	Energy Policy for the Reagan Administration
Plimpton, Francis	1/19/67	The Future of the UN
Podhoretz, Norman	11/29/79	Breaking Ranks
Portocarrero, Adolfo Calero	5/2/83	Re. Central America
Porzio, Ralph	11/14/75	The Right to Die
Powell, Enoch	2/20/84	Is Britain a Giant Humbug?
Powell, Enoch	10/20/70	Britain's Most Controversial MP
Powell, Enoch	2/14/74	Powell and the British Crisis
Powell, Enoch	5/19/69	On British Race Relations
Powell, James	5/16/73	Correspondents Question WFB
Powers, Thomas	3/26/80	CIA and the Mission of Intelligence
Premack, David	10/18/73	Behavioral Control
Preminger, Otto	4/10/67	Movie Production and Censorship
Pressler, Larry	4/27/81	Public TV
Pressman, Gabe	1/10/73	Conservative Challenges in '73
Price, Raymond	12/20/73	Views of a Nixonite
Price, Raymond	4/28/69	Problems of a Chief Executive
Prichard, Edward, Jr.	10/27/82	The Roosevelt Legacy
Pritchett, C. Herman	9/10/70	Supreme Court/Rule of Law/Academic Freedom
Proxmire, William	9/14/71	The Politics of William Proxmire
Purdy, Al	10/21/68	Why Do So Many Canadians Hate America?

Q

| Quinn, Edward | 4/25/77 | The End of Education |

R

Rabin, Yitzhak	5/9/75	Israel and Kissinger Failure
Rabin, Yitzhak	3/15/79	Re. the Israeli–Egyptian Accord
Rabishke, Alan	1/17/80	The Eighties: Domestic Affairs
Rader, Dotson	10/3/72	*Nine Lies About America*
Rader, Dotson	4/12/76	Growing Up at Thirty-seven
Rahim, Abdul	5/26/83	The Afghan Mess
Railsback, Thomas	9/10/74	President's Pardon
Ramos, Oreste	9/25/78	Independence for Puerto Rico?
Rangel, Charles	3/24/86	Let's Legalize Those Drugs
Rapoport, Roger	12/9/69	Why Don't Conservatives Understand?

Rapoport, Roger	6/20/68	Student Unrest—Harvard, Yale, Michigan
Rauh, Joseph	6/10/66	Communists and Civil Liberties
Ravitch, Diane	9/18/87	Problems in Our High Schools
Rawlinson, Peter	7/30/71	Law and Order in England
Reagan, Ronald	1/14/80	Presidential Hopeful (!)
Reagan, Ronald	1/13/78	Panama Canal Debate
Reagan, Ronald	1/5/72	SPECIAL—Conservatives Confront 1972
Reagan, Ronald	7/6/67	Is It Possible to Be a Good Governor?
Reagan, Ronald	7/15/71	Re. Being a Good Governor
Reed, Clarke	12/12/72	The Civil Rights Law
Reedy, George	7/1/70	*The Twilight of the Presidency*
Reems, Harry	12/13/76	*Deep Throat* and the First Amendment
Reeves, Richard	11/4/76	The Electoral Verdict
Reeves, Richard	5/18/77	Nixon Revisited
Reeves, Richard	1/10/73	Conservative Challenges in '73
Reeves, Richard	12/10/75	How We Choose Presidents
Reeves, Thomas	7/15/82	Looking Back at Senator McCarthy
Reich, Otto	6/13/84	The Real Cuba (II)
Reich, Otto	9/3/85	Re. Nicaragua
Reich, Robert	6/1/87	Two Dissenters
Reich, Robert	7/7/83	Is There a New Economics?
Reid, Jimmy	2/13/79	Crisis of the British Trade Unions
Reid, Jimmy	2/18/75	Communist Party and British Policy
Rembar, Charles	6/20/73	Press Shield Laws
Rembar, Charles	6/24/68	Obscenity and the Supreme Court
Revel, Jean-François	11/15/84	Democracy vs. Communism
Reyes, Manolo	3/26/80	What to Do About Cuba
Reynolds, William B.	10/13/83	Debate on Affirmative Action
Rhodes, John	12/9/74	Democratic Moderation
Richards, Ann	11/10/83	Re. Texas
Richardson, Elliot	12/20/73	Future of the GOP
Richardson, Elliot	5/26/71	Free Medicine?
Riddell, Peter	2/21/84	How Is Mrs. Thatcher Doing?
Riddell, Peter	9/15/86	What's Wrong with the U.S.?
Riddell, Peter	6/27/78	*Firing Line*'s British Correspondents
Riddell, Peter	2/8/72	Inquiry into American Conservatism
Riebenfeld, Paul	11/26/75	The Zionist Vote
Riesel, Victor	9/19/66	Abuse of Union Power
Rifkin, Jeremy	6/28/76	Re. People's Bicentennial
Riles, Wilson	1/26/76	The Educator's Dilemma
Rinfret, Pierre	8/26/76	Economic Planks of Both Parties
Rinfret, Pierre	9/20/74	The Economy
Ritchie, Jock	9/13/73	Energy Crisis and Energy Policy

Rivera, Antonio	10/1/87	Young Latin Americans
Roberts, Paul Craig	3/31/80	Approaches to Inflation
Robertson, Pat	4/27/81	Public TV
Robertson, Pat	10/28/87	SPECIAL—GOP Presidential Candidates
Robinson, John A. T.	10/6/67	Is There a New God?
Roca, Eduardo	1/31/77	Should the U.S. Pressure Argentina?
Rocard, Michel	2/23/84	A French Socialist Speaks Out
Roche, John P.	1/7/71	Colleges and the Youth Cult
Roche, John P.	5/15/67	The Liberals and LBJ
Roche, George C.	11/28/79	Re. HEW and Colleges (Title IX)
Roche, George C.	11/7/77	Re. Private Property
Rockefeller, Sharon	4/27/81	Public TV
Rockefeller, Steven	9/27/84	Christianity and Other Faiths
Rodman, Selden	10/8/70	Chile and the Future of South America
Rohatyn, Felix	7/21/82	Should We Default Poland?
Rohrabacher, Dana	6/16/72	Nixon and Young Conservatives
Romandia, Roberto de la Madrid	9/14/77	Illegal Aliens
Rooney, Andrew A.	9/1/71	The News Twisters
Roosevelt, Franklin D., Jr.	3/8/67	The Role of the Third Party
Rosenblatt, Stanley	5/3/83	Medical Malpractice
Rosenfeld, Shalom	5/9/75	Hawks and Doves in Israel
Rosenthal, Mitchell	5/9/80	Marijuana: What's New?
Rossant, James S.	11/2/71	Good Buildings Being Built?
Rostow, Eugene	11/10/69	Negotiating for Peace
Rostow, Eugene	11/28/72	New and Old Foreign Policy
Rostow, Walt	2/22/83	Ideas and Action
Rostow, Walt	9/1/71	Is LBJ Defensible?
Rostow, Walt	11/28/72	New and Old Foreign Policy
Roth, Peter M.	5/8/70	English Youth
Roth, Russell	6/10/74	National Health Insurance
Roth, Toby	12/3/87	Re. War Powers Act
Rothwax, Harold	2/2/69	The Fifth Amendment
Rotunda, Ronald	4/25/86	Politics and Wordplay
Rowny, Edward	12/1/86	How Do We Stand on Disarmament?
Rubin, Jerry	4/12/76	Growing Up at Thirty-seven
Rubinstein, Amnon	1/24/72	Inside Israel
Rubottom, Richard	11/1/85	The Hispanic Rumble
Ruckleshaus, William	11/12/73	Independent Prosecutor?
Rudolph, Lloyd	6/9/83	Was Gandhi for Real?
Ruether, Rosemary	6/24/68	The Rib Uncaged: Women and the Church
Rumsfeld, Donald	10/9/75	Running the White House
Rumsfeld, Donald	1/13/69	The Walker Report

S

Schoenman, Ralph	11/13/67	War Crimes
Scholes, Robert	5/31/85	Yale: Class of 1950
Schomp, Gerald	3/2/71	John Birch Society and the American Right
Schorr, Daniel	4/25/86	Politics and Wordplay
Schorr, Daniel	7/30/86	Crotchets of a Veteran Journalist
Schwartzchild, Henry	9/13/73	Amnesty
Schwarz, Fred	6/29/67	The Decline of Anti-Communism
Scorer, Richard	7/9/75	Ozone Controversy
Scott, Ann	3/30/73	The Equal Rights Amendment
Scoville, Herbert	4/24/78	The Neutron Bomb
Sears, Alan	7/9/86	Pornography and the State
Sears, Hilary	2/27/68	English Youth and Vietnam
Sears, John	7/15/76	Who's More Electable—Ford or Reagan?
Seidman, Bert	8/2/76	National Health Insurance
Seidman, Larry	11/16/71	Eighteen-Year-Old Vote
Seigenthaler, John	11/11/82	Views on the Election
Seignious, George	8/16/79	SALT II: What's to Lose?
Servan-Schreiber, Jean-Jacques	12/9/68	The American Challenge
Shakespeare, Frank	4/27/81	Public TV
Shakespeare, Frank	2/1/73	The USIA
Shakespeare, Frank	6/9/70	Politics and the Media (USIA)
Shakespeare, Frank	9/15/83	On Radio Free Europe
Shanker, Albert	4/10/86	Debate re. Privatization (I and II)
Shanker, Albert	1/6/69	The Issues in the School Strike
Shannon, William	9/20/76	The Claims of Jimmy Carter
Shapiro, Donald	12/13/76	Capital Punishment
Shaplen, Robert	10/1/79	Communist Rule in China
Sharaf, Abdul Hamid	6/1/72	The Arab Side
Shaw, Sullen	11/16/77	Three Journalists on Taiwan
Sheed, Frank	4/21/69	Modernism in the Catholic Church
Sheed, Maisie Ward	4/21/69	Modernism in the Catholic Church
Sheen, Fulton J.	1/6/70	Skepticism and Disorder
Sheen, Fulton J.	6/24/71	Is St. Augustine Relevant?
Shepard, Alan	7/24/73	Was It Worth It?
Shevin, Robert	6/23/79	Capital Punishment
Shiffman, Bernard	1/27/69	How Goes It with the Poverty Program?
Shilling, A. Gary	5/12/78	Public Policy and the Economy
Shockley, William	6/10/74	Shockley's Thesis
Short, Renee	7/30/71	Pornography English Style
Shrum, Robert	1/19/84	Debate Re. President Reagan
Shrum, Robert	4/25/85	Debate re. SDI
Simes, Dimitri and Natasha	7/30/73	Soviet Jewry
Simon, Julian	10/15/81	Is There an Answer to Malthus?

Simon, Paul	7/1/87	SPECIAL—Democratic Presidential Candidates
Simon, William E.	10/13/80	Economic Program for the Eighties
Simon, William E.	12/9/74	Energy and Economy
Simon, William E.	5/12/78	Public Policy and the Economy
Singer, Max	12/10/81	The Enemy in Central America
Skinner, B. F.	10/2/71	The Case Against Freedom
Skinner, B. F.	10/16/73	Mechanism of Moral Development
Smith, Adam	7/1/70	The Stock Market—Ups and Downs
Smith, David	7/7/69	Marijuana—How Harmful?
Smith, Edgar	12/6/71	The Edgar Smith Story (I)
Smith, Edgar	12/6/71	The Edgar Smith Story (II)
Smith, F. Michael	8/2/76	National Health Insurance
Smith, Hedrick	1/8/76	The Russians
Smith, Hedrick	2/25/81	Reagan's Foreign Policy
Smith, Ian	3/14/74	Rhodesia
Smith, J. Brian	6/16/72	Nixon and Young Conservatives
Smith, Liz	7/8/76	Journalists Question WFB
Smith, Tobias	6/23/79	Capital Punishment
Smith, William	12/6/84	Re. Libertarian Theology
Smith, William French	10/1/81	Where on Immigration?
Snepp, Frank	1/30/78	Decent Interval
Snepp, Frank	12/4/80	Are Freedom and the CIA Compatible?
Sobran, Joseph	10/5/82	Debate re. Education
Sobran, Joseph	11/12/81	WFB on the Firing Line
Sobran, Joseph	11/30/82	Debate re. Women vs. Men
Sofaer, Abraham	7/27/87	Re. ABM Treaty and Testing
Solarz, Stephen	10/28/85	Problems in the Philippines
Solarz, Stephen	12/3/87	Re. War Powers Act
Solarz, Stephen	5/2/83	Re. Central America
Solarz, Stephen	6/15/79	Lifting Trade Ban on Rhodesia
Solarz, Stephen	6/22/77	Rhodesia
Solarz, Stephen	7/13/81	Mr. Begin's Preemptive Strike
Solarz, Stephen	9/15/83	Re. South Africa
Solarz, Stephen	9/26/85	Capitalism and Apartheid
Solarz, Stephen	2/22/83	Should U.S. Withdraw from Europe?
Solarz, Stephen	2/25/81	Reagan's Foreign Policy
Solarz, Stephen	6/17/81	Angola and South Africa
Solomon, W. David	1/6/84	Is There a Natural Law?
Soper, Donald	11/1/72	Christianity and Capitalism
Sosland, Morton	11/8/74	Soviet Grain Deal
Soustelle, Jacques	9/22/69	Looking Back on De Gaulle
Sowell, Thomas	4/10/86	Debate re. Privatization (I and II)
Sowell, Thomas	11/12/81	Economic Lot of Minorities
Sowell, Thomas	11/3/83	Economics and Politics of Race

Sparrow, John	7/24/69	Is There a Place for the Old Order?
Spender, Stephen	2/5/75	Intellectual's Responsibilities
Spengemann, William	5/4/87	Uses of the Past
Spock, Benjamin	6/26/67	Vietnam Protests
Spong, John	1/23/87	Anglican Priest-Persons
Spring, Raymond L.	4/19/84	Crime and Insanity
Springs, Dillard P.	4/11/79	Breaking Up OPEC
Staar, Richard	1/17/80	U.S. in the Eighties: Foreign Policy
St. Clair, James	1/19/68	Army–McCarthy Hearings (I and II)
Stans, Maurice	8/28/70	International Trade
Stans, Maurice	5/4/79	Terrors of Justice
Star, Paul	4/10/86	Debate re. Privatization (I and II)
Starr, Roger	5/29/85	Has New York Let Us Down?
Starr, Roger	8/29/77	Abuse of Power
Stayn, Stephanus	11/4/68	Is South Africa Everybody's Business?
Steel, David	5/9/70	British Abortion Act
Steele, Jonathan	10/21/70	British Journalists Question WFB
Stego, Cecilia	11/3/83	Are Young Europeans Suicidal?
Stein, Ben	6/29/79	The Television Machine
Stein, Herbert	4/11/85	Should the Fed Be Tamed?
Steindl-Rast, David	9/27/84	Christianity and Other Faiths
Steinfels, Peter	10/11/79	Impact of the Pope's Visit
Sterling, Claire	6/5/81	What to Do About Terrorism
Stern, Philip	1/15/70	The Oppenheimer Case
Stevas, Norman St. John	3/31/75	Abortion
Stevas, Norman St. John	5/9/70	British Abortion Act
Stockman, David A.	4/2/86	David Stockman Regrets
Stokes, Carl	5/24/68	Governing the Cities
Stone, Clement	1/11/71	The Crisis of Private Insurance
Strachbein, O. R.	12/18/69	Tariffs
Strauss, Robert	11/28/72	Political Financing
Stutman, Robert	2/29/88	Should We Legalize Drugs?
Sullivan, Ronald	12/6/71	The Edgar Smith Story (II)
Surrey, Stanley	1/21/74	Tax Reform
Susskind, David	5/2/66	The Prevailing Bias
Svineri, Shlomo	5/9/75	Hawks and Doves in Israel
Swedan, David	2/26/69	Black Student Power—Five Campuses
Sweezy, Alan	6/23/69	The Population Explosion
Sweisgood, Peter	5/15/72	Alcoholism
Symington, James	5/31/85	Yale: Class of 1950
Szasz, Thomas	5/22/85	Psychiatry: New Explorations
Szasz, Thomas	5/16/73	Drugs Without Prescription?
Szulc, Tad	10/21/74	Recognize Cuba?

T

Tureck, Rosalyn	7/17/85	Re. Musical Performances
Tureck, Rosalyn	9/28/70	Why Are They Afraid of Bach?
Tyrrell, R. Emmett	12/11/84	The Liberal Crack-up

U

Udall, Morris K.	12/12/74	Democratic Presidential Prospects—1976
Ulanovskaya, Nadia	7/26/77	Soviet Intelligence Apparatus
Unruh, Jesse	3/6/67	Do the States Have a Chance?
Utley, Freda	4/25/68	The Middle East

V

Valenstein, Elliot	10/18/73	Psychosurgery/Brain Control
Valenti, Fernando	6/16/72	Music and Modernism
Valenti, Jack	5/4/82	Looking Back on LBJ
van den Haag, Ernest	12/13/76	Capital Punishment
van den Haag, Ernest	10/3/72	Sex Education
van den Haag, Ernest	11/14/75	Crime and Criminals
van den Haag, Ernest	12/11/67	Do We Need Public Schools?
van den Haag, Ernest	12/11/86	Does Sex Education Work?
van den Haag, Ernest	3/25/81	Question of Gay Rights
van den Haag, Ernest	7/12/84	Threat from the Third World
van den Haag, Ernest	7/20/78	What Rights Do Nazis Have?
van den Haag, Ernest	7/7/71	War Crimes
van den Haag, Ernest	9/29/83	Re. Capital Punishment
van den Haag, Ernest	12/3/81	Why Are Intellectuals Dumb?
van den Haag, Ernest	3/31/80	Government by Plebiscite?
van den Haag, Ernest	5/19/69	Cornell and Conflict of Generations
van den Haag, Ernest	6/20/73	Conservatives and Watergate
Vanderjagt, Guy	7/17/80	The Republican Vice-Presidency
Vasey, Lloyd	11/21/77	Asian Policy: From Hawaii
Vatikiotis, P. J.	3/16/79	The Rising Tide of Islam
Vatz, Richard	5/22/85	Psychiatry: New Explorations
Vaughan, Robert	7/8/67	Vietnam
Viguerie, Richard	1/2/79	Conservative Panel
Vin, Im	7/20/78	Cambodia and the Refugee Problem
Vinocur, John	2/24/84	Re. French–U.S. Relations
Vlachos, Helen	5/10/75	U.S.–Greek Relations
von Hapsburg, Otto	7/23/69	Monarchy and the Modern World
von Hapsburg, Otto	7/17/81	European Traditionalist
von Hayek, Friedrich	11/7/77	Re. Private Property
von Hoffman, Nicholas	2/15/80	WFB/Others View America
Vonnegut, Kurt	12/2/85	What Does P.E.N. Have to Offer?

Vorster, John	3/13/74	South Africa
Vree, Dale	1/18/79	Ecumenism and Schism

W

Wagner, Geoffrey	4/25/77	The End of Education
Waldie, Jerome	9/10/74	President's Pardon
Walker, Charls E.	4/1/85	Congress and the Deficit
Walker, Martin	3/9/76	What Is Their CIA Up To?
Walker, Michael	1/9/86	Is Canada's Mulroney a Disappointment?
Walker, Richard	3/25/87	The Role of South Korea
Walker, Richard	5/5/72	Implications of the China Trip
Wallace, George	1/24/68	The Wallace Crusade
Wallich, Henry	12/18/69	Tariffs
Walters, Vernon	5/13/78	Secret Diplomacy
Walters, Vernon	5/27/87	Are We Getting Anywhere in the UN?
Wantland, William	1/23/87	Anglican Priest-Persons
Warbur, Gabriel	3/16/79	The Rising Tide of Islam
Ward, John William	11/23/76	Future of the Private College
Ward, Lynn	6/23/79	Young Republicans on '80 Election
Watkins, John G.	11/12/85	A Look at the Hillside Strangler
Watson, Jack	5/15/80	Responsibilities of the Cabinet
Wattenberg, Ben	11/8/74	Election Rhetoric—1974
Waugh, Auberon	9/22/69	Biafra and English Foreign Policy
Weatherby, Harold	1/13/75	Book of Common Prayer
Weigel, George	5/27/87	Crisis in the Catholic Church
Weinberg, Lee S.	5/22/85	Psychiatry: New Explorations
Weinberger, Caspar	10/14/87	Defense Secretary on Current Crisis
Weinberger, Caspar	3/30/73	Federal Aid to Education
Weinberger, Caspar	6/2/86	Are We Overdoing the Defense?
Weinstein, Allen	3/21/78	Perjury—Hiss–Chambers Case
Weiss, Paul	11/14/66	The Failure of Organized Religion
Weiss, Seymour	5/4/87	Re. the Moscow Talks
Welles, Chris	12/10/75	Is the Stock Market Honest?
Wells, Dee	8/22/73	WFB Questioned About America
Wellstood, Dick	12/9/80	Why Is Jazz Neglected?
Welty, Eudora	12/12/72	The Southern Imagination
Wertham, Frederic	6/20/68	Violence
West, Dame Rebecca	2/26/68	The Role of the Traitor
Westbrook, Yvonne	11/16/71	Eighteen-Year-Old Vote
Westin, Alan	3/30/81	How Much Loyalty to the Boss?
Westmoreland, William	9/20/79	Crisis in Military
Westmoreland, William	1/23/76	Lessons from Vietnam
Westmoreland, William	9/18/81	The Draft and Politics

Wexler, William A.	10/3/72	The Jewish Vote
Weyand, Fred C.	11/21/77	Asian Policy: From Hawaii
Weyrich, Paul	1/13/87	Conservatives and Reagan's State of Union
Weyrich, Paul	10/29/87	Debates and Politics
Weyrich, Paul	5/22/80	Whom Should Reagan Pick as VP?
Whelan, James	3/26/80	What to Do About Cuba
White, F. Clifton	11/4/68	Influence of TV on American Politics
White, F. Clifton	1/13/87	Conservatives and Reagan's State of Union
White, F. Clifton	1/16/67	Presidential Politics
White, F. Clifton	3/24/86	Preliminary Talk About 1988
White, Mark	11/1/85	Democratic Politics Texas Style
White, Theodore	6/23/82	What Was Special About 1980?
White, Theodore	7/22/75	*Breach of Faith* (Nixon)
White, Theodore	9/22/69	The Making of the President 1968
White, Theodore	12/12/78	Our Chinese Policy?
Whitehead, Clay T.	2/1/73	The White House and the Media
Wicker, Tom	3/7/67	Politics and the President
Wicker, Tom	3/10/75	Journalism
Wiley, Richard	9/9/75	FCC and Public Policy
Will, George	1/19/84	Debate re. President Reagan
Williams, C. Dickerman	12/2/74	Kids, Sex and Doctors
Williams, C. Dickerman	2/2/69	The Fifth Amendment
Williams, C. Dickerman	6/20/73	Press Shield Laws
Williams, Edward Bennett	5/3/74	Re. Fifth Amendment
Williams, Lynne	3/3/71	Some Reflections on TV Programming
Williams, Shirley	2/25/73	The Welfare State
Williams, Walter	9/15/83	Re. South Africa
Wills, Garry	1/10/73	The Catholic Crisis
Wills, Morris	10/7/68	Korean War Defectors
Wilson, Sir Harold	5/13/83	The British Elections
Wilson, James Q.	11/14/75	Crime and Criminals
Wilson, Malcolm	6/15/71	Strikes in Defiance of Law?
Wilson, Pete	9/14/77	The Case Against Jerry Brown
Winpisinger, William	3/2/82	Reagan and the Working Man
Wirt, Sherwood Eliot	6/24/71	Is St. Augustine Relevant?
Wolfe, Tom	10/1/81	Is Modern Architecture Disastrous?
Wolfe, Tom	12/17/70	*Radical Chic*
Wolfe, Tom	7/9/75	*The Painted Word*
Woodward, Bob	7/9/74	Journalistic Investigation
Worden, Simon P.	10/3/85	Reflections on Star Wars (I and II)
Worsthorne, Peregrine	10/6/67	The English Conservatives
Worsthorne, Peregrine	9/15/86	What's Wrong with the U.S.?
Worthington, Peter	8/22/78	Newsmen and the Law

Wriston, Walter	5/30/86	Debtors and Creditors
Wurf, Jerry	7/19/79	Carter and the Unions
Wurf, Jerry	10/21/74	Strikes Against the State

Y

Yablonsky, Lewis	9/3/68	The Hippies
Young Americans for Freedom, Directors	8/15/75	Concerns of Young Conservatives
Young Americans for Freedom Group	8/29/77	YAF
Young Americans for Freedom Members	12/8/70	Dialogue with YAF Kids
Yepsen, David	4/18/84	Prospects for Democrats
Yew, Lee Kuan	10/30/78	Singapore
Ying, Diane	11/16/77	Three Journalists on Taiwan
Yoder, Edwin	1/11/78	Journalists Question WFB
Yorty, Samuel	8/28/67	Municipal Government

Z

Zagoria, Donald	11/4/76	What's Going On in China?
Zielenziger, Michael	4/18/84	Prospects for Democrats
Zion, Sidney	1/13/69	The Walker Report
Zion, Sidney	1/19/88	Impasse in Israel
Zogby, James	1/19/88	Impasse in Israel
Zolf, Larry	10/21/68	Why Do So Many Canadians Hate America?
Zumbakis, S. Paul	2/24/87	Returning Ex-Nazis to Soviet Union
Zumwalt, Elmo	7/22/74	SALT II
Zumwalt, Elmo	5/14/76	Political Campaign and Defense

INDEX

Florida, Cuban refugee problem in,
144
Florida primary (1976), 363
Fonda, Jane, 105
Fontaine, Roger, 366, 376–77, 381
food stamps, 310, 311
Foot, Michael, 287–92
Ford, Gerald R., 149–50, 158, 173,
363
Ford Hall, 107
Ford Hour, 256
Ford Motor Company, 138–39, 313,
314–15
foreign policy, 161, 168, 326–62
Founding Fathers, 135, 136, 410
Fourteenth Amendment, 219–20
Francis of Assisi, Saint, 34, 453, 460
Franklin, Benjamin, 410–11
freedom, 7–8, 290, 292, 294, 361–62
as biological response, 82–83
of press, 196–201
socialism and, 288–89
of speech, 114, 196, 201–4,
221–27, 288–89, 328; *see also*
First Amendment
Freedom House, 104
Freedom of Information Act, 124
Freeman, Neal, 9
free market, 67, 69, 70, 71, 134–35,
188, 293, 295, 320–21, 345,
346
free will, 81–92, 235–36, 457–58
Freud, Sigmund, 324
Friedman, Milton, 40, 183, 184, 299,
304, 360
From Bauhaus to Our House
(Wolfe), 263–69

Galbraith, John Kenneth:
conservatism as viewed by,
293–94, 305
debating style of, xxxiv–xxxv,
21–22, 38–42, 56, 72–76
economic views of, xxxiv–xxxv,
14, 38–42, 72–76, 293–96, 311
government as viewed by, 65–70,
298, 425
Gallup polls, 173
gambling, risk and, 298–99
Gandhi, Indira, xxxiii
Gandhi, Mohandas K., 324
Gang of Four, 333
Garreau, Joel, 144
gasoline tax, 146, 147
gas prices, 65–72, 293
General Accounting Office (GAO),
188
General Motors, 68, 313
Genesis, 439–40
George III, King of England, 136,
382, 410
Gephardt, Richard, 61
German language, 271, 272
Germany, Nazi, 22, 33, 85, 86, 134,
212, 279, 389
Gettysburg Address, xxxii, xxxiii,
xxxix
Ghana, 338
Gilder, George, 158, 296–300
Gilmore, Gary, 78, 79
Giscard d'Estaing, Valéry, 387–88
Glazer, Nathan, 296, 314
GNP (Gross National Product), 142
God, existence of, xxxvii, 86–87, 89,
90, 448–58, 461
gold mining, 347, 353
gold prices, 346
Goldwater, Barry:
civil rights and, 52
as conservative, xiv, 158–59, 168,
363, 364
as presidential candidate, xxxi, 24,
299–300, 436

Due Return	Due Return
Date Date	Date Date